Psychology of
Learning & Behavior

Psychology of Learning & Behavior

Barry Schwartz
Swarthmore College

W. W. Norton and Company, Inc.
New York

Library of Congress Cataloging in Publication Data

Schwartz, Barry
    Psychology of learning & behavior.

    Bibliography: p.
    Includes index.
    1. Conditioned response.   2. Behaviorism.
I. Title.
BF319.S38   1978   150   77–27262

Book designed and illustrated by The Whole Works®

ISBN 0 393 09070 1

2 3 4 5 6 7 8 9 0

To the memory of my father, Abraham,
and to Jeannette,
Myrna,
Allison, and Rebecca,
the four people I love.

Contents

3. Basic Methods for the Analysis of Behavior

4. Pavlovian Conditioning I

5. Pavlovian Conditioning II
New Developments and Applications

6. Operant Conditioning:
Necessary Conditions

7. Schedules of Reinforcement   151

8. Discrimination and Generalization   182

9. Aversive Control:
Punishment and Avoidance

222

12. Constraints on Behavior

333

Preface

My introduction to behavior theory, about a dozen years ago, was a book by B. F. Skinner called *Science and Human Behavior*.[1] In that book, Skinner attempted to extend principles which had emerged from a small but growing body of laboratory research to the entire range of human experience. As I read the book, I disagreed with almost all the arguments, but I was unable to rebut them. I decided then that a theory with the sweep and power of this one had to be taken seriously; it could not be dismissed casually. I also became convinced that ultimate judgment about the validity of Skinner's perspective on human nature would have to be based upon an evaluation of the laboratory research program on which that perspective rested.

I have written this text for those undergraduates who are taking their first course in learning, learning and conditioning, or principles of learning. It is intended to introduce these students to the basic principles of Pavlovian and operant conditioning, to provide them with some of the tools which are needed for a proper evaluation of the discipline. In writing the book I wanted first to present a picture of what is at stake, of why the study of learning and behavior theory is important. I wanted undergraduates to know, as they grappled with many specific facts and theories, that each fact and theory carries with it a piece of a general perspective on human nature which touches all of our lives. While particular facts might have little significance in themselves, they have great significance as part of this general picture of human nature.

The first three chapters of this book are directed at this objective. In Chapter 1, behavior theory is discussed as a world view, as a set of beliefs about the nature of man which contrast sharply with traditional beliefs. Chapter 2 attempts to connect behavior theory to its in-

1. New York: Macmillan, 1953.

tellectual antecedents in philosophy and biology, and to display it as an extension of an intellectual movement more than three centuries old. In Chapter 3, the methods of behavior theory are discussed, with particular attention to how these methods are a logical reflection of the world view articulated in Chapter 1 and the intellectual history discussed in Chapter 2.

As a second objective, I wanted to give undergraduates the opportunity to study the discipline critically. I wanted to expose them to some of the contradictions, unsolved problems, and controversies which are a part of behavior theory. There is still much uncertainty about fundamental issues in the field, and students should know this. My aim is to get students involved early with current problems and to have them actively interpreting and manipulating their materials and not just passively recording them. This aim is served by describing clearly not only what behavior theorists agree on, but also what they argue about. Yet at no point do I assume that the students have had any background in the field.

Thus, in two chapters on Pavlovian conditioning (Chapters 4 and 5), students move from a discussion of the conditioning process as conceived by Pavlov, in which contiguity between events is the crucial variable, to a modern view which emphasizes contingency analysis. Similar developments, from contiguity to contingency, are traced for the domain of operant conditioning in Chapter 6. Chapter 7, on schedules of reinforcement, and Chapter 8, on discrimination and generalization, identify central problems which are engaging researchers now, in addition to enumerating the principles which have already been developed. In Chapter 9, on aversive control, a wide range of theories of avoidance learning and punishment is discussed, and a few of the shortcomings of each theory are identified. Chapter 10, which is about the relations between Pavlovian and operant conditioning, provides an account of the difficulties researchers have with this most basic issue. In short, with each content area discussed an effort is made to indicate to students where future research might fruitfully be directed. In addition, an attempt is made throughout the discussion of particular content areas to connect research findings and theoretical disputes to important aspects of ordinary human experience, and to behavior theory's world view.

The last two chapters of the book focus on problems of a different sort. These are problems which question the foundations of the discipline. In discussions of the "misbehavior of organisms" and "constraints on learning," I attempt to indicate clearly and in detail why these research areas are so significant, to specify the challenge they pose for behavior theory, and to discuss general alternatives to behavior theory which might accommodate certain phenomena more comfortably. By the end of these chapters, the student should be able to form a preliminary judgment about the value and validity of behavior theory as an empirical discipline and as a view of human nature.

There are many people whom I must thank for their contributions to this book. I will always be indebted to the two people who trained me. My first teacher was Charles Catania. He convinced me that the discipline this book is about must be taken seriously. He showed me that progress in behavior theory is progress toward a new conception of humanity, and that behavior theory warrants the intellectual commitment of intelligent people. Finally, he showed me how important the language of a science is to its conceptual fabric. My second teacher was David Williams. He and his students worked together on problems concerning the foundations of behavior theory. They showed that the foundations were weak, or at least weaker than one might have guessed by examining the rest of the growing edifice. I have stayed at the foundations ever since, and I have tried to write this book so that the foundations are always clearly in view.

For advice and guidance on the manuscript itself, I am grateful to Robert Bolles, Robert Rescorla, Paul Rozin, and John Staddon, who thoroughly reviewed the entire manuscript and made many suggestions which educated me and improved the book. Charles Catania, Elkan Gamzu, Henry Gleitman, Hugh Lacey, David McFarland, John Nevin, Richard Schuldenfrei, Ken Sharpe, and Alan Silberberg provided many helpful comments on several chapters of the manuscript. Norton editors Don Fusting and Don Lamm always seemed to understand what I wanted to say, and helped me find a way to say what I wanted more gracefully. Among my students, many of whom read and evaluated an early version of the manuscript, I owe special thanks to Jed Brickner, Charlotte Feierman, Carol Harris, Laura Lillien, William Pavlik, Dan Reisberg, Nancy Saito, and John Samuelson. To Winnie Vaules, I have a lasting debt for turning hopeless penmanship into flawless typescript, always promptly and cheerfully. And I am grateful to Didi Beebe and Sue Santa Maria for their extensive assistance with correspondence, copying, and assorted other clerical details which can make book writing a nightmare, but did not.

Finally, I give loving thanks to Myrna Schwartz, whose contribution to this book, and to all of my work, has been most important of all. She has been teaching me psychology now for a dozen years. She finds the weakness in my arguments and helps me strengthen them. She finds the confusion in my thoughts and helps me organize them. Nothing I do reaches the outside world without first having profited from her insight. A great sense of confidence and security comes from knowing that when a piece of work leaves the house, it has already survived its most rigorous test. Without Myrna's help, this book would have been written sooner, but few would have bothered to read it.

Barry Schwartz
Swarthmore, Pennsylvania
July 1977

Psychology of
Learning & Behavior

1
An Introduction to Behavior Theory

We live in an age of science. As citizens of the industrialized, 20th-century world, we take science to be an authority on matters pertaining to the nature of the world and man's place in it, matters which earlier were resolved for us by philosophers, theologians, or statesmen. Where once it was the philosopher's task to uncover the essential nature of reality, now it is the physicist's. Where once it was the theologian who reflected on man's place in the natural order, now it is the biologist. And where once philosopher, theologian, and statesman together laid down rules and offered guidance about proper human conduct, now such judgments are coming to be shared with social scientists.

Our orientation to science for answers to deep, eternal questions has been a long time coming. With the beginnings of modern science in the 16th century, people began to turn to the scientist for an explanation of the physical world. Physics provided us with the principles which governed the behavior of inanimate objects. But it was believed that the principles of physics went only so far: living things shared some vital characteristics which inanimate things did not possess, and which the principles of physics could not explain. With the emergence of scientific biology in the 18th century, however, the domain of science was extended. At least some characteristics of all living things were captured by the methods and theories of science. Indeed, perhaps all characteristics of nonhuman living things were susceptible to a scientific analysis. Still, people were special. Scientific methods had inherent limitations. While they might reveal to us the physical stuff

1

of which people were made, the human capacity for reason and the human soul placed man outside the bounds of physics or biology.

But science could not be contained indefinitely. Perhaps emboldened by its success in other domains, science extended itself to human conduct. In the 19th century, some scientists were suggesting that all aspects of the behavior of all living things could be understood in terms of principles of physics and biology. Those committed to the scientific study of all aspects of human nature broke away from philosophy and established their own discipline—experimental psychology. For the last century, experimental psychologists have been pursuing the natural laws which describe people. Sensation, perception, thinking, learning, memory, motivation, and action are all being subjected to rigorous scientific analysis. While at present the existence of such natural laws is an article of faith and not a realization, people are increasingly willing to put their faith in the scientist.

This book is about one facet of modern psychology, a branch variously referred to as the psychology of learning, learning theory, behavior theory, and behavior analysis. This branch of psychology is explicitly committed to the view that human nature can be revealed and understood with the methods and principles of natural science. It has been at the heart of psychological activity for most of this century. Perhaps more than any other branch of psychology, behavior theory rests upon a general view of the nature of human action which flies in the face of almost 3,000 years of philosophical and religious doctrine. In studying behavior theory, we will spend most of our time describing and evaluating many specific laboratory experiments, typically experiments with rats, pigeons, dogs, or monkeys as subjects. However, these experiments provide the empirical foundation for behavior theory's conception of human nature, and at the same time, they are motivated by this conception. Thus, our evaluation of experiments will also be an evaluation of the conception of human nature.

ASSUMPTIONS OF BEHAVIOR THEORY

The goal of science is the discovery of lawful regularities in nature. The physicist studies the motion of a body down an inclined plane and relates that motion to the motion of the same body in free fall, and to the motion of the planets around the sun. He attempts to arrive at a general theoretical formulation which accurately describes motion in these three situations, and shows how the situations are related. The general formulation allows the physicist to predict the motions of bodies in other, different situations which have not yet been encountered. The physicist's activities are predicated on the view that certain central properties of the physical world are eternal, that phenomena repeat themselves, that bodies will move in the same, orderly way tomorrow as they do today. There would be no point in searching for general physical principles if the physical world changed dramatically from day to day. It is the physicist's view that, while many features of the physical world are always changing, it is just the general principles of physics which do not change. Whatever the nature of the bodies which occupy space in the physical world a thousand years from now may be, they will obey the laws of physics.

When psychologists approach the study of human nature scientifically, they hold the same assumption about the nature of human action as physicists do about the motion of bodies. There are regularities to human action which are eternal, which are a part of the essential nature of man. When these regularities are discovered and properly formulated, they will account for human action in the past and predict human action in the future. If human actions did not repeat themselves, if the conditions under which people behaved and the phenomena of behavior themselves continually changed from one period in time to the next, the pursuit of "laws" of behavior would be futile. We might come to an understanding of human action, perhaps through a study of social and cultural history, but we could not develop scientific laws. Thus, the assumption that behavior and its causal determinants repeat themselves reflects a commitment to the scientific (as opposed to, for example, the historical) study of human action.

There are obvious differences between people and inanimate objects which should make us pause to consider whether psychologists are justified in making the same assumptions about eternal regularities as physicists. People are reasoning, thoughtful, remembering creatures. They are changed as a result of their experiences in a way that falling stones, for example, are not. People carry experiences with them, and develop and learn and change in part as a result of those experiences. How can we seek something eternal in human nature when one of the obvious hallmarks of human nature is changeability?

It is just this characteristic of human nature—changeability or flexibility—which is the main concern of behavior theory. Experience certainly changes people. What behavior theory assumes, however, is that the very process of change is itself eternal. Only certain kinds of experiences will change people, and these kinds of experiences will change people in lawful, predictable ways. The kinds of experience which change people and influence action, and the nature of the change and the influence, are what behavior theory is out to find. Behavior theorists are seeking the laws by which past experience influences future action.

This goal of behavior theory—to find the laws which relate past experience to future action—has two central features. First, the thing to be explained according to behavior theory is action—behavior. People think, people feel, and people remember. At any moment, a multitude of interesting events is occurring within each of us. But science can gain only uncertain access to these internal events. Behavior, on the other hand, is objective. It is something which can be readily observed and measured. For this reason, behavior theorists by and large restrict their attention to behavior. For some behavior theorists the focus on behavior is just a step toward the scientific study of all aspects of human nature, including internal events. To others, a complete account of behavior promises to be a complete account of human nature with no need for any reference to internal events.[1]

Second, behavior theory emphasizes environmental events as playing the key role in determining human behavior. The source of action lies not inside the person, but in the environment. By developing a full understanding of how environmental events influence behavior, we will arrive at a complete understanding of behavior. It is this feature of behavior theory—its emphasis on environmental events as the determinants of human action—which most clearly sets it apart from other approaches to the nature of man. If it is true that human behavior is the reliable product of environmental events, then responsibility for behavior, whether noble or ignoble, rests not in the actor but in the environmental variables which give rise to the action. As behavior theory succeeds, our customary inclination to hold people responsible for their actions, and look inside them to their wishes, desires, goals, intentions, and so on, for the causes of their actions, will be replaced by an entirely different orientation. This new orientation is one in which responsibility for action is sought in environmental events. If this orientation is valid, then behavior theory is a view of the world which will leave no aspect of daily life untouched.

BEHAVIOR THEORY AS A WORLD VIEW

Behavior theorists claim that the causes of behavior lie not within the actor but in the environment. The claim that action is influenced by events in the environment is so obviously true that it is hard to imagine any account of human action worth serious consideration of

1. See Chapter 2, pages 33–35.

which this is not a feature. What distinguishes behavior theory is not the thesis that actions are influenced by environmental events, but that an analysis of how environmental events affect behavior will tell us all we need to know about the determinants of action. An analysis of environmental events will provide a *complete account* of human action. More specifically, behavior theorists expect that the major burden of explanation of human action will be carried by a small set of environmental events, events which we typically call rewards and punishments. The central thesis of behavior theory is that virtually all significant voluntary human actions can be understood in terms of their past relations to rewards and punishments. What controls voluntary action is its past history of association with rewarding or punishing environmental events.

We all acknowledge that some behavior is controlled by rewards and punishments, that to understand what causes people to act as they do, it is necessary to take rewards and punishments into account. We are not surprised when we open our morning newspaper and discover that a public official has engaged in an illegal act for money. It is also no surprise that we reduce our driving speed on a highway when a patrol car comes into view. Rewards and punishments are a palpable part of each of our lives. They are bestowed upon us and we use them ourselves to induce people to act in certain ways. Yet, we would argue, there is more to human beings than that. People do many things because of some inner force which guides them. People do things because it is logical or right or moral or humane to do them. People are happy because they have fulfilled their expectations about themselves, and they are depressed because they have not. Rewards and punishments touch the least human part of people. What we really care about, if we are to understand human action, is what people do when there are no obvious bribes or threats. In evaluating the character of other people, we tend to disregard those acts which are obviously controlled by rewards or punishments, and treat as significant those acts for which rewards and punishments seem absent. Those are the things which tell us about the person.

From the perspective of behavior theory, the acts for which we credit or blame people are not acts for which rewards or punishments are absent. They are acts the rewards and punishments for which are subtle and, as yet, unnoticed. All behavior of consequence is controlled by rewards and punishments. Sometimes the controlling environmental contingencies may be obvious (as when we slow down on the highway after passing a police car), and sometimes they may be subtle, but always they are responsible for what we do. In the words of one of the major figures of behavior theory, B. F. Skinner (1904–   ):

> *An experimental analysis shifts the determination of behavior from au-*
> *tonomous man to the environment— an environment responsible for . . . the*
> *repertoire acquired by each member [of the species]. . . . Is man then "abol-*
> *ished"? Certainly not as a species or as an individual achiever. It is*
> *autonomous inner man who is abolished, and that is a step forward.*[2]

It is hard to imagine a view of human nature more opposed to our ordinary conception of ourselves than this one. We have all grown accustomed to thinking of ourselves as the controllers of our own lives. Society holds us responsible for our actions, and we readily accept that responsibility. We place an extraordinary value on our freedom of choice, and we resent and resist any efforts at coercion. While we readily acknowledge that there are occasionally extenuating circumstances which compel us to act in a particular way—like firing a gun at someone who is pointing a knife at us, or forcing entry into a private building when we smell smoke—these situations arise infrequently. More typically, we *choose* a college, a spouse, a movie, a car, a career, on the basis of emotional characteristics, desires, needs, and rational analyses which are a unique feature of each of us. We formulate our own goals, and we act on the basis of our own preferences and desires, and not in keeping with external pressures.

Behavior theory challenges this conception of ourselves. If you want to know why someone did something, do not ask. Analyze the person's immediate environment until you find the reward. If you want to change someone's actions, do not reason or persuade. Find the reward and eliminate it. The idea that people are autonomous and possess within them the power and the reasons for making decisions has no place in behavior theory.

These characteristics of behavior theory suggest that the widespread application of its principles might result in major changes in our social institutions. If one is not free to act in a particular situation, that is, if there are forces present which demand certain actions, then one cannot be held responsible for engaging in those actions. We accept the principle that transgressions which are committed under duress should not be punished. Acts must be freely chosen before their perpetrators are forced to accept the consequences. But behavior theory rests on the principle that all acts are committed under "duress," in that contingencies of reward and punishment in the environment are responsible for what we do. Acts are never "freely" chosen by the person. They are always determined by rewarding and punishing aspects of the environment, together with the person's past experience of rewards and punishments for similar actions.

2. Skinner, 1971, p. 215.

Thus, we see that behavior theory is guided by a thesis about human nature which challenges deeply held beliefs which have been a part of our culture and our social institutions for perhaps 3,000 years. We have presented the thesis as characteristic of all behavior theory. It is actually most closely associated with the work of a particular theorist, B. F. Skinner. Skinner does not, in general, speak for all behavior theorists. There are many important points of disagreement among behavior theorists and we will encounter some of them throughout the book. Skinner's views are particularly extreme, and many who call themselves behavior theorists would take exception to much that Skinner has written. However, Skinner is the only major figure in behavior theory who has stated a world view. Much of his work has been concerned with specifying the relations between the kinds of research behavior theorists do in the laboratory and central features of ordinary human experience. Because Skinner's general claims about the nature of man are consistent with key concepts in behavior theory, and because no behavior theorist has offered alternative claims which might challenge Skinner's, Skinner must be taken seriously as the spokesman for his discipline.

The thesis about human nature on which behavior theory rests is one which people find repugnant and degrading. Nevertheless, behavior theory is becoming an increasingly influential part of our culture. The reason for its influence is that it has yielded a set of empirical principles which has been applied with some success in social settings as diverse as mental hospitals, schools, and prisons. It has provided people with a set of tools for working with individuals who find it difficult, for whatever reason, to lead fulfilling lives within society. One may ignore the physicist when he limits his domain to laboratory experiments and abstract theory. However, when his domain is extended in application by the engineer to automobiles, airplanes, atomic energy, and so on, he can no longer be ignored. Similarly, when behavior theory is extended in application to areas which touch our daily lives, it also cannot be ignored. This application of the principles of behavior theory to the hospital, the school, the prison, and so on, is referred to as *behavioral engineering,* or *behavior modification.*

APPLICATIONS OF BEHAVIOR THEORY
AN EXAMPLE

In many mental hospitals, a ward is set aside for the "chronic schizophrenic" patients. For these long-term residents, treatment has not worked. They do not get better by themselves as other schizophrenic patients sometimes do. After a period of unsuccessful therapy, they are maintained on the ward with little further attempt at treatment.

They are fed, cleaned, clothed, and kept alive. Often, these patients seem to have retired from living. They slump against a wall for hours at a time, speaking to no one and listening to no one. They do not respond to meal calls, and do not even feed themselves. They do not dress or wash themselves. They do not use the toilet. The world in which they live seems to extend only to the outer limits of their own bodies and they are completely dependent on the nursing staff for sustenance.

A group of therapists who employed principles of behavior theory in therapy entered a chronic schizophrenic ward in an effort to get patients to attend to some of their own bodily needs. The hospital was too understaffed to provide the kind of constant attention that these patients required. The therapists' task was to get the patients to cooperate with the nurses—to feed themselves, clothe themselves, and use the bathrooms. In this way, some nursing personnel could be freed for service elsewhere in the hospital.

The therapists began by trying to get patients to walk to the dining room unassisted and feed themselves. The current practice was for recalcitrant patients to be spoon-fed on the ward by nurses. To the therapists, this practice looked like a reward for recalcitrance. Suppose a patient was interested in receiving attention and support from a nurse. One way to get such attention was to refuse to eat meals. The consequence of refusing meals was personal attention. To test their hypothesis, the therapists eliminated the supportive activities of the nursing staff. Meals were signaled in the usual way by a gong. Patients who did not come to the dining room did not eat. At the first meal, all the patients who usually failed to enter the dining room stayed where they were, waiting to be coaxed and, finally, fed. When this attention was not forthcoming, they missed the meal. They missed the next one also, and the next one.

At breakfast the following day, again nothing happened, but at lunchtime two patients responded immediately to the gong and walked to the dining room. Once inside, they filled their trays, sat quietly at a table, and ate a little in silence. A third patient wandered in, and a fourth. By the end of a week of this new procedure, meal taking became a normal part of everyone's day.

This small improvement in the patients' behavior had an enormous effect on the operation of the ward in general. The nurses were less rushed and were able to be more supportive and attentive to everyone than they had previously been. For the therapists, however, this was only the beginning. Their plan was to use meal taking as a privilege—a reward for doing other things. They began to implement this plan after the voluntary meal taking had been occurring successfully for two weeks. A turnstile was installed at the door of the dining room. Tokens were required to pass through the turnstile. At first, the nurses guided the patients through the turnstile. A little later, they handed the patients tokens at the turnstile which the patients themselves deposited. Still later, the patients were required to come to the nurses for their tokens. These new demands on the patients were made slowly, but successfully.

The next step was an important one. A new, double turnstile was installed at the entrance to the dining room. In order for either one to operate, two patients, each depositing a token, had to enter at the same time. At first, the nurses fed tokens to one side of the turnstile. They next assisted the patients, in pairs, to the turnstile. Finally, the patients had to make their own arrangements. They had to communicate and cooperate. This procedure was fraught with difficulty, but it finally worked. And this minor communication requirement had a major effect. Once each patient had to make room in his private world for another person, he had to attend to the here and now of real social interaction. Fantasies, stupors, and monologues were slowly replaced by conversation. Most of the conversation centered on making it to the next meal, but it was conversation, nevertheless.

Now came the final step. The patients were going to be required to earn their tokens. Each patient was set a few tasks by the nurses and the therapists which, if successfully completed, would produce a token. The tasks were trivial. They centered exclusively on self-maintenance—washing, combing their hair, dressing, going to the bathroom, and the like. The patients performed their tasks readily and, before long, the nurses were almost completely freed from the caretaking functions which had occupied most of their time. The patients looked more alert, clean, active, and in touch with what was going on than anyone could remember.

The therapy program continued. The jobs that could earn tokens were expanded, and so were the things the tokens could buy. Candy, soap, hairbrushes, fresh linen, toys and trinkets, magazines, and cigarettes were available. Jobs involving ward maintenance as well as personal maintenance were introduced. People earned tokens by assisting in the dining room, by assisting with the laundry, with ward cleaning, with recreation, and even by dispensing and keeping records of consumption of the different rewards that were available. Finally, the patients were given the responsibility of establishing a job-and-reward scale: different jobs earned different numbers of tokens, and different rewards cost different numbers of tokens.

The success of the program was limited. No one was cured, and no one left the hospital. However, even this modest success is significant.

The quality of the patients' lives was improved, and in some cases the way was paved for other kinds of therapeutic activity. In addition, sometimes therapy programs like this one result in patient discharge.[3]

Let us consider how the assumptions and goals of behavior theory are exemplified by this case study. First, the problem to be addressed was behavioral. The patients were no doubt full of inner turmoil, and they failed to apprehend events in the environment rationally. But these internal dynamics of the patients were inaccessible to the therapists. They could not be evaluated, much less changed. What could be evaluated, and changed, were abnormalities in the patients' actions. Thus, it was action on which the therapists focused.

Second, in attempting to change the behavior of the patients, the therapists tried to identify events in their immediate environment which might have been serving as rewards. When one works with the assumption that rewards and punishments are responsible for all significant human action, one's first task in confronting a behavior problem is to identify the rewards which are maintaining the behavior. The therapists hypothesized that the reward for complete passivity—for failure to take meals or engage in personal hygiene—was the attention and support it brought from the nursing staff. They eliminated attention as a consequence of passivity. Their expectation, confirmed in this case, was that if attention from the nurses was responsible for the behavior of the patients, then eliminating attention would change the behavior.

The successful application of behavior theory in the schizophrenic ward is not an isolated example. Principles of behavior theory, derived from laboratory research with animal subjects, are being used to treat problems as diverse as alcoholism, cigarette smoking, obesity, stuttering, phobias, and learning disabilities. These principles are being used to control and eliminate behavior problems in schools, and to improve methods of instruction. While attempts to apply behavior theory are not always successful, when they are, they inspire in many the confidence that more success only awaits the further development of principles of behavior theory in the laboratory.

BEHAVIOR THEORY AND EVERYDAY LIFE

Some observers of behavior theory in application view it as a threat to human freedom. They see the developing techniques for behavior

---

3. This case description is fictitious, but it is closely based upon pioneering work on what are called *token economies* by Ayllon and Azrin, 1968. For reviews of research with token economies, see Atthowe and Krasner, 1968, and O'Leary and Drabman, 1971. For numerous other examples of successful application of principles of behavior theory, see Ullman and Krasner, 1965, or Ulrich, Stachnik, and Mabry, 1966, 1970, 1974.

control and behavior change as future tools for a kind of scientific to-
talitarianism. Those people who possess the tools will be able to impose their will on society. How does the behavior theorist reply to
these concerns?

The central component of any reply is that behavior control is a
fact of life. Though we may not have recognized it, individuals and institutions have always depended upon the use of reward and punishment to manipulate our behavior. We have probably used some principles of behavior theory ourselves to gain control over the behavior
of others. Teachers have always induced students to do their work
with the promise of reward and threat of punishment. Churches induce their members to behave in accordance with some moral code
with promise of rewards and punishments. Most people work at their
jobs for financial rewards. Governments induce people to spend their
money in particular ways by introducing tax penalties and incentives.
On a more personal level, we control the behavior of our children
with promise of reward and, more commonly, threat of punishment.
With these principles of behavior control already in operation all
around us, the main impact of behavior theory will be to make their
use more efficient and effective.

The critic of behavior theory might reply to this argument by stating that because something exists is not a justification for its further
existence—not to mention its extension. Perhaps the new awareness
of techniques of control inspired by behavior theory should awaken
efforts to eliminate it wherever it exists rather than to increase its efficiency. The behavior theorist would disagree. Recall that a central
assumption of behavior theory is that an understanding of how rewards and punishments work will provide a *complete* account of
human behavior. What this means is that principles of reward are
facts of nature. They tell us not that reward *can* work, but that it *must*
work. The science of behavior is a description of the way things *are,*
and not a blueprint of the way things ought to be. If it is a valid
description of the way things are, then one can no more change it or
eliminate it than one can change the laws of physics. One cannot eliminate control. One can eliminate an undesirable source of control and
replace it with a more desirable one, but the best way to accomplish
this is by learning the principles of behavior theory and then applying
them.[4]

The critic of behavior theory might reply that showing that the behavior of people *can be* controlled by rewards and punishments is not
the same as showing that it ordinarily is so controlled. It would surprise no one if, by putting a tin bucket over someone's head and bang-

4. Skinner, 1971.

ing on it with a hammer, one could get that person to do anything to have the banging stop. However, a demonstration of this type does not imply that the same person ordinarily does what he does in order to escape from noxious stimulation (or produce pleasant stimulation). The demonstration of behavior control in the laboratory or in the mental hospital may have the same character as the demonstration of behavior control by banging a bucket. Unless this claim can be refuted, the step from claiming that behavior *can be* controlled by reward and punishment to claiming that it *is* controlled by reward and punishment must be taken with great care.[5]

In short, the seriousness of concerns about the consequences of the growing application of principles of behavior theory to aspects of everyday life depends in large part upon our judgment about how accurate a picture of human nature behavior theory provides. If we judge the principles of behavior theory to be valid, and if we judge those principles to account for the major part of human action, then the behavior theorist is right. All that the application of behavior theory entails is the *systematic use* of techniques of behavior control which have always been and will always be a central part of human life anyway. If, however, we judge the principles of behavior theory to be invalid, or to be valid for only a limited portion of human life, then the behavior theorist is wrong. The application of behavior theory entails a change in human nature and in the nature of social institutions.

What we are suggesting is that a proper evaluation of the broad social and ethical implications of behavior theory depends upon an evaluation of the validity and generality of its basic principles. This book is an attempt to provide the reader with an opportunity to evaluate those basic principles. For the most part, we will present behavior theory sympathetically—present its best case. The shortcomings and problems with behavior theory which we encounter in the first ten chapters will be shortcomings of the sort which more research, within the framework of behavior theory, is likely to resolve. In the last two chapters of the book, we will present and evaluate possible shortcomings of behavior theory which may not be resolved simply by more research, but which may require a fundamental change in the nature of the theory and its thesis about the nature of man.

5. I am indebted to Richard Schuldenfrei for this argument.

2

The Science of Behavior

Setting the Context

The pursuit of an understanding of human nature has been at the center of intellectual concern and activity for centuries. Traditionally, people concerned with studying human nature attempted to come to an understanding through careful observation, speculation, and logical argument. Such students of human nature were typically philosophers or theologians.

For the last century, psychology has been in the process of transforming itself from a branch of philosophy into an independent, empirical science. In the course of this transformation, observation, speculation, and argument have taken a backseat to carefully controlled, rigorous experimentation. This new methodology promises significant advances in our understanding of the nature of man.

How has psychology gone about the task of making itself a science? From where have the problems, goals, and methods of modern psychology come? More specifically, what are the origins of modern behavior theory? In the following sections, we discuss first some of the philosophical antecedents of behavior theory, second, some of the biological antecedents of behavior theory, and third, some of the antecedents within psychology of present-day behavior theory.

PHILOSOPHICAL BACKGROUND OF BEHAVIOR THEORY

The history of thinking about human action, at least in the Western world, has been dominated by a few central ideas. These ideas are a part of our own commonsense explanations of the actions of others

13

and of ourselves. We view people as free to act as they choose. They have intentions or purposes, and they act to achieve certain ends. People have reasons for their actions and these reasons provide a sufficient account of human action. Because people are free to act, and have reasons for acting, we hold them responsible for what they do.

Prior to the 16th century, an account of behavior in terms of intentions and goals was not restricted to humans, or even to living things. Explanations of the movements of inanimate physical objects employed concepts which were similar to the ones used to explain human behavior. However, owing largely to the Italian astronomer Galileo (1564–1642), the dominant conception of the physical world began to change. Physical bodies were seen to move in lawlike and predictable ways. Such machinelike regularity was attributed not to forces within the body, urging and directing it, but to forces outside the body. Such outside forces completely determined physical motion. When such forces were understood, we would have a complete account of physical motion which left nothing either to chance or to the goals and desires of the moving body.

Descartes and Hobbes

The application of this mechanical view of the physical world to the behavior of living things, including people, began with French philosopher René Descartes (1596–1650). Descartes divided behavior into two classes—voluntary and involuntary. Voluntary behavior was governed by reason—by the mind. Its source was thus nonmechanical and nonphysical. In contrast, involuntary behavior was purely mechanical, just as the motion of inanimate objects was mechanical. When a child touched a hot flame with a finger, the fire set in motion a nerve in the finger. The motion was transmitted up to the brain where "animal spirits" were released. These spirits traveled back down the nerve, swelling the muscles in the fingers and causing them to be pulled back. Descartes' own analogy was to the mechanism by which one caused a bell at one end of a rope to ring by tugging on the other end of the rope.

Descartes' conceptual machine which accounted for involuntary action has come to be known as the *reflex arc*. A *stimulus* (the fire) is transmitted from the fingers to the brain by a nerve. This stimulus starts the machine which has as its output a motor *response* (finger withdrawal). Somewhere in the brain, stimulus input and response output are *associated* by means of nervous connections. Though the specific understanding of how reflexes worked has undergone many revisions through the years, the broad outline of the reflex arc has basically remained intact. There are countless reflexes in virtually all organisms. Some, like the knee jerk, are easy to observe in ourselves. Others, like the response of the pupil to light, are harder to observe but no less reliable. Still others, like stomach contractions, are only observable with instruments.

For Descartes, the reflex arc accounted for all the behavior of nonhuman animals, and the involuntary behavior of humans. The other domain of human action—voluntary action—was unique to humans. The mind was aware of reflex actions, though it could not control these actions, and it had complete control over nonreflex actions. And

Descartes's illustration of the reflex arc, by means of which stimulation of the foot (B) by fire (A) is transmitted to the brain (D E F). (Reprinted from Descartes, "De Homine" in Philosophical Works, Cambridge University Press, 1911.)

the actions of the mind were not subject to physical laws. They were governed by reason, and if they were subject to any laws, these laws were then unknown.

An argument for a more thorough-going mechanism, which did not exclude any aspects of human action, was made by the British philosopher Thomas Hobbes (1588–1679). Hobbes, like Descartes, viewed voluntary action as the province of the mind. However, unlike Descartes, the activities of the mind could themselves be explained by mechanical laws. Observable actions originated in incipient motions in the mind, which Hobbes called "endeavours." While "endeavours" were unobservable, they were physical and, as such, they behaved in the same lawlike way that reflexes did.[1] "Endeavours" occurred in the service of a set of human motives which, for Hobbes, were fundamentally hedonistic. The pursuit of pleasure and the avoidance of pain were the sole motives for human action. Philosophers before Hobbes had argued about whether pursuit of pleasure and avoidance of pain were good reasons for action. For Hobbes, this was a false issue: whether hedonism was good or bad, hedonism was simply and unalterably human nature.[2]

Thus Hobbes extended the mechanical views of Descartes to all human action and, in addition, he substituted for the view that intelligent human action was governed by reason, a view that action was governed by the pursuit of pleasure.

Associationism

Hobbes argued that the mind worked in accordance with natural laws like the ones that explained the motion of inanimate objects. What were the laws of mental activity? A philosophical tradition known as *British Empiricism* or *Associationism* took as its task the discovery of the laws of the mind. The leading figures in this tradition were John Locke (1632–1704) and David Hume (1711–1776).

For the Associationists, the source of all knowledge was sensory experience. People are born knowing nothing and gradually build up knowledge of the world by accumulating bits of sensory information. The young child looks at a closed book and sees not a book, but a small rectangular patch of color. The older child looks at the book and sees the same patch of color. However, the older child knows

1. Hobbes's notion of an "endeavour" parallels concepts developed for similar reasons by one of the major figures in behavior theory, Clark L. Hull (1884–1952). See Hobbes, 1651; Hull, 1943, 1952; and Peters and Tajfel, 1957.
2. Perhaps the clearest modern exponent of Hobbesian hedonism is B. F. Skinner (for example, 1971).

other things about the book. He knows that inside the book are many other rectangles—thin white ones with even rows of black marks on them. He knows the black marks are words and the words are strung together to form sentences. He knows the book will not stand up and walk away or turn its own pages. The older child knows all this without directly experiencing any of it through his senses. How does the child come to this knowledge? The Associationist answer is that in the past the child has directly experienced the pages of the book, the print on the pages, and so on. These experiences have occurred closely together in time and have occurred repeatedly. These two features of experience, *temporal contiguity* and *repetition,* allow the child to associate the sight of a closed book with its contents. With enough repetition, the sight of the book calls forth a large set of past sensations, or ideas, which are now bound together as a single unit. In this way, the full, detailed idea of a book is compounded out of a history of individual sensory impressions. Hume says:

> *Custom, then, is the great guide of human life. It is that principle alone which renders our experience useful to us, and makes us expect, for the future, a similar train of events with those which have appeared in the past. Without the influence of custom, we would be entirely ignorant of every matter of fact beyond what is immediately present to the senses.*[3]

Based upon the views that all knowledge came from experience, that experience was sensory experience, and that individual sense impressions combined to form complex ideas, the Associationists set out to formulate the laws of association. What was it that determined when and how associations were formed, and how powerful they would be? The basic principle of association was contiguity: two experiences which occurred closely together in time were likely to be associated. But there were other factors which influenced the formation of associations. Thomas Brown (1778–1820) identified some of them:

1. The intensity of the sensations.

2. The recency of their pairing.

3. The frequency of their pairing.

4. The number of associations in which the sensations to be associated were also involved.

3. Hume, 1739, Section V, Part I. Hume is concerned here not only with how we know more than we see at any given moment, but also with how we predict the future from the past. The focus of much of his treatise is on how people come to infer that the book they presently see is like books they have seen in the past and will have similar properties.

5. The similarity of the association to be formed to other, past associations.

In the mind of John Stuart Mill (1806–1873), sensations were like chemical elements. They combined to form compound ideas in the same way that hydrogen and oxygen combined to form water. Just as the science of chemistry was developing laws of combination of physical elements, so also the science of the mind could develop laws of combination of mental elements—a mental chemistry of ideas.

This progress in philosophical speculation about human thinking and action laid a foundation for the study of human nature as a scientific endeavor in search of natural laws. Descartes argued that some human action was lawlike and mechanical. Hobbes argued that *all* human action was lawlike and mechanical. The Associationists began to develop the laws. In addition, Associationism argued that the mind was not preformed, it was shaped by experience, and that in experience, simple elements of knowledge were built, brick upon brick, into complex ideas. These two aspects of Associationism have dominated all of behavior theory.

BIOLOGICAL BACKGROUND OF BEHAVIOR THEORY

When Descartes argued that involuntary human activity was machinelike and postulated a mechanism we have called the reflex arc to account for such activity, virtually nothing was known about the nervous system or nervous conduction. From the middle of the 17th century to the end of the 19th century, major advances in the study of the nervous system produced a conception of the reflex arc which was similar in spirit, if not in detail, to the one proposed by Descartes.

Physiologist John Swammerdam (1637–1680) showed that mechanical stimulation of a nerve was sufficient to produce movement of the muscle attached to the nerve. Work by other physiologists, including David Hartley (1705–1766), made it clear that the "animal spirits" of Descartes were not the source of nervous conduction. By the beginning of the 19th century, people were investigating the possibility that the source of nervous conduction was electrical energy, a view which conforms in large part to our present understanding of nervous conduction. By the middle of the 19th century, it had become known that nerves had specialized functions. Some nerves were sensory: they carried information about body stimulation to the brain. Other nerves were motor: they carried information from the brain to the muscles and produced action. Two critical components of Descartes' reflex arc had thus been identified and studied. So promising was the developing knowledge of the reflex arc that some researchers advanced the view that all behavior could be understood in terms of reflexes, even when the triggering environmental stimulus was not easy to find. The great Russian physiologist I. M. Sechenov wrote in 1863 that:

> *when the external sensory stimulus remains unnoticed—which happens quite frequently—thought is even accepted as the initial cause of behavior. Add to this the extremely subjective character of thought, and you will understand how firmly man must believe in the voice of self consciousness when it tells him such things. In reality, however, this voice tells him the greatest of falsehoods: the initial cause of all behavior always lies, not in thought, but in external sensory stimulation, without which no thought is possible.*[4]

We can see that by the middle of the 19th century there was substantial optimism that the whole of human behavior could be understood in terms of the workings of a physical machine—a reflex machine.

Darwin

Before Descartes, any suggestion that people had something significant in common with animals would have been viewed as preposterous. Descartes argued that the least human part of people— involuntary, unreasoned movement—was produced by the same mechanism that produced *all* animal behavior. Hobbes extended the arguments of Descartes to include all of human behavior as well. Progress in physiology led at least some physiologists to a view like Hobbes's: all behavior, of all organisms, would ultimately be understood in terms of the mechanical action of reflexes.

This developing idea that the behavior of animals was not fundamentally different from the behavior of falling stones, and the behavior of people was not fundamentally different from the behavior of animals, flew in the face of prevailing philosophical and religious views that man, possessed as he was of reason and a soul, was unique among living things. People acted with intelligence and foresight, and in accord with moral principles. Surely, neither stones nor chickens displayed intelligence or moral sense.

The intellectual development which most undercut prevailing views about the special status of man was British naturalist Charles

4. Portions of Sechenov's original work in Russian are translated in Herrnstein and Boring, 1965, p. 32. Part of it is cited by Rachlin, 1976, p. 35.

Darwin's theory of evolution by natural selection. Darwin (1809–1882) spent many years as a careful observer of nature. In 1859, he published *The Origin of Species* in which he proposed a theory of how species changed and how they were related.[5]

Darwin began with the view that life in the natural world was a battle among individual organisms for limited resources. Those individuals that won the battle and obtained the necessary resources would survive and reproduce. Those organisms which lost the battle would die off. The critical insight for Darwin was that not all members of a species were identical. Individuals differed in subtle but important ways. It was these individual variations which gave some members of a species a competitive advantage over others. The successful species members passed on their advantageous qualities to their offspring in some way. The offspring thus also enjoyed a competitive advantage over other species members. In each generation, the organisms that possessed these superior qualities lived longer and had more offspring than organisms which lacked these qualities. Over the course of many generations, more and more of the surviving members of the species shared the qualities which had initially given a handful of individuals an advantage. Ultimately, these qualities became a universal characteristic of the species; all members of the species had them. Thus, the old species, which did not in general have these qualities, would have evolved into a new one which did. And the process of evolution was a continuing one; species change, over the course of thousands of years, was the way nature worked and would continue to work.

Darwin's theory thus contained two crucial elements. First, there was *variation* among members of a species. Second, a process of *natural selection* seemed to increase over time the number of members of a species with characteristics which increased their chances of survival.

What was responsible for the variation among members of a species? Darwin did not know. Indeed, the origins of modern genetics were almost half a century in the future. However, Darwin argued that variation was not purposeful and intelligent; it was random. There was no grand design which insured that an individual species member would develop a characteristic which increased its chances for survival. Many of these individual variations might even be harmful. However, natural selection insured that only the useful individual variations would come, over generations, to characterize the species. Thus, neither nature nor the individual needed to act intelligently. Random variation was quite unreasoning. Natural selection was nature's exercise of intelligence.

5. Darwin, 1859.

Darwin's theory had a major influence on all aspects of the intellectual world. With respect to developing views of human nature, the theory of natural selection suggested that there was continuity among species. That new species very slowly evolved out of old ones suggested that species which were close together in evolutionary time had many characteristics in common. The notion of species continuity made it easier to argue against the prevailing wisdom that people were, in all important respects, unique. If people had reason, they were not necessarily alone among living things. Perhaps more significantly, one could argue that "reason" was something of a myth. Natural selection produced "intelligent" species change by unintelligent means. "Intelligent" behavior by individual organisms might be the product of a similar, unintelligent mechanism.

Spencer

Darwin did not offer this last speculation. However, a contemporary of his, Herbert Spencer (1820–1903), did.[6] Spencer suggested that organisms engaged in essentially random activity. Some of that activity resulted in pleasurable consequences. These pleasurable consequences worked to select the activities which preceded them. In this way, only activities which had produced pleasure (or eliminated pain) would continue to occur. If one makes the not implausible assumption that the things which give organisms pleasure are the very things which promote survival, one has an application of Darwin's theory to the life of individual organisms. Some unknown mechanism produces random variation in behavior. The particular activities which promote survival by producing pleasurable consequences are selected. Ultimately, the behavioral repertoire consists exclusively of activities which promote survival. Is behavior intelligent, planned, and goal-directed? For Spencer the answer was no. It is not the intention of the actor which is responsible for action. It is selection by the environment which determines future action on the basis of the consequences of past actions.[7]

PSYCHOLOGY AS A SCIENCE

Against this background of developing argument from philosophy and biology, it is not surprising that a move to study human nature

6. Spencer, 1880.
7. This principle has come to be called the *law of effect*. As we shall see throughout the book (see especially Chapter 6), it is the cornerstone of a very large part of behavior theory.

scientifically would emerge. All obstacles to the scientific study of man were removed. Descartes had argued that only some human action stemmed from material and mechanical sources. Hobbes argued that all human action could be understood in terms of mechanical principles. Darwin's theory added credibility to the views of Hobbes, while progress in physiology gave life and substance to Descartes' reflex arc. Meanwhile, the Associationists were searching for accounts of the growth of knowledge (complex ideas from simple ones) along the lines being developed by the science of chemistry, and Spencer viewed the development of a behavioral repertoire in the individual as a mechanical, unintelligent analog of the evolution of behavioral repertoires in different species. Not only is it easy to imagine a swell of enthusiasm for a science of psychology, but one can even see the specific lines along which such a science might develop.

One might begin a *scientific* investigation of human nature with the expectation that an explanation of human action would look something like this:

1. The newborn infant is a collection of simple reflexes. Simple stimuli are registered in the brain and trigger simple responses.

2. As the infant gains experience, different simple stimuli get associated with each other. The taste and smell of milk, originally two independent sense experiences, become connected through contiguity. Subsequently, the taste of milk suggests its smell and, conversely, the smell of milk suggests its taste.

3. Since different stimuli are now associated with each other, they begin to trigger each other's reflexes. The smell of milk or the sight of a nipple may trigger sucking. The taste of milk may trigger sniffing.

4. As development continues, more and more stimuli get associated with each other and more and more reflexes get connected. Thus, complex sensory experiences, like the perception of a flag, get built from association of simple experiences of red, white, blue, star, and stripe. Similarly, reflexes get chained together, with the response of one reflex serving as the stimulus for the next.

5. Of all the reflexes which occasionally occur, only some will produce consequences which have survival value (are pleasurable). It is these reflexes alone which remain in the repertoire of the adult organism.

6. Thus, the normal adult may be viewed as someone who has learned to recognize complex stimuli by building up associations of simple ones and has learned to engage in complex sequences of be-

havior by chaining together simple reflexes. We shall see that behavior theory has been dominated by the pursuit of empirical support for this conception of human nature.

FROM EARLY PSYCHOLOGY TO MODERN BEHAVIOR THEORY

The Associationists asserted that there are laws which govern the formation of ideas. If psychology was to be science, assertion had to be replaced by the gathering of empirical evidence. A major step in this direction was taken by the German psychologist Hermann Ebbinghaus (1850–1909). Ebbinghaus conducted an extensive series of experiments with himself as subject. The experiments involved learning lists of nonsense words like TAV, CES, FAX, and so on. Ebbinghaus explored the order in which the lists were recalled, how practice affected recall, what relations or associations got formed among items on a list, and other aspects of the learning and memory for these nonsense words.[8] Ebbinghaus developed a set of empirical laws of association, many of which have survived more than half a century of further investigation.

From our perspective, Ebbinghaus's work is significant for two reasons. First, it was a major step in moving inquiry about human nature into the laboratory. Second, the problem Ebbinghaus chose to work on explicitly incorporated the doctrines of Associationism into scientific psychology. Each nonsense word could be viewed as analogous to a simple element of sensory experience. In his research, Ebbinghaus was asking how these simple elements were combined, through experience, into complex ideas. If, for example, we read TAV, CES, and FAX over and over again, do these individual words become united by experience into a single, complex one—TAV–CES–FAX—so that hearing one calls forth the others? If so, what aspects of our experience with these words contribute to their union? Implicit in Ebbinghaus's research was the view that our understanding of complex ideas reflects a past history of association of simple ones.

Pavlov

While the work of Ebbinghaus was an important step in the building of a science of psychology, and an important precursor to behavior theory, a much more direct influence on behavior theory was provided by the work of Ivan P. Pavlov (1849–1936). Pavlov was a

8. Ebbinghaus, 1885 (translated in 1913).

Nobel Prize-winning Russian physiologist. At around the turn of the century, he shifted his attention from physiology to what he called "psychic reflexes." Pavlov knew that dogs would reliably salivate when food was placed in their mouths. He was studying the role of the "salivary reflex" in digestion. His research on digestion took a permanent detour when he discovered that objects in the environment which reliably appeared just prior to the delivery of food to the dogs (for example, the laboratory coats of the researchers) would themselves make the dogs salivate, even before food was placed in the mouth. What could be producing salivation to stimuli which preceded food delivery? Presumably, salivation to the food itself was a built-in characteristic of dogs. But a connection between the sight of a laboratory assistant and salivation could hardly be built-in. It had to be that aspects of the dogs' experience in the laboratory were responsible for the salivation which occurred to objects other than food. The reflex connection between a lab coat and salivation had to be learned, or *conditioned.* Having observed these psychic or *conditioned reflexes,* Pavlov devoted the rest of his life to a study of the laws of their formation.[9]

Why was Pavlov so excited about his discovery? He saw it immediately as a window to the laws of the mind. It was clear to Pavlov that while inborn reflexes formed a significant part of the behavior of all organisms, an even more significant portion of behavior could not be inborn. That people respond to a flame applied to the finger is almost surely inborn. But that people also respond to "Fire!" is not. The word "fire" must somehow be associated with actual flame so that either the flame or the word will produce the appropriate reflex. Salivation to a lab coat had to be an instance of the association of inborn responses with new stimuli.

Thus, for Pavlov, the study of conditioned reflexes was the study of the laws of association of ideas. Organisms began with a set of simple reflexes, and experience in the world both broadened the range of events which would produce the reflex and combined simple reflexes into complex reflex sequences. All of knowledge and action could be understood in terms of the elaboration through experience of simple, inborn reflexes.

Pavlov's work, like that of Ebbinghaus, contributed to the development of a *science* of associationism. However, Pavlov went a step beyond Ebbinghaus. While Ebbinghaus was investigating "ideas," Pavlov was investigating reflexes—material things which could be seen and measured. In Pavlov, associationism and reflex physiology

9. See Pavlov, 1927. Discussion of the laws of conditioned reflexes is the focus of Chapters 4 and 5 of this book.

were combined. The study of the laws of the mind was transformed into the study of behavior.

Watson and Behaviorism

Though Pavlov's research began at the turn of this century, it was not available in English until 1927. By that time, it had already become a major influence on American scientific psychology. This was largely the result of the efforts of John B. Watson (1878–1958). Watson's career as a psychologist was brief, and in it he made no major substantive contribution. What he did was argue the view that psychology should be the scientific study of *behavior,* and nothing more.[10] He was the leading spokesman for a school of psychology known as *Behaviorism.* Its central tenet was that all there was to human nature was behavior. Thoughts, wishes, images, desires, and feelings had no place in the study of man. All of these words were simply obscure and imprecise labels for muscle movements and neural activity. Associationism was valuable, but not the associationism of Ebbinghaus, not the association of ideas. Instead, one should pursue the assocationism of Pavlov.[11] Here, all mental entities were abandoned in favor of physical ones. The arguments of Hobbes, centuries earlier, came to fruition with Watson and the Behaviorist movement.

Watson's writings influenced virtually all of scientific psychology. For more than 40 years, scientific psychology was, with few exceptions, behaviorist psychology. Though psychology entered an era of great debate among major theorists immediately after Watson, the notion that psychology was the study of behavior was not debatable. That was a view that nearly all theorists shared. It is a view which many researchers in present-day behavior theory still hold.

LIMITATIONS OF THE REFLEX ARC

Watson's popularization of a scientific psychology which would proceed along the empirical lines already drawn by Pavlov fits so nicely with the philosophical and biological background that one might expect that after Watson, all scientific psychologists would have set out in pursuit of the laws of reflexes. The notion that the reflex arc could serve as a model for all the behavior of all organisms does not seem an unreasonable one.

10. See Watson, 1913, 1919.
11. In actual fact, it was not the work of Pavlov, but the work of another Russian physiologist, Bechterev, 1913, which seemed to influence Watson. Bechterev's work was similar to Pavlov's and, though it began later, it was translated from the Russian earlier.

Imagine yourself as a scientific psychologist about 60 years ago. Having adopted the reflex arc as a basic unit of behavior, you begin to develop the laws of the reflex and of association. You study a simple organism in a well-controlled environment in which you, the experimenter, provide the stimuli which trigger the reflexes. Such a strategy enables you to come to understand how reflexes work. As your understanding grows, so does your confidence in the theoretical framework you have adopted. After having developed laws of the reflex in very simple situations, you would increase the complexity of your experiments. You would expect thereby to discover how complex reflexes (which presumably dominate the activities of complex creatures like people) are built out of simple ones.

Thorndike

When the reflex arc concept was applied to moderately complex situations, in which the experimenter did not provide the triggering stimuli, it ran into substantial problems. They can best be discussed with an example, one extensively studied by E. L. Thorndike (1874–1949).[12] Imagine a cat in a cage, the door of which is held fast by a simple latch. Just outside the cage is a piece of salmon in a dish. The cat moves around in the cage, sniffing its corners. Suddenly, it sees the salmon, moves to the part of the cage closest to it, and begins extending its paws through the bars toward the fish, which it cannot reach. The cat reaches more and more vigorously and begins scratching at the bars. After a while, this activity stops and the cat starts moving actively about the cage. A few minutes later, it bangs against the latch and frees it. The door opens and the cat scampers out and eats the fish. The cat is replaced in the cage and a new piece of fish is placed in the dish. The cat goes through the same sequence of activities as before and eventually opens the latch, seemingly inadvertently. This is repeated again and again. Gradually, the cat stops extending its paws through the bars and spends more and more of its time near the latch. Next, the cat begins directing its activity almost exclusively at the latch, now no longer inadvertently. Ultimately, the cat develops a quick and efficient pattern of movements which enables it to open the latch and free itself almost immediately.

12. Thorndike, 1898, 1911. Thorndike's early work was not a response to Watson, but contemporaneous with Watson. Indeed, Thorndike was one psychologist whom Watson often singled out for criticism for having a mentalistic theory. It is clear in retrospect that Thorndike was not offering a return to mentalism. Rather, he was offering a more subtle and sophisticated kind of mechanism than Watson was, one which has much in common with the theories of Darwin and Spencer.

This situation, while still enormously simpler than the natural environment, is considerably more complicated than one in which only reflexes triggered by the experimenter are studied. How can the reflex arc be used to explain the behavior of the cat? The immediate task is to enumerate the reflexes. There might be a sniffing reflex, a looking reflex, a reaching reflex, a jumping reflex, a running reflex, and so on, but could there be a latch-opening reflex? No, but presumably latch opening reflects the development of a complex combination of reflexes. The next task is to identify the stimuli which trigger the reflexes. This is more difficult. What are the odors which trigger sniffing? What triggers agitation? The salmon presumably triggers reaching, but, if so, why does the cat stop reaching? The latch might trigger some set of paw movements, but, if so, why didn't they occur when the cat was first in the cage? And doesn't the salmon have something to do with the latch-opening response? Finally, there is the task of explaining the changes in the cat's behavior in the cage over time.

It is clear that either much work would be required for the reflex arc to provide a satisfactory account of the actions of the cat, or a theoretical framework which established an alternative to the reflex would have to be provided. Thorndike did the latter.

Before we develop the alternative, let us consider a commonsense account of the cat in the cage. One might begin by saying the cat wanted the salmon. When efforts to reach it failed, the cat stumbled around until it accidentally hit the latch and opened it. The next time in the cage, the cat did not realize what part of its behavior had succeeded, so it stumbled around some more. Gradually, with repeated experience, the cat learned how to open the latch efficiently and then continued to do so in order to get the salmon. What triggers latch opening? Nothing. It is not a machinelike reflex, but an action which depends upon goals and intentions. The cat knows what it wants, and eventually comes to know how to get it.

This commonsense explanation denies the basic premises of the reflex arc model. Behavior is not a collection of simple reflexes, and organisms do not work the way machines do. It suggests that if cats are not machines in cages, they are certainly not machines in nature, and people, who are infinitely more flexible than cats, could not possibly be machines, no matter how complexly constructed.

On the other hand, it might be possible to construct a machine which acts with purpose, that is, acts not as a result of some triggering stimulus, but as a result of some anticipated goal. It keeps acting in a particular way until the goal is achieved, and somehow stops doing those things which move it away from the goal and continues doing those things which move it closer.

The Law of Effect

Thorndike provided such a mechanical alternative to the reflex arc. For much behavior, there is no triggering stimulus at all which automatically produces the activity. What primarily influences its occurrence is *feedback*—its consequences. And this influence is automatic. Acts which have favorable consequences will continue to occur, while acts which do not have favorable consequences will stop. Thus the cat spends more of its time around the latch and less of its time pushing its paws through the bars of its cage. Eventually, only efficient latch opening occurs. As with the reflex arc, this feedback mechanism works on simple acts, and complicated ones are merely chains of individual, simple ones strung together.

The idea that behavior is controlled by its consequences Thorndike labeled the *law of effect*. It has much in common with Spencer's application of Darwin's theory of natural selection to the life history of individual organisms. Random variations in activity, a kind of trial and error, occurred, and those variations which led to pleasurable consequences were stamped in or strengthened. The adult organism behaved intelligently because, through the action of the law of effect, only "intelligent" (adaptive) behavior remained in its repertoire. This stamping-in process has come to be known as *operant* or *instrumental conditioning*.

Gestalt Theory

The pursuit of laws of conditioned reflexes, following Pavlov, and the pursuit of a detailed understanding of the law of effect, following Thorndike, have dominated behavior theory throughout its history, and continue to dominate it today. Those researchers who have been critical of behavior theory have developed alternative theories of their own, rather than modifying behavior theory. One such alternative, which is as old as behavior theory itself, is known as *Gestalt Theory*. It has been critical of a number of aspects of behavior theory. It is first critical of the notion that complex activity is nothing but a collection of simple elements. For the Gestalt theorist, the complex is more than and different from a sum of the simple. Breaking events or activities down into basic elements distorts our understanding of the events or activities. For example, a simple melody is more than the sum of the notes which comprise it. We apprehend the melody as a whole all at once and recognize it even if the particular notes which comprise it are transposed on the musical scale. Second, Gestalt theory has argued that activity is generally characterized by purpose and intelligence which cannot be reduced to either the laws of reflexes or the law of effect. For the Gestaltist, organisms do not move blindly or randomly through the world, ending up with a set of activities that happen to work. Instead, they intelligently formulate and test hypotheses about what activities might achieve what ends. Often such hypothesis testing may be covert. An organism might imagine an action and its consequence without actually trying it. As early as 1917, Wolfgang Köhler (1887–1967), one of the leading figures of Gestalt psychology, argued that chimps learned to solve problems in just this covert, insightful fashion.[13] Gestalt theory has not survived into the present as a coherent formulation, but many researchers continue to work with a Gestalt spirit, and thus continue to reject the fundamental tenets of behavior theory.

BEHAVIOR THEORY IN THE PRESENT

In the generation which followed the discoveries of Thorndike and Pavlov, scientific psychology witnessed a theoretical battle among behavior theorists. Four major figures, C. L. Hull, E. R. Guthrie, E. C. Tolman, and B. F. Skinner, offered brands of behavior theory which seemed radically different from one another.[14] The literature was overrun by attempts to create experiments which would provide definitive support for one theory over another. A set of crucial problems emerged, the resolution of which was expected to decide among the competing theories.[15] The most influential theorist in this group at the time was Hull.

The great battle was never won. The crucial problems were not resolved. The critical experiments turned out not to be critical. Perhaps it is because the theories were much more alike than they were different. Consider this statement by Tolman:

> *Let me close, now, with a final confession of faith. I believe that everything important in psychology . . . save, [perhaps] such matters as involve society and words, can be investigated in essence through the continued experimental and theoretical analysis of the determiners of rat behavior at a choice-point in a maze. Herein I believe I agree with Professor Hull and also with Professor Thorndike.*[16]

13. Köhler, 1929.
14. See Hull, 1943; Guthrie, 1935, 1959; Skinner, 1938; and Tolman, 1930, for coherent presentations of the four competing views.
15. See an excellent collection of papers from this period in Goldstein, Krantz, and Rains, 1965. The papers give a good idea of the issues which consumed psychology at this time, and the feeling shared by many that one comprehensive theory of behavior would emerge from all the controversy.
16. Tolman, 1938, p. 34.

What Tolman was suggesting was that an almost complete account of the nature of organisms could ultimately be developed from the study of the behavior of a relatively simple organism in a relatively simple situation. His statement reveals the commitments that:

1. The proper subject of a science of psychology is behavior.

2. That scientific laws of behavior can be discovered.

3. That there is a continuity among species in the laws of behavior.

4. That there are simple elements or units of behavior to be identified.

5. That complex behavior may be understood in terms of these simple units.

Tolman was quite correct in his assertion that he shared these commitments with Hull and Thorndike (and with Skinner, Guthrie, and all the other behavior theorists).

Considered from the broad perspective with which we began this chapter, all behavior theories were close relatives. It was only when the philosophical developments which began with Descartes were fully inculcated in the community of scientific psychologists that the issues which distinguished the different theories seemed major.

Over the years the general theories have evolved into very specific ones. The world views expressed by Hull, Guthrie, and Tolman have few serious advocates, though areas of research and theory retain their distinctly Guthrian, Hullian, or Tolmanian flavor. Skinner is the exception. His general theory has survived and grown over the years so that it now dominates behavior theory.

THE "SCIENCE" OF BEHAVIOR

In discussing the antecedents of modern behavior theory, we have emphasized the development of the notion that "human nature" could be a proper subject for scientific inquiry. Applying the methods of science to a problem means, in part, establishing precise definitions of key concepts, arriving at a sense of what form a satisfactory explanation of a phenomenon will take, and stating hypotheses in such a way that there can be agreement about how they may be verified. We turn now to a discussion of the manner in which behavior theory has made itself into a science.

Objective Definitions and Methods

A big step in the making of a science is taken when a language is developed which enables people to describe their observations with pre-

cision. Such a language consists mainly of a set of terms and their definitions. However, it may also include a set of methods or procedures
which are the standard means for making observations. Consider, for
example, the proposition that the density of water is greater than the
density of ice. This seems like a very straightforward, unambiguous
proposition which requires no translation into more precise, technical
language. We all know what water is and what ice is, and probably we
have a good idea about density. Or do we? Are the water from our
faucet and the water from a mountain stream the same water? How
about the ice in our freezers and the ice atop an alpine peak? For ordinary purposes, they are equivalent. However, to test our proposition,
not only is the substance that comes out of our faucet different from
the substance that trickles through the mountains, but neither of
these substances is water. Water is defined as a chemical compound
consisting of hydrogen and oxygen and nothing more. There is no
rock sediment, no soil trace, no chlorine, and no rust in the water referred to in our proposition, though there may be in mountain
streams and tap water. Indeed, it is possible that our proposition will
be false if tested with tap water. The minerals contained in tap water
may affect the water's response to temperature change. However, if
water is *defined* as distilled H_2O and ice is *defined* as H_2O at $0°$ cen-
tigrade, we will have gained an important advance: our proposition
will be *confirmable*. Since everyone will be sure of what "water" and
"ice" mean, anyone, anywhere will be able to put our proposition to a
test, and if people in different places do so, we may be confident that
in all cases it was the same test.

It may seem a little silly to go to such trouble to define water and ice
since we all know what they are. This is even true in the case of our
proposition since in all likelihood the mineral content of ordinary tap
water will not alter the outcome of a test of the proposition. But suppose we used ordinary tap water and tested the proposition and
found it false. Then we would not know whether the proposition was
false or whether our tap water's response to temperature was influenced by its mineral content. So, to be safe, it is sensible to adopt the
technical, somewhat remote definitions of water and ice in testing the
proposition.

Consider now another proposition: Women are more intelligent
than men. What does this proposition mean and how are we to evaluate it? Clearly, the difficulty centers on "intelligence." What is it and
how do we quantify it? There is a long history of the study of intelligence in psychology. What intelligence has come to mean is performance on certain kinds of tests. Thus, the proposition may be re-
stated precisely as "Women will obtain higher scores on intelligence
tests than men." Now, we have no problem in deciding either what the

proposition means or how to evaluate it. One can test the proposition when it is stated in this way so that everyone will agree on whether or not it has been verified.

What do we mean by "intelligence" in ordinary language? When we use it, we typically refer to some characteristic of a person—some general trait which may be revealed in a wide variety of situations. We cannot see intelligence. We infer it from things we can see. However, having seen these indications of intelligence in an individual, in subsequent discussions of the individual, we use the word "intelligent" with confidence. The precise definition of intelligence just offered has one especially significant property: it refers to events which are all readily observable. We are making explicit the strategy that is generally adopted implicitly in the use of abstract words. But we are doing something more as well. Rather than saying "intelligence" may be *indicated* by a score on a test, we are saying "intelligence" *is* a score on a test. It is nothing more than the set of observations we use to identify it. This strategy of defining concepts and propositions in such a way that they are observable and objective characterizes behavior theory. Definitions which do not have this character are judged to stand in the way of scientific progress.

Let us see what benefits this definitional strategy provides. Two problems with observation, speculation, and argument as methods of inquiry into human nature are lack of agreement about the meaning of words and lack of criteria for verification of propositions. Objective, observational definitions clearly eliminate the first problem, for a definition is good only if it means the same thing to all users of the word. Objective definitions also deal with the problem of verification by insuring that our hypotheses or propositions are formulated in such a way that the means of their verification is obvious.[17]

Problems with Objective Definitions

Defining terms and propositions so that they are observable and easily tested is an important step in turning the study of human nature into a science of behavior. However, such objectification is not without problems. Consider again the definition of intelligence as a score on a particular test. Such a definition insures that all investigators using the word will mean the same thing and that propositions will be verifiable. However, defining intelligence in this way, while solving the problem of objectivity, creates another one. Whatever we may mean by the word "intelligence" in ordinary discourse, it is cer-

17. See Popper, 1959.

tainly something other than performance on a test. One could verify the proposition that women score better on intelligence tests than men and still convince no one that women are more intelligent than men. Here is the danger in providing precise definitions of words like "intelligence." In doing so, we place a barrier between the phenomenon as it occurs in the real world and the phenomenon as it occurs within our precise, testable proposition.

Most of the notions we use in explaining human behavior refer to aspects of people like intelligence that we cannot directly observe. We speak of what people *think,* how they *feel,* what they *desire* or *intend,* what they *remember,* and so on. In the making of psychology into a science, behavior theorists have felt the need either to objectify these terms as we have objectified "intelligence," or to dispense with them altogether. Either strategy would create problems like the one created by our definition of "intelligence." We mean more by "desire" or "intention" than any particular objective definition could capture. How can we take seriously any attempt to explain our behavior which does away with all the important things we know go on inside us? Somehow, behavior theory must find a way to deal with our internal lives. Objective definitions of terms like "intention" or "desire" must be connected to our everyday definitions or, if the concepts are abandoned altogether, it must be shown that a complete account of behavior can be provided without them.

Behavior Theory and Internal Events

In their efforts to develop a set of objective methods for the study of human nature, behavior theorists have been concerned with how internal, subjective phenomena like desires and intentions should be handled. A number of alternative approaches can be identified.

1. One position is that internal events may exist, and that they may be important components of human action, but that they cannot be studied scientifically. They are by their very nature private and unique to each individual. Therefore, scientific techniques which depend upon public verifiability are not appropriate. Behavior theory should work out those principles of human action which can be verified. The rest shall remain the province of philosophers, poets, and social critics. This view is sometimes called *methodological behaviorism.*

This is a rather pessimistic view of the potential value of scientific psychology. By establishing some clear principles of behavior, it will enable speculation about what goes on inside the person to be based upon more reliable and less individualistic observations than used to be the case. It will not, however, be able to get inside the person by it-self.

2. A second view is less pessimistic. It holds that private, mental events cannot be studied directly, as does the first view. However, they may be used as concepts or constructs in developing explanations of behavior. That is, it is appropriate to use terms like intention, memory, feeling and the like, but not in the casual way that everyday observers of human nature use them. Rather, they may be useful if they are well anchored to events in the world which can be observed directly. When used in this way, they are called intervening variables, and they help to organize a large set of experimental observations into a smaller set of more general principles.[18]

What does it mean to say that these private events must be well anchored to observables? Let us take an example. Consider the concept "fear." Fear is a private experience with which each of us is familiar. Yet, because it is private, it probably means something a little different to each of us. However, it can be made into a useful scientific construct. Suppose we could identify a broad set of environmental situations, each of which could lead to one or more of a set of responses which suggested fear. The situations might be a picture of a vampire, a painful electric shock, a parent with a strap, a picture of a person looking down from the ledge of a 100-story building, and so on. The responses might be sweating, running, widening of the eyes, quickening of the pulse, tensing of muscles, grinding of teeth, and so on.

If we attempted to describe the relations between the various environmental conditions and the various responses, we would have a very long, complicated, disorganized list. One way to simplify and organize the list is to introduce the concept "fear." We argue that the various environmental conditions we have identified produce an internal, unobservable state—fear. Fear, in turn, produces the different responses we have listed. The concept of fear is used to highlight the relations among the different environmental conditions and the different responses. Thus, concepts like "fear" can be enormously useful in making order out of the chaos of individual observations. It is important to remember, however, that such concepts are useful only if the situation–response relations they summarize are well established.

3. A third view is still more optimistic. It is at the heart of what is called *radical behaviorism,* the orientation on which the behavior theory of B. F. Skinner is based.[19] This view acknowledges the existence and importance of internal, private events. Furthermore, it argues that

18. MacCorquodale and Meehl, 1948; Miller, 1959.
19. Skinner, 1974.

they can be studied and studied directly. What makes this direct access to internal events possible is that they are caused by the same environmental conditions which cause observable actions. This idea about the nature of thoughts and feelings is so radically different from our customary views that it requires explication. We tend to assume that we do something because of some idea or feeling inside us. First comes the idea, then the action. When we try to guess at what is causing someone else to do something, our reasoning takes the opposite direction. First we see the action, then we infer some internal cause. We assume, however, that the actual causal sequence is the reverse—thought, then action. Well, the view of radical behaviorism is that the causal sequence we use in explaining someone else's behavior is the same one we use in accounting for our own behavior. We interpret our own internal states by watching what we do just as we interpret someone else's internal state by watching what he or she does. In both cases, the behavior comes first and interpretation of what is going on inside comes second. Subsequently, when we experience this internal state, it may lead to action; that is, the causal sequence may be the way we assume it is. The important point is that in learning about our internal states—in developing "self-perception" or "self-awareness"—we use the same evidence that we use in describing the actions of others.[20]

What this means is that by learning which actions or events are responsible for the initial interpretation of internal states, we can learn about the states themselves. Observable behavior is the source material of which internal states are constructed.

Thus, for the radical behaviorist like Skinner, internal, private events have a place in behavior theory. However, they are phenomena which need to be explained and not phenomena which themselves provide explanations.

Behavior Theory as Theory

In an effort to pursue human nature scientifically, behavior theory has set about defining terms and stating propositions so that they are objective and verifiable. But there is more to the making of a science than objectivity. One must have a theory, a coherent formulation which fuses individual observations into a meaningful framework which indicates the relations among the individual observations and

20. This analysis originated in Skinner, 1954. Some experimental support for the view has been obtained by Bem, 1970. Actually, the heart of the analysis is embodied in William James's analysis of emotion (1884), and James's analysis has been supported by the research of Schachter and Singer, 1962.

provides an explanation of them. Most importantly, one needs a theory to help decide which observations should be made, which terms and propositions should be objectified, and how they should be objectified.

Consider an example. Imagine turning on a light switch in one of your rooms. The light flickers for a moment and goes out. Your problem as a scientist is to figure out why. We can identify a number of possibilities:

1. The light bulb is burned out.

2. The switch is bad.

3. There is a loose connection in the ceiling fixture.

4. A fuse has blown.

5. The electric company has just turned off all of your power.

6. An enemy of yours has willed your light to go out.

7. The light bulb was tired.

8. A passing airplane disrupted the flow of energy from the switch to the light.

9. It was an act of God.

The list of possible causes could be extended indefinitely. Now, how does one decide which possibilities are worth investigating and how they are to be investigated? Most of us would probably focus attention on the first five possible causes; the last four would probably not even occur to us. The reason for this selectivity is that we have adopted a very powerful theoretical framework within which to understand electricity—the framework provided by physics. It is this theoretical framework which will dictate the propositions we formulate and test. One could imagine a different theory of electricity (surely a less compelling one than the physical theory) which would influence us to focus attention on one or more of possibilities 6 through 9.

The point of this example is that there are many different propositions one might formulate about human nature, and many different ways of objectifying and testing these propositions. The behavior theorist decides which propositions to test and how on the basis of a conception of which strategy is most likely to enable him to understand the phenomenon he is investigating. In part, he comes to this conception on the basis of past experience with the phenomenon under investigation. It is on this basis that one might decide to test first the proposition that the light bulb has burned out. However, in the main, the behavior theorist depends upon an idea, provided by a theory, of what a satisfactory explanation will look like. He has a goal, an endpoint in view.

We see here that a clearly and precisely stated theory establishes the goals of observation by establishing the form that a satisfactory explanation must take. Our discussion of the philosophical and biological antecedents of behavior theory has highlighted some of the major influences in the development of a scientific approach to human nature. The same influences also largely determined the behavior theorists' conception of what the laws of human nature would look like:

1. They would be laws of behavior.

2. They would be laws of learning by association.

3. They would involve identification of basic elements and rules for their combination.

4. They would be laws which characterized infrahumans as well as humans.

This set of expectations about the form which the laws of human nature would take led in turn to the development of particular methods of investigation which were ideally suited to find such laws. The methods are justified by the theory and the theory comes from three centuries of philosophical inquiry. In the next chapter, we describe the methods of behavior theory. We will see how well tuned they are to the expectations with which behavior theory began about the form which laws of human behavior would take.

3

Basic Methods for the Analysis of Behavior

When one sets out to investigate a phenomenon systematically, one is faced with a difficult decision. What methods should be used to study the phenomenon? This decision will depend upon one's view of what aspects of the phenomenon are most important or interesting. But the judgment of what is important or interesting will depend upon the theoretical perspective with which one approaches the phenomenon in the first place.

The methods which characterize the analysis of behavior have grown out of the theoretical orientation described in the last chapter. In this chapter, we outline the research methods typically used in the study of Pavlovian and operant conditioning, identifying features which they share and features which distinguish them. The justification for these particular methods, their superiority over other possible methods for behavior analysis, stems from the theoretical perspective which spawned them.

THE USE OF ANIMALS TO STUDY PEOPLE

Dating from the work of Pavlov and Thorndike, the analysis of behavior has focused almost exclusively on the study of animals. The principles which gave rise to the technology of human behavior control discussed in Chapter 1 were all developed through the study of animal behavior. That animals have been the subjects of study reflects the assumptions which have guided the analysis of behavior. Most central among them is the view that complex behavior is made up of simple, and virtually universal, elements. Though rats and pigeons display none of the richness and complexity of humans, their behavior may well be comprised of these same simple elements. Thus, if one identifies simple elements of behavior and their rules of combination in nonhumans, one can then apply these elements and combination rules to humans. It is assumed that the difference in complexity between human and nonhuman is only quantitative, not qualitative. For example, computers are infinitely more complex than hand calculators. Yet, both are comprised of the same elements—integrated circuits. If one understands integrated circuits, one can understand both calculators and computers. Analogously, if one understands the basic elements of behavior, one can understand both pigeons and people.

Though these assumptions may justify the study of animals, they do not provide the whole story. What is to be *gained* by studying animals? The answer, quite simply, is control. One can construct very simple environments in which animal behavior can be studied. One can control the past experience of animal subjects, and expose them to conditions of severe stress and deprivation. The same, obviously, cannot be done with humans. In short, an experimenter can create a wholly artificial world in which animals are born, raised, and studied. Potentially significant environmental conditions can be created singly or in combination. With human subjects, one can only approximate this degree of experimental control. While all conditions can be determined for a few hours by the experimenter, the human subject then leaves the laboratory and reenters the world. To what extent do these uncontrollable natural experiences influence the effects of the laboratory experience? There is no way to know. Thus, there is much to be gained by studying animals rather than humans. That nothing significant is lost by this strategy depends upon the assumptions already discussed.

Which animals make the most useful subjects? Pavlov studied dogs and Thorndike studied cats. Use of these species and many others has continued through the years. However, most research in the last 30 years has been done with simpler, smaller, less costly, and more easily maintained species—rats and pigeons. The assumption that the basic principles of behavior control are true of virtually all species makes it reasonable to choose subjects pragmatically. Moreover, once the choice is made, other pragmatic issues operate to keep researchers working with these subjects. Commercially produced equipment is tailored to the commonly used organisms. If one wishes to study the behavior of a different organism, one must build his own equipment.

PAVLOVIAN CONDITIONING

Around the turn of the century, in the course of his research on digestion, Pavlov observed a phenomenon which others had observed, but made little of, in the past. He was investigating the role saliva played in the digestive process. Usually, the dogs he was studying would salivate when food was placed in their mouths. However, after repeatedly seeing a laboratory assistant in a white coat, followed immediately by the delivery of food into the mouth, the dogs began to salivate at the sight of the assistant. This phenomenon was a nuisance which impeded Pavlov's research program on digestion. However, Pavlov recognized it to be also a phenomenon of such great significance that the research on digestion stopped, and was replaced by the study of this other phenomenon, which Pavlov labeled a "psychic reflex."[1]

Consider what Pavlov was observing. That food in the mouth produced salivation was no great surprise. There was simply a salivary reflex, of the sort envisioned by Descartes, such that food on the tongue produced a nerve impulse which went to the brain where it connected with other neurons which in turn triggered salivation. All the circuitry involved in the production of saliva was built into the organism, and it worked in a reliable, mechanical fashion. But how could the sight of something produce saliva? There couldn't possibly be a built-in connection between white coats stimulating the eye and salivation. The dogs had to be learning something. Pavlov thought that these psychic reflexes could be the basic building blocks of all learning. He suggested that by studying the process by which psychic reflexes developed, it might be possible to develop laws of association—principles according to which new stimuli could come to produce already existing reflexes. Finally, he saw the study of psychic reflexes as a way to understand how the brain is structured, and how experience changes the structure of the brain. As a result of these insights, Pavlov began the study of *conditioned reflexes.* He investigated a set of phenomena which now bear his name—Pavlovian conditioning.[2] More significantly, he developed a set of empirical principles, most of which have stood the test of more than 50 years of research.

The Paradigm

The salivary reflex is one of many unconditioned reflexes which are built into the nervous system. An unconditioned reflex has two components. There is first the environmental event or stimulus which

1. Pavlov, 1927.
2. Pavlovian conditioning is also referred to as classical or respondent conditioning. The term Pavlovian will be used throughout this book, but the reader should be aware that other usages are common.

triggers it. This is called the unconditioned stimulus, and is abbreviated either US or UCS. Second, there is the response itself, called the unconditioned response or UR (UCR). The relation between the US and the UR is typically schematized in this way:

US (Food)→UR (Salivation)

The phenomenon of Pavlovian conditioning occurs when some other stimulus, the conditioned stimulus (CS), produces the reflex response. In fact, the response produced by the CS is usually not identical to the UR. Often, it is a component of the UR rather than the entire response. The response produced by the CS is called the conditioned response or CR.

Initially, when the CS is presented to the animal it produces its own reflexive response. For example, if a tone is the CS, when it is first presented to a dog, the dog will usually turn toward the tone and prick up its ears. This reflex is called the orienting reflex. With repeated exposure to the tone, the orienting reflex diminishes substantially. This is the point at which conditioning experience usually begins. The CS (tone) is presented and followed closely in time by presentation of the US (food in the mouth); each of these pairings is a "trial." After a number of pairings of the tone and food (CS and US), the dog begins salivating reliably when the tone comes on, in anticipation of the food. This anticipatory salivation is the conditioned response (CR). The procedure typically employed to produce Pavolvian conditioning is depicted in Figure 3–1.

As Pavlov conceived it, the crucial aspect of the conditioning procedure was the pairing, in close temporal contiguity, of CS and US. This pairing eventually led to a change in the structure of the nervous system such that the occurrence of the CS would excite the part of the brain which usually was excited by the US. In this way, conditioned excitation developed.

Since Pavlov's initial investigations, the methods used for the study of Pavlovian conditioning have broadened significantly in scope. Many other reflexes in many other organisms have been studied. Because of technical problems involved in measuring salivation, much research on Pavlovian conditioning is now done with the eyeblink reflex in rabbits, cats, and often humans, among other species. Also, heart rate, electrical skin resistance, and blood pressure have been frequently studied in a variety of species. In virtually all cases, researchers have observed the same phenomena that Pavlov observed in studying the salivary reflex in dogs. Pavlovian conditioning is a powerful and general phenomenon. Indeed, it is so powerful that it may

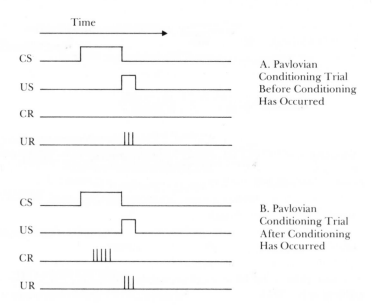

Figure 3–1. The Pavlovian Conditioning Paradigm. *In* A, *early trials are depicted. The CS is presented and followed by the US. URs occur to the US (vertical lines) but there are no CRs. In* B, *after conditioning has occurred, CRs (vertical lines) occur to the CS and before the US.*

set the stage for behavior changes which do not involve reflexes, at least not as central components. Pavlovian conditioning can influence the kind of behavior one would call purposive and goal-directed.

This extension of Pavlovian conditioning is particularly significant when the principles of Pavlovian conditioning are applied to human behavior. Most of human behavior which interests psychology is not reflexive. If the effectiveness of Pavlovian conditioning extended only to reflexes, it would be of limited value in application to humans. Certainly, people salivate at pictures of appetizing foods, and there are heart rate increases at the sight of a car approaching what looks like a head-on collision, but this is not the stuff of which most human action is composed. The human activity of greatest interest to us is voluntary, and for this reason the extension of Pavlovian conditioning to nonreflexive behavior is particularly important.

OPERANT CONDITIONING

At about the same time that Pavlov was beginning his investigation of conditioned reflexes, Thorndike began to explore a different type of conditioning, subsequently called "operant conditioning."[3] Recall the cats learning to escape from a cage to obtain a piece of fish. In discussing that experiment, it became clear that interpreting the behavior of cats as a set of reflexes, conditioned or otherwise, would be difficult. Thorndike conceived it as a quite different kind of learning, learning by trial and error. The cat engaged in a wide variety of activities, only some of which resulted in successfully reaching the fish. These responses, by virtue of having been followed closely in time by a food reward, become stronger (that is, their likelihood of occurrence increased). Other responses which did not result in reward were weakened, and ultimately ceased. In this way, the cat's behavior was shaped, by trial and error, until only those responses which produced reward continued to occur.

To account for the behavior of the cats, Thorndike articulated the *law of effect*. What it said was that responses which were followed by a satisfying state of affairs (reward) would occur with greater and greater frequency over time. On the other hand, responses which were followed by an annoying state of affairs (punishment) would occur less and less frequently over time.[4] It is this commonsensical statement which has formed the basis of practically all the research done on the analysis of behavior and of practically all the methods of behavior technology. As stated in Chapter 1, the law of effect has probably been known and used in some form for centuries, if not millennia. Yet it was Thorndike's demonstration in a well-controlled experimental context which sparked the systematic study of the ways in which reward and punishment influence behavior.

The Paradigm

Thorndike went on to other types of problems after his discovery, and the transformation of this demonstration into a program of research was largely left to others. One of Thorndike's most notable followers, and the one on whom we will focus, is B. F. Skinner. Skinner took up the study of rewards and punishments in the 1930s and developed a set of methods and terminology which have characterized much of the analysis of behavior ever since. To begin with, Skinner made a clear distinction between trial-and-error learning, which he called *operant conditioning* (because the behavior operated upon, or had an effect upon the environment) and Pavlovian conditioning. They are compared diagrammatically in Figure 3–2.

In this diagram, there are two types of connecting lines—broken

3. Operant conditioning is also commonly referred to as instrumental conditioning.
4. Thorndike, 1898.

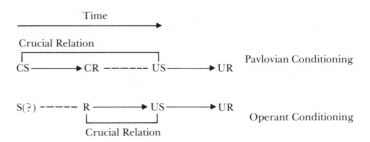

Figure 3–2. Comparison of Pavlovian and Operant Conditioning Procedures. *In both procedures, the sequence of events is the same. However, the crucial components of the sequence are different. In Pavlovian conditioning, it is the relation between CS and US which is responsible for the CR. After conditioning, the CS causes the CR (arrow). In operant conditioning, it is the relation between the response (R) and the US which is crucial (arrow).*

lines and solid lines with arrows. They are intended to signify different things. The broken lines merely indicate that one thing follows another. On the other hand, the arrows are meant to indicate that one thing is caused by or produced by another. Thus, in the now familiar case of Pavlovian conditioning, the US causes the UR and the CS causes the CR, but the CR has no effect. It merely precedes the US. Food is placed in the dog's mouth whether or not it salivates. The situation is quite different in the case of operant conditioning. Though there are presumably some stimuli around in the situation which the animal notices (S?), they do not cause the response. On the other hand, R produces the US. The cat must open the latch (R) to get the fish (US). Once the fish is in its mouth, presumably a UR (salivation) occurs. But the UR is usually not of interest, and thus not measured in operant conditioning experiments.

When the two conditioning paradigms are placed side by side in this way, they appear remarkably similar. They both begin with neutral stimuli, then conditioned responses, then unconditioned stimuli and unconditioned responses. However, the location of the causal arrows makes all the difference. In Pavlovian conditioning experiments, it is the relation between two stimuli, CS and US, which produces the conditioned response. In operant conditioning experiments, it is the relation between response and a stimulus (R and US) which produces conditioning. Note also that in Pavlovian conditioning, the CR and the UR are intimately related; both are reflexes. In contrast, in operant conditioning, the operant could be anything. In the cat example, R is opening a latch, but it could be turning around in a circle, standing on the hind paws, purring, scratching, etc. Any response will do, as long as the animal can make it.

Consider a simple human example of the difference between operant and Pavlovian responses. There are many ways a person can arrange to have a sirloin steak put before him. One could buy a steak at a butcher shop, bring it home, and cook it; one could walk to a restaurant; one could go to a neighbor's backyard barbecue; and so on. Each of these acts is an operant response. On the other hand, when the sizzling steak is actually placed on the table, no matter how it got there, the Pavlovian response will be salivation. This distinction may be stated in a more general and technical way. The operant response bears an arbitrary relation to the US. There is no intrinsic or built-in connection between them. On the other hand, the Pavlovian CR *is* intrinsically related to the US. The form of the CR is powerfully influenced by the nature of the US.

The Unconditioned Stimulus (US) or Reinforcer

Let us now consider the US as it is used in the two types of conditioning paradigms. In the examples discussed thus far, the US was the same—food. In general, stimuli which are USs in Pavlovian conditioning experiments can be (and have been) USs in operant conditioning experiments. All that is required of a stimulus is that it be biologically important, that is, that it produce a strong and permanent unconditioned response. The set of possible USs is rather small, and the set which is commonly used is smaller still. Food, water, and electric shock are the most common USs. It is not always easy to tell whether a stimulus will be a US. Lights and tones do not qualify because, although they produce URs (orienting reflexes), these tend to disappear as the animal's experience with the stimulus grows. On the other hand, if the light or tone is very intense it seems to function in the same way as electric shock, as a painful stimulus which produces relatively permanent URs. Thus, whether a stimulus may be a US is sometimes determined by its intensity. The soft tone is a neutral stimulus while the loud one is a US.

Though Pavlovian USs and operant USs may be the same, they are often referred to by different technical terms. Throughout Chapter 1, operant USs were called rewards. The technical term for them is *reinforcers*. This is a useful term because the presentation of a US like food may be thought of as strengthening or reinforcing the behavior which preceded it. This is really all that the law of effect says. Thus, when food is presented in an operant conditioning experiment it is called a reinforcer, while when it is presented in a Pavlovian conditioning experiment it is called a US.

Reinforcers belong to one of two general classes—positive and negative. The positive reinforcers are USs like food or water which increase the likelihood of the behavior which precedes them. Negative reinforcers, often called punishers, are USs which decrease the likelihood of behavior which precedes them. Electric shock is the most common example. In Pavlovian conditioning experiments, the use of positive and negative reinforcers as USs is typically distinguished by referring to alimentary (positive US) and defensive (negative US) conditioning.

Discrimination

Let us return now to Figure 3–2. What can be said of the peculiar component of the operant conditioning paradigm which is identified as "S(?)"? Any environment, no matter how simple, contains a multitude of stimuli. For the cat in the cage, there are odors, there are the bars of the cage, there is the latch, there are lights, there is some kind of material underfoot, there is air temperature. The list could go on. Which of these stimuli is the CS for latch opening? When this problem was mentioned in Chapter 2, we concluded that none of these stimuli was the CS—that in fact there was no CS. Latch opening is a voluntary response. It is not triggered or elicited by any specific environmental stimulus. It is not a reflex. What controls its occurrence is the food which follows it, not the stimuli which precede it. This is represented by the causal arrows in Figure 3–2. Nevertheless, it is entirely possible that some environmental stimulus could influence the occurrence of latch opening. Suppose that after the cat had learned to open the latch and escape from the cage, the experimenter changed the experiment in the following way: two shapes, a square and a circle, are sometimes placed in the cage. If the cat attempts to open the latch when the square is present, it can succeed and get the fish. However, when the circle is present, the latch is locked from the outside of the cage as well as the inside. No amount of latch-opening behavior can succeed in opening the cage.

When the cat is first exposed to these new conditions, its behavior continues as before. After some experience of failure, though, the cat stops manipulating the latch when the circle is present and continues as before when the square is present. The cat has learned a *discrimination.* It has learned not that squares and circles are different (which presumably it already knew) but that squares and circles provide different information about the potential success of latch opening. Circles mean stop—don't bother; squares mean go. These two stimuli are now exerting control over the cat's latch-opening behavior. We can take the question mark away from the S in Figure 3–2. However, though circles and squares now influence latch opening, they are not CSs. They do not elicit latch opening; they merely set the occasion or provide information as to when latch opening will be reinforced and when it will not be. Latch opening is just as voluntary and unelicited as it ever was. Just as it would be a mistake to claim that red lights elicit a "step on the brake" reflex and green lights a "step on the gas" reflex, so also it would be a mistake to characterize latch opening as a reflex. To emphasize the difference between these stimuli and CSs, they are called by a different name, Stimuli which set the occasion for the emission of a voluntary response are called *discriminative stimuli*. In the cat example, the square would be termed an S^+ since it signals a positive relation between the behavior and the reinforcer. The circle is termed an S^-. The role of discriminative stimuli in the control of behavior will be taken up in great detail in Chapter 8.[5]

Measuring the Operant Response

Once Thorndike had provided the groundwork for research on operant conditioning, investigators could have continued the study of reinforcement and punishment using his methods. There were, however, a few minor details which made them less than optimal. The most serious one was the response that was being measured. Latch opening is a complicated and time-consuming response, and it requires constant intervention of the experimenter. In trying to evaluate the effects of reward on latch opening, it is not clear which characteristics of the response to measure. Should we measure how much time it takes the cat to open the latch from the time it is placed in the cage? Should we measure how long it takes once latch opening begins? Should we measure the smoothness of its execution or the force exerted on the latch by the cat? Skinner suggested that perhaps

---

5. The present argument is that the square is not a CS since it does not trigger latch opening. However, if we diagram the sequence of events in an experiment like this one, we get:

    Square---latch opening---fish--------------------salivation
    S^+---------R--------------------Reinforcement----UR

The careful reader will notice that the S^+ stands in the same relation to food as a Pavlovian CS does. Thus, we could diagram the experiment:

    Square---Salivation---Fish----Salivation
    CS--------CR------------US-----UR

The square can be a CS, but not for latch opening. Rather, it can elicit conditioned salivation as a CR.

the best measure of operant conditioning would be one that allowed an estimate of the likelihood of occurrence of the response (its probability) at any moment. There are difficulties in judging the probability of a response directly, but some idea of its probability can be inferred from its frequency. It is clear that the more often one does something in general, the more likely one is to do at any particular time. Thus, Skinner argued that operant conditioning experiments should measure the frequency or rate of occurrence of the particular response.[6] With this aim, it would be desirable to measure a response which occurs rapidly and with little effort. Furthermore, the experimental situation should allow the animal to make the response repeatedly, without intervention. In this way, one could develop very fine measurements of conditioning as it occurred. The response would perhaps initially occur only occasionally in an hour as the organism explored its environment. As the response was followed by reinforcement, its frequency could increase, ultimately, to perhaps 75 or 100 times per minute. If such a response could be found, one could measure the strength of conditioning (in responses per minute) with ease and simplicity.

The Conditioning Chamber

Having developed this strategy, Skinner set out to develop the experimental situation in which to execute it. The product was an apparatus like the one in Figure 3–3.

The control panel and the rat are enclosed in a soundproof, opaque chamber, usually with a little peephole to permit observation from outside. The lever, feeder, lights, and tone are electrically connected to automated equipment outside the chamber. The response to be measured is the lever press. Each time the rat presses the lever, a switch is closed. This switch closure may be arranged to produce food and at the same time automatically count the responses.

For Skinner, the lever press is an ideal response. It can be made rapidly and repeatedly with minimal expenditure of effort. It is not as ideal for the rat. Left alone, rats will rarely press a lever. If they do, it is often inadvertent. They may brush their tails across it, or bump into it. This creates a minor problem. In order for the law of effect to work—for behavior to be strengthened by satisfying consequences—the behavior must occur at least once so that the satisfying consequence may be produced. The way to solve this problem is to help the rat along a bit by means of a procedure called *shaping by suc-*

6. Skinner, 1950.

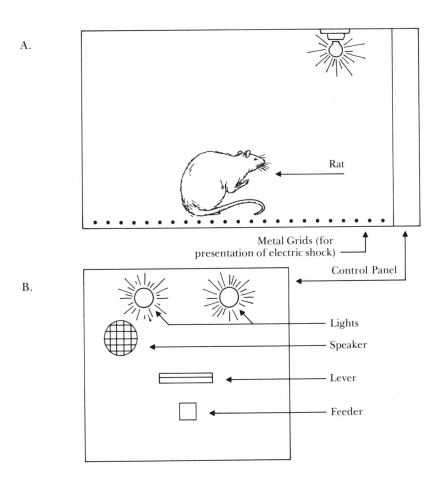

Figure 3–3. The Rat-Conditioning Chamber. *Diagram of a standard conditioning chamber for rats* (A) *and a rat's-eye view of the control panel housed in the chamber* (B).

cessive approximation. The experimenter observes the rat, and, rather than waiting for a lever press to occur, the experimenter waits for some movement toward the lever, then delivers food. This makes movements toward the lever a bit more likely. The experimenter now waits until the rat moves closer to the lever before presenting food. Each food delivery requires a response which is closer to a lever press than the one before it. Within a rather short time, the lever press response may be firmly established using this technique.

Shaping of behavior by successive approximation is so commonplace in the natural environment that we hardly notice it. When we teach children to swim, or to dress themselves, or to write the alphabet, we start with simple, easily executed components and gradually develop the desired response. If we waited for the desired response to occur full-blown before we reinforced it, few children would ever swim or write.

The second very commonly used apparatus is shown in Figure 3–4. All of its constituents are essentially equivalent to those in the rat chamber, but it accommodates a different animal—the pigeon. There is only one major difference between this apparatus and the previous one. Rather than pressing a lever, the pigeons are required to peck at one of the round disks or keys which are mounted above the feeder. Thus, rats press a lever for food and pigeons peck a key for food. The keys themselves are usually transparent and different colored lights can be used to illuminate them from behind. Thus, if one wanted to

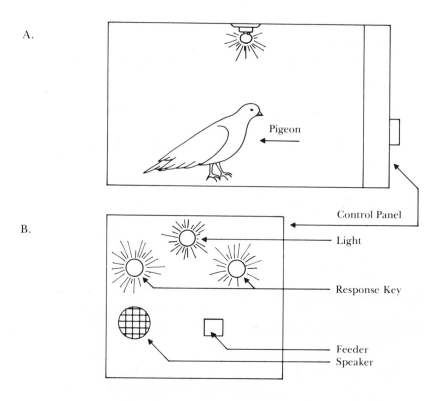

Figure 3–4. The Pigeon-Conditioning Chamber. *Diagram of a standard conditioning chamber for pigeons* (A), *and a bird's-eye view of the control panel housed in the chamber* (B).

train a pigeon to peck a key when it was green but not when it was red (by delivering food reinforcement only when pecks occurred when the key was green), the pigeon would actually be trained to peck *at* the discriminative stimulus (S^+). This makes the typical pigeon experiment slightly different from the typical rat experiment; with rats, if discriminative stimuli are used, they are typically not located on the lever. Thus the rat does not respond *at* them. The pigeon's key peck shares all the desirable properties of the rat's lever press. It is brief, easily repeated, and requires little effort. It has the additional virtue that pigeons can be trained to peck a key more rapidly (usually) than rats can be trained to press a lever.

Thus, the major difference between the rat chamber and the pigeon chamber is the response one measures. However, this difference is only apparent. From the experimenter's point of view, the responses are identical. They are, in both cases, the closure of a switch which sends an electric signal each time the key is pecked or the lever is pressed. The way in which the switch is closed is of little interest. The rat may "peck" the lever (press it with its nose) and the pigeon may "press the key" (hit it with its wings) and it will still be treated as the same response. Indeed, rats and pigeons may make the response in a different way each time.[7] As long as (and only when) the switch is closed, it is a lever press (key peck). This research strategy indicates something very important about operant conditioning. What is conditioned in operant conditioning experiments is not a single response but a whole class of responses. The operant is actually a response class. And the individual members of this class need have only one thing in common—that they close the switch.

THE EXPERIMENTAL ENVIRONMENT
AS "VIEWED" BY THE ANIMAL

It may have occurred to the reader in going through the procedures and terminology of the analysis of behavior that there is nothing obvious about these methods that makes them superior to dozens of others one might have developed. Having learned of Thorndike's findings, one could have attempted to study the behavior of cats in more complex situations. Alternatively, one could have moved to the study of monkeys, or to the study of children learning in school in an effort to ascertain whether cats, monkeys, and children solve prob-

---

7. Though the technical definition of an operant permits this variability from one response to the next, we shall see in Chapter 6 that, in fact, a very stereotyped pattern of switch closing nearly always develops over the course of conditioning.

lems in similar ways. Finally, one could have decided to study cats in their natural habitat, to see whether the law of effect works in nature the way it works in a cage. Each of these alternatives represents an effort to decrease the gap between the situation one studies and the phenomenon one is primarily interested in—the analysis of human behavior. One could have chosen to explore any or all of these methods.

Instead, the analysis of behavior moved in exactly the opposite direction. It sought the simplest possible situation. It developed that situation to be as unlike the natural environment as it possibly could. It chose to study organisms much further removed in complexity from humans than cats. What led to this development? What provided a justification for using so simple and artificial a situation to attempt to develop the laws of human behavior?

For an answer to these questions, we must return to the issues discussed in Chapter 2, which focused upon the role that theories play in guiding one's observations. The methods developed for the experimental analysis of behavior are testimony to the importance of theory. To someone unfamiliar with the theoretical foundation of the analysis of behavior, no methods could be less obviously appropriate than the ones which have developed. However, to someone working within that theoretical framework, no methods could be better. Recall that the reflex arc model suggests that there are simple units of behavior, controlled by simple environmental events. The richness and complexity of behavior as we see it in nature reflects the building of simple units into complex combinations. But the way to understand the complex cases is by understanding their constituents. The standard rat and pigeon experimental environments are places in which almost nothing aside from the simple behavior being measured can occur.[8] In addition, these environments allow so much control by the observer that the only environmental events which occur are the ones the experimenter allows. What better way is there to come to understand the principles which govern the occurrence of simple behavioral units?

The theoretical framework which guides the analysis of behavior has done more than influence the methods of study which have been developed. It has also influenced the way those methods are characterized or described. For the experimental environments, while good at achieving the desired simplicity and control, are not perfect. There

---

8. The word "almost" in this sentence is important. Recent researchers have focused on a detailed analysis of what goes on in the chamber which is not ordinarily recorded and have found some interesting and significant phenomena (see Chapter 6).

is room for disagreement between the experimenter's view of a situation and the animal's. Suppose an experimenter wants to train a pigeon to peck a key when the key is green (S$^+$) and not when it is red (S$^-$). The pigeon comes to respond in this way after some training. The experimenter might assert that the pigeon has learned a discrimination: the pigeon has learned to peck green and not peck red. However, the pigeon might have learned something quite different. The pigeon might have learned to peck the brighter of two stimuli or to peck the key which looks like the grain it eats. The pigeon might have learned to peck the key when it is green, and to strut about the chamber when the key is red. Each of these is a possibility and it would be a very difficult experimental problem to determine which of them is true. The point, however, is that from the theoretical perspective of the analysis of behavior, it does not make much difference. The pigeon may have learned any of these things, or numerous other things, and in each case the learning will be described in the same way: as a discrimination between red and green. It is understood that there is more going on in the chamber than the experimenter knows about. The pigeon may "interpret" the world differently from the experimenter. The theory allows that the solution to this almost insoluble problem is to characterize the learning which occurs from the experimenter's point of view, not the pigeon's. Thus the phrase "learn a discrimination" is an abstraction—a theoretical expression. It becomes a label for a very large number of possible alternative behaviors.

We have completed our discussion of the theoretical foundations and research methods which characterize the analysis of behavior. We are now ready to explore in detail what these methods have enabled us to find out about behavior. In the next part of the book, we will describe some principles of behavior which have emerged from three-quarters of a century of vigorous research on Pavlovian and operant conditioning.

4

Pavlovian
Conditioning I

We are now ready to begin a detailed investigation of what is known about the control of behavior. The first three chapters set the stage for our inquiry by discussing in some detail the underlying assumptions which characterize the analysis of behavior and the methods commonly employed in carrying out the analysis. The next two chapters will explore the principles of Pavlovian conditioning. We will discuss the different kinds of phenomena which have been observed in studies of Pavlovian conditioning, the necessary and sufficient conditions for establishing a conditioned reflex, and some of the ways in which the principles of Pavlovian conditioning have been extended outside the laboratory.

THE CLASSIC CONDITIONING EXPERIMENT

As the reader will recall, Pavlov's pioneering research on conditioned reflexes, begun around the turn of this century, involved the study of salivation in dogs. In a typical experiment, the dog is brought into a soundproof room and strapped into a harness. A salivary gland, which has been moved to the outside of the cheek by minor surgery, is connected to recording equipment which measures salivation in drops. At the start of the experiment, bits of food which serve as the unconditioned stimulus (US) are placed in the dog's mouth, and the number of drops of saliva produced are recorded. Then, the stimulus to be used as the conditioned stimulus (CS) is occasionally presented for brief periods. Typically, the CS does not produce any drops of saliva. It is important to be sure of this before conditioning is attempted, for if the CS produces salivation in its own right, then, when it is paired with the US and salivation occurs, it is difficult to know whether this salivation is the result of the conditioning experience or is directly produced by the CS.

What the CS often does produce is a different kind of reflex, called an investigating or orienting reflex. When the CS is presented, the dog pricks up its ears or looks toward it. This reflex depends upon the novelty of the stimulus, and after a while, with repeated exposure to the CS, the investigating reflex diminishes.[1] Now the time is right to begin conditioning.

The CS is, let us say, a ticking metronome. The US is meat powder placed in the mouth. Every few minutes the CS is presented, and 15 seconds later, while the CS is still on, meat powder is placed in the mouth. Each of these pairings of CS and US is a trial. For the first few trials, there is no noticeable response during the CS and copious salivation during the US. After a dozen trials or so (this varies from animal to animal), the dog begins to salivate during the CS and before the US. This *anticipatory* salivation is the conditioned reflex. If we recorded salivation in each trial, the data might look like those in Figure 4–1.

In the first few trials, salivation only occurs to the US. In the 10th trial, the first drops of anticipatory salivation appear. By the 20th trial, salivation to the CS is at its maximum. Although salivation is what is measured with care in these experiments, other responses appear to be conditioned as well. The dog shows signs of general excitement or agitation when the CS is on, and if sufficient movement is possible, the dog may even sniff at or lick the CS (in this case, the metronome).[2] However, the form of these additional activities, and indeed whether or not they even occur, will differ from one animal to the next. What virtually all animals do in common is salivate when the CS is present.

THE SCOPE OF PAVLOVIAN CONDITIONING

The scope of Pavlovian conditioning extends well beyond the basic demonstration of conditioned salivation in dogs. Modern research is

1. This phenomenon, known as habituation, may be the simplest and most pervasive of all kinds of learning. The phenomenon of habituation has been subjected to intense investigation in recent years. Researchers have found, among other things, that the speed of habituation is a function of the intensity of the stimulus (the more intense the stimulus, the slower the habituation) and its frequency of presentation (the more frequently it is presented, the faster the habituation). The habituated response also seems to recover as time passes without the stimulus (see Thompson & Spencer, 1966; Leaton & Tighe, 1976).
2. An early and influential report of these types of behavior was made by Zener, 1937.

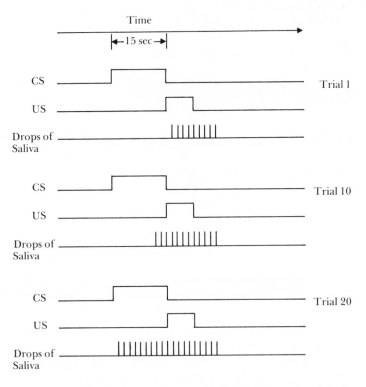

Figure 4–1. Development of a Conditioned Reflex. *In Trial 1, the dog salivates (vertical lines) only after food is presented. In Trial 10, a few drops of saliva come before the delivery of food. By Trial 20, salivation begins at the onset of the CS and continues throughout the trial.*

carried out with animals other than dogs and with responses other than salivation. The extension of Pavlovian research to new situations is partly an attempt to assess the generality of many of the phenomena Pavlov observed. Is Pavlovian conditioning specific only to dogs and salivation, or is it ubiquitous, as Pavlov expected? Obviously, the implications are far more important if Pavlovian conditioning can be demonstrated in animals other than dogs, with CSs other than metronomes, USs other than food, and responses other than salivation.

Types of Conditioned Stimuli (CS)

It does not seem an exaggeration to state that virtually any stimulus to which an animal is sensitive may be used as a CS. Within the auditory domain, clicks, tones, buzzes, musical notes, and the sound of bubbling water are among the stimuli which have successfully served as CSs. Among the visual stimuli employed are colors, patterns of lines, and geometric shapes. In addition, tactile stimuli, from gentle touches to mild electric shocks, odors, and tastes have been successfully used as CSs. Even the passage of time can serve as a CS. It is not of particular importance or interest to catalog all the stimuli which have served as CSs. The mere fact that many different stimuli have been used successfully helps to eliminate possible concern that Pavlovian conditioning may not be a general phenomenon.

That many different stimuli may be used as CSs does not mean that the choice of CS does not influence conditioning. Within each class of stimuli (e.g., tones, clicks, or lights) it is generally true that the more intense the stimulus, the faster conditioning will be. Also, if a CS is made up of a compound of two or more stimuli (a light and a tone) it sometimes happens that one of the stimuli will completely *overshadow* the other. If, after a large number of conditioning trials with the tone and light together, when the CR is firmly established, the two stimuli are presented separately on different trials, it may turn out that only one of them produces a CR.[3] Thus overshadowing refers to the fact that if two stimuli which are effective CSs when presented alone are presented instead as a compound, one of the stimuli may completely dominate the other as a CS.

Types of Unconditioned Stimuli (US)

The stimulus chosen as a US is of great importance in Pavlovian conditioning experiments. Recall that the US partly determines the UR, or unconditioned reflex. If the US is food, then the UR will be a response elicited by food—in the dog, salivation. On the other hand, if the US is a painful electric shock, then the reflexive response will not be salivation. In fact, when a shock is used as the US, the UR is a whole collection of responses: tensing of the muscles directly stimulated by the shock; changes in heart rate, blood pressure, and electrical skin resistance; and, sometimes, whining and urination. What makes this fact particularly significant is that the CR almost invariably bears a close relation to the UR. The two are not usually identical, but they are often very similar. Therefore, one's choice of US imposes powerful constraints on the CR one will obtain.

3. See Kamin, 1968, and Rescorla and Wagner, 1972, for discussions of overshadowing. We will discuss the research of these investigators in detail in the next chapter.

Most research has used either food or electric shock as the US. When food is the US, the observed CR may be salivation, general agitation, approach and contact of the CS, or one of several other responses. For example, in one experiment with rabbits, the CS was a 1-second tone and the US was an injection of saccharin solution into the rabbit's oral cavity. The recorded response was jaw movement, ordinarily a component of the rabbit swallowing reflex. The results of the experiment are presented in Figure 4–2, which plots the percentage of trials which contained at least one anticipatory jaw movement over the course of eight, 40-trial blocks.[4]

When shock is the US, the constellation of responses observed has

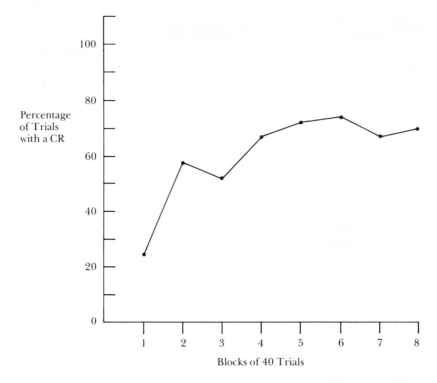

Figure 4–2. Development of Conditioned Jaw Movement in the Rabbit. *Each point represents the proportion of trials out of 40 in which a jaw movement occurred to the CS. In the first block, the rabbit responded in only 25 percent of the trials. In the second block, the rabbit responded in 58 percent of the trials. Responding eventually leveled off at about 70 percent of the trials. (After Smith, DiLollo, & Gormezano, 1966.)*

4. Smith, DiLollo, and Gormezano, 1966.

been given the label "fear" or "conditioned fear." We will discuss studies of conditioned fear in detail in Chapter 9.

Other USs have also been studied, some of them extensively. A very common Pavlovian conditioning procedure is eyeblink conditioning. The US is a puff of air delivered to the cornea, and the UR is a blink. An example of results from this type of experiment, with rabbits as subjects, is presented in Figure 4–3.[5] The data in Figure 4–3 are similar to those in Figure 4–2. Finding similarities like these from rather different experimental situations increases one's confidence that the phenomena of Pavlovian conditioning are not specific to particular experimental settings.

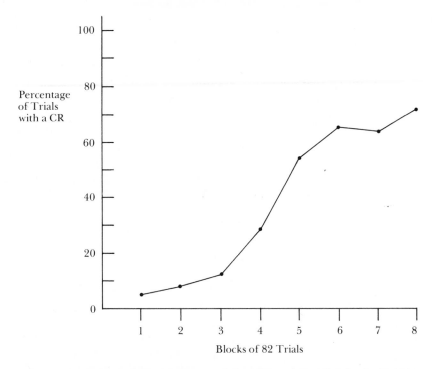

Figure 4–3. Development of Conditioned Eyeblink in the Rabbit. *Each point represents the proportion of trials out of 82 in which an eyeblink occurred to the CS. Very little responding occurred in the first three blocks. In the fourth block, the rabbit responded in 28 percent of the trials. By the sixth block, responding occurred in 65 percent of the trials, much as in Figure 4–2. (After Schneiderman, Fuentes, & Gormezano, 1962.)*

5. Schneiderman, Fuentes, and Gormezano, 1962. For a detailed discussion of experiments of this type, see Schneiderman, 1973.

There are also some experiments which employ less common but more intriguing USs. A variety of sublethal poisons have been used as USs with a number of animals, though mostly with rats. The response to the poison can best be described as general malaise. The poisoned animal looks sick; it is sluggish and uninterested in food until the illness wears off. This type of US differs dramatically from the others discussed so far. Unlike food, shock, or air puffs, which are brief and discrete, poison takes a while to have its effect and the effect lingers.

As in the case of different CSs, the type of US makes a difference in conditioning. First, the US will largely determine the form of the CR. Second, as with CSs, the intensity of the US plays a role in determining the strength of conditioning. In general, the more intense the US, the higher the asymptotic level of conditioning will be.[6]

Types of Organisms

While the wide variety of CSs and USs which can be used successfully in studies of Pavlovian conditioning makes it clear that Pavlov was not investigating a very limited and specialized phenomenon, there is still a question about whether conditioning phenomena are observed across different species. Here, the evidence is most impressive of all. Pavlovian conditioning has been studied in detail in monkeys, dogs, cats, rabbits, and a variety of birds and fish. It has been demonstrated in human infants as well as human adults. Pavlov's discovery was as general and important as he thought it was. Pavlovian conditioning seems to be a form of learning which is nearly universal in the animal world. Hence, an understanding of the laws of Pavlovian conditioning would be a major step toward the understanding of the behavior of organisms in general.

TEMPORAL ARRANGEMENT OF CONDITIONED AND UNCONDITIONED STIMULI

In discussing and comparing the different CSs and USs that have been used in Pavlovian conditioning experiments, we have assumed that they were used in a standard Pavlovian conditioning procedure. But what is a standard Pavlovian conditioning procedure? Obviously, there must be a CS and a US, but how are they arranged? In fact, there is no standard procedure. Rather, there is a family of procedures which are commonly used. In his initial investigations, Pavlov focused much attention on the temporal relation between CS and US,

6. Rescorla and Wagner, 1972.

that is, how they were arranged in time. No doubt he was influenced by the laws of association which preceded his investigations. In discussing the association of ideas, the Associationists placed great emphasis upon temporal contiguity. Two events which occur closely together in time (like the sight and smell of bread) are more likely to be associated than two events which occur further apart in time (like the sound of an alarm clock and the smell of breakfast). Let us investigate, then, how conditioning is affected by the temporal relations between CS and US.

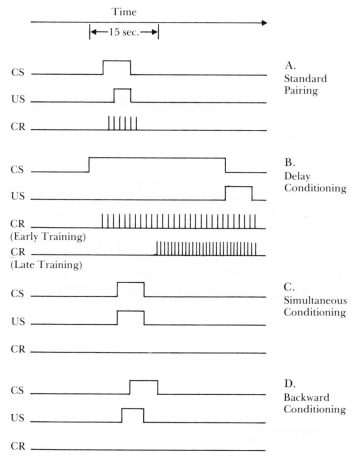

Figure 4–4. Schematic Drawing of Some Common Pavlovian Conditioning Procedures. *The bottom line of each drawing indicates the pattern of conditioned responding typically observed on these procedures.*

Figure 4–4 depicts a variety of common arrangements of CS and US. The upward deflections of the lines indicate the times when the CS or US is present. The type of procedure we have discussed thus far is diagrammed in Figure 4–4A. It is labeled *standard pairing,* and it is characterized by a fairly short interval between the CS (which comes first) and the US. In the diagram, the CS–US interval (which is measured from the onset of the CS to the onset of the US) is 2 seconds. There have been many experiments performed to determine what CS–US interval optimizes conditioning. The answer to this question is somewhat complicated. For some reflexes, like the eyeblink, the optimum CS–US interval is about 0.5 second. For other reflexes, the optimum CS–US interval is appreciably longer—up to 5 seconds. These details need not concern us here: the standard-pairing diagram is meant to represent an optimal Pavlovian conditioning procedure.[7]

Delay Conditioning

What happens if the CS–US interval is quite long? This type of procedure is depicted in Figure 4–4B. The procedure is called *delay conditioning.* Conditioned responses can be produced with the delay procedure just as with the standard pairing procedure. What is interesting about the delay procedure is the temporal pattern of conditioned responses. Early in training, when CRs first begin to occur, they tend to start at the beginning of the CS and continue right through the onset of the US. However, late in training, when the animal is experienced, the temporal pattern of CRs changes. Now, when the CS comes on, there are no CRs. Conditioned responses begin to occur about midway through the CS, and from that point increase in frequency until the end of the trial. It seems as though the CS has become two CSs—CS(early) and CS(late). The animal seems to learn that the US is not going to come when the CS first comes on, with the absence of CRs a result of this learning. The delay conditioning procedure seems to be a discrimination procedure, like the square and circle example discussed in the last chapter. Here, the stimuli discriminated are not different shapes, but different time intervals.

Are animals able to discriminate time intervals? The answer is yes. Evidence for temporal discrimination comes from a Pavlovian conditioning procedure which is not depicted in Figure 4–4. It is called *temporal conditioning.* If a US is presented at regular intervals, say once a minute, and there is no CS at all, conditioned responses will begin to

---

7. See Beecroft, 1966, for a review.

occur toward the end of the minute between US presentations. What is the CS? What can it be but the passage of time since the last US?

Simultaneous Conditioning

Figure 4–4C represents a procedure which is not commonly used in Pavlovian conditioning experiments—called *simultaneous conditioning*. Here, both onset and offset of CS and US are coincident. The reason this procedure is not often studied is that it typically does not produce conditioning. This seems a bit peculiar. Here, the temporal contiguity of CS and US is perfect, and since temporal contiguity seems an important determinant of conditioning this procedure ought to succeed. Why doesn't it? Recall the discussion of the phenomenon of overshadowing (p. 57). If two ordinarily effective stimuli are presented as a compound CS, then one may completely overshadow the other so that only the dominant CS comes to produce CRs. This same principle may explain the failure of simultaneous conditioning. If CS and US, say light and shock, are presented together, the shock may so dominate or overshadow the light that the light is not even noticed. By presenting the light even a fraction of a second before the shock, one can insure that it will be noticed and that conditioning will occur.

Backward Conditioning

Finally, Figure 4–4D depicts a procedure which is just like the standard-pairing procedure, with one important exception—the CS comes *after* the US. The procedure is appropriately called *backward conditioning*. Like simultaneous conditioning procedures, backward conditioning procedures fail to produce conditioned reflexes. If a tone is sounded after food is delivered to a dog's mouth, the tone will not produce salivation. Again, this seems to pose a problem for the simple view that temporal contiguity is all that is needed for conditioning to occur. The temporal contiguity between CS and US is the same in Figures 4–4A and 4–4D. Yet one procedure is optimal and the other is a failure. Thus it seems that temporal contiguity is not enough—the CS must precede the US.

Counterconditioning

The failure of backward conditioning raises an interesting issue. Suppose that the CS in an experiment was a very mild electric shock—one that tingled slightly—and the US was food. If CS preceded US, we would expect to observe conditioned salivation to the shock. If US preceded CS we would expect no conditioning to occur. Now suppose, however, that the intensity of the shock was increased. When shock preceded food we would observe no conditioning, while, when food preceded shock, food would produce conditioned fear responses. This is not a case of successful backward conditioning. The point is that when shock is intense, it can be a US but not a CS. Indeed, when shock is intense, food can be a CS. What this means is that the designation of a stimulus as a US or CS is a relative, not an absolute judgment. Pavlov made the point that there is a kind of hierarchy of reflexes. Some are more potent than others. A US for one reflex could be made the CS for another reflex only if the first reflex were less potent than the second one. Thus the mild-shock/food procedure works as an instance of forward pairing while the strong-shock/food procedure fails as an instance of backward pairing. The procedure of making a stimulus which is usually a US into a CS for some other reflex is called *counterconditioning*.

Counterconditioning has significant implications for a variety of situations in which Pavlovian conditioning is used as a therapeutic technique. For example, Pavlovian conditioning methods have been used successfully in treating alcoholism. One common procedure involves administering drugs to alcoholics, just after they take a drink, which induce intense nausea and vomiting. The expectation is that the taste of the alcohol will become associated with stomach illness, and be sufficiently aversive that the alcoholic will no longer drink. Note that this procedure will only work if the unpleasant response to the drug is more potent than the pleasant response to alcohol. If not, the procedure becomes an instance of backward conditioning.

Higher Order Conditioning

At this point one might be wondering about how these subtle distinctions among Pavlovian conditioning procedures make contact with everyday life. After all, how many USs occur in the normal course of one's day? There is food and presumably people salivate at the sight and smell of food, but what else is there? How often are we confronted by noxious or aversive USs? Normal, everyday experience is not littered with CS–US pairings. There is, however, another Pavlovian conditioning phenomenon which seems much more relevant to the real world than the ones discussed thus far. It is called *higher order conditioning*.

Suppose a dog is exposed to a procedure in which a tone is paired with painful electric shock. After a number of trials, the tone reliably elicits a fear response as the CR. Now the dog is subjected to two different types of procedures on alternate days. On some days, tone–shock pairings occur as usual. On other days, a light is paired with the tone and no shock is presented at all. After a while, conditioned fear responses will be produced by the light even though it has never been paired directly with the shock US. This phenomenon is called *second-order conditioning*. The light is a second-order CS which is paired with a first-order CS (tone) until both the light and the tone elicit CRs.

In principle, one could establish third- and fourth-order CSs as well. In practice, however, this proves exceedingly difficult. Nevertheless, the fact of second-order conditioning goes a long way toward extending the generality of Pavlovian conditioning to ordinary human experience. While the occurrence of USs may be rare, the occurrence of stimuli which have been paired with USs is less rare. If these stimuli are regularly preceded by other stimuli, then these other stimuli can become second-order CSs.

Consider an example. Suppose someone was afraid of thunder. The sound of thunder was a US for a set of fear responses. Lightning reliably precedes thunder, and we would not be surprised if conditioned fear responses were produced by lightning. The presence of thunder and lightning are sufficiently rare that this person's fear of them would not be especially noticeable or debilitating. However, there are a variety of other stimuli which reliably precede lightning: temperature reduction, wind increase, and a darkening of the sky are among them. Any of these could conceivably become a second-order CS so that, for example, wind came to elicit conditioned fear. If this happened, the person's seemingly harmless fear response to thunder could grow, through Pavlovian conditioning, to a problem of major proportion.

WHAT IS LEARNED IN CONDITIONING?

When an animal experiences Pavlovian conditioning trials, what does it learn? How is it changed? We can identify a number of possibilities—two of which are diagrammed in Figure 4–5.

In Figure 4–5*A*, a broken line (representing learning) connects the CS with the UR. According to this view, the conditioning subject learns to associate the CS with the response, tone with salivation. Figure 4–5*B* depicts a learned association between the CS and the US, between tone and food. The question, in short, is whether the subject learns a stimulus–response (S–R) association as in *A*, or a stimulus–stimulus (S–S) association as in *B*.

Researchers have attempted to answer this question for years with

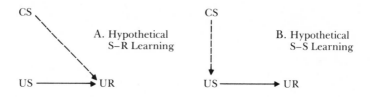

Figure 4–5. Two Theoretical Models of What Is Learned in Pavlovian Conditioning Experiments. *The broken lines indicate hypothetical learned associations between CS and UR in A, and between CS and US in B.*

equivocal results.[8] One can find evidence supporting both S–R and S–S views of the conditioning process. Thus, we cannot resolve the issue. What we can do is present some of the evidence which has accumulated in support of each view.

Consider the following experiment. A dog receives a large number of trials in which a buzzer is paired with a light. No USs are presented. After this initial training, the light is paired with shock to the leg, which produces a UR of leg withdrawal. After a number of trials, the light comes to elicit anticipatory leg withdrawal. Now, the buzzer is sounded. Does the buzzer alone elicit leg withdrawal? What might we expect on the basis of the two hypothetical learning processes depicted in Figure 4–5? If conditioning involves S–R association (Figure 4–5*A*), then the buzzer should not produce leg withdrawal. When the buzzer was being paired with the light, leg withdrawal was not occurring. If, on the other hand, conditioning involves S–S association, the buzzer might well elicit leg withdrawal, for the S–S association between buzzer and light could have been formed before shock was introduced into the experiment. The results of the experiment are clear. The buzzer does elicit leg withdrawal responses.[9] This phenomenon is known as *sensory preconditioning,* to highlight the fact that sensory conditioning (between two CSs like buzzer and light) occurs prior to any conditioning of either CS with a US (shock). The sensory preconditioning procedure is diagrammed in Figure 4–6*A*.[10]

This result might seem to resolve the issue of what the animal learns in a conditioning experiment. The matter is complicated, how-

8. See Mackintosh, 1974, especially pages 85–97.

9. Brogden, 1939.

10. For years there was substantial controversy about whether sensory preconditioning procedures produced any conditioning at all. It now seems clear that sensory preconditioning is an effective procedure if one does the experiment properly. For recent demonstrations, see Prewitt, 1967, and Tait, Marquis, Williams, Weinstein, and Suboski, 1969.

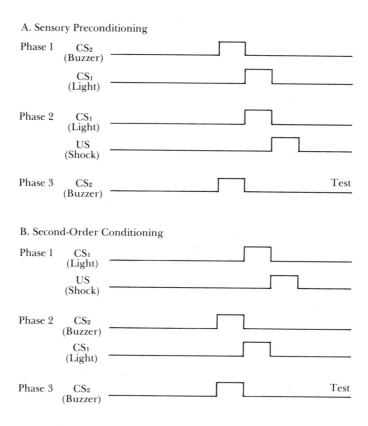

A. Sensory Preconditioning

Phase 1 CS₂
         (Buzzer)

         CS₁
         (Light)

Phase 2 CS₁
         (Light)

         US
         (Shock)

Phase 3 CS₂   Test
         (Buzzer)

B. Second-Order Conditioning

Phase 1 CS₁
         (Light)

         US
         (Shock)

Phase 2 CS₂
         (Buzzer)

         CS₁
         (Light)

Phase 3 CS₂   Test
         (Buzzer)

Figure 4–6. Diagrams of Sensory Preconditioning (A) and Second-Order Conditioning (B) Procedures. *The procedures differ only in that the order of phases 1 and 2 is reversed. That is, in sensory preconditioning, pairing of CS_2 and CS_1 precedes pairing of CS_1 and US, while in second-order conditioning, pairing of CS_2 and CS_1 follows pairing of CS_1 and US.*

ever, by results of experiments employing procedures like the one depicted in Figure 4–6*B*. This is a diagram of the *second-order conditioning* procedure. A CS (CS_1) is paired with a US. Then a new CS (CS_2) is paired with CS_1 and we look for conditioned responses to CS_2. Sensory preconditioning and second-order conditioning procedures are nearly identical. They differ only in that in sensory preconditioning, pairing of CS_2 and CS_1 precedes pairing of CS_1 and US, while in second-order conditioning, pairing of CS_2 and CS_1 follows pairing of CS_1 and US.

Suppose one did a second-order conditioning experiment, pairing

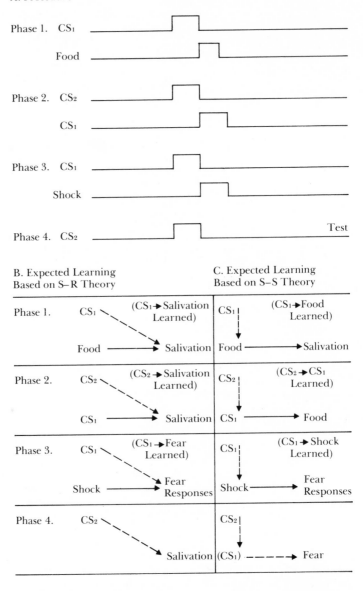

A. Procedure

Phase 1. CS₁

          Food

Phase 2. CS₂

          CS₁

Phase 3. CS₁

          Shock

Phase 4. CS₂   Test

B. Expected Learning Based on S–R Theory

C. Expected Learning Based on S–S Theory

Phase 1. CS_1 → (CS_1 → Salivation Learned)
Food ───→ Salivation

CS_1 ↓ (CS_1 → Food Learned)
Food ───→ Salivation

Phase 2. CS_2 → (CS_2 → Salivation Learned)
CS_1 ───→ Salivation

CS_2 ↓ (CS_2 → CS_1 Learned)
CS_1 ───→ Food

Phase 3. CS_1 → (CS_1 → Fear Learned)
Shock ───→ Fear Responses

CS_1 ↓ (CS_1 → Shock Learned)
Shock ───→ Fear Responses

Phase 4. CS_2 → Salivation

CS_2 ↓
(CS_1) ––––→ Fear

Figure 4–7. Diagram of a Second-Order Conditioning Experiment and Expected Results Based upon S–R and S–S Theories. A *depicts a second-order conditioning procedure.* B *depicts the learning which an S–R theory of conditioning would predict the procedure should produce. The subject learns a CS_2–salivation association so that changing the stimulus (US) paired with CS_1 does not change the response produced by CS_2.* C *depicts the learning which an S–S theory of conditioning would predict the procedure should produce. The subject learns a CS_2–CS_1 association so that changing the US from food to shock (phase 1 vs. phase 3 of A) will change the response produced by CS_2 from salivation to fear.*

CS$_1$ with food until CS$_1$ produced anticipatory salivation, then pairing CS$_2$ with CS$_1$ until CS$_2$ also produced salivation. Then suppose one paired CS$_1$ with shock until CS$_1$ elicited leg withdrawal. Now, when CS$_2$ was presented alone, would the animal salivate or withdraw its leg? Let us go back to Figure 4–5 and see what the two models of conditioning we outlined would lead us to expect. The S–R model (*A*) suggests the view that when CS$_2$ and CS$_1$ are paired, the animal learns an association between CS$_2$ and salivation, not between CS$_2$ and CS$_1$. Thus, when CS$_2$ is presented, the animal should salivate. On the other hand, the S–S model (*B*) suggests that CS$_2$ is associated with CS$_1$. If CS$_1$ is now associated with shock, and not food, the animal should withdraw its leg when CS$_2$ is presented. What the animal does is salivate.[11] An outline of the experimental procedure and the results one would expect on the basis of the two models in Figure 4–5 is presented in Figure 4–7.

There are two lessons to be learned from these experiments. The first is that we cannot provide an unequivocal answer to the question "What is learned?" Sensory preconditioning studies suggest that an S–S association is learned while second-order conditioning studies suggest that an S–R association is learned. The second lesson is that procedural differences from one experiment to the next which seem minor may have major consequences. Notice again, in Figure 4–6, how similar the sensory preconditioning and second-order conditioning procedures appear. Despite the procedural similarity, they seem to have dramatically different effects. It appears that the student of behavior who ignores procedural details may do so at the cost of misunderstanding or misconstruing the principles of behavior analysis.

PAVLOVIAN CONDITIONING AND INHIBITION

Pair a tone with food and an animal will eventually salivate to the tone. Pair a light with shock and the animal will display fear to the light. Pair a click with a puff of air to the eye and the animal will blink when the click sounds. These are three very different Pavlovian conditioning phenomena. Yet they are all instances of the same general phenomenon—Pavlovian *excitatory* conditioning. Through pairing of CS and US, the CS comes to excite a CR. But what happens if, after excitatory conditioning has occurred, the subject receives presentations of the CS without the US so that, for example, a tone which has been paired with food and elicited salivation is presented repeatedly

11. Konorski, 1948. This result has also been substantiated in more recent experiments involving somewhat different procedures (Rizley & Rescorla, 1972).

to a dog without being followed by food? Behaviorally, it is easy to tell what happens; the dog stops salivating to the tone. This phenomenon is called *experimental extinction,* or just *extinction.* The question is whether extinction involves the erasure of the conditioned reflex so that the animal that has undergone conditioning and extinction is more or less the same as an untrained animal, or whether extinction does something different. Pavlov thought that extinction involved the development of active inhibition of the conditioned response rather than simply the erasure of a CS–US connection.

What is inhibition? This seems like such an obvious question that one wonders why it needs to be asked. We use the word frequently in everyday language to describe a force within us which keeps us from doing certain things. Thus there are sexual inhibitions, inhibitions about performing in front of strangers, inhibitions about speaking one's mind, and so on. As a descriptive term in common use, "inhibition" seems straightforward enough. However, what could inhibition possibly mean as a property of a reflex? Recall our simple model of the reflex arc. A stimulus triggers a neural impulse which goes to some part of the brain. There it *excites* another neural impulse which in turn triggers the reflex. In short, a US excites a UR. Food excites salivation. How could a US inhibit a UR? If there is no connection between the US and the UR, the UR will not occur, but is that what we mean by inhibition? Do we wish to say that a puff of air to the eye *inhibits* salivation because salivation does not occur? Clearly not. Air puffs neither excite salivation nor inhibit it. They are simply independent of it. Inhibition refers to the *active suppression* of some behavior which would, under other circumstances, be expected to occur. Therefore, if inhibition genuinely exists at the level of the relex, it must be specifically attached to the US or the UR.

Using this model, Pavlov found that there existed both excitatory and inhibitory reflexes and that Pavlovian conditioning could produce both excitatory and inhibitory *conditioned* reflexes. Indeed, Pavlov's view was that the highest level of the nervous system, the cerebral cortex, had as much to do with inhibition as with excitation. Hence, we need briefly to discuss inhibition as a property of the nervous system.

Inhibition in the Nervous System

The nervous system has an important property which makes inhibition possible. When a particular set of neurons is at rest, that is, not stimulated, these neurons are still active. Said another way, a resting neuron is still being activated and sending signals. It sends signals at a fairly constant rate, as depicted in Figure 4–8A. When the neuron is stimulated, the effect of the stimulation is to *increase* the rate at which the neuron fires. This increase is what is detected elsewhere in the nervous system. Figure 4–8*B* depicts the rate at which the stimulated neuron may fire. Now, if the neuron receives an inhibitory signal, its rate of firing will decrease below resting level, as depicted in Figure 4–8*C*. Thus, because neurons send signals even when at rest, it is possible to both increase (excite) and decrease (inhibit) the rate at which the signals are produced.

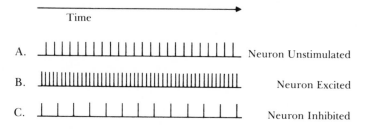

Figure 4–8. Schematic Drawing of a Neuron Firing When Unstimulated (A), When Excited (B), and When Inhibited (C). *Each vertical line indicates a firing of the neuron.*

Research in the last 30 years has established not only the presence of inhibition in the nervous system, but its pervasiveness. Moreover, Pavlov's view that the cortex plays a critical role as an inhibitory influence is now well established. The cortex seems to inhibit the occurrence of many reflexes which would otherwise be excited in subcortical parts of the nervous system. When organisms suffer cortical damage of one sort or another, these reflexes are released from the cortical inhibition and begin to appear. One sees these reflexes in infants, before the cortex has fully developed. When cortical development is complete, the reflexes disappear. Then, when cortical damage occurs, the reflexes reappear.[12] Inhibition is also important for voluntary movement. It is the presence of inhibitory capacity in the nervous system which permits the development of smooth and well-coordinated sequences of movement. Without inhibition, movements would be rather unskilled and herky-jerky.

Conditioned Inhibition of Behavior

With a sense of inhibition as a property of the nervous system now established, we can turn to the study of inhibition in Pavlovian condi-

12. See Teitelbaum, 1967, and Peiper, 1963.

tioning. The study of conditioned inhibition poses methodological problems which are not present in the study of conditioned excitation. A sign of conditioned excitation is the presence of some response which was not present before conditioning. However, a sign of conditioned inhibition is the absence of a response we might otherwise expect to occur. But the mere absence of that response does not guarantee that conditioned inhibition is present. The response could be absent for a host of other reasons. A nonlaboratory example will help clarify this problem.

Imagine being at a large, boisterous, friendly party. Everyone seems to be having a good time. There is just one man sitting off by himself in a corner looking blank. How are we to account for the man's behavior? Two possibilities immediately present themselves. Perhaps the man is shy and lacks confidence. Although he is anxious to meet some of the people at the party, he is too inhibited to get up and introduce himself. Therefore, he sits alone, actively suppressing the urge to mingle. The second possibility is that he is bored—utterly uninterested. He is not suppressing anything because there is nothing to suppress. This, in capsule, is the problem in ascertaining the presence of inhibition. Are we to explain the man's behavior in terms of inhibition or in terms of lack of excitation? Both accounts are consistent with his sitting by himself, and with the absence of salivation, fear, eyeblink, or other CR when a CS is presented. How can we separate inhibition from lack of excitation?

Detecting Inhibition

There are a number of ways to detect inhibition, many of which were initially identified by Pavlov. All of the procedural devices used in studying inhibition assume that excitation and inhibition interact. Thus, the general strategy for detecting inhibition involves, first, establishing some excitation, and second, presenting the supposedly inhibitory stimulus. If the stimulus really is inhibitory, then its presence should reduce the amount of excitation one observes.[13]

External Inhibition and Disinhibition • Suppose a dog has been exposed to a procedure in which a light is paired with food. After a number of trials, the dog reliably salivates to the light. Now, on one trial the light is presented and the dog begins to salivate. In the middle of the trial a tone, which has never been presented before, is sounded. Salivation stops. Pavlov called this phenomenon *external inhibi-*

---

13. For a detailed review of research on conditioned inhibition, see Rescorla, 1969.

tion. He interpreted it as an indication that a novel external stimulus can inhibit whatever neural processes are taking place in the cortex. If excitation of salivation is taking place, the novel stimulus will inhibit salivation. If excitation of fear is taking place, the novel stimulus will inhibit fear.

But what if *inhibition* is taking place? Now, according to Pavlov, presentation of a novel stimulus will *inhibit inhibition*. But what does this mean? Well, suppose that salivation to a CS has been extinguished and that extinction produces inhibition. The CS is presented and the dog does not salivate. If a novel stimulus is now presented along with the CS, the dog will start to salivate. This inhibition of inhibition is called *disinhibition*. Pavlov saw it as a way to differentiate inhibition from a lack of excitation. If a dog is inhibiting salivation, then a novel stimulus will produce it. If, on the other hand, a dog is not salivating simply through lack of excitation, then a novel stimulus will have no effect on salivation.

Stimulus Compound Tests • Consider another example. Two dogs are exposed to a procedure in which a light is paired with shock until conditioned fear responses have been established. Prior to this conditioning, one of the dogs had had experience with a tone. The tone was presented repeatedly until it was no longer novel, that is, no longer an external inhibitor. The other dog also experienced the tone, but in a procedure designed to make it a conditioned inhibitor of fear. Now, periodically, in the midst of their experience with light–shock pairings, the dogs are presented with a compound of light and tone. If the tone has become a conditioned inhibitor of fear, then we would expect the second dog to show less sign of conditioned fear than the first dog to the light–tone compound.

A variant of this compounding procedure involves taking two dogs and giving them the same experience with tones as before. For one dog, it is a neutral stimulus and for the other it is (supposedly) a conditioned inhibitor. Now, the dogs are exposed to *training* with light + tone paired with shock. If the tone has become a conditioned inhibitor, one would expect the second dog to take longer than the first to develop conditioned fear responses.

Inhibition of Operant Behavior • There is a third procedure which has become more common than the others, and is in many ways of greater potential applicability to human affairs. The first step in this procedure is to train animals in an operant conditioning task. To take a common example, one would train rats to press a lever to avoid an electric shock. It is commonly assumed that in the course of learning the task the rat develops fear responses, and these fear responses play an important role in keeping the rat pressing the lever. When the task is well learned, Pavlovian conditioning begins. A stimulus becomes established as a conditioned inhibitor, or excitor, of fear. Now the animal is returned to the operant conditioning chamber. While it is pressing the lever to avoid electric shock, the Pavlovian CS is occasionally presented. If it is an excitor of fear, one would expect the CS to increase the degree of fear already present in the rat. This in turn would lead to an increase in the rate at which the rat presses the lever. If, on the other hand, the CS is a conditioned inhibitor of fear, one would expect the rat's level of fear, and rate of lever pressing, to decrease. Thus, this method allows the assessment of both Pavlovian conditioned excitation and Pavlovian conditioned inhibition.

While other techniques for assessing inhibition have been developed, there is no need to go into them here. We are now ready to investigate the circumstances under which conditioned inhibition may develop.

CONDITIONS WHICH PRODUCE INHIBITION

Extinction

A dog has been exposed to pairings of tone and food until a strong CR to the tone has developed. How can the conditioned reflex be eliminated? If the dog is simply removed from the experiment and not exposed to tone–food pairings for a year or so, and then placed back in the experimental situation, it will salivate profusely on the very first tone presentation. Thus, conditioned reflexes are not easily forgotten. However, if the dog is simply exposed to presentations of the tone without food, conditioned salivation will gradually disappear. This phenomenon is called *extinction*. Just as CRs can be established by pairing CS and US, so they can be eliminated by presenting CS alone.

What happens during an extinction procedure? At the end of the procedure, we are left with a subject that looks just like a naive subject. The CS is presented and no CR occurs. It is possible that extinction literally amounts to the unlearning or erasure of the previously conditioned response, and that a naive subject and one that has undergone conditioning followed by extinction will be undifferentiable. Pavlov had a different view. He thought that extinction was not unlearning, but new learning. He thought that in extinction procedures the previously excitatory CS became inhibitory. By using one of the devices for detecting inhibition outlined above, one could presumably show that the naive subject and the one whose reflex had been extinguished were quite different.

Surprisingly, there is little evidence available to decide this issue. Experiments involving the compounding technique described above have found that the extinguished CS does not appear to have inhibitory properties.[14] It seems to work like a neutral stimulus. On the other hand, Pavlov showed that if an extinguished CS, which previously elicited salivation, is presented along with a novel stimulus (external inhibition), disinhibition is the result and salivation reappears. Thus, while positive evidence that an extinguished CS becomes inhibitory exists, it is difficult to view the issue as unequivocal. Clearer evidence for inhibition comes from other Pavlovian procedures.

Inhibition of Delay

By referring back to Figure 4–4, one will be reminded of the delay conditioning procedure. A long presentation of a CS is followed by a US. After extended training, subjects tend to make CRs only in the latter part of the CS. The question to focus on here is what is going on early in the CS? Is the early part of the CS simply nonexcitatory, or could it actually be inhibitory? Pavlov thought the latter was true, and his evidence came from the use of external inhibition as a research tool. When a novel stimulus was presented in the latter part of a CS in a delay conditioning procedure, it inhibited the salivary CR. If, on the other hand, the novel stimulus was presented early in the CS when no salivation was occurring, it produced salivation. Pavlov interpreted this as an instance of disinhibition; the external inhibitor inhibited the process currently in force, which was itself inhibition. The net result was excitation.

Similar results were obtained with delay conditioning procedures using very different methods.[15] In one experiment, dogs were trained to make operant responses to avoid getting electric shocks. After a few days of this training, they were making about 6 responses per minute. They were then exposed to Pavlovian conditioning of fear. A 20-second tone was paired with painful electric shock. When the tone was subsequently presented to the dogs while they were responding to avoid electric shocks, it had two different effects. Late in the tone, the rate of operant responses was about 9 per minute. This was an increase of 50 percent over response rate with no tone and clear evidence of conditioned fear. Early in the tone, response rate was 3 per

14. LoLordo and Rescorla, 1966.
15. Rescorla, 1967b, 1968.

minute, a decrease of 50 percent from response rate with no tone and
clear evidence of inhibition of fear. Thus, evidence that inhibition is
occurring early in the long CS of delay conditioning seems unequivocal. Data from this experiment are presented in Figure 4–9.

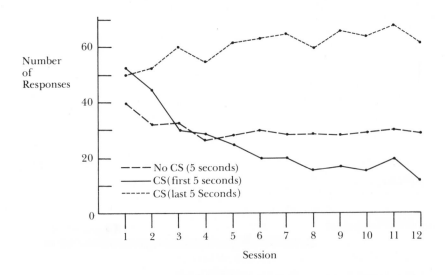

Figure 4–9. Inhibition of Delay in Pavlovian Conditioning. *The
graph indicates the number of responses per session made by dogs in
5-second periods prior to a CS for shock, in the first 5 seconds of the CS,
and in the last 5 seconds of the 20-second CS. Responding early in the CS
is lower than responding without the CS (inhibition of delay), and responding late in the CS is higher than responding without the CS (conditioned fear). (After Rescorla, 1967b, Figure 3.)*

Discrimination and Generalization

Imagine a dog exposed to the following procedure: on some trials,
a tone is paired with food; on other trials, a light is presented and not
followed by food. If we plotted the development of conditioned salivation over the course of conditioning trials, it would look something
like the curves in Figure 4–10. Early in the procedure, conditioned
salivation occurs to both the tone and the light. This phenomenon is
called *stimulus generalization.* Conditioning experience with one stimulus (in this case, the tone) is generalized to other stimuli (in this case,
the light). After a while, however, while conditioned salivation to the
tone continues to grow, conditioned salivation to the light begins to
wane. The two curves continue to diverge until salivation occurs to

the tone on nearly every trial and salivation never occurs to the light. We describe this result as the development of a *discrimination* between the tone (CS⁺) which is paired with food, and the light (CS⁻) which is not.

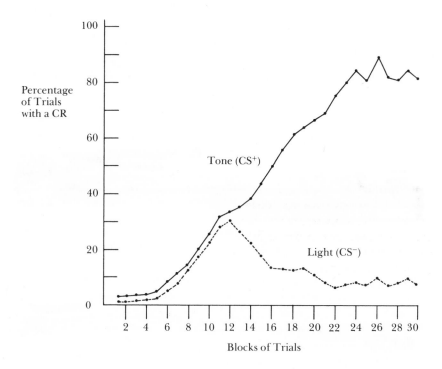

Figure 4–10. Hypothetical Development of a Pavlovian Discrimination. *Initially, the animal responds to both the CS⁺ and the CS⁻. After some training, responding to the CS⁻ drops off while responding to the CS⁺ continues to increase.*

The question which concerns us is whether, in the course of discrimination training, the CS⁻ remains a neutral stimulus or becomes an inhibitory one, and the evidence is clear and compelling. Virtually all the techniques for uncovering inhibition already discussed have been used in assessing the status of a CS⁻ and all have provided evidence that the CS⁻ is a powerful conditioned inhibitor.[16] In addition, there is another source of evidence for inhibition which has not yet been discussed. It comes from the study of generalization gradients.

16. See Rescorla, 1969.

Excitatory and Inhibitory
Generalization Gradients

Let us return for a moment to the hypothetical dog which has been exposed to Pavlovian discrimination training and produced the data in Figure 4–10. Let us suppose that the tone CS^+ was a pure tone of frequency 800 Hz (tonal frequency corresponds to what we call pitch). Let us further suppose that the light CS^- was of wavelength 500 nm (wavelength of light corresponds to what we call color). Now, suppose that in addition to presentations of the CS^+ and CS^-, the dog also received occasional presentations of tones which differed in frequency from the CS^+, and lights which differed in wavelength from the CS^-. None of these stimuli was followed by the US. If the experimenter recorded the percentage of trials in which the various tones elicited a CR, he would observe a pattern of responding like that in Figure 4–11*A*. This pattern is called an excitatory generalization gradient. The CS^+ produces the most responding and, as other tones become more and more different from the CS^+, the amount of responding they produce decreases.

What about the different lights though? The CS^- produces no salivation, as we know. If this is due merely to the absence of excitation, then we would also expect other colors to yield no salivation. On the other hand, if the CS^- is inhibitory, then we might expect other colors to be somewhat less inhibitory (just as other tones are somewhat less excitatory than the CS^+). If this is so, we would expect salivation to *increase* as the light presented moves further and further away from the CS^- in wavelength. This, in fact, is what is observed, as can be seen in Figure 4–11*B*.[17]

The phenomena of generalization and discrimination are of crucial importance when these conditioning principles are applied to behavior technology. Therapy which is successful in the therapist's office means nothing. Success is determined by the patient's ability to generalize to the real world. Indeed, finding ways to insure generalization of treatment from the office or hospital to the outside world is one of the most difficult problems confronting behavior technology.

What makes the problem especially difficult is that sometimes generalization can go too far. One can imagine the problems in living which would be created if a relatively harmless conditioned fear response, as for example, to lightning as a CS for thunder, generalized to other loud noises (e.g., airplanes) and other bright flashes of light

---

17. For more on generalization in Pavlovian conditioning, see Moore, 1972.

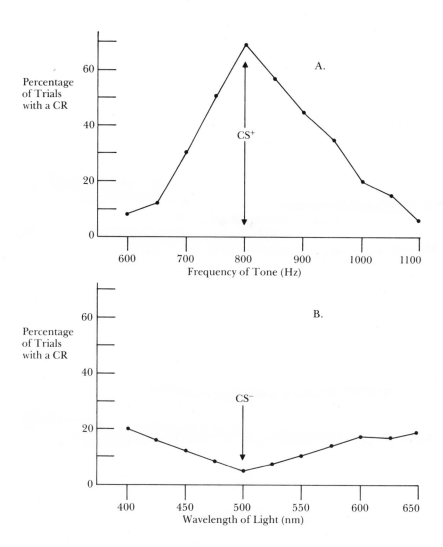

Figure 4–11. Hypothetical Generalization Gradients of Excitation (*A*) with a Tone as CS⁺, and Inhibition (*B*) with a Light as CS⁻. *In* A, *maximum responding occurs to the CS⁺ and drops off systematically as the tones presented are more and more different from the CS⁺. In* B, *minimum responding occurs to the CS⁻, and responding increases as lights are more and more different from the CS⁻. The inhibitory gradient* (B) *is less sharp than the excitatory one, a typical research finding.*

(e.g., car headlights). Such a phenomenon would result in almost complete disruption of a person's behavior in a normal urban environment. Thus, the behavior technologist is faced on the one hand with fostering generalization of successful treatment from the hospital to the real world and, on the other hand, with preventing overgeneralization of harmless or even appropriate conditioned responses to inappropriate and debilitating extremes.

Backward Conditioning

There is one other condition under which inhibition is produced—backward conditioning. Recall that if a US *precedes* a CS (backward conditioning), conditioning does not occur. This assertion can now be modified. Conditioning does occur, but not excitatory conditioning. Rather, the CS becomes a conditioned inhibitor. Consider what a sequence of trials in a backward conditioning experiment would look like. Figure 4–12 depicts such a procedure. The most obvious characteristic of this procedure is the temporal contiguity of CS and US, with US coming first. Despite this contiguity, excitatory conditioning does not occur. This suggests that Pavlovian conditioning requires a process of looking forward in time rather than backward. But suppose the animal looks forward in time from the CS. What does the CS tell the animal? The CS tells it that the US is over. Said another way, the CS is paired with the *termination* of the US. This may be sufficient to make the CS inhibitory. Indeed, there is ample evidence, from experiments like some we have already described, that a CS which is paired with the termination of a US is an inhibitory stimulus.[18]

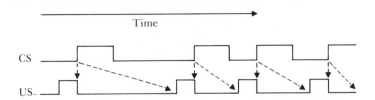

Figure 4–12. Diagram of a Sequence of Backward Conditioning Trials. *The arrows indicate two possible associations between CS and US which would make the CS inhibitory. That is, the CS might be inhibitory because it signals the end of the last US, or because it signals a long period before the occurrence of the next US.*

18. Rescorla, 1969.

Though there is substantial agreement that backward conditioning makes a CS inhibitory, the means by which this occurs is controversial.[19] So far, we have claimed that it is the pairing of a CS with US termination that is responsible, but there is another possibility. To see this, it may help to imagine oneself as a subject in the experiment. Periodically, a painful shock (US) occurs, followed by the sounding of a tone (CS). The tone tells us that shock is about to end, but so what. We already know that. The shocks are rather brief, and we have experienced them before. Besides, it is probably the onset of the shock which is most fear provoking and uncomfortable. In other words, the tone does not give us much valuable information with regard to the termination of shock. On the other hand, the tone tells us that the intertrial interval, a period in which no shocks will occur, is coming. It is a signal for a prolonged period of safety. Perhaps it is the pairing of tone and intertrial interval that makes the tone an inhibitor of fear. There is a way to test this. Suppose one arranged the intertrial interval so that while it was a few minutes long on the average, it was sometimes very, very short. Now, the tone would still signal shock termination and the intertrial interval, but the intertrial interval would no longer signal safety from shock. If it is the pairing of tone with intertrial interval which makes the tone an inhibitor of fear, it should not become one in this procedure. In fact, it does not become one.[20] Therefore, the backward CS seems to become inhibitory because it signals a period of safety from shock.

Why have we made so much of this phenomenon? The reason is that we have introduced some ideas which did not come up in dealing with other conditioning phenomena. Instead of saying the CS was *paired with* the intertrial interval, we said it *signaled* the intertrial interval. The CS in fact was paired with both the end of the US and the intertrial interval. We suggested that this first characteristic was not terribly useful or informative while the second one was. What do words like "signal," "useful," and "informative" mean? What do they have to do with Pavlovian conditioning? It has appeared that Pavlovian conditioning results from the mechanical pairing of CS and US. But words like "useful" and "informative" seem to suggest something less mechanical and more selective. It is as though the animal evaluates dif-

---

19. There is actually evidence that backward pairing procedures can produce excitation (Cautela, 1965; Heth & Rescorla, 1973; Wagner & Terry, 1975), but a recent experiment (Heth, 1976) indicates that this excitation may be transitory. Nevertheless, even transitory excitatory effects require an explanation and none is presently available.
20. Moscovitch and LoLordo, 1968.

ferent sources of information and focuses on the most reliable or most important one. As we shall see in the next chapter, this seems to be precisely the reason that Pavlovian conditioning occurs when it does—not because the CS is *paired* with the US, but because it provides *information* about the US. The last decade has brought a small revolution in our understanding of the most fundamental aspects of Pavlovian conditioning: the conditions which are necessary and sufficient for its occurrence.

5

Pavlovian Conditioning II

New Developments and Applications

Our understanding of Pavlovian conditioning has undergone a major transformation in the last 10 years. For Pavlov and most of his followers, conditioning involved the simple, mechanical association of two events which occurred closely together in time. Special moments of contiguity between CS and US stamped in a connection between them. It is now becoming apparent that conditioning is neither this simple nor this mechanical. Animals seem to evaluate the information conveyed by various stimuli, and to associate selectively the most informative ones with USs. For conditioning to occur, a potential CS must tell the animal something about the US which it would not otherwise know.

NECESSARY CONDITIONS FOR PAVLOVIAN CONDITIONING

In 1967, Yale psychologist Robert Rescorla suggested that contiguity of CS and US, while perhaps necessary for conditioning to occur, was not sufficient. What was necessary in addition was that there be a differential *contingency* between CS and US.[1] What is the difference between contiguity and contingency?

Let us consider a commonplace example. Imagine a person who habitually listens to the forecast of the next day's weather. Sometimes the weather report predicts rain and the next day it rains. Sometimes the weather report predicts warmth and sunshine and the next day it

---

1. Rescorla, 1967a.

is warm and sunny. There are, therefore, numerous instances in which the forecast is paired with the actual weather, that is, the forecast is accurate. One might expect that the forecast would influence this person's behavior.[2] If the weather report were always this accurate, we could describe it mathematically in the notation of probability theory in this way:

$$p(\text{rain}/\text{rain forecast}) = 1.0 \tag{1}$$
$$p(\overline{\text{rain}}/\overline{\text{rain}} \text{ forecast}) = 1.0 \tag{2}$$
$$p(\text{rain}/\overline{\text{rain}} \text{ forecast}) = 0.0 \tag{3}$$
$$p(\overline{\text{rain}}/\text{rain forecast}) = 0.0 \tag{4}$$

These four probability statements may be read as follows:

(1) The probability that it will rain given that the forecast was rain is 1.0, that is, every time the forecast is rain, it will rain.

(2) The probability that it will not rain given that the forecast was no rain is 1.0, that is, every time the forecast is no rain, it will not rain.

Statements (3) and (4) follow necessarily from (1) and (2) and may be translated in the same way. In describing the relation between weather forecasts and the weather, we would say that a differential contingency existed between forecast and weather such that the forecast provided *information* about the weather. If weather forecasting were this good, one could choose clothing each night with complete assurance that it would be appropriate for the next day's weather.

But let us be more realistic. Suppose that it rained every time the weatherman said it would, but that it also rained about once in every 10 times that he said it would not. Now, our probability statements would look like this:

$$p(\text{rain}/\text{rain forecast}) = 1.0 \tag{5}$$
$$p(\text{rain}/\overline{\text{rain}} \text{ forecast}) = 0.1 \tag{6}$$
$$p(\overline{\text{rain}}/\overline{\text{rain}} \text{ forecast}) = 0.9 \tag{7}$$
$$p(\overline{\text{rain}}/\text{rain forecast}) = 0.0 \tag{8}$$

2. Notice that this example does not itself involve Pavlovian conditioning. Choosing what clothes to wear or something of the sort on the basis of a weather forecast is in no sense a conditioned reflex. However, the issue of contingency in contrast to contiguity extends well beyond Pavlovian conditioning (see Chapter 6).

The weather reports are still quite helpful. Whenever they say rain, it will rain, though occasionally it will rain when they say it won't. It still is sensible to pay attention to the weather report.

But now, let us suppose that the probability statements looked like this:

$$p(\text{rain}/\text{rain forecast}) = p(\text{rain}/\overline{\text{rain}} \text{ forecast}) = 0.2 \qquad (9)$$

$$p(\overline{\text{rain}}/\text{rain forecast}) = p(\overline{\text{rain}}/\overline{\text{rain}} \text{ forecast}) = 0.8 \qquad (10)$$

What do these expressions convey? What (9) says is that rain is just as likely to come when the forecast is no rain as when the forecast is rain. The probability of rain is 0.2, which means that one day in five, on the average, it will rain, and listening to the forecast will provide absolutely no information about the next day's weather. Whether it rains and whether the forecast predicts rain are independent of each other.

If this were the state of the art in meteorology, it would make no sense to listen to weather forecasts. Notice, however, there are still occasions in which the forecast of rain (or no rain) is paired with the outcome rain (or no rain). Thus, this last situation represents a case in which contiguity continues to exist between CS and US but a *differential* contingency between CS and US is absent.

Let us return now to the Pavlovian conditioning experiment. Imagine a standard procedure in which a tone is paired with shock (see Figure 5–1*A*). In the language of probability, the procedure could be described as follows:

$$p(\text{shock}/\text{tone}) = p(\overline{\text{shock}}/\overline{\text{tone}}) = 1.0 \qquad (11)$$

$$p(\text{shock}/\overline{\text{tone}}) = p(\overline{\text{shock}}/\text{tone}) = 0.0 \qquad (12)$$

Now suppose we added some extra tones so that only half the tones were followed by shocks:

$$p(\text{shock}/\text{tone}) = 0.5 \qquad (13)$$

$$p(\text{shock}/\overline{\text{tone}}) = 0.0 \qquad (14)$$

The tone is not as informative as it was before (there are frequent false alarms), but it still provides valuable information: shock will *never* come unless a tone has come first (see Figure 5–1*B*).

But now suppose we added some extra shocks as well—shocks which occurred during the intertrial interval (see Figure 5–1*C*). Indeed, suppose we added enough shocks so that shock was just as likely

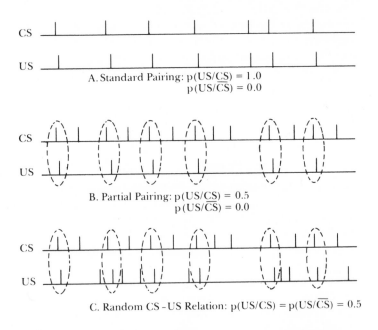

Figure 5–1. Diagram of Informative and Noninformative CS–US Relations. *In A, every CS is followed by a US. In B, seven additional CSs are added to the CS–US pairings. Now the CS is no longer a perfect predictor of the US, though it is still a good predictor. In C, seven additional US presentations are also added. Now, the occurrence of the CS is no longer a good predictor of the US.*

to come in the absence of the tone as in its presence. In probability terms,

$$p(\text{shock/tone}) = p(\text{shock/}\overline{\text{tone}}) \tag{15}$$

As in the case of the weather report, here the tone provides no useful information about the shock. Tone and shock continue to be paired as they were at the start of the experiment; they are sometimes contiguous. However, the extra tones and extra shocks have eliminated the differential contingency between tone and shock that was present at the start of the experiment.

What Rescorla proposed was that if a subject were exposed to this last procedure, conditioning would not occur, despite the presence of CS–US pairings. To confirm this, he trained dogs to make operant responses to avoid electric shock. He then exposed them to a variety of Pavlovian fear-conditioning procedures. One group of dogs (*A*) received standard CS–US pairings. A second group (*B*) received the same number of CSs and USs but they were always unpaired. What would we expect the effect of this procedure to be? From Pavlov's contiguity view of conditioning, we would expect that this procedure would produce no conditioning. From the contingency view, we would expect something different:

$$p(shock/\overline{tone}) > p(shock/tone) \tag{16}$$

The absence of the tone predicts shock, while the presence of the tone predicts safety. Thus, just as in the case of backward conditioning, we would expect the CS to inhibit fear as a result of this procedure.

A third group (*C*) also received the same number of CSs and USs, but they were neither paired nor unpaired; they were independent. The occurrence of the CS provided no information about the occurrence of the US, though pairings occasionally occurred by chance. Here, the contingency view would predict no conditioning to the CS. Finally, a fourth group (*D*) also received independent presentation of CS and US with one important exception: if the US was scheduled to be delivered more than 30 seconds after the most recent CS, it was automatically cancelled. Thus, while the number of accidental CS–US pairings for these last two groups would be the same, the groups would differ in that for the last group,

$$p(shock/tone) > p(shock/\overline{tone}) \tag{17}$$

since some shocks scheduled in the absence of the tone would not actually be delivered. Thus, the contingency view would predict conditioned fear in this last group. These four procedures and the expected results are depicted in Figure 5–2.

The results of the experiment confirmed Rescorla's analysis. When the tone CS was occasionally presented while the dogs were making avoidance responses, for the first (standard pairing) and last (positive contingency) groups, it increased the rate of avoidance responding, which as we saw earlier is an indication of conditioned fear; for the third group (pairing but no contingency) it had no effect, and for the second group (no pairing but a negative or inhibitory contingency) it reduced the rate of avoidance responding.

It therefore seems clear that our understanding of Pavlovian conditioning requires a fundamental change. Up until 1967, it was believed that simple, mechanical association of two stimuli contiguous in time would result in conditioning. However, Rescorla's experiments

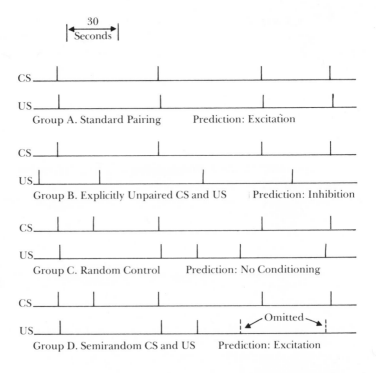

Figure 5–2. Diagram of Procedures Used to Test the Contingency Theory of Conditioning. *Group A receives only pairings of CS and US. The expectation is that this "standard" pairing procedure will produce excitatory conditioning. Group B receives only unpaired presentations of CS and US. The contingency theory of conditioning predicts inhibitory conditioning in this group. Contiguity theory would predict no conditioning, either excitatory or inhibitory. Groups C and D receive the same number of CS–US pairings. They differ only in that, for Group D, USs scheduled to come more than 30 seconds after the last CS are omitted (broken lines). According to contiguity theory, the groups should not differ. However, according to contingency theory, the CS should be informative for Group D and not for Group C so that only Group D should show excitatory conditioning.*

demonstrated that the organism is sensitive to the degree to which one stimulus provides *information* about the other. In some way the organism computes probabilities—of US/CS and of US/CS—and the outcome of this computation determines whether a potential CS will actually be an effective CS. A general characterization of this view and of what kinds of procedures will result in what kinds of conditioning is presented in Figure 5–3.

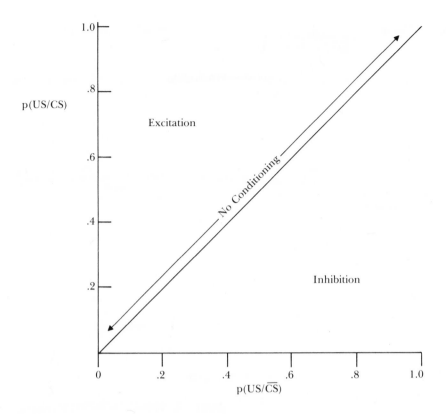

Figure 5–3. Diagram of the General Pavlovian Contingency Space. *According to the contingency theory, all procedures which fall above the diagonal line should result in excitatory conditioning, because the US is more likely to come if the CS has come than if it has not. All procedures which fall below the diagonal line should result in inhibitory conditioning, because the US is less likely to come if the CS has come than if it has not. All procedures which fall on the line should result in no conditioning, because the US is neither more nor less likely to come if the CS has come than if it has not.*

INFORMATIVENESS, REDUNDANCY, AND THE BLOCKING EFFECT

In the last chapter (p. 57), the phenomenon of overshadowing was mentioned. If the CS is a compound of two stimuli, and one of them is more salient or noticeable than the other, nearly all the conditioning which occurs may be controlled exclusively by this more salient stimulus: the less salient one may be completely overshadowed.

What conditions make one stimulus more salient than another? Often it is simply a matter of the intensity of the two stimuli: a loud tone is more salient than a dim light, and a bright light is more salient than a soft tone. Sometimes, for particular species, one stimulus modality is more salient than another. It seems, for example, that for hungry pigeons visual stimuli are more salient than auditory ones, while for rats the reverse is true. The most interesting case, however, is when one stimulus becomes more salient than another because of an animal's experience with it.

The effect of an animal's experience with stimuli on their salience was demonstrated in an important and dramatic series of experiments by Princeton psychologist Leon Kamin.[3] The basic experiment involved the following procedure: rats were exposed to 16 trials in which noise was followed by electric shock. Then they were given 8 trials in which a compound stimulus of the noise and a light were followed by shock. Finally, they were given a presentation of the light alone to see whether it produced any conditioned responses. What might we expect the result of such an experiment to be? The noise alone provides information that shock is coming, and the rats presumably learn this in the first 16 trials. Then light and noise together are followed by shock. What does the light tell the animal? As far as one can tell, everything to be known in this situation can be learned from the noise. The light is a redundant, noninformative addition to the situation. Thus, despite pairing of light and shock, the contingency view would predict that the light will not produce conditioned responses. And it doesn't. That this effect is due to the experience the rats have with the noise alone is clear from another procedure Kamin tried. If light and noise are presented as a compound from the beginning, and then light is tested by itself, it produces strong conditioned responses. This overshadowing of control by one stimulus as a result of experience with a second stimulus has been called the *blocking effect* to distinguish it from the overshadowing which results from unconditioned properties of the stimuli themselves.

Since Kamin's original experiments, a few variants have been designed to elucidate the mechanism which underlies the blocking effect. Suppose rats receive 16 trials of noise–shock followed by 8 trials where light and noise are given together. On these last 8 trials, however, there is no shock. Is the light still redundant? In this case, because the light is telling the animal that shock is not coming, the light is not redundant. On the contrary, the light becomes an extinction

3. Kamin, 1968.

stimulus. After 8 of these trials, the noise is again presented alone. Although 8 extinction trials would usually be sufficient to reduce substantially the amount of conditioned responding obtained, one discovers that on this procedure the noise has undergone virtually no extinction. It is the light which has been associated with no shock while the noise has been blocked or protected from extinction. Consider what this phenomenon requires the animal to do. The animal first notices the light, a new stimulus. Then, the animal fails to receive a shock, a new event. If there had been no new stimulus, extinction to the noise would have begun. Instead, the animal seems to associate the change in the US with the change in the CS.

In a similar experiment, noise–shock pairings were followed by noise + light–shock pairings. With the compound, however, the shock was more intense. When the light was tested alone, a substantial amount of conditioning was revealed. Here again, the introduction of the light was correlated with an important change in the US. As a result, the light was not a redundant stimulus. Hence these results are consistent with the concepts of informativeness and redundancy.

THE RESCORLA–WAGNER THEORY

The research of Rescorla and Kamin, among others, seems to demand a change in our conception of the conditioning process. Animals do not evaluate pairings of CS and US in a vacuum. These pairings are evaluated against a background which may include other presentations of CS and US unpaired, or include presentations of other CSs which are also reliable predictors of the US. Conditioning occurs only when an evaluation of the entire context reveals that a particular CS is a good (perhaps the best available) predictor of the US. This new conception of Pavlovian conditioning makes the conditioning process seem a lot more complex than it used to seem. It also raises an immediate and insistent question. How do animals do it? By what mechanism are they able to keep track of CSs and USs, estimate probabilities, compute probability differences, and ultimately make CRs to the CS? The requirements of the task seem sufficiently arduous to tax human intellectual capacity. Yet it is claimed that something of the sort is accomplished routinely by nonhumans. It seems clear that probability calculations of this type are automatic, in just the way that calculations of the trajectory of a thrown ball, which allow one to catch the ball, are automatic. However, we still need an account of the mechanism by which this automatic calculation might occur.

Recently, a possible account of how animals might discover the informativeness or predictiveness of potential CSs was proposed by Robert Rescorla and another Yale psychologist, Allan Wagner.[4] Their theory explains complex contingency analysis in terms of simple associations of the sort Pavlov had in mind. It can account for most of the old, familiar phenomena of conditioning as well as for the new dramatic ones. Finally, it has the virtue of precision. The theory is specified in such clear detail that one can derive from it predictions about the behavior of a subject in untried experimental situations.

Consider the idealized representation of a standard conditioning curve shown in Figure 5–4. Curves of this form are called negatively accelerated. The changes in the value of conditioning strength (*y* axis) with conditioning trials (*x* axis) are very substantial early in training. However, as training proceeds and the leveling-off point, or asymptote, is approached, changes in strength of conditioning with each

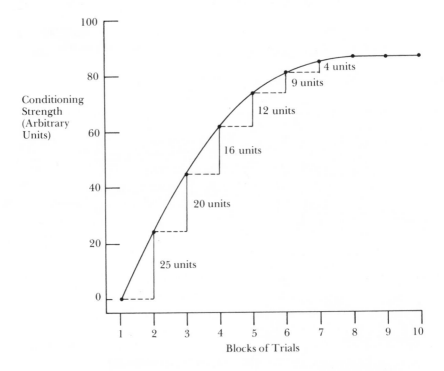

Figure 5–4. Idealized Learning Curve. *The curve is negatively accelerated, which means that the amount of change in conditioning strength (in arbitrary units) gets smaller and smaller with repeated trials.*

4. Rescorla and Wagner, 1972; Wagner and Rescorla, 1972.

trial get smaller and smaller. The intuition captured by a negatively accelerated curve like this is that the experimental subject does not profit equally from each trial. How much one profits depends upon how much one already knows. When one knows nothing, profits are substantial. When one knows a great deal, profits from further trials are small. Rather than learning a fixed amount with each trial, one seems to learn a fixed proportion of the difference between one's present level of learning and the maximum. As that difference gets smaller (as one learns more), the amount of new learning produced by further trials gets smaller.

The Rescorla–Wagner theory begins with the fact that the typical learning curve for Pavlovian conditioning has this negatively accelerated form. With this as a starting point, the theory attempts to characterize the learning curve mathematically. The theory describes the growth of asociative strength (V) with repeated conditioning trials.[5] The change in associative strength on any trial, n (ΔV_n) is expressed as follows:

$$\Delta V_n = K(\lambda - V_{n-1}) \tag{18}$$

where K = a constant between 0 and 1, the value of which is determined by the CS and US; λ = the asymptote or leveling-off point of conditioning, determined by the US. It is assumed that different USs, or different magnitudes of the same US, will support different asymptotic levels of conditioning. For example, the more intense the shock which serves as the US, the higher we might expect the asymptote of conditioning to be. The constant K reflects the idea that some CSs (the more salient ones) and some USs produce faster conditioning than other CSs and USs. Thus, the value of K influences the rate of conditioning while the value of λ influences the asymptotic level of conditioning.

What equation (18) expresses is simply that the changes in associative strength on trial n (ΔV_n) will be proportional to the difference between λ (the asymptote) and the previous associative strength, V_{n-1}. Since the value of V will grow from trial to trial, the quantity $(\lambda - V_{n-1})$ will get smaller and smaller, so that ΔV_n will also get smaller and smaller. But this is simply a description of the negatively accelerated learning curve.

Let us work through an example. Suppose $V = 0$, $K = 0.3$, and

5. Associative strength is a theoretical quantity. It is assumed to map fairly directly into behavioral measures of conditioning, like drops of saliva, frequency of eyeblinks, or changes in heart rate.

$\lambda = 90$ in Trial 1 of a conditioning experiment. If we apply equation (18) to repeated trials, we get:

Trial 1: $\Delta V_1 = .30(90 - 0)$ $\quad = 27.0$

Trial 2: $\Delta V_2 = .30(90 - 27)$ $\quad = 18.9$

Trial 3: $\Delta V_3 = .30(90 - 45.9) = 13.2$

Trial 4: $\Delta V_4 = .30(90 - 59.1) = \quad 9.3$

Trial 5: $\Delta V_5 = .30(90 - 68.4) = \quad 6.5$

Total associative strength after five trials $= 74.9$

Associative strength grows 27 units on Trial 1, 18.9 on Trial 2, 9.3 on Trial 4, and only 6.5 on Trial 5. Clearly, the change in associative strength on any trial gets smaller and smaller as conditioning proceeds, which is what the negatively accelerated learning curve requires. To examine the effect of the value of K on learning rate, the reader might work through the above example with $K = 0.5$. Under these conditions, after five trials associative strength will be about 87 units.

Let us now examine how this simple, elegant theory can be applied to the phenomena of overshadowing and blocking.

Rescorla–Wagner Theory and Compound Stimuli

What does the Rescorla–Wagner theory say about conditioning involving compound stimuli? Let us call CS_1 "A" and CS_2 "X." According to the theory,

$$V_{AX} = V_A + V_X \tag{19}$$

In short, the associative strength of a compound stimulus is equal to the sum of the associative strength of its parts. If we did an experiment in which tone and light were presented as a compound CS right from the start, the growth of associative strength would look like this:

$$\Delta V_{A(tone)} = K(\lambda - V_{AX}) \tag{20}$$

$$\Delta V_{X(light)} = M(\lambda - V_{AX}) \tag{21}$$

The only difference between (20) and (21) is in the constants K and M. Recall that part of what determines the value of that constant is the salience of the CS. If tone and light were equally salient, then $K = M$ and (20) = (21). If so, we would expect the associative strength of both tone and light to grow in equal steps. If, after presenting them together for 50 trials or so, we tested each of them alone, we would expect each of the stimuli to yield exactly half of the associative strength of the compound.

Overshadowing • But suppose that the tone was much more salient than the light, so that $K = .7$ while $M = .1$. Let us chart the course of conditioning predicted by the theory, assuming that $\lambda = 90$.

$$\Delta V_{A(tone)} = K(\lambda - V_{AX})$$

Trial 1: $\Delta V_A = .70(90 - 0) \quad = 63.0$

Trial 2: $\Delta V_A = .70(90 - 72) \quad = 12.6$

Trial 3: $\Delta V_A = .70(90 - 86.4) = \quad 2.5$

Trial 4: $\Delta V_A = .70(90 - 89.2) = \quad 0.6$

$$\Delta V_{X(light)} = M(\lambda - V_{AX})$$

$\Delta V_X = .10(90 - 0) \quad = 9.0$

$\Delta V_X = .10(90 - 72) \quad = 1.8$

$\Delta V_X = .10(90 - 86.4) = 0.3$

$\Delta V_X = .10(90 - 89.2) = 0.1$

After four trials, the associative strength of A would be about 79 units; the associative strength of X would be about 11 units. X would be *overshadowed* by A. And note that A plays a crucial role in the low degree of conditioning to X. Since A conditions rapidly, the asymptotic level of strength to AX is reached rapidly, though X makes rather little contribution. If we did the experiment with X alone, keeping the values of λ and M the same, the first four trials would look like this:

$$\Delta V_{X(light)} = M(\lambda - V_{AX})$$

Trial 1: $\Delta V_X = .10(90 - 0) \quad = 9.0$

Trial 2: $\Delta V_X = .10(90 - 9) \quad = 8.1$

Trial 3: $\Delta V_X = .10(90 - 17.1) = 7.3$

Trial 4: $\Delta V_X = .10(90 - 24.4) = 6.6$

After four trials, the associative strength of X would be 31 units instead of 11. Thus, the theory makes it clear that the less salient of two stimuli in a compound is overshadowed by the more salient stimulus.

Blocking • Now let us consider blocking. Recall that in Kamin's experiments on blocking, one CS (a noise) is paired with shock for a number of trials, and then a second CS (a light) is added, so that trials contain noise + light followed by shock. Under these conditions, the light does not acquire any associative strength. Suppose a noise is paired with shock for six trials with $\lambda = 90$ and $K = 0.7$ as before. After six trials (the reader can work it out) the associative strength of the noise is about 89 units. Now, the noise and light are presented together, followed by shock. Assuming that the noise and light are equally salient (i.e., $K = M = .7$) this is what the theory predicts:

$$\Delta V_A = K(\lambda - V_{AX}) \qquad\qquad \Delta V_X = M(\lambda - V_{AX})$$

Trial 1: $\Delta V_A = .70(90 - 89) = 0.7 \qquad \Delta V_X = .70(90 - 89) = 0.7$

It is apparent from this trial that the theory predicts that virtually no conditioning will occur to the light. Since V_{AX} is already so close to asymptote, further trials will result in only the most minimal increases in associative strength. Thus, prior conditioning with the noise (A) "blocks" subsequent conditioning to the light.

But suppose that when we introduce the light we double the intensity of the shock. As we have seen, according to the theory, changing the intensity of the US will change the asymptote, or λ. Suppose our new λ, with the higher shock intensity, is 150. Now let us examine what just the first noise + light followed by shock trial should produce.

$$\Delta V_A = K(\lambda - V_{AX}) \qquad\qquad \Delta V_X = M(\lambda - V_{AX})$$

Trial 1: $\Delta V_A = .7(150 - 89) = 42.7 \qquad \Delta V_X = .7(150 - 89) = 42.7$

It is clear that the theory predicts that if introduction of the light as a CS with the noise is accompanied by an increase in US intensity, the light will not be blocked from conditioning. And as we saw in describing Kamin's experimental results earlier, the light is not blocked under these conditions.

Applications of the Rescorla–Wagner theory extend far beyond overshadowing and blocking. The theory can account for all the inhibitory phenomena we discussed in the last chapter. It can account for the fact that a random relation between CS and US produces no conditioning, and for the fact that a negative relation between CS and US (one in which they always occur unpaired) makes the CS inhibitory. What this means is that simple trial-by-trial changes in associative strength, in the manner specified by the theory, may represent the mechanism which underlies the probability calculation and information evaluation which phenomena like blocking and contingency learning seem to require.[6]

THE ADAPTIVE NATURE OF THE CONDITIONED RESPONSE

We have been concerned thus far with the necessary and sufficient conditions for conditioning to occur. We have reached the conclusion

---

6. For detailed presentation of both the theory and the evidence which supports it, see Rescorla and Wagner, 1972, and Wagner and Rescorla, 1972.

that conditioning depends upon the existence of a relation between CS and US whereby the CS provides information about the imminent occurrence of the US. The question before us now is what does the organism *do* with that information? How does conditioning facilitate survival? How does the capacity for conditioning give organisms that possess it an adaptive advantage over organisms that do not? To answer these questions, we must focus on the nature of conditioned responses.

Pavlov's view of the conditioning process was that the CS becomes a literal substitute for the US. Whatever responses the US triggers are also triggered by the CS once conditioning has occurred. Thus, if food triggers salivation, licking of the lips, and general agitation, an effective CS will trigger salivation, licking of the lips, and general agitation. If a puff of air triggers tensing of facial muscles and an eyeblink, a CS will trigger tensing of facial muscles and an eyeblink. This account of conditioning is typically referred to as the *stimulus substitution* view.

There is now substantial evidence against the view that CRs invariably mimic URs. While they sometimes mimic URs, they are sometimes unrelated to URs and sometimes even the direct opposite of URs. What all CRs seem to have in common is that they are adaptive—they enhance the animal's chances for survival in its natural environment.

An example of the adaptiveness of the CR comes from studies where electric shock is a US. We have been describing the UR produced by electric shock as fear. In fact, shock produces a variety of skeletal and autonomic responses which can be separately measured. The most dramatic UR to shock seems to be general mobilization of the sympathetic nervous system: heart rate and blood pressure increase when shock is presented. What would be the adaptive value of an anticipatory increase in heart rate to a CS for shock? Such a CR would seem to be maladaptive. It would serve to increase the strain on a cardiovascular system which is already being strained by the shock. A much more adaptive CR would be a *decrease* in heart rate, in direct opposition to the unconditioned response. Such a CR would indicate the ability of the body to anticipate cardiovascular strain and compensate for it in advance. It turns out that cardiac *deceleration* is the most common result of Pavlovian fear-conditioning experiments. In the well-trained animal, the CS decreases heart rate and the US increases heart rate.[7]

Consider another particularly dramatic example of the adaptiveness of the CR. Rats were given injections of insulin every other

7. For a detailed discussion, see Obrist, Sutterer, and Howard, 1972.

day. The effect of insulin is to reduce the amount of glucose in the blood, to produce hypoglycemia. Hypoglycemia is a very dangerous condition which can sometimes put organisms into a severe state of shock. The diabetic coma results from hypoglycemia. Now the question is this: If the injection procedure itself becomes a CS, and insulin is a US, and hypoglycemia is the UR, what will the CR be? Nothing could be less adaptive than a CR which was the same as the UR. When rats were injected with salt water to test for the CR produced by the injection itself, it turned out that the injection produced an *increase* in the level of blood sugar, not a decrease. The conditioning process worked to compensate for the potentially lethal effects of the US.[8]

There is even substantial evidence for the adaptiveness of the CR in Pavlov's own research. For Pavlov, the measured CR was the same response as the UR—salivation. However, Pavlov did not permit the animals to do much more. The subject was strapped into a harness so that the possibility for movement was limited. Moreover, food was delivered into the mouth. The animals were not required to move to the source of food and ingest it. Thus it is possible that the kinds of effects observed by Pavlov were determined by the methods he used, and that a modification of these methods which permitted animals to move about freely would reveal conditioned responses which were not a normal part of the conditioned reflex.

This is indeed the case. If one looks closely at a harnessed dog during conditioning, one observes orientation of the head toward the CS. If one permits the dogs to move about, one observes movement toward and contact with the CS, but also movement toward the place where the US will be delivered. Now the unconditioned response to food in the mouth is salivation. Movements directed at the CS do not mimic the UR at all. Nevertheless, they enormously increase the adaptive value of the conditioning process.

In the natural environment, the most common CS for food is either its visual appearance or its odor. While no doubt these stimuli produce salivation, if they also produce movement directed at them they

8. Siegel, 1972. Evidence is emerging that, in general, when pharmacological agents are used as USs, the conditioned response to the injection itself is the opposite of the response to the drug. If the US is glucose, which increases blood sugar, the CR to the injection is a decrease in blood sugar (Deutsch, 1974). If the US is morphine, which reduces pain sensitivity, the CR to the injection is heightened pain sensitivity (Siegel, 1975). Siegel, 1977, recently suggested that the general phenomenon of drug tolerance (with repeated administrations of a drug, larger and larger doses must be used to produce the same effect) is the result of CRs to the injection which are opposite in direction to the URs to the drug. Thus, for example, after repeated injections of morphine, the drug must overcome a super-sensitivity to pain which has been conditioned to the injection. Before conditioning occurs, morphine only has to dull ordinary pain sensitivity. Thus smaller doses can be successful early in treatment but not late in treatment.

will draw the animal toward the food. This will, of course, increase the likelihood that the food will actually be ingested. Salivation without this directed movement does not produce the food. In the real world, unlike the laboratory, food does not come to the animal—the animal must go to the food.

Pavlov knew this. His book contains numerous references to the adaptiveness of the conditioning process. He knew that something important was being omitted when his own research focused exclusively on salivation. He did so nevertheless because salivation permitted a degree of quantification which the other responses one might observe did not. In Pavlov's words:

> *It is essential to realize that each of these two reflexes—the alimentary reflex and the mild defense reflex to rejectable substances—consists of two distinct components, a motor and a secretory. First the animal exhibits a reflex activity directed towards getting hold of the food and eating it . . . ; and secondly . . , an immediate secretion of saliva occurs. . . . We confined our experiments almost exclusively to the secretory component of the reflex. . . . It allows an extremely accurate measurement of the intensity of the reflex activity. . . . It would be much more difficult to obtain the same accuracy of measurement for any motor reflex, especially for such complex motor reactions as accompany reflexes to food. . . .*[9]

In a clear statement of his own view of the adaptiveness of the conditioning process, Pavlov wrote:

> *This comparatively simple experiment explains how a decerebrate dog can die of starvation in the midst of plenty, for it will only start eating if food chances to come in contact with its mouth or tongue. Moreover, the elementary nature of the inborn reflexes, with their limitations and inadequacy, are clearly brought out in these experiments, and we are now able to appreciate the fundamental importance of those stimuli which have the character of signals.*[10]

In Pavlov's view, the movement toward and ingestion of food requires conditioning of the sight (or smell) of food to food in the mouth. Without this experience, dogs would die of starvation. That conditioning has major survival value is obviously implied by this view. Thus, Pavlov's own orientation was toward adaptiveness, though his

9. Pavlov, 1927, pp. 17–18.
10. Pavlov, 1927, p. 23.

methods precluded a detailed appreciation of the adaptiveness of conditioned reflexes.

This concludes our discussion of the basic principles and phenomena of Pavlovian conditioning. Let us summarize our major conclusions: Conditioned excitation occurs when a US is preceded by a stimulus which predicts or provides information about its occurrence. When a situation includes a number of potential CSs, conditioning seems to occur to the one which is most predictive. Conditioned inhibition occurs when a stimulus reliably predicts the absence, or lowered probability, of a US. The conditioned responses which develop are typically responses which promote the animal's survival by improving its adaptability to the conditions of the immediate environment.

PAVLOVIAN CONDITIONING AND PSYCHOPATHOLOGY

The phenomena being investigated by Pavlov began to have a serious influence on American psychology around 1910, and almost from the beginning American psychologists were interested in the potential applicability of Pavlov's principles to the problems of ordinary life.[11] In dealing with psychopathology, one has two concerns. One concern, obviously, is to develop a treatment or mode of therapy which is effective. Often, this concern is sufficient. On the other hand, some researchers and theorists have tried to go beyond the development of effective therapy to an understanding of what produces pathological behavior in the first place. An effort to develop a model of the *causes* of pathology as well as the cures has been particularly evident in the sphere of Pavlovian conditioning, though it has occasionally appeared in the sphere of operant conditioning as well.

What is to be gained from such an effort? Why bother to understand what produces pathology if one can develop effective therapy without such an understanding? There are two answers to this question.

First, it is not easy to develop an effective therapy. The use of behavioral technology is very much a trial-and-error operation; try one method, then another, then another, until you find one that works. A useful model of what produces pathology would greatly enhance the chances of finding an effective treatment without too many false starts. Second, and far more important, is the fact that only an understanding of the causes of pathology will allow the development of

11. See Watson and Raynor, 1920.

means of prevention. Thus, before describing in detail the ways in which Pavlovian conditioning is used to treat pathology, let us consider a few ideas about how Pavlovian conditioning can produce pathology.

Sources of Pathology: Experimental Neurosis

A dog has been trained on a Pavlovian discrimination procedure. The CS⁺, a circle, is followed by food. The CS⁻, an ellipse, is not followed by food. The dog learns the discrimination and at the end of training salivates only to the CS⁺. Now the procedure is changed. The CS⁺ becomes an ellipse, but one that looks almost like a circle. The CS⁻ is also an ellipse, but one that looks more like a circle than the old CS⁻. Despite the greater similarity between CS⁺ and CS⁻ than before, the dog once again learns the discrimination. The procedure is changed again. CS⁺ and CS⁻ are both ellipses, but even more like each other than before. Again, with greater difficulty, the discrimination is learned. Finally, a new pair of ellipses is chosen, and now the dog finds it impossible to make the discrimination. However, the dog does not simply salivate to both stimuli, nor does it simply stop salivating. It shows tremendous agitation. It barks and howls and attempts to escape the harness. It shows signs of distress that have not been observed before. If the dog is returned to the original discrimination between circle and ellipse, it fails to master the discrimination. The dog seems to have broken down.

Pavlov observed this phenomenon and called it an *experimental neurosis*.[12] He saw it as a result of strong, conflicting tendencies toward excitation and inhibition produced by the same stimuli. It did not happen to dogs exposed from the first to the impossible discrimination. In these dogs, strong excitation and inhibition presumably never developed. However, in dogs with the history of experience described above, experimental neurosis sometimes occurred.

Experimenters in recent years have not had much success in producing experimental neuroses, so the reliability of the phenomenon is in considerable doubt. Moreover, whether experimental neurosis, when it does occur, results from a conflict in the cortex between excitation and inhibition is uncertain. Still more uncertain is whether the neurosis which is a commonplace in modern life bears a causal resemblance to experimental neurosis. Nevertheless, it is tempting to view neuroses as reflecting self-doubt, conflict, uncertainty, and opposed tendencies to action which result generally in a good deal of emo-

12. Pavlov, 1928.

tionality coupled with a lack of any effective behavior. What Pavlov's demonstration showed is that a very specific, isolated conditioning experience can transform the general behavior of an animal. It is not implausible that some human neuroses might stem from particular conditioning experiences of this sort.

Anxiety and Conditioned
Emotional Responses (CER)

In the literature of clinical psychology, a distinction has long been maintained between fear and anxiety. Fear is said to be objective: it is focused on particular objects or situations. It is usually "rational." Anxiety, on the other hand, is subjective: it is unfocused or diffuse. It is difficult or impossible to specify the source of the anxiety, and thus, difficult or impossible to prevent it from occurring. Anxiety, rather than fear, is thought to be the main component of many types of psychopathology. People occasionally find themselves emotionally paralyzed without being able to identify the source of the paralysis. This leaves them withdrawn, unable to act, and miserable.

There is much evidence of conditioned fear. Procedures using shocks as USs and tones or lights as CSs reliably produce fear to the light or tone. However, if anxiety rather than fear is at the heart of much of pyschopathology, it is not clear that a Pavlovian conditioning model of pathology will have much to offer. Is there something to be said about anxiety from a Pavlovian point of view? In the last few years, research in Pavlovian conditioning has produced some important insights into the nature and origins of anxiety. To discuss these insights, it is best to begin with an example.

Suppose a rat has been pressing a lever for food. Lever pressing occurs at a high and steady rate. Now, a tone is occasionally sounded, and followed by a painful electric shock. These tone–shock pairings produce Pavlovian conditioned fear which is indicated by a change in the rate at which the rat presses the lever. During the tone, lever pressing is substantially, sometimes entirely, suppressed. Notice that lever pressing has nothing to do with the shock, and that the failure to press the lever costs the (hungry) animal food. Despite this, suppression of lever pressing occurs reliably. This phenomenon is called *conditioned suppression* or *conditioned emotional response* (CER).[13]

From what we know about Pavlovian conditioning, what should one expect to happen if instead of being paired, tone and shock are explicitly unpaired. Shocks occur during the session, but never just

13. Estes and Skinner, 1941.

after a tone. Such a procedure ought to make the tone a conditioned inhibitor of fear. One might expect to observe suppression of lever pressing in the absence of the tone, and frequent lever pressing in the presence of the tone. This, indeed, is what happens. Now suppose the tone and shock are neither paired nor unpaired: the occurrence of tone provides no information about the occurrence of shock, or, in the notation of probability:

$$p(shock/tone) = p(shock/\overline{tone})$$

Since we know that Pavlovian conditioning depends upon an informative relation between CS and US, we would expect that this procedure would not produce conditioning. But what does that mean with respect to lever pressing? Does it mean that lever pressing will continue at the same steady rate as before the shock was introduced?

Indeed, such a procedure does not produce conditioned fear. Rats behave no differently in the presence of the tone than in its absence. What they do is suppress lever pressing at all times. Again, although lever pressing has nothing to do with shock, and although failure to press costs the rats food, they stop pressing the lever altogether. In addition, the rats do not simply stop pressing the lever, they also huddle in a corner of the chamber, frozen with terror. Even more dramatic is the fact that when these rats are examined after the experiment, stomach dissection reveals a substantial number of ulcers— ulcers not produced by the shock itself (since animals exposed to the tone–shock pairings fail to develop ulcers) but produced by the *unpredictability* of the shock.[14]

In the situation in which tone is paired with shock, the animal becomes afraid of the tone, but when the tone is gone, the animal is safe. It can relax. The fear is objective and while it is certainly debilitating, it ends when the objective stimulus ends. On the other hand, in the situation in which shock is unpredictable, there is no stimulus which might prepare the animal for the shock. Shock may come at any time, without warning. Hence the animal cannot in any way mitigate its effect. The result is akin to what clinicians call anxiety: an emotional state which is generally and profounding debilitating and which completely suppresses effective action. It may be that exposure to unpredictable aversive events is what produces anxiety—in humans as well as in rats.[15]

14. Seligman, 1968, 1969, 1975 (Chapter 6).
15. The Rescorla–Wagner theory would treat what we are calling anxiety as conditioning to the background stimuli in the environment.

Imagine a child in a doctor's office. The doctor's style with children is honesty. When something is going to hurt, he says so; when there is no likelihood of pain, he also says so. The behavior which results bears an interesting resemblance to the behavior of rats that receive tone–shock pairings. Children are deathly afraid when the doctor warns them about impending pain, but otherwise are relaxed and cooperative. Now imagine a different doctor. This one, in order to avoid having to deal with wrought-up children, always tells his patients that his procedures will involve no pain. Then, before they can resist, he catches them by surprise with the injection or whatever else must be done. At first, this second doctor will have less trouble than the first. Ultimately, however, his patients will become generally frightened and resistent to treatment of any kind. While there are no danger signals to produce crying and tensing, there are also no *safety signals* to produce relaxation.

We have come to the other side of the coin of the contingency theory of Pavlovian conditioning. Stimuli which predict significant future events are important not only because of what they predict, but also because of what their absence predicts. Pavlovian conditioning is important not only because CSs signal USs and produce adaptive conditioned responses, but because the absence of these CSs provides important information which allows relaxation. Conditioned fear implies conditioned relaxation. Both are probably critical to the emotional well-being of organisms. A therapy program designed to eliminate anxiety would probably require a restructuring of the patient's environment so that both danger signals and safety signals were plentiful.

This, then, is the Pavlovian view of anxiety. When it is coupled with Pavlovian accounts of other kinds of psychopathology, like neurosis, we are left with a detailed model of the origins of pathologies of various kinds. And, of course, the model suggests particular kinds of treatment.

Pavlovian Conditioning as a
Therapeutic Tool: Counterconditioning

In Chapter 4 we described a phenomenon known as counterconditioning. By pairing food as a CS with painful electric shock as a US, one can establish conditioned fear responses to the food. What makes this phenomenon unusual is that food ordinarily evokes its own unconditioned responses. Yet the pairing of food and shock can result in fear rather than salivation to the food.

Counterconditioning procedures have played an important role in therapeutic situations. We have already mentioned that alcoholics have been successfully treated with procedures in which the ingestion of alcohol is paired with chemically induced nausea and vomiting. A far more common therapeutic procedure, which is based upon counterconditioning, is known as *systematic desensitization.* Its main developer has been Joseph Wolpe.[16] Most often, it is used to deal with pathological fears or anxieties.

Systematic Desensitization

A typical program of desensitization therapy will proceed roughly in this fashion: first, in a clinical interview, the source of the patient's fears will be identified in as concrete a fashion as possible. For example, let us assume that a patient enters therapy with a fear of enclosure. Once this is established, patient and therapist together will develop a list of different imaginary situations which are related to this fear. The situations might range from reading about a jet fighter pilot in his cockpit, to imagining a ride on an elevator, to imagining being trapped in a mine shaft. After a few dozen of these situations are created, the patient is asked to rank them in terms of the severity of the fear reaction they produce. Now the therapy can begin.

The patient is trained in deep muscle relaxation. This is a procedure which resembles hypnosis, in which a state of complete relaxation is achieved. This training is sometimes facilitated by the use of relaxing drugs. Once deep relaxation can be produced reliably in session after session, the patient begins by relaxing, and then he or she is asked to imagine one of the fear-producing situations which were created earlier. In the beginning, the patient is asked to imagine the least fearful situation. If this does not provoke fear, the therapist introduces a slightly more fearful situation. This continues until the patient begins to feel discomfort. Then the session is terminated. The next session also begins with relaxation, and the patient moves slowly up the list of fear-provoking situations. Each time, the session stops at the first sign of fear. The therapy is concluded when the patient can imagine the most fearful situation, and even actually be exposed to it, without showing a fear reaction.

What is the theory behind this therapy? Simply, it is assumed that deep relaxation and fear are incompatible. The imaginary scenes which provoke a low level of fear are paired with relaxation. Because the level of fear they provoke is low, it is expected that relaxation will successfully compete with fear and become the new CR produced by

16. Wolpe and Lazarus, 1969.

those scenes. As relaxation is strengthened as a CR, fear will automatically be weakened. The more this occurs, the greater will be the power of relaxation to compete successfully with fear. In this way, the patient can move up the hierarchy of fearful situations, from least fearful to most fearful, and slowly have relaxation as a CR to replace fear for all of the situations.

Desensitization is a successful therapeutic tool. While it has been used to treat a wide variety of fears, it depends critically on the patient's ability to describe those aspects of his or her life which provoke fear. If the patient cannot do so, then it is impossible to construct a hierarchy. For this reason, desensitization is less effective in dealing with what clinicians call diffuse, unspecified anxiety reactions. Here, a patient is afraid but has difficulty identifying the source of the fear. Nevertheless, for the domain in which desensitization is effective, it is more effective than any other program of therapy yet developed.

Systematic desensitization is a long way from simple reflexes. Let us examine this procedure more closely. What is the US? There does not appear to be one. The CS is paired not with another stimulus, but with a response or set of responses (muscle relaxation). Is muscle relaxation a CR or a UR or both? Finally, what is the CS? What kind of a stimulus is "imagining a situation"? None of these questions seems to have an answer at present. To further complicate the situation, there is reason to believe that relaxation alone is not sufficient for counterconditioning to occur. It seems critically important that the patient have *control* over relaxation. If relaxation is entirely drug-induced, the effectiveness of the therapy is greatly diminished.[17] If, on the other hand, drugs are simply used to enhance relaxation which is largely produced by the patient himself, the effectiveness of the therapy is greatly improved. What kind of a stimulus is "control," and what is its place in conditioning? We will have much to say about this in the next chapter. For now, it is enough to point out that the connection between Pavlovian conditioning in the laboratory and desensitization therapy is not a simple and straightforward one.

This raises an interesting issue. Desensitization therapy may be an example of technology which was conceived entirely on the basis of a particular theory (Pavlov's theory), but has turned out, on close inspection, to be only superficially related to that theory. There is an important sense in which this discrepancy between theory and application does not matter. The mere fact that the theory gave rise to the application is a credit to the theory even if the application does not follow perfectly from the theory. However, the discrepancy between

17. Seligman, 1975.

theory and application raises the possibility that the theory is in error. It may be that the facts of the application can contribute to a reworking of the theory until one is in line with the other. In short, it is possible that desensitization therapy may contribute to another reformulation of the principles of Pavlovian conditioning. As yet, this has not happened. The road between basic principles and technology has been a one-way street in the analysis of behavior: all information has moved from the laboratory to clinical settings. However, one should be open to the possibility that technological developments may inform the theory on which they are based. Such a mutual influence between basic principles and technology would be an exciting development indeed.

We have come a long way in these two chapters. We began by discussing the basic phenomena of Pavlovian conditioning, as uncovered by Pavlov. We next discussed in detail the phenomenon of inhibition and the theory which attempts to capture it. Next, we introduced a wholly new conception of how conditioning occurs—one based on contingency and information rather than contiguity. The new conception has refocused attention on the complex abilities which conditioning may require. The simple reflex as a model of Pavlovian conditioning must undergo a radical reformulation or be abandoned. Finally, we indicated the ways in which Pavlovian conditioning has been an effective tool of technology—both in the development of theories of the causes of psychopathology and in the development of therapies for the cure of psychopathology.

It is time now to move on to the other major conditioning process we have discussed—operant conditioning. Since it is concerned with voluntary activity, far the bulk of the behavior of most higher organisms, it has commanded a great deal of attention from researchers and behavioral engineers alike. It will similarly command a great deal of attention in this book. The next four chapters will be concerned with different facets of operant conditioning. Our discussion will begin with an analysis of the most basic issue concerning operant conditioning: What are the conditions which are necessary and sufficient for its occurrence? Dealing with this issue will take us through a series of steps which parallel almost exactly developments in Pavlovian conditioning.

6

Operant Conditioning

Necessary Conditions

In this chapter we will enter the domain of voluntary behavior. We are accustomed to describing such behavior as being controlled by the individual, self-initiated, purposeful, intentional, and goal-directed. Voluntary behavior is the stuff of human action, and a theory of behavior which could not provide us with the principles that determine its occurrence would be hopelessly inadequate.

The approach to the study of voluntary behavior which has proven most successful over the years was developed by B. F. Skinner. We have already seen in Chapter 2 that the Skinnerian framework attempts to account for behavior which seems purposive and goal-directed with a set of principles which make no reference to purpose. The central component of these principles is the law of effect. Behavior is controlled by its past consequences. Positive or reinforcing consequences increase the likelihood of the behavior they follow, while negative or punishing consequences decrease the likelihood of the behavior they follow. The law of effect works in an automatic or mechanical fashion to determine what organisms will do. On this view, control of behavior is removed from the individual and placed in the environment. We do not initiate acts *in order to* produce results of a particular kind. Rather, the results of acts determine whether we will initiate the same acts in the future.[1]

The goal of research on the law of effect and voluntary behavior is

1. In *Beyond Freedom and Dignity*, 1971, Skinner defines voluntary behavior as behavior which is controlled by its consequences. The apparent paradox of defining "volition" in terms of an external controlling agent dramatizes the difference between Skinner's view and traditional ones. His view, of course, is that all behavior is controlled by something, and his aim in this definition is to distinguish operant behavior from reflexes.

the *functional analysis* of behavior. To understand the meaning of functional analysis, it is best to contrast it with a different type of goal—structural analysis. If one were interested in understanding the human body, one could approach the problem in at least two different ways. First of all, one could attempt to isolate and identify different body parts, both internal and external. One would discover that such things as arms, kidneys, livers, veins, and so on, were integral units of the body, and that each of these contained intact subunits. When the analysis was complete, one would know the *structure* of the human body—the human anatomy.

On the other hand, one could begin the study of the human body by identifying certain bodily *functions*: digestion, respiration, reproduction, excretion, and so on. Then, one could begin to analyze the body in terms of these functions. How is respiration accomplished? How does reproduction occur? This functional analysis would yield different information than the structural analysis. The functional units of the body are different from the structural units of the body. Many different structures are involved in a single functional system like the digestive system.

Skinner sought to divide the behavior of an organism into functional units. First, he thought functional units of behavior would be more accessible to the psychologist than anatomical units of behavior. Second, he thought the functional *effects* of behavior—its consequences—were the major determinant of its future occurrence. In developing a functional analysis of behavior, Skinner's goal was to develop functional relations between behavior on the one hand and its consequences on the other. What went on inside the organism—how behavior was organized by the nervous system—was of no immediate concern. Skinner thought that a rather complete account of behavior could result solely from an understanding of the functional relations between behavior and environment.[2]

The most significant influence of Skinner's functional orientation is that it led directly to the research methods he developed. The goal of his work dictated the means to the goal. The experimental situation and all of its constituents were functionally defined.

CENTRAL CONCEPTS OF OPERANT CONDITIONING

To begin with, Skinner took as a given that the law of effect was valid. Reinforcement increases the likelihood of behavior that precedes it and punishment decreases the likelihood of behavior that

2. See Skinner, 1935, for a discussion of his functional approach.

precedes it. Then, Skinner defined three central terms: stimulus, operant, and reinforcement.

The Stimulus

A *stimulus* is anything an organism can detect. But how can one tell that an organism detects the stimulus? One can tell by determining whether the stimulus can gain control of behavior. If one can show that an organism's behavior is different in the presence of a stimulus than in its absence, one can be sure that the organism detects the stimulus. Thus, a stimulus is defined functionally in terms of its power to control behavior.

Suppose, for example, one trains a rat to press Lever 1 when a red circle is present and to press Lever 2 when a green triangle is present. What are the stimuli? Are they colors, shapes, or both? Suppose that on one test occasion the rats are exposed to a red triangle, and on a second occasion they are exposed to a green circle. If they press Lever 1 on the first occasion, and Lever 2 on the second occasion, one concludes that "the stimulus" is color. If they press Lever 2 on the first occasion and Lever 1 on the second occasion, one concludes that "the stimulus" is shape. In either case, the stimulus is not all that is objectively present in the rat's environment, but that aspect of the environment which controls the rat's behavior.[3]

The Operant

How does one define the response or *operant*? This is the place where Skinner's functional approach is most telling. For Skinner, the operant is defined functionally—in terms of its effects on the environment. The operant is not a single response, but a class of responses with a common element. What is the common element? It is just that property of the responses on which reinforcement depends.[4] Thus, for example, if food is delivered to a rat every time a switch mounted beneath a lever is closed, the operant is switch closure. Whether the rat accomplishes this by pressing the lever, biting the lever, sitting on the lever, or whatever, each instance of switch closure is a member of the same operant class. If food delivery depends not only on closing the switch, but on keeping it closed for, say 2 seconds, we have a new

---

3. Matters concerning the determination of which stimuli control behavior and by what process they do so are discussed in detail in Chapter 8.
4. For a detailed discussion of these definitions and some of the logical problems they entail, see Schick, 1971.

operant. Again, how this switch closure is accomplished is irrelevant. All instances of switch closure for 2 seconds are treated as members of a single class. Thus, an operant can be defined in an almost limitless number of ways. We say almost because some definitions will be better than others. If one defines and reinforces the operant of, say, "lever presses while the sun is shining," one may discover that this class is not influenced in an orderly way by reinforcement. If so, then one has chosen a bad definition of the operant. Therefore, the experimenter defines the operant functionally, and the orderliness of the animal's behavior tells the experimenter whether the definition was a good one.

It should be clear that this approach to analyzing behavior is quite different from an anatomical approach. The only thing which unites a potentially infinitely large set of responses into a single class is not a

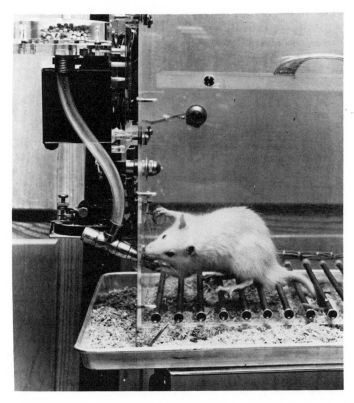

A rat trained to press a lever for water reinforcement. (Photo courtesy of Pfizer Inc.)

property of the responses themselves, nor of the organism that emits them, but a property of the environment. Sitting, biting, and paw movement may have nothing whatever in common, save the fact that they all result in the closing of a switch, on which reinforcement depends.

Reinforcers

Next, there is the definition of a reinforcer (or punisher). Reinforcers and punishers are stimuli, but a special and especially important class of stimuli. A reinforcer is any stimulus whose presentation increases the likelihood of the operant which precedes it and a punisher is any stimulus which decreases the likelihood of the operant which precedes it. Notice how these definitions assume the validity of the law of effect. If a stimulus is presented immediately after a response (e.g., one steps off a curb and immediately hears the blast of an automobile horn), and the likelihood of the response neither increases nor decreases, there can be two possible explanations of this effect. One is that the stimulus (car horn) is neither a reinforcer nor a punisher. The second is that the law of effect does not always work. But Skinner, in defining reinforcers and punishers in terms of their power to influence behavior, ruled this second possible account out.

Consider, by analogy, a physicist observing an act of levitation.[5] There are two possible accounts of levitation. One is that accelerations can occur without an applied force (the levitation is an acceleration), and the other is that there is a force being applied to the rising body which is not readily apparent. But the physicst "knows" that accelerations do not occur without applied forces. Therefore, only the second possible account exists for the physicist, who might well spend many days attempting to identify the elusive applied force. The possibility does not exist for the physicist that the levitation could occur with no force applied. So also the possibility does not exist for Skinner that a reinforcer could be presented without increasing the likelihood of the operant it followed; if a stimulus does not increase the frequency of the behavior it follows, it is simply not a reinforcer. One of the implications of this view is that the same stimulus may be a reinforcer at some times but not at others. Food, for example, may not control the behavior of an organism that has just eaten. What this means is that the power of a stimulus to increase the likelihood of an operant is not an inherent property of the stimulus, but a relation between the stimulus, operants, and states of the organism.

5. Meehl, 1950.

Why should we define a reinforcer in this way instead of searching for some objective property which all reinforcers have in common, since, by attempting to identify reinforcers independently of the law of effect, we would not need to assume its validity. In fact, a number of attempts to find the property common to all reinforcers have been made. Central among them was the theory that reinforcers all satisfied some bodily need or *drive*. Water, for example, was a reinforcer if an organism needed it or was deprived of it. What made it a reinforcer was its ability to reduce the need. Similarly, one could identify a hunger drive, a sex drive, and perhaps a few more.

As soon as drive theory was precisely enough articulated to be tested, researchers started discovering exceptions to it wherever they looked. Thus, rats, monkeys, and other animals will press a lever to turn on a light. There is no apparent bodily need which is satisfied by the light, yet it can serve as a reinforcer. While satisfaction of a need may be sufficient to make a stimulus a reinforcer, it is certainly not necessary. As exceptions to drive theory accumulated they led to revisions in the theory, which in turn led to further exceptions, until finally, after almost half a century in pursuit of a theory of drive, the concept has been largely abandoned.[6]

Reinforcer Relativity • Some of the more dramatic indications of the problems with identifying the reinforcing power of a stimulus with the satisfaction of needs or drives came from a program of research by David Premack and his collaborators.[7] Premack argued that reinforcers were not stimuli per se (e.g., water), but opportunities to engage in behavior (e.g., drinking). In addition, he argued that whether a particular activity was reinforcing was not absolute. Whether or not drinking would be a reinforcer would depend entirely upon what it was reinforcing. Thus, drinking might reinforce lever pressing, but it might not reinforce eating, even though the animal was equally in need of water in both cases. The way one could know which activities drinking would reinforce and which it would not was by measuring the frequencies of a set of different activities in circumstances in which the animal could freely engage in any.

Suppose, for example, a rat had free access to food, water, and an exercise wheel, so that it could eat (Activity A), drink (Activity B), or run (Activity C). Suppose that the rat ate more often than it drank, and drank more often than it ran. We could thus rank the activities in terms of their frequency. Premack argued that the opportunity to

6. For a thorough account of the drive concept, see Bolles, 1967, 1975.
7. Premack, 1959, 1962, 1965.

engage in an activity would reinforce only activities which were less frequent than it. Thus, in our example, eating (A) could reinforce both drinking (B) and running (C) because the frequency of $A > B > C$. Drinking could reinforce only running, however, and running could reinforce neither eating nor drinking. If, under other circumstances, the frequency was $C > A > B$, then the opportunity to run would reinforce eating and drinking. Premack showed that rats would drink in order to run under just those conditions in which his theory predicted it.

What Premack's theory suggests is that the power to reinforce is not an absolute property of either stimuli or activities, but is relative to other activities which may be available at the moment. Though recent research has posed some problems for Premack's theory, it is clear from Premack's research that an attempt to identify a reinforcer in other than functional terms is likely to meet with great difficulty.[8] Certainly, drive theory fails to accomplish this end. Thus Skinner's approach seems to have anticipated the difficulties encountered by others and avoided them.

The Principle of Transsituationality

These definitions of stimulus, operant, and reinforcer reveal more than the fact that the analysis of behavior is functionally oriented. Consider how interdependent the definitions are. Stimulus and reinforcer are defined in terms of behavior, and operant is defined in terms of reinforcement. It seems as though the definitions of these very basic terms assume what needs to be proved: that the law of effect operates on and controls behavior. Without the law of effect as a given, the definitions would not make sense. But with the law of effect as a given, what is left to be investigated? Many people have noticed this relation between the definitions and the things which need to be proved and suggested that the law of effect is a tautology—a statement which is necessarily and trivially true.[9]

However, Paul Meehl saw and articulated a way in which the law of effect could be freed of its tautological character. He called it the principle of transsituationality.[10] Meehl argued that when a rein-

---

8. See Timberlake and Allison, 1974.

9. Among the most insistent and influential critics of the relation between the law of effect and the set of definitions which guide the analysis of behavior is Noam Chomsky (see Chomsky, 1959; 1975, Part 1). Criticisms take the form that the law of effect is like the statement "Either it will rain today or it won't rain." Such a statement is necessarily true (whatever the truth value of its individual premises, the statement as a whole is always true) but it is also vacuous. It tells us nothing about the world. It does not allow us to make useful predictions about the weather or anything else.

10. Meehl, 1950.

forcer is defined by its ability to increase the likelihood of behavior (e.g., food is a reinforcer since its presentation increases lever pressing), then the situation *in which it is defined* cannot be used to substantiate the law of effect. Here, the very definition of the reinforcer assumes the law of effect to be valid. However, if the same stimulus is now employed as a reinforcer in a situation which is completely different from the one in which it was defined (e.g., rats learning to run through mazes for food) and it has the same effect, this can be taken as support for the law of effect. As long as a stimulus which is defined as a reinforcer in one situation works as a reinforcer in other situations, the seemingly tautological relation between the law of effect and the definition of a reinforcer is broken. Thus, to give the law of effect meaningful content, reinforcers must be *transsituational.*

The same principle may be applied to the definition of operants. The tautological relation between the operant and the reinforcer which is a part of the definition of operants can be broken as long as an operant which is defined with respect to one reinforcer can also be controlled in a situation involving a different reinforcer. Again, transsituationality gives the definition of the operant a measure of independence from the definition of a reinforcer. Finally, the definition of a stimulus, in terms of whether it produces a measurable difference in behavior, can be freed from its dependence on behavior if it can be shown that a stimulus which is defined in one situation works as a stimulus in other situations.

In short, for the most basic operant conditioning concepts to be meaningful, the findings obtained in a particular experimental situation must generalize to other situations. Ideally, it will turn out that all stimuli which affect behavior in a particular way in one situation will affect behavior in the same way in all other situations, and that the same transsituationality will be true of operants and of reinforcers. In general, if any individual member of the class of stimuli, of operants, or of reinforcers can be employed from one situation to the next and yield the same experimental outcomes, then the concepts stimulus, operant, and reinforcer, though defined *interdependently,* can be said to operate *independently* in the analysis of behavior.

The "Arbitrary" Operant • Skinner was aware of the importance of transsituationality when he was developing methods for the study of operant conditioning. He saw that it was especially important to choose an operant which was not intrinsically related to the reinforcer. Not only would such a relation undermine the integrity and independence of the basic definitions, but it would also raise doubts about the generality of experimental results. To see this, consider an example. Suppose one trained rats to jump to escape an electric shock delivered to the feet. When they jumped, the shock was turned off. If one found the rats jumping, one might be tempted to conclude that turning off a noxious stimulus can reinforce an organism's responses. The trouble is that shock often makes rats jump. There is a relation between painful stimulation of the paws and jumping which is built into the rat; it jumps even when jumping fails to turn off the noxious stimulus. The fact that the rats come to jump to turn off shock may have resulted exclusively from this special relation between jumping and shock which is characteristic of the rat. But if this is so, then all one can conclude is specifically that rats can jump to turn off shock,

A pigeon pecking a lit key for food reinforcement. (Photo by W. Rapport, courtesy of B. F. Skinner.)

not that any organism's behavior can be maintained by elimination of a noxious stimulus.

Suppose, however, that the rat had been trained to press a lever to escape shock, and it still learned. Since lever pressing is not something which is built into rats (when escaping shock or doing anything else), one could safely conclude that the rat's learning was not attributable to some special characteristic of rats, lever pressing, and shock, but to some general principle involving responses and escape from noxious stimulation in all or most organisms.

Therefore, to insure the maximum generality of the principles uncovered in the analysis of behavior, it is critical to study operants which bear no intrinsic relation to the stimuli or reinforcers being used: it is critical to establish operants which are *arbitrary*. But how does one know in advance that an operant bears no intrinsic relation to the reinforcer one is using? Skinner saw that the safest way was to invent the response. If the response was something that the organism simply never did before entering the experiment, it could not possibly have a built-in relation to the reinforcer being used. Thus, the lever press, and later, the key peck, came into being. It was assumed that lever presses by rats and key pecks by pigeons had the same relation to food (an arbitrary one) that most human behavior had to its reinforcers. Typing, answering telephones, making automobiles, doing civil engineering, practicing law, etc., were related to their reinforcers (food, clothing, shelter, and other things money could buy) in the same arbitrary way that lever pressing was related to its reinforcers. All of these activities were easily distinguished from salivation, which bore an intrinsic relation to its reinforcer (food). Thus, the operant was defined by Skinner functionally—in terms of its effects on the environment—both because it was premature to define behavior anatomically and because functional definition was the surest way to equate the disparate activities of disparate species.

CONDITIONING BY CONTIGUITY

When an animal is being trained to make a particular response, the experimenter waits for an approximation of that response to occur, and then delivers reinforcement. As a consequence of that reinforcement, the response becomes more likely. When it next occurs, the reinforcer is delivered again. This operation is repeated until the animal spends virtually all of its time making the response. If one exposed a rat to sessions of lever-press training which included 50 reinforcements each, the acquisition of lever pressing, measured in responses per minute, would look like the curve in Figure 6–1. If, after

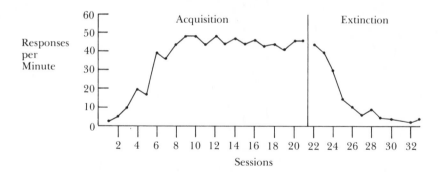

Figure 6–1. Acquisition and Extinction of Lever Pressing. *This hypothetical curve depicts the growth in the frequency of lever pressing over the course of a number of experimental sessions, followed by its extinction when reinforcement is discontinued.*

a number of sessions (21 in Figure 6–1), reinforcement were discontinued, response rate would diminish, ultimately returning to zero. This phenomenon is called experimental extinction and is the exact analog to extinction of Pavlovian conditioned reflexes.

What aspect of the relation between the reinforcer and the response is crucial for conditioning to occur? As with Pavlovian conditioning, accounts of how reinforcement works have emphasized temporal relations. When a reinforcer is delivered, whatever response has just preceded it will be strengthened or increased in frequency. Thus temporal *contiguity* of response and reinforcer has viewed as the critical characteristic of the operant conditioning process.

Evidence for the importance of response–reinforcer contiguity comes from experiments in which the delivery of reinforcement is delayed: the response occurs and, only some seconds later, the reinforcer is presented. If one plots the frequency of responses maintained by reinforcement which is delayed, as in Figure 6–2, one finds that the greater the delay of reinforcement is, the lower response rate is.[11]

Superstition

More dramatic evidence for the importance of response–reinforcer contiguity comes from a classic but simple experiment.[12] Skinner trained pigeons to eat grain from a feeder. He then exposed them to a

11. Azzi, Fix, Keller, and Rocha e Silva, 1964.
12. Skinner, 1948.

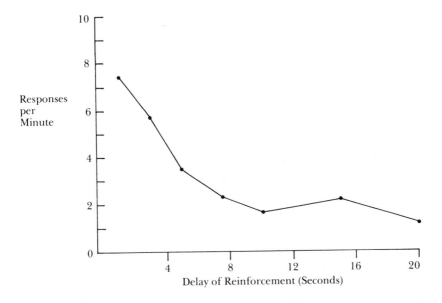

Figure 6–2. Effects of Delay of Reinforcement on the Rate of an Operant Response. *As delay of reinforcement increases, responses per minute maintained by reinforcement decreases. The subjects were rats, and the operant response was a lever press. (After Azzi, Fix, Keller, & Rocha e Silva, 1964, Figure 1.)*

procedure in which the feeder was made available at regular intervals irrespective of what the pigeons were doing—that is, pigeons were not *required* to do anything to get food. Skinner's reasoning in doing this experiment was roughly this: when food was delivered, the pigeons would certainly be doing something. They might be strutting about the cage, grooming, flapping their wings, turning around, pecking at a screw on the wall, etc. While one could not be sure of what the pigeons would be doing at any particular moment, one could be sure that they would be doing something. When reinforcement occurred, it would be paired with whatever response the pigeons had just emitted. Though this response did not produce the reinforcer, the temporal contiguity of response and reinforcer would be sufficient to strengthen (increase the likelihood of) the behavior.

If this happened, then the next time food was delivered, the pigeons would be more likely to be engaging in that particular activity than before (as a result of the first reinforcement). Therefore, it was likely that reinforcement would follow that response again. If so, the likelihood of the response would increase still further. This chain of events would continue to repeat itself until the pigeons were spending most of their time engaged in this activity. Though the activity would differ from one pigeon to the next, Skinner expected that each pigeon would ultimately be engaged in some activity with a high frequency. And this is what Skinner observed. One pigeon turned counterclockwise about the cage. One thrust its head into one of the upper corners of the cage. One tossed its head about. Two developed side-to-side pendulumlike movements. One pigeon made pecking movements at the floor. Only two of eight pigeons in that experiment failed to develop a stereotyped and frequent pattern of movement.

Skinner called this phenomenon *superstition.* He saw the process by which the response developed as a parallel of the development of human superstitions. Some response which is irrelevant to the actual production of reinforcement is nevertheless paired with it, and strengthened as a result. Thus, according to Skinner, the bowler uses "body english" to direct the ball down the lane, the gambler mutters a catechism as the dice are about to be rolled, the salesman wears his "lucky suit" when he visits a new prospective client, and so on. All that is required is a few accidental pairings of response and reinforcer. As Skinner says, "To say that a reinforcement is contingent upon a response may mean nothing more than that it follows the response. It may follow because of some mechanical connection or because of the mediation of another organism: but conditioning takes place presumably because of the temporal relation only, expressed in terms of the order and proximity of response and reinforcement."[13]

That occurrence of a reinforcer strengthens a response whether or not the response actually produces the reinforcer does not mean that there is no difference between the effects of a reinforcer when it is accidental and when it is response-produced. Suppose pigeons are trained to peck a key for food and are exposed to this procedure until they peck the key at a fairly constant rate. At this point, reinforcer delivery is made independent of the pigeons' behavior. The pigeons will continue to peck the key, but the frequency of key pecking will decrease dramatically (see Figure 6–3).[14]

From the data in Figure 6–3, one might conclude that organisms can distinguish response-produced from accidental reinforcers, but this is not necessarily the case. The organism will not spend all of its time engaged in the superstitious response. As a result, occasionally when the reinforcer occurs, it will be delayed a few seconds from the most recent occurrence of the superstitious response. As we have al-

13. Skinner, 1948, p. 168.
14. Herrnstein, 1966.

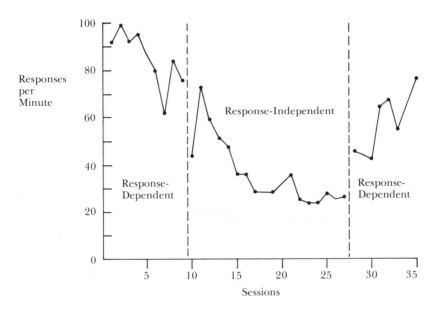

Figure 6–3. Effects of a Dependency Between Response and Reinforcer on Response Rate. *When food delivery is dependent upon responding, the pigeon pecks the key about 80 times per minute. When food is then delivered at the same rate, but independent of responding, response rate decreases to about 25 pecks per minute. Reintroduction of the dependency results in an increase in response rate. (After Herrnstein, 1966, Figure 1.)*

ready seen in Figure 6–2, delayed reinforcers are less effective than immediate reinforcers. Thus, the decrease in responding observed when the reinforcer is changed from being response-dependent to being response-independent may be the result of the delay of reinforcement entailed by the second procedure. What a dependency between response and reinforcer does is insure that the reinforcer will always follow the response immediately.

There have been a few attempts to extend the investigation of superstitious behavior to humans. It is one thing to call a laboratory phenomenon "superstition," and claim that it mimics superstition as we ordinarily use the term. It is quite another thing to show that human superstitions can be attributed to the same underlying process as pigeon superstitions. A first step in that direction is to show that people, like pigeons, will engage in stereotyped responses if these responses are accidentally followed by a reinforcer.

In one experiment of this type, college students were instructed to push one of two buttons whenever a light flashed.[15] The reinforcer for button pushing was an increment of a counter which the students could see. In fact, all that was required to produce the reinforcer was to push the right-hand button. Pushing the other button had no effect at all. Nevertheless, owing to occasional occurrences of left-push/right-push/reinforcer sequences, nearly every subject pushed the left button frequently. Indeed, for most subjects, a rather stereotyped sequence of left–right responses developed. When subjects were later questioned about what they were doing and why, they accurately described their behavior, but misperceived the requirements of the situation. In general, they stated that some combination of left and right button presses was necessary for the reinforcer. Thus, it seems that for people, the mere contiguity of response and reinforcer is sufficient to maintain the response.

Assumptions Underlying Superstition

This evidence of superstitious behavior in pigeons as well as people suggests that all that is necessary for operant conditioning to occur is the temporal contiguity of response and reinforcer. However, such a view of how reinforcers work is not *sufficient* to explain superstitious behavior. There are two additional assumptions regarding the effects of reinforcers which are essential if the account of superstition offered here is to make any sense. Let us try to reconstruct the moment-by-moment development of a superstition from Skinner's interpretation. The pigeon is placed in the chamber, and engages in a variety of activities. Then, food is made available. The delivery of food immediately follows something the pigeon was doing—say, grooming. What is the effect of the very first reinforcer? According to Skinner, even a single reinforcer makes the activity it follows more likely. In order for his account of superstition to work, this must be so. Otherwise, when the next reinforcer came, the pigeon would probably be doing something other than grooming, perhaps strutting; with the next reinforcer, the pigeon might be pecking. If the reinforcer kept following a different response each time, no particular response would be strengthened. Thus, the very first reinforcer must increase the probability of the response it follows enough so that that response is likely to precede the reinforcer the next time. This is the first of the two assumptions: a single reinforcement is sufficient to strengthen the response it follows.

15. Catania and Cutts, 1963.

Let us return to the pigeon. It has just experienced a food delivery while grooming and, granting the first assumption, it continues to groom. It grooms for five seconds, ten seconds, twenty seconds without the occurrence of another reinforcer. But this nonreinforcement of grooming should produce extinction (see Figure 6–1). Grooming should decrease in frequency. Before the next reinforcer occurs, grooming might cease altogether. If this indeed happened, then the development of superstitious behavior would be very unlikely. Whatever response was strengthened by the first reinforcement would be extinguished before the second reinforcement. Thus, there is a need for a second assumption: the strengthening effects of a reinforcement last longer than the time required for extinction to weaken the response.

It is difficult to evaluate these assumptions empirically. Suppose one is training a pigeon to peck a key for food. The training method is the method of successive approximations (see Chapter 3, p. 49). The experimenter waits for the pigeon to approach the key and then delivers the reinforcer. How is one to measure the effects of this reinforcer? Will approaching the key increase in frequency? Perhaps it will. However, it is unlikely that the experimenter's criterion for delivering the reinforcer will match the pigeon's organization of its behavior after just a single reinforcement. While the pigeon was approaching the key, it may also have been bobbing its head, looking around, fluffing its feathers, and so on. The reinforcement may increase the frequency of one of these activities, but which one? If the experimenter is not recording everything the pigeon is doing (which is itself impossible) he may miss the fact that reinforcement strengthened anything. The immediate effect of a reinforcer will only be apparent if it strengthens a response which the experimenter happens to be measuring. This is true every time a reinforcement occurs. While it follows the response which produced it, it also follows other responses which are irrelevant to its production. The way conditioning ultimately occurs is that over successive reinforcer presentations, only the criterion response will consistently precede the reinforcer. Other responses which occur concurrently with the criterion response will differ from one reinforcement to the next, and ultimately will not be strengthened. Because of this inherent uncertainty about which behavior will actually be influenced by the delivery of a single reinforcer, it is difficult to determine whether a single reinforcement is enough to increase the likelihood of a response. All one can do is watch the organism carefully, and hope to detect a general change in its behavior with a single reinforcement. Informal observations of this sort do suggest that a single reinforcement alters an organism's behavior.[16]

Evaluating the second assumption—that extinction is slower than conditioning—is also difficult. Usually, when extinction is studied, it is after organisms are well trained. Under these conditions, it will often take many sessions before the response is extinguished entirely. Unfortunately, this kind of evidence is not relevant to the explanation of superstition, for the account of superstition offered here requires that extinction be slow even after a single reinforcement. The pigeon is grooming when food is delivered. The next food delivery will be, say, 30 seconds later. Will the single reinforcement be sufficient to withstand 30 seconds of extinction? Since it is difficult to assess an increase in responding as a result of reinforcement, it is similarly difficult to assess a decrease in the same response over 30 seconds of extinction. Thus the two principles on which this account of superstition depends seem destined to remain assumptions. Perhaps the best support for the assumptions is the fact of superstitious behavior itself. Unless an alternative account can be provided, it seems reasonable to accept the present one and its underlying assumptions. We shall see shortly that there is an alternative account of superstition—an account which may require a fundamental change in our understanding of the operant conditioning process.

We have seen that the traditional view of operant conditioning treats the temporal contiguity, or pairing, of response and reinforcer as the crucial determinant of conditioning. The mere presentation of a reinforcer will strengthen the response which precedes it whether or not that reinforcer actually depends upon the response. The major difference between response-dependent and response-independent reinforcement is that in the former case the activity which is strengthened is determined by the experimenter and not by chance.

This view of the operant conditioning process parallels the traditional view of Pavlovian conditioning. We saw that recent evidence has required a revision of that view: that contiguity without contingency is not sufficient to produce conditioning. We will now turn to evidence that the same revision is required in the domain of operant conditioning. We shall see not only that organisms can distinguish sit-

16. This basic uncertainty about what behavior a reinforcer will influence goes to the problem discussed in Chapter 3 of evaluating the Skinner box from the point of view of the animal. One cannot assume that the experimental subject interprets its environment in the same way the experimenter does. Indeed, the real effect of conditioning may be to get the animal's interpretation of the environment to match the experimenter's.

uations in which their behavior controls reinforcer delivery from situations in which it does not, but that the exercise of control is itself reinforcing, while the lack of control may have profound negative consequences.

CONDITIONING BY CONTINGENCY

Imagine setting out to design an ideal organism, one which is perfectly adapted to its environment. Unless the environment is to remain remarkably constant, it is important to build into the organism the ability to modify its behavior. But what form should this behavior modification mechanism take? While a mechanism based upon temporal contiguity between response and consequence will often be valuable to an organism, it can also often lead an organism astray. The acquisition of superstitions not only gains nothing, but it costs the organism energy expenditure. Moreover, an organism engaged in superstitious behavior may be missing the opportunity to engage in alternative activities which are genuinely effective in adapting to the environment. It would be far more valuable for an organism to distinguish situations in which its behavior produced reward from situations in which its behavior was merely paired with reward.

Such an ability would allow the organism to select its activities in the same efficient way that a contingency-oriented Pavlovian conditioning mechanism allows an organism to select its information. While it would make our conception of conditioning less automatic and simple than the contiguity view suggests, as we saw in the last chapter, the ability to select information and learn about contingencies can still be viewed as an automatic process. Evidence of superstition suggests that contiguity of response and reinforcer is sufficient to produce conditioning. Is there any evidence to the contrary? Is there any indication that organisms distinguish dependence between response and reward from independence?

Learned Helplessness

Consider the following experiment. Two dogs are to be trained to make a response to avoid a painful electric shock. The required response will be jumping over a barrier from one side of a box to another. Before that training occurs, they are placed in a very different type of situation. They are brought into separate rooms so they cannot see or hear each other, and are strapped into Pavlovian harnesses so that movement is restricted. Near their noses is a small metal panel. If they touch the panel with their noses, the movement of the panel operates a switch (just as the rat's lever press does). Both of these dogs occasionally receive painful shocks. One dog, called the "control" dog, can turn off the shock by pushing the panel. The second dog, called the "yoked" dog, cannot exercise any control over the shock. Whenever the "control" dog is shocked, the "yoked" dog is shocked. Whenever the "control" dog turns off the shock by pushing the panel, the "yoked" dog's shock is also terminated. Thus, the two dogs receive an identical number and temporal pattern of shocks. Not surprisingly, the control dog learns to push the panel and eventually escapes shock on nearly every trial.

Now, the two dogs are placed in the apparatus in which they must jump a hurdle to avoid shock. The "control" dog quickly learns to make this response and, in a short time, is receiving virtually no shocks. Similarly, an untrained dog which has not been exposed to the shock in the harness learns quickly to avoid shock by jumping over the hurdle. For the "yoked" dog, however, it is a different story. When that dog receives a shock, it whines and yelps and seems distressed. In addition, it makes no movement across the hurdle. As trial after trial goes by, this dog continues to whine but grows more and more passive. Ultimately, the dog simply lies down, hardly moving, with its muscles almost completely flaccid, and makes no effort at all to escape or avoid the painful shock. The dog has become completely helpless. This phenomenon has been identified in the literature as *learned help-lessness*.[17]

What could be responsible for this complete failure to learn by the "yoked" dog? It must have been something that happened to the dog in the harness, for both "control" and untrained dogs learned to jump the hurdle with great ease. But what could the helpless dog have learned in the harness? There are two clear alternatives. One is based upon the arguments used to explain superstition. While in the harness, whatever the animal is doing when shock comes is punished, through temporal contiguity of the response and shock. As a result, most of the dog's behavior is punished. This may result in the "passivity" which is subsequently observed in the hurdle-jumping situation. A variant of the account is that some posture which the dog accidentally adopts reduces the amount of current which actually passes through the dog when shock is delivered. If so, this posture might be reinforced and might be generalized to the hurdle-jumping situation. Then, it might compete with the development of hurdle jumping, for if the dog continues to adopt that posture during shock, the actual in-

17. For a thorough account of learned helplessness, see Seligman, 1975, or Maier and Seligman, 1976.

tensity of the shock will continue to be reduced. Thus the adoption of that posture will continue to be reinforced. While it is difficult to find evidence which directly supports this interpretation, it is plausible, particularly since it seems to account successfully for the phenomenon of superstition.

The second alternative is that what the dog learns in the harness is that important events (shocks) are *independent* of its behavior. It learns that nothing it does makes a difference. In the language of probability, the dog learns that p(shock/response A) = p(shock/response B) = p(shock/response C) = ... = p(shock/$\overline{\text{response}}$). When subsequently placed in the hurdle-jumping situation, this dog's previous learning about the independence of behavior and consequence interferes with its learning that now its behavior does matter.

Consider the implications of this second alternative. First, it is directly opposed to the idea that temporal contiguity of response and consequence is all that is necessary to produce conditioning. Indeed, it is directly opposed to the idea that such temporal contiguity produces superstition. It says that organisms are able to distinguish situations in which reward is response-dependent ("control" dogs) from situations in which reward is independent of responding ("yoked" dogs). This is a distinction which the contiguity interpretation of conditioning explicitly denies. Moreover, this alternative account says that even when response and consequence are independent, the organism learns something general. The organism learns that important environmental events are not subject to its control and this learning may produce a profound inability to learn in situations in which important events are controllable. This view of the operant conditioning process is depicted in Figure 6–4.

Contiguity versus Contingency

How is one to decide between the two views. The contiguity view has two things in its favor—simplicity, and the demonstrable existence of superstitious behavior. The second view also has two things in its favor. First, it is a view of the learning process which seems much more adaptive than the contiguity view. Second, it is a view of operant conditioning which parallels our present understanding of Pavlovian conditioning. In both cases, it is contingency (between CS and US or between behavior and consequence) rather than contiguity that produces conditioning.

It would be satisfying if the same underlying process of contingency analysis could account for both operant and Pavlovian conditioning. While one could endeavor to choose between the two accounts on the

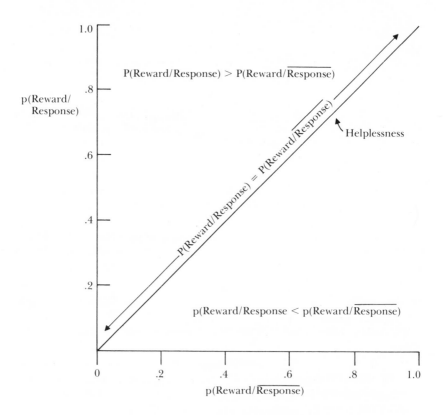

Figure 6–4. Diagram of the General Operant Contingency Space. *At all points above the diagonal line, reward is more likely given the response than given no response. Under these conditions, the response should increase in frequency. At all points below the diagonal line, reward is less likely given the response than given no response, and the response should decrease in frequency. Note that if the situation involves a punishing stimulus like shock instead of a reward, conditions above the diagonal should produce a response decrease while conditions below the diagonal should produce an increase. The diagonal itself represents independence of response and consequence. These are the conditions which produce learned helplessness.*

basis of their theoretical usefulness, ideally, one would like to appeal to an empirical phenomenon which was consistent with one account but not the other. There is such a phenomenon.[18] Suppose helplessness results from the superstitious development of passivity. If so, then actually training an animal to be passive should result in even more dramatic helplessness. If, on the other hand, helplessness re-

18. Maier, 1970.

sults from learning that behavior and consequence are independent, then training an animal to be passive (a case where consequence does depend on behavior) will not result in helplessness.

To decide the issue, groups of "control" and "yoked" dogs were established as before. The difference was that in order to escape electric shock, the "control" dogs had to remain still for a period of time. The dogs learned this task, and after considerable training in which "control" and "yoked" dogs received an identical number and pattern of shocks, all dogs were tested in the hurdle-jumping situation. If the learning of passivity produced helplessness, we would expect the "control" dogs to be more helpless than the "yoked" dogs. If the learning of independence between behavior and consequence produced helplessness, we would expect only the "yoked" dogs to be helpless. This in fact is what was observed. "Control" dogs rapidly learned to jump the hurdle while "yoked" dogs sat, whined, and took the shock. It seems, therefore, that the phenomenon of helplessness provides a clear indication that organisms can discriminate response-dependent from response-independent environmental events.

Contingency Learning in Infants

The demonstration of learned helplessness is especially significant for two reasons. First, it shows that a specific conditioning experience can produce a general breakdown. We will elaborate this when the relevance of helplessness to human pathology is discussed later in the chapter. Second, if helplessness in fact results from learning that one has no control over important environmental events, then helplessness demands a reinterpretation of the basic process of operant conditioning along the same lines which Rescorla's work suggested about Pavlovian conditioning. If organisms can learn that they lack control, they must also be able to learn that they have control. Temporal contiguity between response and reinforcer cannot account for either of these kinds of learning. We will turn now to other dramatic evidence that organisms can distinguish response-dependent from response-independent reward. In this case, the organisms in question are 3-month-old infants.

Consider an infant subject lying in its crib with its head resting on a pillow. Under the pillow is a switch which operates whenever the infant turns its head. Mounted on the opposite side of the crib is a mobile. For one group of infants, whenever they turn their heads on the pillow and close the switch, the mobile moves for a few seconds. These infants quickly learn to turn their heads to move the mobile. When the mobile moves, they smile and coo and seem delighted. For a second group of infants, movement of the mobile is out of their control. The mobile is *made to move* roughly as often for these infants as the infants who control the mobile's movement make it move. Not surprisingly, the infants in this group do not increase the frequency with which they turn their heads on the pillow. This is not surprising because there is no particular reason to expect reinforcement (moving mobile) to follow head movement instead of something else. What is surprising is the infants' response to the mobile. Early, they smile and coo just as the control infants do. However, after a few appearances of the mobile, the smiling and cooing stops. Apparently, the reinforcing character of the mobile depends upon the infants' power to make it move, or on the synchrony between the infants' behavior and the mobile's movement. It is only in the relation between behavior and consequence that the experience of the two groups of infants differs. Yet, the response of these two groups to the mobile is dramatically different. It thus appears that even young infants distinguish response-dependent from response-independent reinforcement.[19]

PARALLELS BETWEEN PAVLOVIAN AND OPERANT CONDITIONING

Research on learned helplessness and on operant conditioning in infants provides clear evidence that organisms can distinguish situations in which reinforcement depends on their behavior from situations in which reinforcement is independent of their behavior. The mere pairing of response and consequence does not seem to provide a sufficient explanation of the operant conditioning process.

It is tempting to conclude from this research that a single mechanism underlies both Pavlovian and operant conditioning. We can divide the possible relations between CS and US, or response and reinforcer, into three classes:

19. See Watson, 1967, 1971. It is worth noting, parenthetically, that the demonstration that infants can distinguish control from lack of it is surprising and significant only within the context of learning theory. For researchers with different theoretical orientations, things could hardly be otherwise. In the theoretical framework created by the celebrated developmental psychologist Jean Piaget, Watson's findings are so expected that one would hardly do the research to uncover them. In proposing a theoretical account of very early development in children, Piaget, 1951, distinguishes two stages of development purely on the basis of awareness of control. In one stage, infants seem to do things which have *surprisingly* interesting consequences. In the next stage, they do the same things *precisely in order to produce* these consequences. However, when the consequences are produced for them, they are not interested. It seems, indeed, that what is interesting for them is not the consequence itself, but the relation between it and their behavior. Watson's research serves in a way to highlight the differences between Piagetian theory and learning theory.

(1) $p(US/CS) > p(US/\overline{CS})$ $p(Rft/Resp) > p(Rft/\overline{Resp})$

(2) $p(US/CS) = p(US/\overline{CS})$ $p(Rft/Resp) = p(Rft/\overline{Resp})$

(3) $p(US/CS) < p(US/\overline{CS})$ $p(Rft/Resp) < p(Rft/\overline{Resp})$

The first pair of statements indicates a positive contingency between either US and CS or reinforcer and response. Under these conditions, Pavlovian and operant conditioned responses develop. The second pair of statements indicates conditions in which there is no contingency between CS and US or response and reinforcer. The effect of these procedures is complicated. Under some conditions they would be appropriate as control procedures against which to evaluate a positive or negative contingency. However, we have seen that under other conditions they produce rather profound behavioral effects in their own right. If the situation is traumatic, then independence between CS and US produces a generalized debilitation which we called anxiety in Chapter 5. Similarly, independence of response and reinforcer under traumatic circumstances produces a general debilitation which we have called helplessness. Whether generally debilitating or not, however, it is clear that independence of CS and US or response and reinforcer yields effects which are quite different from the effects of a positive contingency. Finally, the third pair of statements describes conditions in which there is a negative contingency between CS and US or response and reinforcer. We saw in the last chapter that such a contingency produces Pavlovian conditioned inhibition. We have not discussed the effects of operant procedures of this type. It is clear that such negative contingencies eliminate the particular activity under study. If reinforcement depends upon not pecking a key, then pigeons already trained to peck the key will stop.[20]

The parallels between the two types of conditioning are quite striking. However, while Pavlovian conditioning research demands the view that contingency is necessary for conditioning, the research discussed in this chapter does not demand the same interpretation of operant conditioning. The helplessness and infant-conditioning experiments show two things: first, they indicate that response-dependent consequences *can* be discriminated from response-independent consequences; second, they indicate that the former are preferred to the latter. Neither of these points rules out the possibility that conditioning can occur, via superstition, even when reinforcement is response-independent. As long as the superstition phenomenon occurs reliably, we seem forced to conclude that contingency between re-

20. See, for example, Reynolds, 1961a.

sponse and reinforcer is not necessary for conditioning to occur—
unless the superstition phenomenon can be given a different explanation.

ANOTHER LOOK AT SUPERSTITION

In 1971, John Staddon and Virginia Simmelhag published a paper
which may turn out to be one of the most important contributions to
the analysis of behavior in many years.[21] The paper had two major
sections. The first was an experiment—a replication of Skinner's superstition experiment. The second was a lengthy and detailed discussion of the implications of the experiment—one which suggested a
significant reinterpretation of what the law of effect actually does.

First, consider the experiment. Pigeons that had never been
trained before were trained to approach and eat from a feeder. When
they did this reliably, they were exposed to daily sessions in the conditioning chamber in which the feeder was made available every 12 seconds. The sessions terminated after 64 food deliveries. The procedure was very much like Skinner's initial procedure. The main
difference came in the recording of data. Staddon and Simmelhag established 16 behavioral categories, including wing flapping, walking,
turning in circles, putting the head in the feeder, raising the beak to
the ceiling, and pecking at one or another part of the chamber. They
then observed the pigeons continuously during the sessions, and
pushed buttons which corresponded to these behavioral categories
whenever the appropriate response occurred. At the end of each session, they had a record of the frequency with which these different
responses occurred, and the order in which they occurred. Thus,
their observations were much more detailed and systematic than Skinner's.

Before discussing the results of their experiment, let us consider
what our present understanding of superstition might lead us to expect. At the time of the very first food delivery, the pigeons might be
engaged in any one of the 16 responses categorized by Staddon and
Simmelhag (or perhaps one which was not included in their set of categories). The effect of that first food delivery would be to increase the
frequency of whatever response had preceded it. This, in turn, would
make it likely that the same response would be occurring when the
next food delivery occurred, thus increasing its frequency still more.
Ultimately, we would expect to find each pigeon spending most of its
time engaged in one particular activity—different from one pigeon to

21. Staddon and Simmelhag, 1971.

the next, but quite reliable from minute to minute and session to session for each pigeon.

This is not what Staddon and Simmelhag observed. Indeed, at the start of the experiment, all of the pigeons spent their time doing different things. Furthermore, early food deliveries followed different responses by different pigeons. However, within about five sessions, all pigeons wound up doing the same thing—pecking. They directed their pecks at different places, but they were all pecking at something. Responses of the sort Skinner observed did occur. Just after a food delivery, the pigeons would engage in a sequence of nonpecking responses. The sequence differed from pigeon to pigeon, but was fairly constant for each pigeon. By about the sixth second after the food delivery, though, all of the pigeons were pecking. One pigeon would reliably turn a circle, put its head in the empty feeder, then peck. Another pigeon would flap its wings, then peck. A third would turn a circle, peck at the floor, put its head in the feeder, then peck. Nonpecking behavior occurred early in the interval between food deliveries, but virtually all of these intervals terminated with pecking.

Staddon and Simmelhag observed another remarkable thing. When the pigeons were switched to a procedure in which food was available every 12 seconds, but they had to peck a response key to produce it, almost nothing about their behavior changed. Even though food now depended on a peck, pecking was no more frequent than when food was response-independent. Moreover, behavior other than pecking tended to occur early in the interfood interval, only to be replaced by pecking toward the middle of the interval. The only important difference in behavior between the response-independent procedure and the response-dependent procedure was in the pecking response itself. Whereas the location of the peck in the response-independent procedure varied from moment to moment, in the response-dependent procedure virtually all pecks were directed at the response key. This, of course, was required to produce food, but it is important to note that the response requirement did not affect the frequency of pecking—only its location.

It is clear that Skinner's account of superstition cannot explain the findings of Staddon and Simmelhag. It is not temporal contiguity of response and reinforcer that determines which activity will occur in a superstition experiment. One might infer from this that temporal contiguity of response and reinforcer is not *sufficient* to produce conditioning under any circumstances. When there is a dependency between response and reinforcer, organisms detect this dependency, and this is what produces conditioning. But if temporal contiguity does not determine the behavior of an organism in a superstition experiment, what does?

Terminal and Interim Behavior

In attempting to answer this question, Staddon and Simmelhag recast the law of effect in an evolutionary perspective. They first distinguished the responses observed late in the interfood interval (pecking), which they called *terminal behavior,* from the responses they observed early in the interfood interval, which they called *interim behavior.* Interim behavior, they argued, is not controlled by the law of effect. It consists of species-characteristic behavior patterns which appear when (a) the organism is in a particular state of deprivation (hunger, thirst, etc.), (b) the organism is in a situation in which that deprivation is usually satisfied, and (c) there is no opportunity to satisfy that deprivation at a particular moment. That is why interim behavior was restricted to the early part of the interfood interval in their experiment. Of more immediate concern to us is the terminal behavior. This behavior is subject to influence by the law of effect, but the law of effect does not provide a complete explanation of its occurrence. Terminal behavior occurs when (a) the organism is in a particular state of deprivation and (b) the opportunity to satisfy that deprivation *is* available. To understand what form terminal behavior will take, it is necessary to introduce another pair of terms.

Behavioral Variation and Behavioral Selection

In order to understand behavior, one must understand two different sets of principles: *principles of behavioral variation* and *principles of behavioral selection.* The first set of principles determines the range of things an organism might do in a particular situation. It was principles of variation which determined that the responses which comprised Staddon's and Simmelhag's 16 categories, and virtually no others, would occur in the superstition situation. Principles of selection then operate as the organism has experience in this situation to determine which of the many responses which might occur (determined by principles of variation) actually will occur. Thus, in the superstition experiment, principles of variation establish pecking as one of many possible responses and principles of selection then operate so that pecking predominates. But what are these principles of variation and selection?

Staddon and Simmelhag identify a number of different principles of variation. We will only mention a few here. First, certain species-specific behavior patterns are called forth by particular situations. Thus, there are defensive responses, aggressive responses, reproductive responses, and feeding responses which are built into the members of different species, ready to appear in the appropriate situation. Second, there are principles of transfer. Behavior which has come to dominate in one situation will be generalized or transferred to other situations which are similar. Third, there are principles of Pavlovian conditioning. Pavlovian conditioning endows previously neutral stimuli with the power to evoke a set of responses which may mimic responses to the US or prepare organisms for the US. These principles (the first innate, the last two experiential), among others, determine what an organism *might* do in a particular situation.

What of principles of selection? Staddon and Simmelhag discuss only two. The first and less general of the two is Pavlovian conditioning. It is Pavlovian conditioning which selects behavior in the superstition experiment. The CS is temporal—the passage of 12 seconds. The US is food. The response observed—pecking—happens to be the pigeon's consummatory response to food. Thus the superstition experiment seems to boil down to Pavlovian conditioning of pecking. If the US were water, or shock, and all other aspects of the situation remained the same, then some response other than pecking would have been selected by the Pavlovian contingency.

The reader will notice that Pavlovian conditioning is both a principle of variation and a principle of selection. That is, it influences both what an organism might do and what an organism will do. This is not the case for the second principle of selection. Staddon and Simmelhag call it the principle of reinforcement. We have been calling it the law of effect. According to Staddon and Simmelhag, reinforcement does not strengthen, or increase in frequency, the response which produces it; rather, it *selects* that response from the set of possible responses in a situation. More accurately, those responses which do not produce reinforcement are eliminated. Only those responses which do produce reinforcement remain. In the superstition experiment, the frequency of pecking was no higher when reinforcement depended upon it than when reinforcement was independent of responding. The difference was that in the former case, pecking was directed at a particular place—the key. Key pecking was *selected* because off-key pecking, along with a host of other responses, was eliminated.[22]

Also consistent with this view is the fact that when an extinction procedure is instituted after conditioning, one of its first effects is to increase the variability of behavior.[23] Though the response continues to occur at high frequency for some time, the locus, force, and tem-

22. If we relate this account to the data we presented in Figure 6–3, we might conclude that the reduction in rate of key pecking which follows a shift from response-dependent to response-independent food delivery reflects not a change in the *rate* of pecking, but a change in the locus of the pecks.
23. See Antonitis, 1951; Guthrie and Horton, 1946; Warden and Lubow, 1942.

poral characteristics of the responses vary much more than they did during conditioning. There seems almost to be a reversal of the sequence of behavioral changes which occur early in training. We have already mentioned that when a rat is being trained to press a lever, the form of the response is remarkably different from one occurrence to the next until, with extended training, an efficient and stereotyped lever press develops. In extinction, with the principle of selection (law of effect) no longer operating, before the lever press stops occurring altogether, the stereotyped and efficient behavior dissolves into the much broader set of responses which occurred early in training. The adaptive value of a mechanism which broadens the set of responses which occurs as soon as the responses which used to work stop succeeding, should be clear. And this, indeed, seems to be the way organisms behave.

This interpretation of the law of effect makes it an almost exact parallel to natural selection. In evolution, principles of variation (genetics) determine the range of possible attributes the members of a species might have. Selection pressure (in terms of efficient food getting and reproduction) eliminates those variants of the species (and the gene pool) that are ill-equipped to survive. The best suited members remain. They reproduce themselves until they have filled the ecological niche. Similarly, in the behavior of an individual organism, principles of variation determine the range of possible responses. Selection pressure (in terms of what responses do or do not produce reinforcement) eliminates those behavioral variants which do not serve survival. The best suited responses remain and fill up the "behavioral niche."[24]

---

24. Other researchers, Skinner among them (1966; 1971, Chapter 1), have pointed out the possible parallels between the action of reinforcement (law of effect) and natural selection. For Skinner, Darwin's theory of natural selection provided a mechanism by which seemingly enlightened, intelligent, purposive, and goal-directed species change could occur automatically and mechanically. That is, organisms did not *try* to develop new body characteristics in order better to cope with the environment. Some (then unknown) process which occurred in reproduction produced in individuals random variations from the normal structure of the species. Those inheritable variations which made the organisms better able to survive and reproduce increased in frequency (due to more successful breeding) over generations. Those which were injurious to survival or reproduction did not increase. After many thousands of years, the better adapted members of the species would have completely replaced the more poorly adapted ones. In this way, species change occurred. In this context, what is most important about Darwin's contribution is that the responsibility for species change was largely removed from the individual organism and placed in the environment. Natural selection was a perfectly mechanical account of how species could evolve always in the direction of greater adaptiveness without having that goal in view. The law of effect also serves to remove responsibility for change from within the individual organism and to place it in the environment. Behavior which we call purposive, intelligent, and freely chosen is

Implications of the Staddon and Simmelhag Argument

On Superstition • Skinner's concept of superstition is difficult to reconcile with the framework established by Staddon and Simmelhag. Independence of response and consequence means the absence of selection by reinforcement. The mere temporal contiguity of response and reinforcer cannot account for the stereotyped behavior which emerges. The contiguity view of superstition is analogous to "taking a population of white mice, breeding them for 20 generations without further selection for color, and then attributing the resulting white population to the results of 'accidental selection.' In this case, as in the case of response-independent reinforcement, the outcome reflects a characteristic of the initial population (i.e., the mice gene pool, the nature of the organism), and not a non-existent selection process."[25] A direct consequence of this view is that organisms distinguish response-independent from response-dependent environmental events, and only the latter class is sufficient to produce operant conditioning (selection by reinforcement). This does not imply that superstition, especially in humans, does not exist; rather, it implies only that the source of human superstition is not temporal contiguity of response and consequence.[26]

If we accept this view, how can we account for the results Skinner obtained? Recall that Skinner did indeed observe responses other than pecking in his superstition experiment, and, on the face of it, Skinner's results are quite inconsistent with the view put forth by

said to be mechanically selected by contingencies of reinforcement operative in the environment.

Just as Darwin posited his theory in advance of any knowledge of the mechanism by which the variation on which natural selection operated occurred (a mechanism which the study of genetics has illuminated), so Skinner studied selection by the law of effect without paying much attention to the mechanism by which behavioral variation occurred. One of the important contributions made by Staddon and Simmelhag was to highlight the distinction between variation and selection of behavior, and make clear that the law of effect applied only to the latter.

25. Staddon and Simmelhag, 1971, p. 21.

26. There is a long history of research on what might be called the attribution of causality in humans—both adults and children. In recent years, a great deal of work has been done on processes of attribution in the field of social psychology. If this line of investigation has any relevance to the phenomenon of superstition in humans, it suggests that superstition results not because people equate causality with temporal contiguity, but because people actively explore a wide range of hypotheses about causes and effects, in much the way that scientists do experiments. Unlike scientific experiments, however, people often are required to make judgments about what causes what based upon very incomplete information. As a result, they can occasionally be "tricked" into the confirmation of a false hypothesis. For a detailed discussion of this approach to human behavior, see Kelley, 1967.

Staddon and Simmelhag. While there is no way to know for sure, a possible account of Skinner's results is this: when pigeons are deprived of food and extremely active, their heads bob back and forth a great deal in pecklike fashion. When the bobbing is not directed at a particular place, like a lit key, it is easily overlooked, or treated as simply a sign of general activity. It is much less dramatic than responses like wing flapping or turning in circles. It is possible that Skinner observed pecking which was directed at nothing in particular and disregarded it, focusing instead on other, more dramatic responses. The responses which Skinner did observe were also observed by Staddon and Simmelhag, and were also observed to increase in frequency. But Staddon and Simmelhag classed these responses as "interim" activities. Skinner may simply have overlooked, or not counted, the "terminal" response of pecking in his experiment.

On the Relation between the Law of Effect and Learning • When reinforcement is viewed as selecting rather than strengthening behavior, it becomes clear that reinforcement only operates on what is already there. What this means is that reinforcement has rather little to do with learning, *as learning is ordinarily conceived.* Typically what people mean by learning is the development of new responses, or the development of an ability to do new things. But this, according to Staddon and Simmelhag, is the province of principles of variation, not principles of selection. Reinforcement will determine what an organism *will do* at any particular time. It has little to say about what an organism *can do.*[27] This distinction between "will" and "can" has taken a number of forms over the years. Many years ago, the distinction was introduced as one between learning (can) and performance (will). Presently, the distinction is a very central one in the interpretation of language. Its current form is as a distinction between competence (can) and performance (will).

The law of effect seems less central to an understanding of human behavior when learning is removed from its purview. It may not be necessary to do this, however. If one conceives of learning as involving not so much the development of new responses as the development of new combinations of old responses, then the relevance of the law of effect to learning reappears. The formation of an operant is an instance of the recombination of old responses into new units.

On the Operant as a Behavioral Unit • We have already had occasion to discuss both the strategy and reasoning behind the definition of

27. This should not be taken as a criticism of Skinner. Skinner has made this point himself repeatedly over the years. See, for example, his account of language (1957), especially the introduction.

operants and the way in which the form of the operant changes with experience. Skinner realized that it would be hopelessly premature to try to characterize responses in terms of the movement of individual muscles. He also saw that it was important to study a response which was not intrinsically related to either the stimuli that preceded it or the reinforcer that followed it. He opted, therefore, for a strategy which involved the creation of an operant class, functionally defined. When one watches an animal early in training, it becomes immediately clear that while the operant class exists for the experimenter, it does not exist for the animal. The rat engages in a series of different responses, some of which include a seemingly inadvertent press of the lever. When food follows the lever press, the rat spends more and more time around the lever. It still engages in the same wide range of responses as before, but now they tend to occur in the area of the lever almost exclusively. As a result, lever presses, and reinforcements, are more frequent. Gradually, the rat learns that rearing on its hind paws is not necessary to produce food, but landing on the lever is. The rat learns that turning in circles is not necessary to produce food, but swishing its tail against the lever is. The rat learns that licking and chewing and grooming are not necessary to produce food, but biting on the lever is. The rat learns that keeping its paws on the lever is not necessary to produce food, but that depressing and releasing the lever is.

All of these lever-press responses initially occur as parts of very different behavioral sequences. They have two things in common: they depress the lever and they produce food. As training proceeds, the "lever press," which is merely a collection of responses which the rat has engaged in many times in the past, emerges as a new, integral, functional unit of behavior. Something has been added to the rat's repertoire—not a brand-new sequence of muscle movements, but a new organization of old and familiar muscle movements. The principle of reinforcement has selected; it has selectively eliminated those components of the rat's behavior which did not produce food, until only the effective components, lever presses, remain.

It may be that much human learning involves new combinations of old responses. If so, then Staddon's and Simmelhag's view that reinforcement selects rather than strengthens behavior makes reinforcement a critical component of the learning process. Just how critical becomes clear when one speculates about the way in which new behavioral units are defined and taught to people. Human behavior tends to be described and organized in terms of the goals it serves. Thus, "mailing a letter" or "getting to 42nd Street and Broadway" are operant classes which subsume an indefinitely large set of possible responses. Their common element, which defines the operant, is just the characteristic which produces the goal. But lever-press operants are defined in precisely the same way. And the role of reinforcement in establishing the operant as a behavioral unit may go a long way toward explaining the creation of more complicated behavioral units such as the ones which characterize human behavior.

On the Law of Effect and Creativity • One of the most frequent criticisms of the law of effect as both a theoretical tool and a technological one relates to the matter of creativity. On the technological side, it is often argued that behavior technology will make people into machines: that people will learn what responses produce what consequences and then simply repeat those responses again and again when the relevant consequences are desired. Somehow, this set of behavior–consequence relations will interfere with or even eliminate people's ability to arrive at novel solutions to problems. This criticism is leveled especially at efforts to introduce technology into the classroom. Critics have the view that training which suggests one and only one correct answer to any question will produce inflexible and uncreative approaches to learning. They argue that the real goal of education is not to establish behavioral repertoires which succeed again and again in familiar situations, but to establish a kind of intellectual competence which will allow people to find adaptive responses in novel situations.

On the theoretical side, it has been argued that the law of effect is utterly unable to account for behavior which is inherently creative. While the law of effect may tell us why people will do again what they have done before, it cannot tell us why or how people will do what they have never done before. The most obviously creative aspect of human behavior is the use of language.[28] Students of language argue that virtually every human utterance is unique: only rarely do people say exactly the same thing twice.

The distinction offered by Staddon and Simmelhag between principles of variation and principles of selection sheds light on both the theoretical and technological criticisms of the law of effect. In essence, the theoretical criticism is upheld. The underlying human ability which makes possible the production of novel utterances must be treated as a principle of variation. This ability determines the range of things a person might say, and the range of things a person definitely will not say, in any particular situation. Principles of selection (the law of effect) may then operate to influence what actually will be said in one situation or another. However, it has nothing to offer as an explanation of the inherent creativity of language ability.

28. See, for example, Chomsky, 1959.

The technological criticism is more difficult to evaluate. On the one hand, the view that reinforcement *selects* behavior implies that the law of effect is the very antithesis of creativity. As long as one activity "works" in a situation, others will be eliminated, and stereotypy will result. Indeed, if there were a response which "worked" in every situation, principles of selection would ultimately produce an organism whose behavior was remarkably mechanical and stereotyped. But this is neither surprising nor undesirable. One would hardly expect people continually to come up with novel solutions to the problem of mailing a letter if there was a mailbox outside the front door of their homes. The real question is this: What happens if, after 20 years of mailing letters outside the door of one's home, one goes to mail a letter one morning and discovers that the mailbox is gone. The data suggest that extinction experience has the immediate effect of increasing the variability of behavior. Principles of variation are called into action, the number of different things an organism does in a situation increases dramatically, and ultimately a new effective behavior (if one is possible) is selected.

The implication of this fact for human behavior is that the machine-like stereotypy which results from the operation of the law of effect when behavior is effective will be replaced immediately by novelty and variability when behavior stops being effective. In short, people will behave like machines only if their behavior is effective in all situations. However, principles of selection do not alter or eliminate principles of variation. As a result, when behavior stops being effective, novel solutions to problems will emerge. Again, as with language, the matter of human creativity is the province of principles of variation, not principles of selection. Just as the law of effect cannot produce creative capacity, so also it cannot eliminate it. What critics of the application of behavior technology must show is not that reinforcement limits creativity, but that some other method of instruction enhances it or, in Staddon's and Simmelhag's terms, broadens the scope of the principles of variation.

OPERANT CONDITIONING AND UNDERSTANDING PATHOLOGY

Operant conditioning principles can be used effectively in the treatment of various forms of psychopathology. The case of the chronic schizophrenics described in Chapter 1 depended upon the most basic of operant conditioning principles—the law of effect itself. The nurses stopped fussing over the patients and assisting them in feeding and cleaning, and reinforcement was provided for self-maintenance. The reinforcement at first was food. Later, however, tokens were substituted for food. This procedure greatly enlarged both the types of responses which could be reinforced and the types of reinforcers which could be offered. Each patient could exchange tokens for desired objects. In this way, some reinforcer could be found to suit everyone. What made the tokens reinforcing? This is simply a specific restatement of a more general issue: What reinforces most human behavior in the natural environment? In this chapter, we have talked of food, water, and aversive stimulation. All of these stimuli are related directly to the biological well-being of organisms. But people seem to behave in general for reinforcers like money, approval, and status. What makes these reinforcers?

We have seen that attempts to identify a set of characteristics which all reinforcers have in common have repeatedly failed. The best we can do right now is identify the common property of all reinforcers as their capacity to control behavior. We will discuss, in Chapter 10, some notions about how things like money or tokens become reinforcers. We will have nothing to say about approval or status as reinforcers, except that they do seem to control behavior in accordance with the law of effect.

The case of the schizophrenic patients, and many others like it, offers one valuable lesson to students of psychopathology. The lesson is that one can know little or nothing about the origins of pathology and still make great strides in treatment simply by analyzing the contingencies of reinforcement which are operative at the moment. The origins of the schizophrenics' problems were difficult to determine, for not only were the origins of their disorders far in the past, but they were likely to be different in each individual case. Nevertheless, analysis and modification of existing reinforcement contingencies opened the way to successful therapy.

While this is a valuable contribution to methods of therapy, it is not enough. As we saw at the end of Chapter 5, methods of treatment without some theory about the origins of a disorder make it impossible to prevent the development of psychopathology. If one understood the origins of pathology, one could employ technology to restructure the environment so that pathology was less likely to develop.

Depression and Learned Helplessness

In the last few years a provocative theory about the origins of one type of pathology has been developed. It is a theory about the origins of certain types of depression, which is probably the most common of all types of psychopathology, and it is based upon the phenomenon of learned helplessness.[29]

Helplessness results from the experience of independence between one's behavior and important environmental events. Profound helplessness effects have been demonstrated in a variety of subhuman species. More specific helplessness effects have been demonstrated in humans by Martin Seligman and his colleagues. The general form of these demonstrations is this: one group of people is exposed to a situation in which their behavior can control the occurrence of an aversive event while another group is exposed to the same situation except that the aversive event is beyond their control. Both groups are then exposed to a completely different kind of situation in which learning is required. The typical finding is that people who have had control learn in the new situation much faster than people who have not had control. Indeed, many in this latter group do not learn at all, though the required task is usually quite simple.

It is the learning of independence between behavior and consequence—the learning of helplessness—which, according to Seligman, is at the root of many cases of depression. There are many parallels between the symptoms of depressive patients and the symptoms of helpless animals. Both are passive; both have difficulty learning in situations in which responses are effective; both fail to display aggression in situations which usually call it forth. Both lose weight, appetite, and interest in social interaction. Moreover, if patients classified as depressive are exposed to learning tasks, they behave in the same way as nondepressive people who have just been exposed to lack of control.

Still more impressive is that therapy which seems to alleviate depression also seems to alleviate laboratory-induced helplessness, and vice versa. Electroconvulsive shock and the administration of certain psychoactive drugs have been used effectively to mitigate depression for some time. When they are administered to animals that have been exposed to helplessness-inducing lack of control, the helplessness syndrome is broken. Similarly, "therapy" which has effectively eliminated helplessness in dogs seems to break up depression in people. If dogs that have been made helpless are dragged back and forth over a hurdle which nonhelpless dogs hop over to avoid electric shock, after a good deal of dragging the helpless dogs learn to make the responses themselves.[30] They are cured of helplessness. Likewise, if depressive patients, who assert that they are unable to do anything effectively,

29. Seligman, 1975.
30. Seligman, Maier, and Geer, 1968.

are forced to engage in simple tasks at which they cannot fail, the difficulty of the tasks can gradually be increased until they are performing normally. The depressive must be forced to experience success; it is necessary to demonstrate that his or her behavior can control environmental events. Once made, the demonstration seems to break up the depressive syndrome.

Finally, Seligman suggests that the laboratory phenomenon of helplessness can also teach us how to prevent depression. Recall that if dogs are exposed to uncontrollable electric shocks *after* they have had experience controlling shock, helplessness does not develop. The possible parallel to depression is clear. If people, in the course of development, are exposed to many situations in which their behavior is effective, then subsequent exposures to lack of control (some of which, after all, are inevitable) ought not to produce depression. We have already seen that even young infants can distinguish response-dependent from response-independent environmental events. What that suggests is that the potential for development of helplessness, or of immunization from it, is present at a very young age.

Seligman's efforts to relate helplessness to depression offer a prime example of the way in which basic research can provide important insights into practical problems. The phenomenon of helplessness has led to a new and promising view of the most common of all emotional disorders. It has suggested new means of treatment, and possible means of prevention. Though the ultimate generality and utility of helplessness as a model of depression remains to be decided, the idea has already done great service to the understanding of pathology.[31]

PAVLOVIAN AND OPERANT CONDITIONING SIMILARITIES AND DIFFERENCES

The last four chapters have been organized around the principle that there are two basic kinds of learning, or perhaps more accurately, two different sets of principles of behavioral control. In Chapter 3, the basic procedures employed to study Pavlovian and operant conditioning were outlined, and some basic terminology was defined. In Chapters 4 and 5, Pavlovian conditioning was discussed in detail, and in this chapter we began a detailed discussion of operant conditioning. Since the distinction between these two kinds of conditioning has

31. It should be pointed out that the interpretation of the helplessness effect offered by Seligman and his collaborators is controversial (see Glazer and Weiss, 1976a and 1976b, for recent alternative views). However, while some of these alternatives have merit when applied to the study of helplessness in laboratory animals, none is particularly cogent when applied to human helplessness studies.

been so central to the organization of this book (and, indeed, to the organization of the study of behavior theory generally) it is important to establish clearly and precisely what it is that makes the two kinds of conditioning different. This seems like a simple enough task. The trouble is that as soon as one starts comparing Pavlovian and operant conditioning, what emerges from the comparison is not their differences, but their enormous similarities.

In a classic and exhaustive text on animal learning published more than 15 years ago, Gregory Kimble devoted an entire chapter to the comparison of Pavlovian and operant conditioning.[32] As he discussed one phenomenon after another, he concluded again and again that the particular phenomenon under discussion characterized both kinds of conditioning. If one compares the two types of conditioning in terms of acquisition of responses, extinction, discrimination, generalization, temporal characteristics, the effects of deprivation, and so on, one can produce these phenomena with both kinds of conditioning, and they tend to have the same characteristics. We have already provided evidence of the similarity between the two types of conditioning in this book. If one looked at a graph of response acquisition (e.g., Figures 4–2, 4–3, and 6–1), and the graph were not labeled, there would be no way to tell from the graph alone whether salivation or lever pressing was being charted.

In the 15 years since Kimble's book was published, no one has uncovered any new phenomena which make it easier to distinguish Pavlovian and operant conditioning. On the contrary, the major new conceptualization of Pavlovian conditioning—that it depends on contingency rather than contiguity—has been matched by a similar reconceptualization of operant conditioning, as witnessed by the work of Staddon and Simmelhag, and Seligman, among others. It seems clear that if one is to find a fundamental difference between the two types of conditioning, it will have to be something other than the phenomena which characterize them.

We have, ourselves, been using two criteria for distinguishing the two types of conditioning without really having justified them. The first is that the *procedures* used to investigate them are different. The second, which is more central and more theoretical, is that Pavlovian conditioning affects reflexive, elicited, nonvoluntary behavior while operant conditioning affects nonreflexive, emitted, voluntary behavior. It is time now to evaluate these criteria to see whether they can sustain the distinction between Pavlovian and operant conditioning.

It is clear that historically Pavlovian conditioning research has been

32. Kimble, 1961.

restricted to the study of reflexes while operant conditioning research has been restricted to the study of voluntary acts. The question is whether these restrictions reflect historical accident or natural necessity. Can reflexes be conditioned with an operant procedure? Can voluntary behavior be conditioned with a Pavlovian procedure? Research in the last few years has provided affirmative answers to both of these questions.

Before discussing the research, we should establish a criterion for distinguishing voluntary from involuntary behavior. Two possible criteria are immediately apparent. First, we might argue that if a response is triggered by an antecedent stimulus, it is involuntary. The problem with this criterion is that behavior which is clearly voluntary, while not elicited by an antecedent stimulus, can certainly be controlled by one. The phenomenon of operant discrimination learning, mentioned in Chapter 3 and discussed in detail in Chapter 8, is a case in which antecedent stimuli control voluntary behavior. Since antecedent stimuli can control both voluntary and reflexive behavior, this criterion boils down to a distinction between "controlled by" and "elicited by." But if we knew how to make this distinction, we would already know how to classify behavior as voluntary or reflexive. Thus this criterion assumes the answer to the question it is trying to help answer.

The second criterion is more promising. We can call a behavior voluntary if it is sensitive to its consequences, if reinforcement increases its frequency and nonreinforcement decreases its frequency. More precisely, if an organism can learn *not* to make the response in order to produce reinforcement just as well as making it, or to decrease its frequency in order to produce reinforcement as well as increase its frequency, then the response in question is voluntary. Can a dog be trained *not* to salivate to obtain food? If so, salivation may be considered voluntary.

Operant Conditioning of Reflexes

When this criterion of voluntariness is applied, we discover that it is satisfied by most behavior we have been calling reflexive. Consider salivation. If a dog is exposed to a Pavlovian conditioning procedure which is modified so that the US (food) is delivered *only if* the dog does not salivate during the CS, the dog does not learn not to salivate.[33] It continues to salivate in most trials even though salivation costs it food. This certainly makes salivation appear reflexive. How-

33. Sheffield, 1965.

ever, if the same procedure is employed with water rather than food, a dog can learn either to salivate or not to salivate (depending on the requirements of the task) to obtain water.[34] Does this mean that salivation is voluntary or not? If we are to make any sense of this question we must look at salivation not as an isolated response, but as part of a relation between a response and a stimulus (food or water). From this perspective it seems that we must conclude that salivation may be reflexive as part of one relation and voluntary as part of another.

Let us consider other "reflexive responses." Neal Miller and his associates have been conducting a program of research on the operant control of reflexive behavior for a number of years.[35] Without describing the procedures, which are rather complicated, let us briefly review some of the more striking observations Miller has made. First, rats can be trained, using operant conditioning procedures, to increase or decrease their heart rate. If the reader were asked to increase his or her heart rate, the initial response would no doubt be bewilderment. How can one make one's heart beat faster? Of course, exercising will increase heart rate. But the rats in Miller's experiments did not exercise because they were paralyzed, precisely in order to prevent skeletal movement which increased heart rate as a by-product. Contingent reinforcement seemed to increase (or decrease) heart rate directly with no mediation by muscles which were clearly under voluntary control.

Along similar lines, Miller demonstrated that operant contingencies could be used to control the rate of formation of urine in the kidneys of rats and the rate at which blood flowed through the rat's ears. It is difficult to think of either of these responses as voluntary. Yet, they satisfy our criterion of sensitivity to their consequences. It is beginning to look as if either our criterion or the distinction between reflexive and voluntary as the province of Pavlovian and operant conditioning, respectively, will have to be abandoned.

Pavlovian Conditioning of Voluntary Responses

The relation between voluntary behavior and reflexes grew even more complex in 1968 as a result of a very simple experiment.[36] Pigeons were exposed to a Pavlovian conditioning procedure: a light was projected on the response key periodically and was followed by

34. Miller and Carmona, 1967.
35. See Miller, 1969.
36. Brown and Jenkins, 1968.

food delivery. After 50 or so pairings of keylight and food, all pigeons began pecking the key and they continued to do so reliably. This phenomenon was called *autoshaping* (for automatic shaping). It is now seen as an instance of Pavlovian conditioning of key pecking. However, initial attempts to explain the phenomenon centered on the concept of superstition, in Skinner's sense. Whatever it was that produced the first key peck, once it occurred it was followed closely in time by food and, thereby, reinforced. The significant experiment which ruled out this interpretation and established unequivocally that autoshaping is Pavlovian conditioning was done with the aid of an experimental procedure (already mentioned) which had been used to establish that conditioned salivation in dogs was reflexive.[37] A key light was lit periodically and followed by food *only if* the pigeons did not peck the key. This identical procedure had failed to eliminate salivation in dogs. Similarly, it did not eliminate key pecking in pigeons. Pigeons continued to peck the key in trial after trial even though each key peck cost them food. Not only did this result parallel the experiment with dogs, but it eliminated superstition as a possible explanation. The only response the pigeons might emit which *could not* be followed by food was pecking the key. Yet that is precisely what they did.

These findings have created quite a storm among researchers in operant conditioning. The pigeon's key peck, after all, is the most often studied "operant" behavior. Now here is evidence which strongly suggests that the key peck is not voluntary at all—that it is not a prototype of human goal-directed activity, but a reflex, just like salivation. This concern has generated extensive research on autoshaping in the few years since its discovery. Virtually all of the evidence points to autoshaping as an instance of Pavlovian conditioning. Autoshaping is determined by contingency rather than pairing, as Rescorla showed was the case in Pavlovian conditioning.[38] The form of the autoshaped response often mimics the form of the unconditioned response. Pigeons make "feeding pecks" at the key if the US is food and "drinking pecks" at the key if the US is water.[39] Two recent reviews of the research which has been done on autoshaping establish the parallels between it and traditional Pavlovian conditioning unambiguously and unequivocally.[40]

37. Williams and Williams, 1969.
38. Gamzu and Williams, 1971.
39. Jenkins and Moore, 1973.
40. Hearst and Jenkins, 1974; Schwartz and Gamzu, 1977.

We will reserve discussion of the significance of autoshaping with respect to the assumptions which underly research on operant conditioning for Chapter 11. The phenomenon of autoshaping undermines the view that key pecking is an arbitrary, voluntary behavior which may be taken as the prototype of all voluntary behavior, and much more will be made of this matter later on. In the present context, the demonstration of autoshaping suggests either that our criterion for distinguishing voluntary and reflexive behavior, or the distinction itself, must be abandoned. Thus far, efforts to distinguish Pavlovian and operant conditioning have continued to point to their similarity.

From a Process Distinction to a Paradigm Distinction

What we seem to be left with as a means to distinguish Pavlovian and operant conditioning is the difference in the experimental paradigms in which they are studied. Pavlovian conditioning studies manipulate the contingencies between stimulus and reinforcer (CS and US), and generally do nothing about the response but record it. Operant conditioning studies focus on the contingencies between the response and the reinforcer. In fact, any study of one type of contingency may also contain the other type. It is nearly impossible to create a pure Pavlovian or operant conditioning situation.

In studies of conditioned salivation, attention is focused on the CS–US relation, but salivation in anticipation of food may have consequences. It is possible that food tastes better when salivation has occurred than when it has not. It is possible that food is more quickly and easily chewed when salivation has occurred than when it has not. That these possibilities exist means that they may contribute to the occurrence of salivation, even though it is clear that the main determinant of salivation is the CS–US contingency. Similarly, when a rat is trained to press a lever for food, there are a variety of Pavlovian contingencies in the situation. When the feeder operates, it makes a noise. This noise is a signal for food. To what extent does this contribute to the maintenance of lever pressing? It is hard to say. In an operant discrimination experiment in which, let us say, lever presses when a light is on produce food while lever presses when the light is off do not, the light is paired with food while the dark is not. Thus an operant discrimination is at the same time a Pavlovian discrimination. If one is interested in the operant features of such a procedure, one measures lever pressing. If one is interested in Pavlovian control of behavior, one measures salivation. The point is that even the classification of procedures as either Pavlovian or operant is a complex problem.

What are we left with? We cannot find any criterion for hard and fast distinctions between Pavlovian conditioning *as a process* and operant conditioning *as a process*. We cannot even find criteria other than the interest of the experimenter for distinguishing Pavlovian conditioning as an experimental paradigm from operant conditioning as an experimental paradigm. What remains is to distinguish them as relations. Pavlovian conditioning is *defined* as the relation between two stimuli, CS and US, S⁺ and reinforcer, one of which is of innate biological significance to the organism. Operant conditioning is *defined* as a relation between a response and a stimulus, operant and reinforcer, CR and US. Both relations may control the same class of behavior. Some responses may be more susceptible to control by one relation than another. The relations may have facilitating effects in some situations and antagonistic effects in others.

This is the distinction between Pavlovian and operant conditioning with which we are left. We will have occasion throughout the remainder of the book to call upon Pavlovian conditioning principles and identify Pavlovian conditioning relations in situations the main focus of which is operant behavior. We will view any activity, in any situation, as potentially influenced by both types of relations. The distinction between the two kinds of learning will serve as an analytic tool rather than as a behavioral classification.

7

Schedules of Reinforcement

In virtually all of the experiments discussed in Chapter 6, the contingency relation between behavior and consequence was clear and simple. Every response would produce food, or every response would turn off electric shock, and food would not be forthcoming (and shock would be) without the response. If contingencies of reinforcement control human behavior in the natural environment, they are certainly very different from the types of contingencies described thus far in this book. The difference is that in the natural environment few responses are reinforced each time they occur. Rather, reinforcement is *intermittent;* it may or may not follow a response and there is a degree of uncertainty about whether a particular occurrence of the response will result in reinforcement. Reinforcement is not forthcoming each time you purchase a lottery ticket, or each time you answer the telephone, or each time you study. Though you study nearly every day, praise and good grades come only at examination time and not always at that time either. Though there may be intrinsic rewards for studying, surely everyone's education includes interludes in which the subject is dull. If the rewards for study are infrequent, why doesn't studying extinguish? Surely a rat would not continue to press a lever day after day if its lever presses were reinforced so irregularly. Or would it?

The study of the control of behavior by intermittent reinforcement has not been neglected in the analysis of behavior. On the contrary, it has been one of the most prominent areas of investigation in the last 20 years. It has been concerned first with describing how the patterning of reinforcement in time (different types of intermittency) affects the patterning of behavior in time. Second, it has been concerned with discovering the mechanism by which intermittent reinforcement of various types produces these different patterns of behavior. This area of research is generally referred to as the study of *schedules of reinforcement*. A reinforcement schedule is simply a rule which specifies how often and under what conditions a particular response will be reinforced.

BASIC SCHEDULES OF REINFORCEMENT

All schedules of reinforcement have one thing in common: reinforcement depends upon the occurrence of a response. With schedules in which each response is reinforced, called *continuous reinforcement (CRF) schedules,* a single response is all that is required for reinforcement. With other schedules, reinforcement may depend upon something in addition to a particular response, either the passage of a certain amount of time (*interval schedules*) or the occurrence of a certain number of previous responses (*ratio schedules*). Each of these types of schedules can be subdivided. The intervals required for reinforcement may be fixed (each interval is the same) or variable. Similarly, ratios may be fixed (each reinforcement depends upon the same number of responses) or variable. These four types of schedules—*fixed interval, variable interval, fixed ratio,* and *variable ratio*—are the most basic types of reinforcement schedules.[1]

Fixed-Interval (FI) Schedules

When reinforcement is arranged on an FI schedule, a single response after the passage of a fixed amount of time produces reinforcement. If the value of the interval is 1 minute (FI 1-min), then one lever press or key peck, a minute or more after the interval has begun, produces reinforcement. Responses *during the interval* do nothing. The passage of the interval by itself does nothing. Reinforcement depends upon both the passage of time and a single response. If the experimental subject could tell time, then it could simply relax until a minute was up and then make a single response, thereby producing a maximum amount of reinforcement with a minimum amount of effort. While organisms do not perform quite this efficiently on FI schedules, they do learn to predict the length of the interval.

---

1. The research program which really provoked interest in schedules of reinforcement was conducted by C. B. Ferster and B. F. Skinner, 1957.

Variable-Interval (VI) Schedules

On variable-interval schedules, reinforcement also depends upon the passage of time and a single response. However, unlike FI schedules, the time between reinforcements on VI schedules varies from one reinforcement to the next. The value of the VI schedule is the average time between reinforcements. Thus, for example, a VI 2-min schedule might make the first reinforcement available after 1 minute, the next 2 minutes later, the next 4 minutes later, the next 30 seconds later, and so on. Although it is possible to obtain reinforcement for each response on a VI schedule simply by waiting for the interreinforcement interval to elapse, there is no way for the subject to predict the length of a particular interreinforcement interval. This difference between VI and FI schedules results in a striking difference in the pattern of responding maintained by the two types of schedules.

Fixed-Ratio (FR) Schedules

On a fixed-ratio schedule, reinforcement depends upon the completion of a certain number of responses; time is irrelevant. If the value of the ratio is 50 (FR 50), every 50th response is reinforced. If the subject responds rapidly, reinforcements may be only seconds apart, and if the subject responds slowly, reinforcements may be many minutes apart. The passage of time does not make reinforcement any more likely.

Variable-Ratio (VR) Schedules

On a variable-ratio schedule, the number of responses required for reinforcement varies from one reinforcement to the next. On a VR 50 schedule, the animal might first have to make 60 responses, then 30, then 85, then 50, then 15, then 70, then 40, and so on. The value of the VR schedule specifies the *average* number of responses required for reinforcement.

PATTERNS OF BEHAVIOR MAINTAINED BY REINFORCEMENT SCHEDULES

How do the different schedules of reinforcement influence behavior? To explore this question, we need a new measuring instrument—the *cumulative record*. Cumulative records provide a visual represen-

A duck trained to retrieve rings by looping them around its neck. The reinforcement schedule is a fixed ratio 4, that is, the duck must retrieve 4 rings for each reinforcement. (Courtesy of Animal Behavior Enterprises.)

tation of the pattern of responding in time (see Figure 7–1). A pen rests on a piece of paper which is moved by a motor at a constant speed. As the paper moves beneath the pen, the pen makes a horizontal line on the paper. The pen is connected electrically to the switch behind the response key (or lever), so that each time the switch is closed, the pen moves up vertically, a small, fixed amount. Thus, each response moves the pen up a notch, and each instant of time moves the pen horizontally. The resulting curve traced by the pen depicts responses (y or vertical axis), over time (x or horizontal axis). The slope of the curve at any point (y/x) indicates the rate at which responses are occurring at that point.

Typical cumulative records of responding maintained on the four

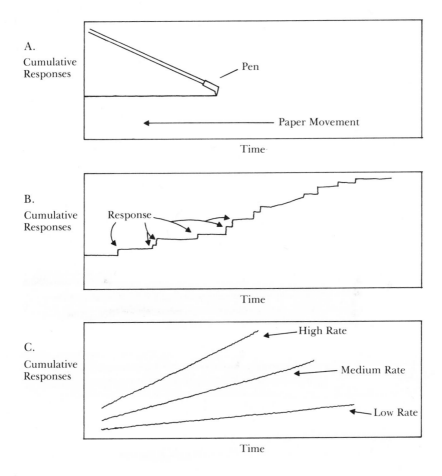

Figure 7–1. Schematic Drawings of Cumulative Records. *In* A, *the pen is moving across the paper and no responses are occurring. In B, the animal is making an occasional response. In C, the three lines represent steady patterns of responding at high, medium, and low rates. The actual rates can be read from the record as the slope of the lines.*

basic reinforcement schedules are depicted in Figure 7–2. The downward marks of the pen indicate occurrences of reinforcement. It is clear from Figure 7–2 that the different schedules produce strikingly different patterns of responding. Variable-ratio and variable-interval schedules are similar in that they produce relatively constant patterns of responding in time. They differ in that variable-ratio schedules maintain higher rates of responding then variable-interval schedules. Similarly, fixed-ratio schedules generate higher rates of responding

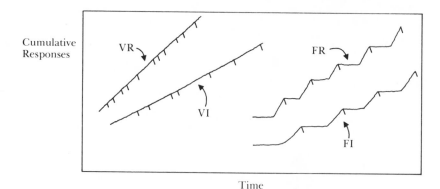

Time

Figure 7–2. Typical Patterns of Responding Generated by the Four Basic Reinforcement Schedules. *The downward strokes indicate reinforcements and the rate of responding at any point in time is represented by the slope of the curve at that point. Note that variable-ratio (VR) and variable-interval (VI) schedules maintain steady rates of responding, with VR response rate higher than VI response rate. Fixed-ratio (FR) and fixed-interval (FI) schedules maintain patterns of responding characterized by a pause after each reinforcement.*

than fixed-interval schedules—when the organism is responding at all. The most noticeable characteristic of both FR and FI schedules is that for some time after each reinforcement there is no responding.

It should not be thought that the different schedules produce response patterns like those in Figure 7–2 independent of their values. The value of the schedule (i.e., VI 1-min vs. VI 10-min, or FR 10 vs. FR 200) also influences the pattern of responding. However, the effects of variations in the value of the schedule depend upon the nature of the schedule itself.

On VI and VR schedules, increases in the value of the schedule (decreases in the frequency of reinforcement) do not change the shape of the cumulative record; as long as reinforcement is frequent enough to maintain responding at all, responses occur at a uniform rate. Changes in the frequency of reinforcement change the *slope* of the curves (i.e., the rate of responding). Within limits, the more frequent reinforcement is, the steeper the slope of the curve is.

On FR and FI schedules, the effect of the schedule value is different. Changes in schedule value primarily affect the length of the pause after reinforcement. Once responding occurs, it tends to occur at a high, steady rate whatever the schedule value may be. Small fixed ratios, like FR 10 or FR 20, may result in no postreinforcement pause at all. The cumulative record for an FR like that would look like the cumulative record for the VR in Figure 7–2. Very large fixed ratios, like FR 200, may produce long postreinforcement pauses, followed by a burst of responses, then another long pause, then another burst, and so on until the ratio is completed. These pauses after responding has begun are taken as signs of what is called *ratio strain*. That is, the value of the ratio is almost too large to maintain responding. Within these limits, fixed-ratio schedules produce patterns of responding like that in Figure 7–2: there is a pause after reinforcement, whose duration varies with the size of the ratio, followed by a uniform, high rate of responding until the ratio is completed.

On FI schedules, the schedule value primarily influences the postreinforcement pause. Well-trained animals may not emit their first response until two-thirds of the interval has elapsed. Once responding starts, one sometimes observes response patterns like those on FR schedules—responding begins at a high rate and stays at that rate until reinforcement. More often, when responding starts, it starts slowly and builds up gradually to the high rate which characterizes the end of the interval. Thus, one observes gentle, elbowlike curves in cumulative records of performance on FI schedules. The pattern is referred to as an *FI scallop*.

SCHEDULES OF REINFORCEMENT IN THE NATURAL ENVIRONMENT

This chapter began by suggesting that intermittency is much more characteristic of reinforcement in the natural human environment than is continuous reinforcement. The study of schedules of reinforcement amounts to the study of the effects of different types of intermittency on behavior. How well do the basic schedules of reinforcement characterize intermittent reinforcement in the real world?

It is not too difficult to find examples of human behavior which are maintained by one or another of the basic reinforcement schedules, and when such examples are found, the pattern of behavior maintained is remarkably like the records in Figure 7–2.

Fixed Ratios

It used to be quite common for factory workers to be paid on a piece-work basis: every hundred suits pressed, or hems sewn, or transmissions installed produced a certain payoff. These fixed-ratio schedules generated very high rates of responding, with brief pauses after each ratio, as shown in Figure 7–2. This kind of salary arrangement was very desirable to management for a variety of reasons. It maintained high outputs. In addition, it made wages a direct part of unit costs. When business was good, and much was produced, employees earned high wages. When business was bad, employees were given less work, completed fewer ratios, and earned less money. Employers were not required to pay constant wages (as by the hour) independent of whether there was a great deal of work or only a little.

Employees found the piecework system undesirable. This was partly—but not exclusively—because their wages would rise and fall uncertainly from week to week. What made piecework undesirable is that the schedule made employees work too hard to earn their wages. The schedule generated behavior at a rate which left workers nervous and exhausted at the end of the day. It was the daily strain of working at high speeds, and hesitating to rest or go to the bathroom since taking time out would cost money, which made ratio schedules aversive.

One might wonder why employees did not simply slow down. To ask this question is to assume that individuals have autonomous control over their actions. The view of the behavioral engineer is that the source of control over behavior lies largely in the environment, not in the individual. That people work at high rates which they find aversive is no surprise; that is simply the effect of ratio schedules on the behavior of people. The faster one responds, the more frequent is reinforcement. Slowing down costs. Even if one is willing to decrease the frequency of reinforcement by decreasing response rate, one cannot intentionally slow down to a comfortable rate. The ratio schedule will generate a high rate. One's only alternative is to escape the situation. This, indeed, is what more and more employees have done as their unions have been able to exercise control over management. Piecework systems have been replaced by hourly wage systems. It is difficult for one to change the pattern of behavior which is generated by a reinforcement schedule, but one can change the schedule.[2]

Variable Ratios

In the case of variable-ratio schedules, there appears to be a natural environment example which fits the laboratory case perfectly. Slot machines are programmed to pay off on variable-ratio schedules. The

2. Pigeons apparently have the same reaction to ratio schedules as people do. If a pigeon that is pecking a lit key for food reinforcement on a ratio schedule is given the opportunity to peck another lit key, the sole consequence of which is to turn off the light on the ratio key briefly, the pigeon will reliably peck this key to "escape" from the ratio. There is no alternative source of food, so this behavior gains nothing but temporary respite from the ratio schedule. Despite the clear aversiveness of the ratio schedule, when the ratio key is lit, the pigeon's behavior conforms to the model of ratio-schedule performance depicted in Figure 7–2. (See Appel, 1963, for an example.)

passage of time between coin insertions has no effect on the likelihood of payoff; only responses are relevant. As anyone who has ever fed coins into slot machines can attest, this reinforcement schedule generates a high and steady rate of responding.[3]

Variable Intervals

Variable-interval schedules also appear to be relatively easy to find in the human environment. Imagine trying to complete a telephone call when the line is busy. Reinforcement depends on both a response (dialing the number) and the passage of time; the more time passes, the more likely it is that the number you want will not be busy. Consider also the way in which most parents attend to the cries of their young children. While some parents reinforce each response, most expect their infants to occupy themselves periodically without parental attention, and allow their infants to fuss for a while before attending to them. The requirement for reinforcement is both the passage of time and the occurrence of a response (crying). The schedules operative in both of these situations generally result in a steady rate of responding, as depicted in Figure 7–2.

Fixed Intervals

It is difficult to find pure examples of fixed-interval schedules operating in the natural environment. While there are a large number of situations which are fixed-interval-like, most of them differ in one or more important respects from FI schedules as studied in the laboratory. Consider a few examples. Most people are paid salaries at regular intervals—one week, two weeks, or a month. The schedule in operation seems to be an FI. However, what is the response which

3. People who play slot machines are often reluctant to leave them, especially if they have emitted a large number of unreinforced responses. Their concern is that as soon as they leave, someone else will win all the money they have just deposited. Their understanding about slot machines is that the likelihood of a payoff increases as the number of unreinforced responses increases. There are ways to program variable-ratio schedules where this conception is true. On VR schedules which are comprised of a fixed set of different ratios, it *is* the case that the probability of reinforcement increases as the number of unreinforced responses increases. However, there are other ways to program VR schedules so that the probability of reinforcement is constant no matter how many unreinforced responses have just occurred. This schedule is sometimes called a *random ratio* instead of a variable ratio. This is the way slot machines are programmed, so that one's chances of a jackpot are independent of the number of unreinforced responses which have just occurred. This same distinction also applies to interval schedules. On variable-interval schedules composed of a finite set of intervals, the probability of reinforcement increases as time passes; on *random interval* schedules, the probability of reinforcement is constant from moment to moment.

is actually reinforced? Perhaps it is walking to the pay window or to one's mailbox. Reinforcement depends upon both the passage of a fixed amount of time and the occurrence of this response. Thus, walking to the pay window is reinforced on an FI schedule. But reinforcement also depends upon behavior *during* the interval. Walking to the pay window is reinforced only if one has done his job all week long. On true FI schedules, behavior during the interval is irrelevant.

When pigeons are exposed to a schedule which is more like the standard work week than is the FI, an interesting effect is observed. In one experiment, pigeons were trained to peck a key for food on an FI 15-min schedule. When performance was stable, the pigeons were making about 300 responses in each interval. The experimenters then introduced a fixed-ratio requirement in addition to the FI. In order to produce food, the pigeons had to peck the key x times during the 15 minutes (x varied from procedure to procedure). This additional contingency substantially *reduced* the amount of pecking that occurred.[4] Thus, there is reason to believe that the pattern of behavior maintained on weekly pay schedules will differ from behavior patterns maintained on FI schedules.

As another example, consider cooking, or, more accurately, checking on the progress of the items being cooked. The required cooking time of most dishes is fixed, and checking on stews or breads or roasts before that time has elapsed has no effect. Once the time has elapsed, checking the progress of the item is reinforced. Thus, cooking seems like a perfect example of an FI. However, consider what would happen if the required cooking time were 1 hour and one checked after 2 hours. The dish would be overcooked and ruined. Thus, reinforcement for "checking the roast" depends upon a response after time x, *but before time y.* On ordinary FI schedules, this additional requirement, called a *limited hold,* is not present. When a limited hold is added to an FI schedule, the behavior of a pigeon looks more like FR behavior than FI behavior.

As a final example, imagine taking a course in which a paper was required every 2 weeks. The reinforcer for writing the paper would presumably be the completion of the assignment and satisfaction of the course requirement. While the reinforcement contingency bears some similarity to an FI schedule in that the interreinforcement intervals are regularly spaced, the actual contingency between responses and reinforcement is the opposite of an FI. Responses during the interval are reinforced. Responses after the interval has elapsed (late papers) are not reinforced, and may even be punished. Despite this

4. Herrnstein and Morse, 1958.

seemingly large difference between an FI schedule and the writing of bi-weekly papers, the pattern of behavior observed in courses which require work of this sort very much resembles an FI scallop. After a paper is turned in, the student does little or nothing for a few days (perhaps a week), then does occasional work for a few days, and finally works at a very high rate as the interval draws to a close. The fact that one observes FI-like behavior patterns even though the schedule is not an FI raises a question about just what facet of FI schedules (and schedules in general) determines the patterning of behavior in time. Is it a general relation between rate of responding and rate of reinforcement that determines schedule performance? Is it simply the temporal pattern of reinforcement, independent of the responses which produce it? Or is it something about the relation between response rate and reinforcement at the moment in which reinforcement occurs? To begin to consider these possibilities, we must turn to an analysis of the mechanisms by which reinforcement schedules control behavior.

ANALYSIS OF REINFORCEMENT SCHEDULES

In discussing the different patterns of responding maintained by different schedules, we will focus on two questions: first, why do fixed schedules produce different behavior patterns than variable schedules, and second, why do ratio schedules produce higher rates of responding than interval schedules?

The Post-Reinforcement Pause

Attempts to answer the first question have focused on the analysis of the post-reinforcement pausing which occurs on both FI and FR schedules. With respect to the pause observed on FI schedules, both the FI schedule and the pattern of responding it maintains resemble Pavlovian delay conditioning. In discussing delay conditioning in Chapter 4, we provided evidence that responding is actively inhibited early in the CS. The evidence comes from studies in which a novel stimulus, which inhibits whatever underlying process is currently active, is presented both early and late in the CS. When it is presented late, CRs which ordinarily occur stop; when it is presented early, CRs which do not usually occur are produced. This inhibition of inhibition (disinhibition) by a novel stimulus indicates that Pavlovian delay conditioning produces inhibition of CRs early in the CS. The same kinds of experiments have been performed with FI schedules, and the uniform result is that a novel stimulus presented early in the interval results in the occurrence of operant responses.[5] Thus, the FI scallop seems to result from temporal inhibition which is analogous if not identical to the inhibition which Pavlovian delay conditioning procedures produce.

Since on fixed-ratio schedules the duration of the post-reinforcement pause is directly related to the size of the ratio, it would seem reasonable to speculate that the two are causally related: that the number of responses for reinforcement determines the length of the post-reinforcement pause.[6] However, the situation is not that simple. Once responding begins on a fixed ratio, it tends to occur at roughly the same rate whatever (within broad limits) the size of the ratio. Thus, an animal will pause longer after reinforcement on an FR 200 schedule than on an FR 50, but once it begins to respond, response rate on the two FR schedules will be very similar. What this means is that the time between reinforcements on a ratio schedule is directly related to the number of responses required; FR 50 and FR 200 differ both in the response requirement (determined by the experimenter) and the interreinforcement interval (determined by the animal). It is therefore possible that pauses on FR schedules are controlled by time in the same way that pauses on FI schedules are controlled by time: that the FR pause reflects inhibition of delay. In an experiment which compared post-reinforcement pauses on ratio and interval schedules in which interreinforcement times were identical, there was no difference in response patterning on the two schedules.[7] This suggests that the post-reinforcement pause which occurs on FR and FI schedules is the product of temporal inhibition in both cases. The implication is that if a novel stimulus is presented during the post-reinforcement FR pause, disinhibition will occur and responses will result. This experiment has not been done.[8]

While it is theoretically neat and simple to explain post-reinforcement pausing on FR and FI schedules by a single mechanism, this should not suggest that the two types of schedules have identical effects on behavior. When responding occurs, it is almost invariably at a higher rate on FR schedules than on FI schedules. Similarly, as depicted in Figure 7–2, response rate is higher on VR schedules than on VI schedules. How are we to explain this difference in response rate between ratio and interval schedules, whether fixed or variable?

5. Flanagan and Webb, 1964; Hinrichs, 1968; Singh and Wickens, 1968.
6. Felton and Lyon, 1966.
7. Killeen, 1969.
8. The possibility that both FI and FR schedules produce temporal inhibition assumes that animals exposed to these schedules are sensitive to the temporal regularity of food delivery. There is substantial evidence in support of this assumption, at least in the case of FI schedules. See Staddon and Innis, 1969; Catania, 1972; and Kello, 1972.

Reinforcement Schedules as
Strengtheners of Responding

One of the factors which influences response rate on any schedule is the rate of reinforcement. Thus, response rate is higher on a VI 1-min schedule than on a VI 2-min schedule. In general, the more frequent reinforcement is on any schedule, the more frequent responding is.[9] Thus, reinforcement might be said to strengthen (increase in frequency) responding, and the more frequently reinforcement occurs, the more responding will be strengthened. On an interval schedule, reinforcement will never be more frequent than the value of the interval. Responding will be strengthened to some level, depending on the value of the interval, and remain fairly steady at that level. Whether the animal responds 10 times per minute or 100 times per minute, reinforcement on a VI 2-min schedule will occur no more than 30 times an hour. On the other hand, on a ratio schedule there will be a dynamic interaction between response rate and reinforcement rate. The organism will respond at some moderate rate and produce reinforcement. The reinforcement will increase the frequency of responding. This in turn will increase the frequency of reinforcement, which will increase the frequency of responding still more, which will increase the frequency of reinforcement still more, and so on, until some physical limit of response rate is reached.

On ratio schedules, unlike interval schedules, response rate directly determines reinforcement rate: a response rate of 10 per minute on FR 50 will produce 12 reinforcements per hour while a response rate of 100 per minute will produce 120 reinforcements per hour. This relation between response rate and reinforcement rate on ratio schedules can explain why response rate is higher on ratio schedules than on interval schedules. It can also explain why pieceworkers work at rates which they find aversive: the faster they work, the more frequent is reinforcement. The more frequent reinforcement is, the faster they work, and so on.

If this account of the difference between interval and ratio schedules is correct, we would expect that ratio and interval schedules which provided identical frequencies of reinforcement would maintain identical rates of responding. Since on ratio schedules the subjects and not the experimenter determine rate of reinforcement, this straightforward proposition is not so easy to test. One way to do it is to use what is called a yoking procedure. One set of animals is exposed to a variable-ratio schedule. The rate of reinforcement is determined by the rate at which animals respond; it is beyond the experimenter's

9. See Catania and Reynolds, 1968; Herrnstein, 1970.

control, and likely to be different from one animal to the next. For each animal exposed to the VR schedule, there is a matched or yoked animal in another chamber. Whenever the VR animal produces reinforcement, reinforcement becomes available to the yoked animal for its next response. Effectively, the yoked animal is being exposed to a VI schedule, the value of which is determined by the obtained rate of reinforcement of the VR animal. Suppose, for example, that the VR animal is exposed to a VR 50 schedule, and the first 10 ratios of the schedule are those depicted in Figure 7–3. This hypothetical animal responds 50 times per minute. The reinforcements are obtained at the intervals shown in Figure 7–3. These intervals constitute a VI schedule (in this case, VI 1-min) for the yoked animal. If rate of responding is a direct function of rate of reinforcement, then the VI animal should respond at roughly the same rate as the VR animal. If,

Required Ratio	Time to Complete Ratio
20	24 sec
60	72 sec
75	90 sec
35	42 sec
25	30 sec
85	102 sec
15	18 sec
40	48 sec
80	96 sec
65	78 sec

Total   500   600 sec

Average   50   60 sec

Figure 7–3. Hypothetical Behavior of an Animal on a VR 50 Schedule. *The value of each ratio is depicted on the left and the time to complete the ratio is on the right. These times would determine the values of a VI schedule for an animal yoked to the VR animal. A single response after the appropriate amount of time had elapsed would produce reinforcement. A yoking procedure like this one would permit comparison of response rates maintained by VR and VI schedules when the frequency and temporal pattern of reinforcements provided by these schedules was identical.*

on the other hand, there is something else about the reinforcement schedules in addition to the rate of reinforcement they provide which determines response rate, then the response rates of the VR and yoked VI animals might differ.

When this experiment was performed initially, four pigeons were exposed to a VI schedule of reinforcement. Then two pigeons were shifted to VR schedules while the other two became their yoked, VI partners. Despite the identical frequency and distribution of reinforcements on VR and yoked VI, the VR animals responded three to four times as rapidly as the VI animals.[10]

A few years ago, the experiment was repeated in the author's laboratory, using rats as subjects. After a few weeks of exposure to a VI 1-min schedule, the 20 rats were divided into 10 pairs with the members of each pair matched as closely as possible for rate of responding on the VI schedule. Then, one member of each pair was exposed to a VR 40 schedule while the other member was exposed to a yoked VI. After 15 sessions like this, the conditions were reversed: yoked VI rats were shifted to VR 40 and VR 40 rats were shifted to yoked VI. The results are presented in Figure 7–4. The VR schedule maintained substantially more responding than the yoked VI schedule and when the animals exposed to each type of schedule were switched, response rates also switched to match the schedule. It seems clear, therefore, with rats as well as pigeons, that ratio schedules maintain higher rates of responding than interval schedules, even when the frequency of reinforcement on both schedules is identical. An account of the control of behavior by reinforcement schedules which is based solely upon the relation between response rate and reinforcement rate is leaving out something important: the possibility that different types of reinforcement schedules actually shape or select particular patterns of responding.

Reinforcement Schedules as Selectors of Response Rate

Unlike interval schedules, ratio schedules reinforce different response rates differently. Low rates of responding are followed by reinforcement less frequently than high rates of responding. Consider the possibility that animals can detect the rate at which they respond: that response rate, or, more precisely, the time between responses (*interresponse time* or *IRT*) can be an effective stimulus for an animal. If this is so, then it is possible that animals can learn that short inter-

10. Ferster and Skinner, 1957, pp. 400–406; see also Thomas and Switalski, 1966.

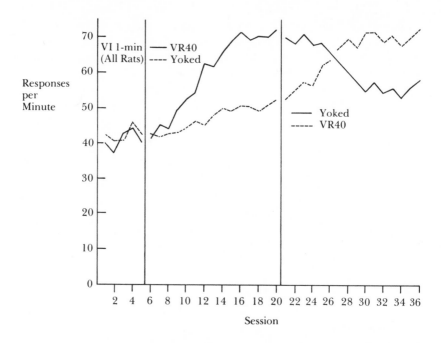

Figure 7–4. A Yoked VR–VI Experiment. *Rate of responding over sessions is averaged across 10 rats in each of two groups exposed to a VI 1-min schedule and then to a VR 40–yoked-VI procedure. After five sessions of VI 1-min reinforcement, 10 rats were exposed to a VR 40 schedule and 10 to a yoked VI schedule. After about 10 sessions, the rats on the VR 40 schedule were responding about 20 times per minute more than the rats on the yoked-VI schedule, although reinforcement frequency was equal for the two groups. When the yoked-VI rats were switched to VR, their response rates increased about 20 responses per minute. Similarly, when the VR rats were switched to yoked VI, their response rates decreased about 15 per minute.*

response times (IRTs) are followed frequently by reinforcement, while long IRTs are followed only infrequently by reinforcement. If animals could learn this, how would it influence their behavior? Clearly, we would expect them to emit many more short than long IRTs. Just as an animal learns that pecks on a red key produce food while pecks on a green key do not, and subsequently emits almost all of its pecks when the key is red, so also an animal might learn that pecks with short IRTs produce food far more frequently than pecks with long IRTs, with the result that most of its pecks have short IRTs.

A mechanism of this sort can easily explain the difference in responding between ratio and interval schedules. Figure 7–5 presents the frequency of reinforcement which would obtain on different ratio and interval schedules if animals were responding at different rates. For the sake of simplicity, it is assumed that responses occur at constant intervals, that is, for a given rate of responding, every IRT is the same.

Response Rate (IRT in Seconds)

Schedule	10 (6 sec)	20 (3 sec)	50 (1.2 sec)	100 (0.6 sec)
FI (VI) 1-min	63	61.5	60.6	60.3
FI (VI) 5-min	303	301.5	300.6	300.3
FR (VR) 50	300	150	60	30
FR (VR) 250	1500	750	300	150

Figure 7–5. Effect of Response Rate on Reinforcement Rate on Different Reinforcement Schedules. *The rows indicate different reinforcement schedules and the columns indicate different response rates. The entries in the cells indicate the average time between reinforcements (in seconds) when a particular response rate occurs on a particular schedule.*

For the interval schedules (first two rows) variations in response rate between 10 and 100 responses per minute produce a minimal change in rate of reinforcement. On a VI 5-min schedule, 10 responses per minute will produce a reinforcement every 303 seconds on the average, while 100 responses per minute will produce reinforcement every 300.3 seconds. The extra 90 responses per minute result in only a trivial increase in reinforcement rate.[11]

For ratio schedules, frequency of reinforcement is dramatically af-

11. To see why response rate has any effect at all on reinforcement rate on VI schedules, imagine an animal responding once every 10 seconds. When reinforcement becomes available, the animal will be somewhere in the midst of its pause between responses. If it has just responded, it will not respond again for 10 seconds. Thus, reinforcement will come 10 seconds later than it might have. If, on the other hand, the animal has paused 10 seconds, then it will respond just as reinforcement becomes available. In this way, the same programmed interval between reinforcements, e.g., 60 seconds, can effectively be a 60-second interval or a 70-second interval. If we assume that on the average the animal will be in the middle of its pause when reinforcement becomes available, then 5 seconds will be added to the programmed interreinforcement interval and a VI 60-second schedule will effectively be a VI 65-second schedule. If, however, the animal responds once a second, then a VI 60-second schedule will effectively be a VI 60.5-second schedule. This is the reasoning behind the computation of interreinforcement intervals in Figure 7–5.

fected by response rate. Ten responses per minute will produce a reinforcement on VR 250 every 1500 seconds (25 minutes); 100 responses per minute will produce a reinforcement every 2.5 minutes. Thus, on ratio schedules short IRTs produce payoffs far more frequently than long IRTs. On interval schedules, IRT length has almost no effect on reinforcement rate. Just as we would not expect an organism to respond differently to a red key than a green key if pecks on both keys provided the same frequency of reinforcement, so also we would not expect short IRTs to dominate longer ones on interval schedules.[12] Since response rate varies inversely with the average IRT (response rate = 1/average IRT) we would expect schedules which select short IRTs to maintain higher response rates than schedules which select no particular IRTs. Thus, the difference in responding maintained by ratio and interval reinforcement schedules can be explained in terms of the selection of particular, short IRTs by the former but not the latter.

Reinforcement Schedules as Strengtheners and Selectors of Response Rate

If reinforcement simply strengthened behavior, that is, increased its frequency, we would expect that the more frequently reinforcement occurred, the more frequently responding would occur. We would expect IRTs to get shorter and shorter as reinforcement became more and more frequent. As we have already seen, this is sometimes true. However, such a view cannot explain the differences in response rate maintained by different types of schedules which deliver reinforcement at the same rate. For example, the VR–yoked-VI experiment showed that ratio schedules maintain higher response rates than interval schedules when both provide the same frequency of reinforcement. The view that reinforcement selects response rates can explain these schedule differences. However, it cannot explain the changes in response rate which occur when the frequency of reinforcement on a single schedule is varied. Why is response rate higher on a VR 25 schedule than on a VR 200 schedule? Both schedules should select the same IRTs. Similarly, why is response rate higher on a VI 1-min schedule than on a VI 3-min schedule?

It appears that neither the strengthening view nor the selecting view can account for all of the phenomena observed in the study of reinforcement schedules. It must be the case that reinforcement does

12. See Morse, 1966.

both things: it strengthens the responses on which it depends, and it selects the responses on which it depends.[13]

THE SIGNIFICANCE OF SCHEDULES OF REINFORCEMENT

Early in the chapter, we suggested a number of natural human situations (like the piecework system of wages) in which reinforcement delivery seemed to conform to one or another schedule of reinforcement. Although continuous reinforcement (CRF) was uncharacteristic of the natural environment, intermittent reinforcement, in accord with one or another schedule, typified reinforcement in the natural environment. While this chapter has suggested no reason to doubt the assertion that reinforcement in the natural environment is intermittent, there is good reason for skepticism about the relevance of the analysis of schedules of reinforcement in the laboratory to the operation of intermittent reinforcement outside the laboratory.

Schedules of reinforcement seem to shape or select particular rates of responding; interresponse time (IRT) analysis provides a crucial component of our understanding of how schedules work. But how often does one observe people emitting the same response over and over again until reinforcement occurs? Though reinforcement for working is intermittent, most jobs require a variety of different responses. A secretary who has just finished typing a letter when his or her paycheck arrives will not repeat that response (retype the letter) or even, necessarily, emit a similar reponse (type another letter) because typing produced reinforcement. The secretary will also answer the telephone and take dictation and file correspondence even though these responses have not just been followed by reinforcement. Though there is no doubt that there will be a general correlation between the frequency of all of these responses and the frequency (or more likely, the magnitude) of reinforcement, it is quite unlikely that a weekly paycheck will reinforce particular IRTs between letters typed or phones answered.

Human behavior tends not to be repetitive in the way that key pecks and lever presses are. What we mean by response "strength" is that at any point in time, or in any particular situation, some response may be very probable (e.g., lifting up the telephone receiver when the phone rings). However, what that means is that the behavior is likely to occur *once* at that time—more likely than some other behavior. The

13. Morse, 1966, p. 81.

study of intermittent reinforcement tells us that such behavior will continue to be probable even if it is only occasionally followed by reinforcement. In order for our understanding of schedules of reinforcement to be usefully applied to the natural environment, there will have to be some way to connect rate of responding in the laboratory to the probability of one response rather than another, or of time apportioned to one activity rather than another in the real world.

It has been assumed that by measuring rate of responding one could estimate probability; the more frequently something occurred over time, the more likely it was to occur at any particular moment. Thus, response *rate* could be viewed as an index of response *probability*. That animals respond at higher rates on ratio schedules than on interval schedules would mean that ratio reinforcement makes a response more probable at any given moment than does interval reinforcement. The view that response *rate* can be translated simply and directly into response *probability* seems to answer the concerns just expressed about the relation between schedules of reinforcement in the laboratory and intermittent reinforcement in the natural environment.

Unfortunately, perhaps the most significant implication of the view that reinforcement schedules *select* response rates is that response rate cannot be taken as an index of response probability. Indeed, IRT analysis seems to eliminate response rate as an *index* of anything. Rate of responding is itself shaped or selected by reinforcement. It is as much a property of the operant as is its force and its locus. Just as one cannot use the locus of the response as an index of anything other than the contingency of reinforcement in operation, so also one cannot use response rate as an index of anything except the schedule in effect. That an organism responds 80 times a minute on a VR schedule and 40 times a minute on VI does not mean that response strength is greater on the VR than the VI; it only means that different responses (short vs. long IRTs) are being reinforced. In situations in which behavior is not repetitive, response *rate* cannot be shaped. Thus it seems that reinforcement schedules work as they do precisely because the target behavior is repetitive. If it were not, IRT analysis would not make sense. But if this is the case, then IRT analysis (and, as a consequence, schedule analysis) cannot be applied to intermittent reinforcement in the natural environment, nor can response probability in the natural environment be inferred from response rate in the laboratory.

Thus, our understanding of schedules of reinforcement poses a serious problem for the very methods used to study them. The analysis of behavior has taken response rate as its primary measuring instrument. But rate of responding is suspect as a measuring instrument. What can be used to replace it or supplement it? Since we are primarily interested in the probability of a particular response relative to others, or in the time spent in a particular activity relative to others, perhaps we can study these variables directly. Perhaps we can give organisms a choice among alternative responses and take their preference for one alternative over another as our primary measuring instrument.

THE STUDY OF CHOICE: CONCURRENT SCHEDULES OF REINFORCEMENT

Suppose a pigeon is confronted with two response keys, pecks on each of which produce food on a VI schedule. A well-trained pigeon will peck a few times on one key, then switch to the other, then switch back to the first, and so on, obtaining reinforcement for pecks on both keys. Procedures of this type are referred to as *concurrent schedules,* which are more generally defined as two or more schedules which operate simultaneously and independently, each for a different response. The behavior of animals exposed to concurrent VI schedules is remarkably reliable. It turns out that responses are emitted to the two keys (or levers) in direct proportion to the frequency of reinforcement obtained for those responses. If we call the response keys A and B, then

$$\frac{\text{Responses on A}}{\left(\begin{array}{c}\text{Responses}\\\text{on A}\end{array}\right) + \left(\begin{array}{c}\text{Responses}\\\text{on B}\end{array}\right)} = \frac{\text{Reinforcements on A}}{\left(\begin{array}{c}\text{Reinforcements}\\\text{on A}\end{array}\right) + \left(\begin{array}{c}\text{Reinforcements}\\\text{on B}\end{array}\right)}$$

or

$$\frac{R_A}{R_A + R_B} = \frac{r_a}{r_a + r_b}$$

The relative frequency of responding on an alternative matches the relative frequency of reinforcement for responses on that alternative. This relation is called the *matching law.*[14]

This matching law provides an accurate description of the behavior of a wide variety of organisms in a wide variety of choice situations. It is as true of lever-pressing rats as of key-pecking pigeons; it is as true

14. See Herrnstein, 1970.

of situations involving aversive stimuli as of situations involving food.[15] Similarly, it is as true for differences in magnitude or delay of reinforcement between two alternatives as for differences in frequency of reinforcement.[16]

How does the use of choice as an index of behavior control free us from a dependence upon response rate and all the problems it entails? After all, choice is merely one response rate divided by another. If the two components of the ratio are imperfect indices of responding, will the ratio not be just as imperfect?

To answer these questions, we must consider two different ways that matching might come about. One possibility is that an animal confronted with two alternatives will spend about half of its time responding on each, but will respond on the two at different rates. Thus, on a concurrent VI 2-min VI 4-min schedule, a pigeon might peck the VI 2 key 60 times a minute when it is pecking the VI 2 key at all, and peck the VI 4 key 30 times a minute when it is pecking that key at all, but spend about the same total amount of time pecking each key. A second possibility is that the animal will peck both keys at the same rate, but spend twice as much time pecking the VI 2 key as the VI 4 key. The ratio $R_A/(R_A + R_B)$ is usually computed over an entire session, so if the animal followed either strategy the result would be matching.

To see this, consider a concrete example. Suppose a pigeon is exposed to 1-hour sessions of a concurrent VI 2 VI 4 reinforcement schedule. If the pigeon divides its time equally between the two keys, but responds 40 times a minute on the VI 2 key and 20 times a minute on the VI 4 key, in the entire session one would obtain 30 (min) × 40 (responses per minute) = 1200 responses on the VI 2 key and 30 (min) × 20 (responses per minute) = 600 responses on the VI 4 key. Now suppose instead that the pigeon pecked both keys at a rate of 30 times per minute, but spent 40 minutes on the VI 2 key and 20 minutes on the VI 4 key. This would result in 30 (responses per min) × 40 (min) = 1200 responses on VI 2 and 30 (responses per min) × 20 (min) = 600 responses on VI 4. The end result in both cases is the same:

$$\frac{R_A}{R_A + R_B} = \frac{1200}{1200 + 600} = \frac{r_a}{r_a + r_b} = \frac{30}{30 + 15} = .67$$

15. deVilliers, 1974.
16. Chung and Herrnstein, 1967; Catania, 1963. For a more general review, see Catania, 1966.

If, in fact, an animal matched response rate to reinforcement rate using the first strategy, then all of the problems with response rate as an index would be true of choice ratios as well. It turns out, however, that animals follow the second strategy. There is now substantial evidence that when animals match, they match the time spent on the alternatives to reinforcement frequency while rate of responding remains fairly constant.[17] Thus, if one evaluates the time spent on each of two alternatives, one can obtain an index of responding which is independent of rate of responding itself. This not only circumvents the problems with response rate as an index of the control of behavior, but it also provides direct assessment of a feature of responding (time spent at an activity) which is more clearly applicable to natural environmental conditions than measures of response rate. Indeed, one would expect that if the concurrent schedules were a VI and a VR which delivered reinforcement at the same rate, time spent on the two schedules would be equal even though response rate on the VR would be higher, due to differential reinforcement of short IRTs.

An Example of the Matching Law

Much recent research on concurrent schedules and choice generally has suggested that choice situations may be an extremely powerful analytic tool. The matching law provides an accurate description of the effects of many different variables on behavior, and it even describes the effects of some of these variables in combination.[18] A particularly impressive example is an experiment which investigated the effects of reinforcement magnitude and reinforcement delay in combination (see Figure 7–6). Pigeons were confronted with two white response keys. If they pecked the right white key 15 times, all the lights in the box went out for 10 seconds. Then the two keys came on again, one red and one green. A peck on the red key immediately produced 2 seconds access to food while a peck on the green key produced 4 seconds access to food, after a delay of 4 seconds. Fifteen pecks on the left white key also turned off all the lights for 10 seconds. Now, however, when the lights came back on only the left key was lit, with green light. A peck on the green key produced 4 seconds of food after a 4-second delay.

What might we expect the pigeons to do in this experiment? Consider first their choice between red and green keys. A red key peck

17. Findley, 1958; Catania, 1966; Baum and Rachlin, 1969.
18. See deVilliers, 1977, for a review.

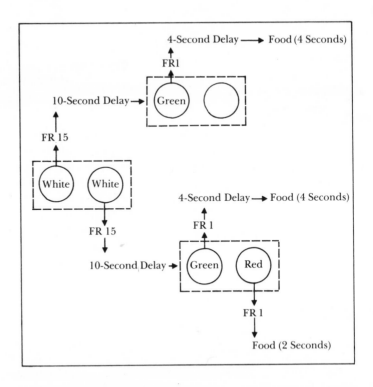

Figure 7–6. Diagram of a Procedure to Study Effects of Magnitude and Delay of Reinforcement on Choice. *Animals are initially confronted with a choice between two white keys. Fifteen pecks on the left key commits them, 10 seconds later, to the availability of 4 seconds of food with a 4-second delay. Fifteen pecks on the right key gives animals a choice, 10 seconds later, between 4 seconds of food with a 4-second delay and 2 seconds of food immediately.*

produces 2 seconds of food immediately while a green key peck produces 4 seconds of food after a 4-second delay. The matching law tells us that relative rate of responding on the two keys will be affected by both the magnitude and the delay of reinforcement, so that:

$$\frac{\text{Responses on red}}{\left(\begin{array}{c}\text{Responses}\\\text{on red}\end{array}\right) + \left(\begin{array}{c}\text{Responses}\\\text{on green}\end{array}\right)} = \frac{\dfrac{\text{Reinforcement magnitude in red}}{\text{Delay in red}}}{\dfrac{\left(\begin{array}{c}\text{Reinforcement}\\\text{magnitude}\\\text{in red}\end{array}\right)}{\text{Delay in red}} + \dfrac{\left(\begin{array}{c}\text{Reinforcement}\\\text{magnitude}\\\text{in green}\end{array}\right)}{\text{Delay in green}}} \quad (1)$$

or

$$\frac{R_{red}}{R_{red} + R_{green}} = \frac{\dfrac{M_{red}}{D_{red}}}{\dfrac{M_{red}}{D_{red}} + \dfrac{M_{green}}{D_{green}}} \tag{2}$$

By substituting the values of M and D arranged in the experiment, we get:

$$\frac{R_{red}}{R_{red} + R_{green}} = \frac{\dfrac{2}{\text{about } 0}}{\dfrac{2}{\text{about } 0} + \dfrac{4}{4}} \tag{3}$$

Since the numerator of this expression approaches infinity, we would predict on the basis of the matching law that most of the pigeons' responses would be on the red key.

Now let us apply the analysis to pecks on left or right when both keys are white:

$$\frac{R_{left}}{R_{left} + R_{right}} = \frac{\dfrac{4}{10+4}}{\dfrac{4}{10+4} + \dfrac{2}{10+0}} = .60 \tag{4}$$

The matching law leads us to expect that the pigeon will choose the left key about 60 percent of the time because at the point of choice between left and right keys a 10-second delay of reinforcement must be added to the delays arranged after pecks at the red or green key.

Now consider how unlikely these two expectations are in combination. We are claiming that the pigeon will prefer the left white key to the right one even though pecks on the left key put the pigeon in a situation in which 4 seconds of food with a 4-second delay is the only possible outcome. When given an immediate choice between that outcome and another one (immediate 2 seconds of food) the pigeon prefers the other one. Thus, even though the pigeon should prefer immediate small reinforcement to delayed large reinforcement (red to green), if we make it commit itself far enough in advance (left white key vs. right white key) it will choose a delayed large reinforcement over an immediate small one.

The results of the experiment confirmed expectations based on the matching law. When choosing between red and green, pigeons pecked red virtually all the time. But when choosing between left and right white keys, they pecked left 65 percent of the time.

It is clear that the variable which will determine which white key the pigeon prefers (everything else held constant) is the time interval between the left–right choice and the red–green choice. There should be some duration between these choices at which pigeons will be indifferent between left and right. We can guess at this duration by turning again to the matching law:

$$
\frac{R_{left}}{R_{left} + R_{right}} = .50 = \frac{\dfrac{4}{x+4}}{\dfrac{4}{x+4} + \dfrac{2}{x}} \tag{5}
$$

By solving for x in this equation, we find the value of x at which pigeons should peck left and right white keys with equal frequency is 4 seconds. When the experimenters systematically varied the time between the initial choice between left and right and the later choice between red and green, they obtained the data presented in Figure 7–7. The prediction, based upon the matching law, that with a delay of 4 seconds between the initial choice and the final response, pigeons should be indifferent between left and right keys, was exactly confirmed.[19]

As the authors of this experiment noted, this particular instance of the matching law has potential therapeutic application. We could characterize the behavior of the pigeon when it is confronted with a choice between red and green as a choice of a less useful outcome (2 seconds of food) over a more useful outcome (4 seconds of food) because the former is immediate. We get the pigeon to choose the more useful alternative when the commitment occurs so far in advance that both outcomes are substantially delayed. Then, the relative immediacy of one outcome over another becomes unimportant. One can imagine many human choices as between immediate small reinforcement and delayed large reinforcement as, for example, the choice between going to the movies and studying on a particular eve-

19. Rachlin and Green, 1972.

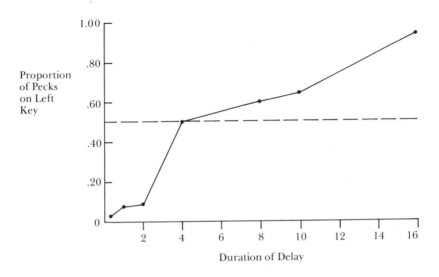

Figure 7–7. A Test of the Matching Law. *The figure depicts the proportion of left-key choices as a function of the delay imposed between early choice and later reinforcement. The point of indifference between left and right keys falls just where the matching law predicts—at 4 seconds delay. (After Rachlin & Green, 1972.)*

ning. If we arranged contingencies so that people had to commit themselves to one or the other outcome well in advance, the chances of commitment to studying rather than going to the movies might increase. It is possible that many problems in "self-discipline" or "self-control" might be ameliorated if contingencies involving early commitment were instituted.

Implications of the Matching Law

This extended example of the power of the matching law has a few implications. First, it shows that the study of choice may allow us to ask and answer difficult questions. In essence, the red and green keys in the example were associated with reinforcers of different *value*. The magnitude of a reinforcer influences its value, and so, apparently, does its delay. The matching law allows us to assess the relative contributions of magnitude and delay to the value of a reinforcer. Moreover, the matching law may allow us to make intelligent comparisons between qualitatively different reinforcers, like food and water. One might reinforce responding on one key with food delivered at a given frequency, then evaluate how frequent water reinforcement for responses on the other key has to be so that the animal is indifferent between the two keys.

More generally, the development of methods for the study of choice speaks to a major philosophical objection to the analysis of behavior as an approach to the nature of action. It is the claim of some philosophers that the essence of human action—indeed, perhaps the defining characteristic of human beings—is that acts are *chosen*. Virtually no human behavior of consequence is of a mechanical, automatic character. While one could construe a simple, single-response situation as involving choice (whether or not to respond at any moment), one can get a good deal closer to what is ordinarily thought of as choice by providing explicit alternatives. And when one does so, one discovers that choice is characteristic of nonhumans as well as humans, and that it obeys a set of concrete, quantifiable, and simple principles.

APPLICATION OF REINFORCEMENT SCHEDULES

As therapeutic instruments, schedules of reinforcement can be extremely valuable. The main problem with behavior therapy is in managing transfer from the therapy situation to the outside environment. One of the major problems one faces is that reinforcement in the natural environment is so intermittent that the newly modified behavior may extinguish. Schedules of reinforcement may provide a solution to this problem, as a result of one of the most reliable phenomena in the realm of operant conditioning—the partial reinforcement effect.

The Partial Reinforcement Effect (PRE)

The partial reinforcement effect (PRE) refers to the finding that extinction after partial reinforcement on one schedule or another is much slower than extinction after continuous reinforcement (CRF). This phenomenon has generated an enormous amount of interest, research, and controversy over the years.[20] The reason for this interest is that the PRE was viewed, when initially discovered, as a paradox. One would assume that the stronger a response is, the more slowly it will extinguish. Further, one would assume that a response which is reinforced every time it occurs will be stronger than a response which is only occasionally reinforced. These two assumptions imply that ex-

---

20. See Amsel, 1958, 1962, 1967, 1972; Capaldi, 1967, 1971; and Mackintosh, 1974, Chapter 8.

tinction after CRF will be slower than extinction after partial reinforcement, yet the reverse is true.

Since extinction after partial reinforcement is slower than after CRF, the behavior therapist has a tool to facilitate the transfer of behavior from the clinic to the outside world. As part of the therapy, one introduces a schedule of reinforcement and gradually decreases the frequency of the reinforcer. In this way, one can help sustain the behavior when the patient encounters intermittency of reinforcement outside the therapy situation. Though little research on the use of partial reinforcement in therapy situations has actually been done, the evidence available at present suggests that it may facilitate transfer from the therapy situation to the outside environment.[21]

Reinforcement Schedules as Research Tools

At present, the major application of schedules of reinforcement is as a research tool for the investigation of other problems. Because reinforcement schedules produce extremely reliable patterns of behavior, the rate and pattern of responding on a particular schedule can be used as a baseline against which to assess the effects of a variety of variables. For example, in recent years research on the behavioral effects of various drugs (behavioral pharmacology) has flourished, owing largely to the use of reinforcement schedules as research tools. One can administer drugs to animals and look for changes in responding on one or another reinforcement schedule. One can evaluate both immediate and cumulative effects of drugs in this way. Since a reinforcement schedule generates the same pattern of behavior day after day, even small fluctuations as a result of drug administration can be taken seriously.

For similar reasons, reinforcement schedules have become an important tool in the study of the relation between behavior and the nervous system. One can destroy various areas of the brain, administer neurochemicals or deplete neurochemicals, and assess the effects of these manipulations against a baseline of stable responding on one or another reinforcement schedule. In this way, one can gain insights into how various parts of the nervous system influence motivation, emotion, and memory among other things.[22]

21. Kazdin and Polster, 1973.
22. See Dews, 1963; Teitelbaum, 1966; Brady and Harris, 1977; Thompson and Boren, 1977; Satinoff and Henderson, 1977.

THE VALUE OF ANALYZING SCHEDULES
OF REINFORCEMENT

We began this chapter by suggesting that schedules of reinforcement go a long way toward extending the analysis of behavior to conditions which were more characteristic of the natural environment than the very simple ones with which the discipline began. The analysis of reinforcement schedules suggested, on the one hand, that reinforcement both increases the frequency of behavior and selects characteristics of behavior, and it suggested, on the other hand, that the applicability of reinforcement schedules to an account of behavior in the natural environment was less obvious than first appeared. The problem lay in the finding that rate of responding could not be taken as a simple estimate of probability of responding. An alternative to response rate is choice (concurrent schedules). The matching law— that relative response rate equals relative reinforcement rate, or magnitude (or perhaps, value)—provides an accurate description of most of the results of choice experiments.

What should one conclude about schedules of reinforcement? Should one conclude, as some have, that an understanding of the control of behavior in general cannot proceed without a thorough understanding of reinforcement schedules?[23] Or should one conclude, as others have, that the significance of reinforcement schedules does not warrant the complexity of analysis which seems necessary to understand them?[24] On balance, the latter view is probably more appropriate:

It may be said that we have the option of whether or not to attempt an exhaustive analysis of schedules. The status of reinforcement schedules in experimental psychology is not coordinate with the status of reproduction in experimental biology. Reproduction is a given and, in the development of biological science, there has been no alternative but to analyze its mechanisms in detail. Schedules of reinforcement, on the other hand, are an invention and it is possible to choose whether or not to analyze in detail the effects they produce. There are interesting analogies between reinforcement schedules as arranged by psychologists and the circumstances of behavior at large. The analogies are, however, probably not as close as popular treatments of reinforcement schedules may suggest. Neither men nor animals are found in nature responding repeatedly in an unchanging environment for occasional reinforcement. In any case, experimental arrangements that resemble natu-

23. Dews, 1963; Reynolds, 1968.
24. Jenkins, 1970; Mackintosh, 1974, especially pp. 181–182.

*ral occurrences are not necessarily the ones best suited to advance the devel-
opment of a science. An important consideration in choosing phenomena for
intensive analysis is simplicity of determination. Neither free operant nor
discrete trial schedules are at all attractive in that respect. There is no need
to allow the complexities of any given experimental arrangement to force
upon us an extensive program of analysis.* [25]

This view of reinforcement schedules is that they may best be considered as an analytical (and therapeutic) tool. And, like all tools,
when they add to rather than diminish the difficulties of the task at
hand, they should be abandoned and replaced by other, more suitable
tools. The study of choice may provide the tool which supplants simple schedules of reinforcement in the analysis of behavior.

25. Jenkins, 1970, p. 107; also in Mackintosh, 1974, p. 182.

8

Discrimination and Generalization

The discussion of operant conditioning in the last two chapters focused almost exclusively on the control of behavior by its consequences. We have seen how a dependency between response and reinforcer shapes and maintains behavior, and how the scheduling of reinforcers influences the occurrence of responses. There is another critical aspect of operant conditioning which we have not discussed. Operant behavior is controlled not only by its consequences, but also by stimuli and events in the environment which precede or accompany the behavior. Animals learn not only that a particular response produces a particular consequence, but also that the consequence is available under particular environmental conditions.

For example, if a pigeon's key pecks are reinforced when the key is green but not when the key is red, the pigeon learns to peck the key only when it is green. What is controlling the pigeon's behavior in a situation of this sort? Certainly, that the pigeon pecks the key at all is the result of the relation between key pecks and reinforcement. However, that the pigeon only pecks the key when it is green must be the result of the relation between green and reinforcement. The pigeon has learned a *discrimination*: it has learned that pecks are followed by reinforcement only in the presence of the green stimulus. As a result, key pecking is controlled not only by reinforcement, but also by the presence of a *discriminative* stimulus—the green key.

Examples of discriminative control of human behavior are ubiquitous. Almost no human behavior is reinforced in all circumstances. People are constantly required to learn the circumstances in which a particular response will be reinforced. For example, learning to cross city streets requires more than learning to step on and off curbs without tripping. It is essential to learn that crossing is reinforced when the light is green, but not when the light is red, and that crossing at the end of the block is reinforced while crossing in the middle is not. The child being taught to cross the street already knows the difference between red and green (as does the pigeon). What must be learned is the difference in the relation between each of these stimuli and the consequences of crossing the street.

While discriminative control of operant behavior may be ubiquitous, it is imperfect. Frequently, behavior which is reinforced under one set of environmental conditions will occur under other, similar conditions. Thus, the pigeon that has learned to peck a green key but not a red key is likely to peck the key if it is yellow. In this case, the pigeon's pecking has *generalized* from familiar training conditions (green key) to new but similar conditions (yellow key). This phenomenon of *stimulus generalization* is as common a characteristic of human behavior as discrimination. The teacher who gives successful lectures at one university may give the same ones when he teaches at a different university. The golfer who swings a seven iron successfully on the fairway may swing the same way in tall grass.

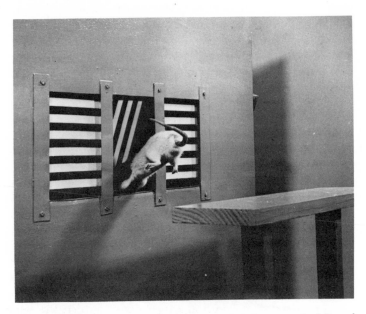

A rat performing a complex discrimination. Reinforcement is delivered only if the rat jumps at the "odd" card, the one that differs from the others. (Photo by Frank Lotz Miller from Black Star.)

This chapter will be concerned with how operant behavior is controlled by stimuli. It will be organized around the phenomena of discrimination and generalization. We will see what they look like in laboratory situations, under what conditions they occur, and what variables affect them. In addition, we will explore a number of theoretical accounts of the processes which underlie them. First, however, let us distinguish the kinds of questions with which the study of discrimination and generalization are concerned from other kinds of questions about the relation between organisms and the stimuli which surround them.

SENSORY CAPACITY, THE PERCEPTUAL WORLD, AND PERCEPTUAL LEARNING

Sensory Capacity

In attempting to delineate the relation between an animal and its environment, there are a number of very different questions one could ask. What stimuli in the environment is the animal capable of detecting? That is, *what are the limits of sensory capacity of the animal?* This question is not concerned with the behavior of the whole animal; it is concerned with the behavior of that animal's sensory systems: vision, audition, smell, taste, etc. Generally, researchers with this interest have attempted to determine the weakest stimulus that each sensory system is able to detect and the smallest difference between two stimuli that each sensory system is able to detect. Just as one can specify the weakest radio signal that an audio receiver is able to pick up, and the receiver's capacity to differentiate signals of different frequency (the different radio stations), so also one would like to be able to specify these characteristics of an animal's auditory system. Research on this problem involves both the study of the physiology of sensory systems and the testing of an animal's ability to "report" the presence of or difference between barely detectable stimuli. The matter of sensory capacity is not the main concern of research on discrimination and generalization. One simply chooses stimuli which are well within the animal's capacity for detection and discrimination.

The Perceptual World

There is a second question one might ask about the behavior of sensory systems, a question which does concern the whole animal. How do internal states of the animal like food deprivation, fear, or reproductive readiness determine what stimuli it will detect from all of the stimuli it is capable of detecting? *What is the perceptual world of an animal at any particular moment?*

The fact is that different species, and even members of a single species at different times, perceive, organize, and respond to their environment differently. The objective world, and the world as seen through the eyes of a human observer, are only a rough approximation of the world as it appears to nonhuman species. Consider a particularly impressive example: if a snail is held suspended by a bracket, and a small stick is placed under its foot, the snail will climb onto the stick if the stick is stationary, and move away from the stick if it is moving. If the stick is tapped against the snail's foot one, two, or three times a second, the snail will turn away. If the stick is tapped four or more times a second, the snail will climb onto it. An object which moves four or more times a second is perceived as stationary by the snail. One-quarter of a second is a "moment" for a snail. For people, a moment seems to be $1/18$ of a second. A number of different sensory systems respond to on-off oscillations more rapid than 18 per second as if the stimuli were always present. Thus, what is "a snail's pace" to a person is not to a snail.[1]

Specifying the perceptual world of a particular species is partly a matter of specifying the sensory capacity of that species. However, other factors also must be considered for sometimes the perceptual world is influenced by the internal state of an animal at a given moment. For example, the herring gull responds to the color of its eggs when it is retrieving them for incubation in the nest. On the other hand, when it is raiding the nests of other birds for food, it responds to the shape of the eggs.[2] Certain butterflies respond to color only when they are seeking food. Though they clearly possess the capacity for color vision, their behavior only reveals this capacity when they are deprived of food.[3]

Perceptual Learning

There is still a third question one might ask about the relation between animals and objects in their environment. Can animals learn to perceive relations among objects or distinctions between objects, and if so, how does such learning occur? From where does the ability to distinguish different letters of the alphabet come? Are all children born with this ability, or do they acquire it? And if they acquire it,

1. See von Uexküll, 1957, for an elegant discussion of the perceptual worlds of animals.
2. Baerends, 1958.
3. Tinbergen, 1951.

what are the important characteristics of the process of acquisition? How does a person learn accurately to distinguish different vintages of a particular variety of wine? While the understanding of *perceptual learning* must be related to the sensory capacity of organisms, it is clear that knowledge of sensory capacity can only establish the limits of perceptual learning—what can and cannot be learned—and not what will be learned and how.[4]

STIMULI AND THE CONTROL OF BEHAVIOR

How do the concerns of the studies of sensory capacity, the perceptual world, and perceptual learning differ from the concerns of the study of discrimination and generalization? These other approaches attempt to specify what events and objects in the environment are perceivable by organisms, or what, in any given situation, the effective stimulus might be. In contrast, students of discrimination and generalization are concerned with identifying the processes by which the stimulus, whatever it is, comes to exert control over behavior. The key word here is "control" (indeed, the phenomena of discrimination and generalization are sometimes subsumed under the heading "stimulus control"). When the pigeon is exposed to discrimination training between red and green, it can already detect the difference between those colors. What it must learn is the relation between each of those colors, pecking, and food. As the pigeon learns the discrimination, we observe the development of control over the pigeon's pecking by the color of the key.

We can illustrate the differences among these different approaches by referring to a standard pigeon experimental situation. Suppose a food-deprived pigeon is trained to peck a green key with grain as the reinforcer. There is an overhead white light (houselight) which provides general illumination of the chamber. There is a wire mesh grid on the floor. An exhaust fan, which ventilates the chamber, provides a steady rumble in the background. Someone with an interest in sensory capacity might wonder whether the pigeon had color vision and, if so, how finely the pigeon could distinguish among different colors. To study this issue, the researcher might establish a procedure in which pecks when the key was green produced food and pecks when the key was red did not. If a difference in responding to red and green developed, the researcher would conclude that pigeons could see color.

---

4. For a discussion of research and theory in the study of perceptual learning, see Gibson, 1970.

The student of the perceptual world of the pigeon might at this point wonder whether the pigeon's perception of color depended in some way on food deprivation. He might feed the pigeon, then create fear by administering painful electric shocks to the pigeon and determine whether color vision was still manifest under these conditions. Alternatively, he might ask what other aspects of the situation were a part of the pigeon's perceptual world. Would the pigeon's behavior be affected if the sound of the exhaust fan ceased, or if the wire mesh floor were replaced by plywood, or if the light on the key flashed on and off rapidly instead of being on constantly?

The student of perceptual learning might wonder whether the pigeon's ability to discriminate colors was the result of previous experiences with colors outside the chamber, and if so, what these particular experiences might have been. Though this question could not be answered for this particular pigeon, other pigeons could be raised under a variety of conditions which differed with respect to experience with color, and then exposed to the red–green discrimination procedure. Differences among the pigeons might elucidate the process by which the discrimination of color develops.

All of these lines of inquiry take for granted the one characteristic of the situation which interests the student of discrimination and generalization—that stimuli correlated in one way or another with reinforcement will control behavior. They all assume that if one stimulus is correlated with food while the other is not, the pigeon will respond differently in the presence of the two stimuli. They would all interpret a failure to observe differential responding as an indication of how the pigeon perceives the stimuli in its environment, and not as an indication of how stimuli control behavior. For the student of discrimination and generalization, it is assumed that differences among stimuli can be detected and the problem is in specifying the conditions which are necessary in order for the stimuli to exert differential control over responding. It is this matter which will concern us in this chapter. We will generally be asking not what is the stimulus, but how does the stimulus control behavior.[5]

OPERANT DISCRIMINATION AND GENERALIZATION

We have already discussed the phenomena of discrimination and generalization in Pavlovian conditioning in Chapter 4. A dog which is exposed to trials in which a tone (CS[+]) is followed by food, while a

---

5. Some researchers have exploited the principles of discriminative control to investigate the sensory capacity of different animals. See Blough and Blough, 1977, for a review.

light (CS⁻) is not, will initially respond to both tone and light. After this initial generalization, the dog begins to respond differentially to the two stimuli: salivation to the tone increases while salivation to the light decreases, approaching zero (see Figure 8–1). If the dog is exposed to tones differing in pitch from the CS⁺, it will salivate to these tones, with the amount of salivation decreasing as the tones become more and more different from the CS⁺. The resulting curve is called an excitatory generalization gradient (Figure 8–2A).

If the dog is exposed to lights differing in hue from the CS⁻, it will salivate to these lights, with salivation increasing as the hues become more and more different from the CS⁻. This U-shaped curve is called an inhibitory generalization gradient (Figure 8–2B).

Successive and Simultaneous Discrimination

The phenomena of discrimination and generalization in operant conditioning parallel those in Pavlovian conditioning, though the procedures used to study them are more varied. In one type of discrimination-learning procedure, called a *successive discrimination,* the stimuli are presented successively, and the animal learns to respond when

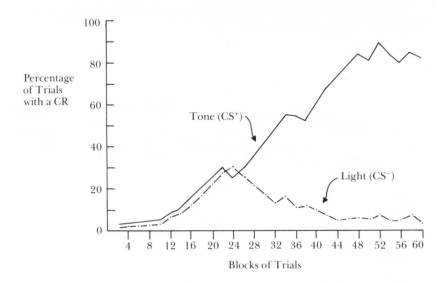

Figure 8–1. Development of a Pavlovian Discrimination. *Initially, the animal responds to both the CS⁺ and the CS⁻. After some training, responding to the CS⁻ drops off while responding to the CS⁺ continues to increase.*

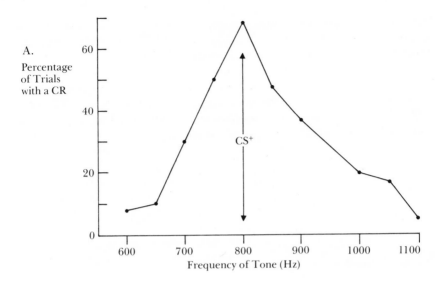

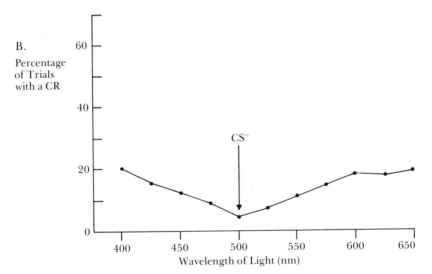

Figure 8–2. Pavlovian Generalization Gradients of Excitation (*A*) with a Tone as CS⁺ and Inhibition (*B*) with a Light as CS⁻. *In* A, *maximum responding occurs to the CS⁺ and drops off systematically as the tones presented are more and more different from the CS⁺. In* B, *minimum responding occurs to the CS⁻ and responding increases as lights are more and more different from the CS⁻.*

one stimulus is present and not when the other stimulus is present, or to make one response in the presence of one stimulus and a different one in the presence of a second stimulus. The example which began the chapter, of the pigeon trained to peck a green key but not a red one, is a successive discrimination procedure. Successive discrimination procedures in which one or the other stimulus is always present, rather than being present during trials and absent during intertrial intervals, is called a *multiple schedule.* Learning to cross streets with traffic lights is analogous to a multiple-schedule procedure. One or the other light, but not both, is always present. Learning to swing only at good pitches in baseball is analogous to a discrete trial successive discrimination. Sometimes an S$^+$ (good pitch) is presented and sometimes an S$^-$ (bad pitch) is presented, and most of the time an intertrial interval (no pitch) is presented.

The second common type of discrimination procedure is called a *simultaneous discrimination.* Here, two stimuli are presented together,

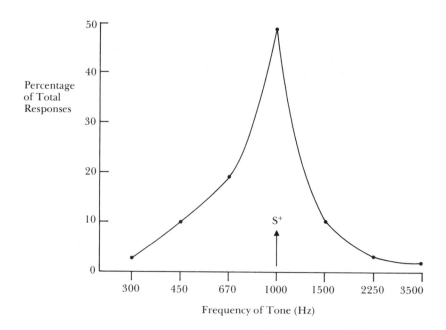

Figure 8–3. Excitatory Generalization Gradient for Tone Frequency in a Pigeon. *The S$^+$ had been a 1,000-Hz tone. The points represent the percentage of all responses made during the generalization test which were made to each particular stimulus. (After Jenkins & Harrison, 1960.)*

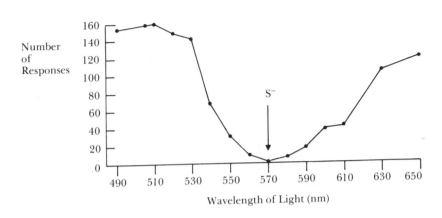

Figure 8–4. Inhibitory Generalization Gradient for Wavelength in a Pigeon. *The S⁻ had been a 570-nm light. Responses increased as the distance between the test stimulus and S⁻ increased. (After Terrace, 1971.)*

and the organism must choose between the alternatives. When the stimuli are always present, the procedure is called a concurrent schedule (see Chapter 7).

When animals are exposed to operant discrimination training, the results are much like those in Figure 8–1; after an initial period in which animals respond to both S⁺ and S⁻, differential control of responding by the two stimuli develops until little or no responding occurs in the presence of the S⁻. When animals are presented with stimuli similar to the S⁺, a generalization gradient much like that in Figure 8–2*A* results. Figure 8–3 presents a generalization gradient for tones of different pitch produced by a pigeon trained to peck a key for food in the presence of a 1,000-Hertz (Hz) tone. Similarly, when animals are presented with stimuli similar to S⁻, a generalization gradient much like that in Figure 8–2*B* results. Figure 8–4 presents a generalization gradient for lights of different wavelength produced by a pigeon for which a stimulus of 570 nanometers (nm) was S⁻.

The similarity between the phenomena of discrimination and generalization observed in operant conditioning procedures and those observed in Pavlovian conditioning procedures certainly suggests that a single account might explain them both. It is not surprising, therefore, that efforts to explain discriminative control of operant behavior have employed concepts which we have already encountered in discussing Pavlovian conditioning. Let us turn, then, to an exploration of the mechanisms which seem to underlie discrimination and generalization.

THE PROCESS OF DISCRIMINATION

Before we can begin to specify the conditions which produce discriminative control, we need a device or procedure with which to detect such control if it is present. Such a device is provided by the generalization test.[6] As Figure 8–3 shows, an animal trained with a particular stimulus as S^+ responds to other, similar stimuli. However, it responds less and less to those stimuli as they become less and less similar to S^+, that is, the generalization gradient has a peak at S^+. The fact that responding changes as the stimulus changes implies that the stimulus is controlling the response. Suppose one administered a generalization test for color to a pigeon that had been trained to peck a green key for food, and one obtained a gradient like that in Figure 8–5A. The gradient is completely horizontal, or flat. Apparently, the pigeon generalizes completely from green to all colors. When flat generalization gradients such as these are observed, we infer that the stimulus dimension being varied (in Figure 8–5A, key color) is not controlling the pigeon's behavior. Why might this be? What can account for the failure of a stimulus to control operant responding?

Predictiveness and Redundancy

To answer this question, let us review some conclusions we reached in Chapter 5 on Pavlovian conditioning. We concluded that in order for conditioning to occur, a differential (predictive) contingency must exist between the CS and the US; if the US is no more likely in the presence of the CS than in its absence, there is no conditioning. If more than one predictive CS is present, then conditioning will occur to the CS which is most predictive. If a number of equally predictive CSs are present, then conditioning might occur to all of them. Alternatively, the presence of one especially salient CS might *overshadow* conditioning to any of the others.

How do these facts relate to the case of the pigeon pecking the green key? Suppose that, by analogy with Pavlovian conditioning, in order for a stimulus to control operant responding, it must be a differential predictor of reinforcer availability. Does the green key meet

6. The generalization test has been the most popular method in recent years for making inferences about the discriminative control of responding by particular stimuli. However, as Mackintosh, 1977, has recently pointed out, it is not the only method, and not always the best one. Alternative tests for discriminative control include removing the putative controlling stimulus altogether and looking for cessation of responding, or transferring the putative controlling stimulus to a new situation and looking for more rapid learning by animals experienced with the stimulus than by inexperienced animals.

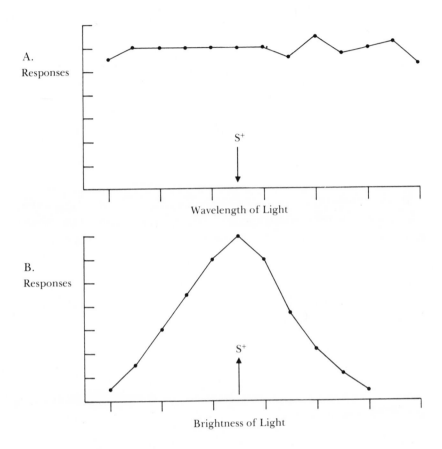

Figure 8–5. Hypothetical Generalization Gradients. *The gradient in A is flat and indicates lack of control over responding by wavelength of light. The peaked gradient in B indicates control of responding by intensity or brightness of light.*

this criterion? Considered in contrast to stimuli outside the chamber, it does. Reinforcement is available in the chamber, but not outside it. Therefore, green is a differential predictor of reinforcer availability. However, green is not the *best* predictor of reinforcer availability. The green key shares its predictive relation to reinforcer availability with the houselight, the wire mesh floor, the sound of the exhaust fan, and a host of other stimuli which are present in the chamber and absent outside it. Any one or more of these stimuli might overshadow the green light and effectively control pecking. Suppose, for example, the pigeon's responding were controlled by the brightness of the key and not by its color. If this were true, then a generalization test in which stimuli were different colors but the same brightness would be presenting the same *effective* stimuli to the pigeon again and again. Though the objective stimulus would be changing as color changed, that aspect of the stimulus which was exercising control would remain constant. Control of key pecking by brightness could be revealed in a second generalization test, one in which the color of the key remained green but its brightness was varied. Such a test might yield the gradient in Figure 8–5B. If so, one could conclude that the stimulus controlling pecking was the brightness of the light on the key and not its color.

When there are a number of redundant (equally predictive) signals for reinforcer availability, which of them will control responding is influenced by a number of factors. First of all, one stimulus may be inherently more salient than the others, and overshadow them. For example, in one study, pigeons were trained to peck a lit key for food in the presence of a tone. Both the tone and the key light were always present as redundant signals for food. After this training, generalization tests for tone frequency yielded flat gradients like the one in Figure 8–5A. In contrast, a second group of pigeons was trained to peck a key in the presence of the tone, but in total darkness. For this group, generalization tests for tonal frequency yielded gradients like the one in Figure 8–5B.[7] Clearly, for the first group of pigeons, the key light overshadowed the tone in controlling pecking.

The relative salience of a stimulus may also be influenced by an animal's past experience. Suppose a pigeon has had previous experience in which a tone was a signal for reinforcer availability. The pigeon is then exposed to a procedure in which a tone and a light are redundant signals. It is likely that the tone will control responding. Without the prior experience with the tone, the light might well control responding. In a confirming experiment, two groups of pigeons were trained to peck a lit key for food in the presence of a 1,000-Hz tone. Key light and tone were redundant signals. Prior to the experiment, one of the groups had received prolonged experience in which the delivery of the daily ration of food to the pigeons in their home cages was signalled by the 1,000-Hz tone. When, after training, both groups were given generalization tests for tonal frequency, the group with no preexperimental experience with the tone produced a flat gradient, as in Figure 8–5A, while the group with preexperimental experience produced a peaked gradient, as in Figure 8–5B.[8] Thus, prior

7. Rudolph and Van Houten, 1977.
8. Thomas, Mariner, and Sherry, 1969. For further supporting evidence, see Lawrence, 1949, 1950.

experience in which a stimulus is a nonredundant signal seems to insure control by that stimulus in situations in which it competes with other equally predictive stimuli.

In summary, we have seen that in situations in which a number of different stimuli bear an equally predictive relation to the availability of food, the particular stimulus which will effectively control responding is largely beyond experimental control. The inherent salience of different stimuli and the relevant past experience of the experimental subject will combine to determine what the effective stimulus will be. The experimenter is not helpless, however. The way to insure control of responding by a particular stimulus is to make that stimulus the best predictor of reinforcer availability. And the way to do this is by discrimination training.

Discrimination Training as a Stimulus Selector

The Best Predictor Controls Behavior • Consider the following experiment. One group of pigeons was trained to peck a green key with a vertical white line superimposed on it. After some training, they were given a generalization test with lines which differed from the vertical in 22.5-degree steps. The resulting flat gradient of generalization is presented in Figure 8–6*A*.

A second group of pigeons was given discrimination training. The vertical line on a green background was the S$^+$; key pecks in its presence produced food. The green key by itself was the S$^-$; pecks in its presence did not produce food. After the pigeons had learned to peck the S$^+$ and not the S$^-$, a generalization test for line orientation was administered. The resulting, sharply peaked gradient, is depicted in Figure 8–6*B*.

Finally, a third group of pigeons was given discrimination training in which green + vertical was the S$^+$ and red without a line was the S$^-$. The subsequent generalization test for line orientation produced the flat gradient depicted in Figure 8–6*C*.[9]

Let us attempt to explain these data. The flat gradient in Figure 8–6*A* suggests that some stimulus other than the line was controlling pecking. Since the line and the green key color and a host of other stimuli were all equally predictive of reinforcer availability, control of responding by the line could have been overshadowed by many different things.

This possibility was eliminated for the pigeons whose data are in

9. Newman and Baron, 1965.

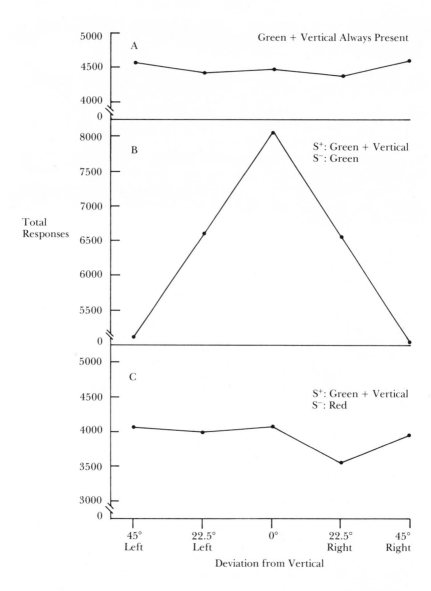

Figure 8–6. Effect of Discrimination Training on Stimulus Selection. *Each part of the figure presents a generalization gradient for line orientation for a different group of pigeons. Group A was simply trained to peck a green key with a white vertical line for food. Group B had green + vertical as an S⁺ and green without vertical as an S⁻. Group C had green + vertical as S⁺ and red without vertical as S⁻. (After Newman & Baron, 1965.)*

Figure 8–6*B*. For this group, pecks were only reinforced when the line was present. Green was also present at this time, as were other aspects of the situation, like the houselight and the exhaust fan. However, green was also present during periods when pecks were not reinforced. Thus, discrimination training established the vertical line as the *best predictor* of reinforcement, with the result that the line controlled pecking, as witnessed by the peaked generalization gradient.

The discrimination training received by the group whose data are in Figure 8–6*C* also established the vertical line as a better predictor of reinforcement than most other aspects of the situation. Environmental stimuli such as the houselight and exhaust fan noise were present during S⁻ periods as well as S⁺ periods. Thus, these stimuli should have been eliminated from competition with the line for control of responding. Notice, however, that the line was not the *best* predictor of reinforcement; the green key was equally good (S⁻ was both the absence of the line and red on the key). The resulting flat generalization gradient suggests that green overshadowed the line and controlled pecking when the two stimuli were equally predictive of reinforcement.

We see, therefore, that discrimination training can be used to insure control of responding by a particular stimulus. It accomplishes this by establishing that stimulus as the best predictor of reinforcement. All other aspects of the environment which might potentially control responding are present all the time, both when reinforcement is available and when it is not. The S⁺ is only present when reinforcement is available.

There are other experiments which support the view that behavior is controlled by the stimulus which is the best predictor of reinforcement. In one such experiment, rats were trained to press a lever with a light always on, with one tone (S⁺) signalling reinforcement availability and another tone (S⁻) signalling nonreinforcement. Under these conditions, the light exerted little control over responding; the tone which was the S⁺ was a better predictor of food than the light. When the procedure was changed so that the two tones were presented but no longer correlated with the availability of the reinforcer (that is, either tone might appear during periods in which reinforcement was available), the light exerted powerful control over responding. The relation between light and food was the same in both procedures; the difference between the procedures was that in the first procedure the tone was a better predictor of food than the light, and in the second procedure there was no better predictor of food than the light.[10]

10. Wagner, Logan, Haberlandt, and Price, 1968.

Discrimination Training and
Incidental Stimuli

The effects of discrimination training need not always be so dramatic, shifting control of responding entirely from one aspect of the situation to another (as suggested by the data in Figure 8–6). It is also possible that in the absence of discrimination training, numerous background or *incidental stimuli* share control of responding so that each of a variety of generalization tests will yield moderately peaked gradients, and that discrimination training eliminates control by all stimuli but the S^+, with the result that the generalization gradient about the S^+ is sharpened.

In a test of this proposition, two groups of pigeons were trained to peck a colored key for food. Generalization tests with other colors yielded a moderately peaked gradient. One of the groups was then given additional training pecking the colored key (now with a white vertical line superimposed on it) and a second generalization test for color. The second gradient was no more peaked than the first one. The other group was given discrimination training: the same color on the key as before was S^+ and a white vertical line on a dark key was S^-. A generalization test for color after this discrimination training produced a much sharper gradient than before.[11]

We can speculate that in the absence of discrimination training, key pecking was controlled by the color of the key in addition to, perhaps, the brightness of the key and a number of aspects of the situation completely unrelated to the key, like the houselight, the noise of the fan, the wire mesh screen underfoot, and so on. If we consider the controlling stimulus to be a compound, including key color and also a host of background or incidental stimuli, then it is not surprising that the pigeons pecked so much at colors other than the training stimulus.[12] When these other colors are presented, other elements of the compound are still present. Thus, when the pigeon pecks at the colored key, it is a peck under the control of color + brightness + fan + houselight, etc. Changing the color of the key represents a rather small change in the total stimulus compound, so that the relatively small change in responding is not surprising.

When we expose the pigeon to a discrimination between the color and the vertical line, the former signalling reinforcer availability and

11. Switalski, Lyons, and Thomas, 1966.
12. The term "incidental stimuli" is often used to refer to background aspects of the environment which may be influencing the response. That these stimuli may influence responding indicates that they are "incidental" from the experimenter's point of view, not the subject's.

the latter signalling its absence, we establish key color as the best predictor of reinforcer availability. By doing this, discrimination training effectively eliminates control of responding by incidental stimuli. No longer is the controlling stimulus a compound which includes color; now, the controlling stimulus is effectively color alone. The colors presented during generalization testing are a lot less similar to the training stimulus under these conditions (when incidental stimuli are irrelevant) than under the previous, nondiscriminative conditions.[13]

Another set of experiments makes this same point about incidental stimuli more graphically.[14] Some pigeons were trained to peck a key for food in the continual presence of a 1,000-Hz tone. A generalization test with other tonal frequencies produced the gradient depicted in Figure 8–7A. Other pigeons learned a discrimination: the 1,000-Hz tone signalled reinforcer availability (S$^+$), and no tone signalled nonreinforcement (S$^-$). This group produced the generalization gradient depicted in Figure 8–7B.

A final set of pigeons also learned a discrimination: the 1,000-Hz tone was S$^+$ and a 950-Hz tone was S$^-$. This group produced the generalization gradient in Figure 8–7C.

Based upon the preceding discussion, we would conclude that the flat gradient in Figure 8–7A is the result of the overshadowing of the tone by other, equally predictive but more salient, "incidental" stimuli. Discrimination training makes the tone a better predictor of reinforcement than any other stimulus, and the result is the peaked gradient in Figure 8–7B, indicating control of responding by the tone. But what aspect of the tone is exercising control? Is it pitch, or loudness, or loudness and pitch in combination? For the group of pigeons whose data are in Figure 8–7C, even this source of competition among potential controlling stimuli is eliminated. The only difference between S$^+$ and S$^-$ is pitch (1,000 Hz vs. 950 Hz). Not only is the tone a better predictor of reinforcement than incidental stimuli, but the frequency or pitch of the tone is a better predictor of reinforcement than any of its other characteristics. As a result, the generalization gradient for tonal frequency produced by this group is even more peaked than the one in Figure 8–7B.

Let us summarize the data in Figure 8–7 as a way of summarizing the entire section. When there is no best predictor of reinforcement, almost any aspect of the experimental situation might control re-

13. This kind of analysis originates with Hull, 1952. See Mackintosh, 1974, 1977, for detailed discussion.
14. Jenkins and Harrison, 1960, 1962.

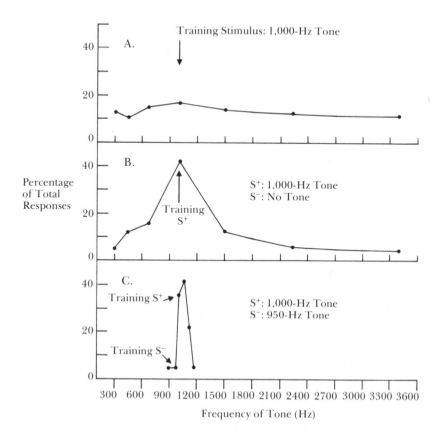

Figure 8–7. Discrimination Training as a Sharpener of Generalization Gradients. *The figure presents the percentage of all responses made during generalization testing which were made in the presence of each different tone. The gradient in A, after nondiscriminative training, is flat. The gradient in B, after discrimination training with a 1,000-Hz tone as S⁺ and no tone as S⁻, is peaked. The gradient in C, after discrimination training between 1,000 Hz (S⁺) and 950 Hz (S⁻) is even more peaked. (After Jenkins & Harrison, 1960, 1962.)*

sponding (Figure 8–7A). When the presence of a tone is established as the best predictor of reinforcement, then one or more aspects of the tone will control responding, and control by incidental stimuli will be eliminated (Figure 8–7B). When the frequency of the tone is the best predictor of reinforcement, then that *specific* aspect of the tone will control responding and control by other aspects of the tone will be eliminated (Figure 8–7C). In general, the way to assure control of responding by any particular aspect of a situation is to make that aspect the best predictor of reinforcement.

Attention

If we were to describe the results in Figure 8–7 less formally, we would be inclined to say that discrimination training teaches animals to *pay attention.* It teaches them on which parts of the environment to focus and which parts to ignore. When a tone is S^+ and no tone is S^-, then the animal learns to pay attention to the tone. When a 1,000-Hz tone is S^+ and a 950-Hz tone is S^-, then the animal learns, more specifically, to pay attention to the frequency of the tone. There is a long history of attempts to investigate attention as a critical part of the process of discrimination learning, and we turn now to a discussion of some of the issues involved in the study of attention.

Consider the following experiment. Two pigeons were trained to peck a key for food. Pecks were reinforced on a VI schedule when the response key had a white triangle superimposed on a red background. When the key had a circle superimposed on a green background, pecks were not reinforced. The pigeons were required to learn a discrimination: pecks at triangle plus red produced food while pecks at circle plus green did not. After a number of sessions, the responding of the two pigeons was well controlled by the stimuli. Figure 8–8*A* depicts the responding which occurred to red–triangle (S^+) and green–circle (S^-).

The question is this: What stimulus or stimuli were in fact controlling the pigeons' pecking? Were red and green controlling responding, or were circle and triangle, or were all four? A way to find out is to occasionally present the four stimuli individually: red without triangle, green without circle, triangle without red, and circle without green. When these tests were performed, the results, depicted in Figure 8–8*B,* were unequivocal. The responding of Pigeon 1 was controlled by color while the responding of Pigeon 2 was controlled by shape. If both color and shape were controlling responding, one might have obtained results like those in Figure 8–8*C.* This experiment is an impressive demonstration that two animals exposed to the identical situation may pay attention to different aspects of the situation with the result that their behavior is controlled by different stimuli.[15]

What does it mean to say that an animal is "paying attention" to a

15. Reynolds, 1961b. There is a peculiar aspect of the data in Figure 8–8. Figure 8–8*B* suggests that Pigeon 1 was responding only to color and Pigeon 2 was responding only to shape. Yet both pigeons pecked their respective controlling stimuli at only half the rate that they pecked red triangles (Figure 8–8*A*). If Pigeon 1 were literally ignoring shape altogether, we would expect responding to red to be roughly equal to responding to red triangles. Perhaps the pigeons responded to a color–shape *configuration* when they were together, but ignored one aspect of the configuration when it was separated into parts.

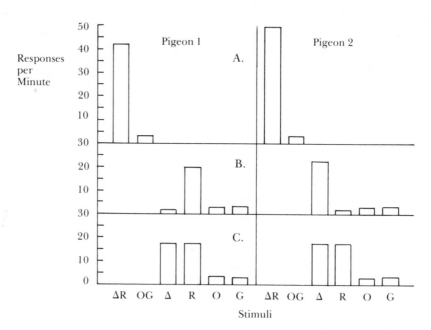

Figure 8–8. Attention in the Pigeon. A. *Responses per minute to red plus triangle and green plus circle by two pigeons that had been subjected to discrimination training in which pecks at red plus triangle produced food while pecks at green plus circle did not.* B. *Responses per minute to the four stimuli when they were presented separately (A and B after Reynolds, 1961b).* C. *Hypothetical responses per minute if both shape and color had been controlling responding.*

stimulus aside from the fact that the animal's responding is controlled by that stimulus? Can we somehow separate paying attention from the more general characteristic of an animal's behavior in a discrimination-learning experiment that it responds appropriately in the presence of the S+ and S−?

These questions have been confronted by numerous investigators over the years. A number of different answers have been proposed, but many have the same general character. Discrimination learning is conceived as a two-step process: first, one learns what stimuli are relevant—what one must pay attention to; second, one learns to do specific things in the presence of specific stimuli.[16] As an example, consider a young child learning to cross city streets. What the child

16. See Lovejoy, 1968; Mackintosh, 1975; Sutherland, 1964; Sutherland and Mackintosh, 1971; Trabasso and Bower, 1968; Zeaman and House, 1963.

might learn first is that traffic lights and vehicles are the relevant stimuli. Then, the child would learn to walk when the light is one color but to wait when the light is a different color, and to walk when the vehicles are stopped or far away, but to wait when the vehicles are moving and close by.

Transfer of Training • Attempts to show that "paying attention" is a separable part of discrimination learning have often involved experiments on *transfer of training*. Animals trained on one kind of discrimination problem are then given a different kind, and the measure of interest is the extent to which training on the first problem affects, or transfers to, learning the second one.

In one kind of transfer-of-training experiment, two groups of subjects first experience different discrimination problems. For example, both groups might receive circles or squares which are red or green. For Group 1, red stimuli are S^+ and green stimuli are S^-, regardless of shape. For Group 2, squares are S^+ and circles are S^-, regardless of color. As the animals master the discrimination, we might imagine the learning process as involving the following steps:

1. For Group 1, color is relevant and shape is irrelevant. That is, color is predictive of reinforcement availability while shape is not. For Group 2, shape is relevant (predictive of reinforcement) and color is not.

2. For Group 1, specifically, red predicts reinforcement and green predicts its absence. Therefore, responses should only occur when red is present. For Group 2, squares predict reinforcement and circles its absence. Therefore, responses should only occur when squares are present.

Alternatively, the discrimination process might involve only a single step—learning specifically about S^+ and S^- and not first about the dimensions (color or shape) of which they are a part.

This phase of the experiment, and a second, test phase, are depicted in Figure 8–9. What might we expect the effects of Phase 1 to be when the groups are exposed to Phase 2, in which blue is the S^+, yellow is the S^-, and diamonds and triangles are irrelevant? Note first that the specific stimuli being employed are all different in Phase 2 from those in Phase 1. However, the relevant dimension in Phase 2 is color—the same dimension that was relevant in Phase 1 for Group 1, but a different dimension from what was relevant in Phase 1 for Group 2. If learning a discrimination involves first learning to attend to the relevant dimension and then learning which specific stimulus is

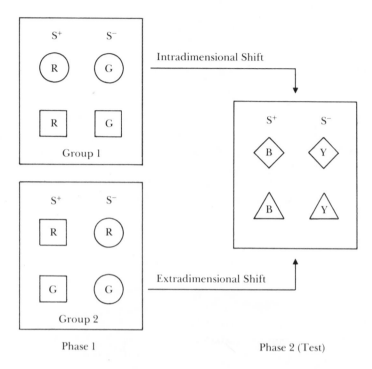

Figure 8–9. The Intradimentional Shift vs. the Extradimensional Shift. *Groups 1 and 2 must learn to respond to blue (S⁺) and not yellow (S⁻) in Phase 2, after prior training. Group 1 has previously learned to respond to red (S⁺) and not green (S⁻). For this group, the new problem represents an* intradimensional shift. *S⁺ and S⁻ are different in Phase 2 from Phase 1, but they are on the same dimension (color). Group 2 has previously learned to respond to squares but not circles. For this group, the new problem represents an* extradimensional shift. *Both the specific S⁺s and the dimension on which they fall are different in Phase 2 from Phase 1.*

S⁺, Group 1, having already learned to attend to color, should learn faster in Phase 2 than Group 2. If, on the other hand, discrimination learning involves simply learning to respond to S⁺ and not S⁻, neither group should be helped more than the other by past experience, since the specific S⁺ and S⁻ (blue and yellow) were not a part of the previous training.

These experiments are described as pitting *intradimensional shift* (different values on the same dimension: blue and yellow instead of red and green, as in Group 1) against *extradimensional shift* (different relevant dimensions: colors as S⁺ and S⁻ instead of shapes, as in Group 2). The reliable observation in rats, pigeons, monkeys, human children, and human adults is that the intradimensional shift is learned faster than the extradimensional shift, providing support for the view that discrimination learning involves learning to pay attention to relevant (predictive) stimulus dimensions.[17] In fact, to be more accurate, the evidence seems clear that discrimination learning involves both learning to pay attention to relevant dimensions and learning to *ignore* irrelevant dimensions. Animals like those in Group 1 in Figure 8–9 seem to learn in Phase 1 not only that color is relevant, but that shape is irrelevant. There is even evidence that learning to ignore irrelevant stimuli may be the major reason for the advantage that Group 1 has over Group 2. For example, if Group 1 subjects are exposed in Phase 1 to a red–green discrimination with all stimuli circles and Group 2 is exposed to a circle–square discrimination with all stimuli red, the difference between the groups in Phase 2 substantially decreases. While Group 1 maintains an advantage over Group 2 in learning to pay attention to color, it no longer has the advantage of learning to ignore shape. And, in the absence of this advantage, the difference between the two groups almost disappears.[18]

The Process of Discrimination
Summary and Conclusions

In learning a discrimination, animals learn to pay attention and to respond to the best predictor of reinforcement. When there are multiple, equally good predictors, they may each control responding, or some may be overshadowed by others. Overshadowing seems to depend upon both past experience with various stimuli and nonexperiential predispositions to perceive some stimuli as more salient than others. Explicit discrimination training establishes one stimulus (the S^+) as a better predictor of reinforcement than any other. As a result, control of responding by that stimulus is enhanced and control of responding by other, incidental stimuli is eliminated. Indeed, animals seem to learn that these other stimuli are irrelevant.

Is this all there is to the matter of discriminative control? The answer is no. Why, in generalization testing, is there a *gradient* of responding? We know that the pigeon has little difficulty distinguishing

17. For demonstrations, see Mackintosh and Little, 1969; Shepp and Eimas, 1964; Shepp and Schrier, 1969; and Wolff, 1967. There are other kinds of transfer-of-training studies the evidence from which also points to paying attention as a critical component of discrimination learning. See Kendler and D'Amato, 1955, and Kendler and Kendler, 1962, for examples, and Sutherland and Mackintosh, 1971, for a critical discussion.
18. Kemler and Shepp, 1971. See Mackintosh, 1973, 1975, for further discussion of "learned irrelevance."

among different colors. The reason it pecks a red key after having been trained to peck a green one is not that it cannot distinguish red from green. Such a discrimination is readily learned when the relation between each of the stimuli and reinforcement availability is different. Nor does it peck the red key because its responding is not controlled by color; the fact that the generalization gradient has a peak at S^+ clearly indicates that key color is controlling responding. It is possible that key color is not the *only* stimulus controlling responding, that is, that stimuli such as the houselight and the fan noise also exert control. If this were so, then during generalization testing for color, these other, incidental stimuli would be present no matter what color was on the key, and might be responsible for the responding which occurred to the different colors. While this account might explain why some responding occurs to colors other than the S^+, it cannot explain why different amounts of responding occur to different colors, as a function of how different they are from the S^+. Thus, there must be more to the phenomena of stimulus control of operant behavior. While the predictiveness of the relation between S^+ and reinforcement availability may account for the *discriminative* control of responding, something else is required to account for the *generalization* of responding.

THE PROCESS OF GENERALIZATION EXCITATION AND INHIBITION

You will recall that we discussed discrimination and generalization in Pavlovian conditioning in terms of the concepts of conditioned excitation and inhibition. Excitation builds up as a CS^+ is followed by food in trial after trial, and inhibition builds up as a CS^- is presented without food. When excitation and inhibition have developed sufficiently, they reliably produce or inhibit the CR. In discussing generalization, Pavlov made clear his view that excitation and inhibition, though conditioned to particular CSs, were not confined to those stimuli. Rather, they were also produced by other stimuli which were similar to the CSs. Similarity could be judged on a variety of dimensions: color, pitch, loudness, brightness, size, location, and so on. The appropriate dimension in any particular situation depended both on the nature of the CS, and on that aspect of the stimulus which controlled the subject's responding. One could judge whether the dimension chosen for study was appropriate by determining whether, in generalization testing, one obtained orderly, peaked gradients like the ones depicted in this chapter (see Figures 8–2*A*, 8–3, 8–5*B*, 8–6*B*, 8–7*B*, and 8–7*C*).

An account of stimulus generalization in operant conditioning which parallels Pavlov's has had a long and prominent history, owing principally to the writings of Kenneth W. Spence.[19] Spence's theory of discrimination and generalization states that when a stimulus is associated with reinforcement, a gradient of excitation develops around that stimulus. Peak excitation is produced by the training stimulus, with orderly decreases in excitation as stimuli are further and further removed from it. In short, the theoretical excitatory gradient looks like the one depicted in Figure 8–3. Similarly, when a stimulus is associated with nonreinforcement, a gradient of inhibition, like the one depicted in Figure 8–4, develops about it. This may not seem like much of a theory since it does nothing more than describe obtained data. However, it should be noted that the theory *preceded* the data. Virtually all of the techniques and experimental results of studies of generalization came after the theory had been put forth.

What does an animal learn when it comes to respond to S^+ and not S^-? There are three different "rules" an animal might follow, each of which would lead to excellent discrimination performance, but only one of which would involve both excitation and inhibition.

1. *Respond if S^+; otherwise, do not.* According to this rule, the animal's responding would be controlled by the S^+ and its absence. There would be an excitatory gradient about the S^+, but no inhibitory gradient, since no specific stimulus was controlling not responding.

2. *Do not respond if S^-; otherwise, do.* By this rule, the animal would not respond to the S^- and one would observe an inhibitory gradient about it. The occurrence of responses would be controlled by the absence of the S^-; no specific S^+ (thus no excitatory gradient) would control responding. In most discrimination procedures in which either the S^+ or the S^- is always present, an animal that learned only to respond whenever the S^- was absent would end up responding at all times when reinforcement was available.

3. *Respond if S^+; do not respond if S^-.* This rule indicates specific excitatory and inhibitory control. The animal learns both the stimulus which predicts reinforcement and the stimulus which predicts nonreinforcement. Responding according to this rule would yield both excitatory and inhibitory generalization gradients.[20]

---

19. Spence, 1936, 1937. While Spence is responsible for the specific theory we are discussing in this section, he developed it against an elaborate and detailed theoretical foundation established by Clark L. Hull, 1943, 1952. The interconnection of Spence's theory with Hull's framework has led some writers to label Spence's theory the Hull–Spence theory of discrimination.
20. This analysis was developed by Jenkins, 1965.

The Spence theory of discrimination clearly views the animal as learning Rule 3: Excitation develops to the S^+ and similar stimuli, and inhibition develops to the S^- and similar stimuli.

The Peak Shift

What is the relation between the excitatory gradient and the inhibitory one? If the S^+ and the S^- are chosen from independent stimulus dimensions, like the color of light as S^+ and the pitch of tone as S^-, there is no relation between the gradients. However, if both S^+ and S^- are taken from the same stimulus dimension, for example, red light versus green light, the gradients interact.

In particular, according to the Spence theory, the gradients add together algebraically. To determine the net excitatory capacity of any stimulus, one simply subtracts its inhibitory value (taken from the inhibitory gradient) from its excitatory value (taken from the excitatory gradient). In this way, a resultant gradient, derived by subtracting inhibitory value from excitatory value for every stimulus, may be obtained.

Let us consider an example. Suppose a pigeon is trained with a 500-nm stimulus as S^+ and a 540-nm stimulus as S^-. The theoretical excitatory and inhibitory gradients are depicted in Figure 8–10A. These curves depict theoretical quantities, excitatory and inhibitory strength. It is assumed that they translate fairly directly into response rate. If the values of the inhibitory gradient are subtracted from the values of the excitatory gradient, the resulting gradient is what appears in Figure 8–10B. There are two important features of this gradient. First, it is not symmetrical. The points on the side of S^+ near S^- are much lower than the corresponding points on the side of S^+ away from S^-. Second, the peak of the gradient is not at S^+; rather, it is shifted away from S^-. The peak in Figure 8–10B is at 480 nm instead of 500. Indeed, Figure 8–10B would lead one to expect more responding to the 460-nm stimulus than to the S^+. Thus, the Spence theory makes the remarkable prediction that animals trained with S^+ and S^- on the same dimension will respond more, in generalization testing, to a novel stimulus than to the one with which they were trained.

This phenomenon, known as *peak shift*, reliably occurs in generalization tests which follow discrimination training. Some typical data from an early observation of peak shift are presented in Figure 8–11. One group of pigeons was trained to peck a 550-nm stimulus and there was no S^-. A second group was also trained to peck the 550-nm stimulus and S^- was a 590-nm stimulus. The generalization gradient

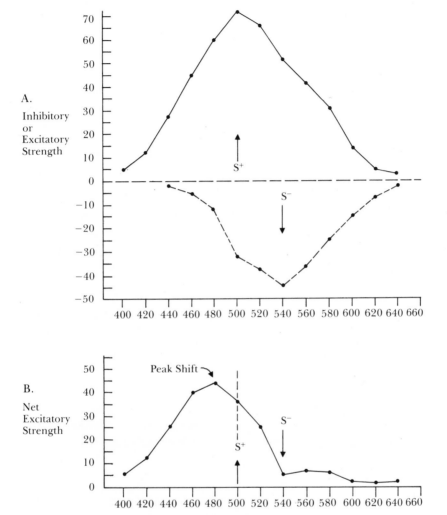

Figure 8–10. Spence's Theory of Discrimination and Generalization. *Hypothetical gradients of excitation about S⁺ and inhibition
about S⁻ are depicted in* A. *The resultant gradient when excitatory and
inhibitory gradients are combined is depicted in* B. *Note that the peak of the
resultant gradient is shifted away from S⁻.*

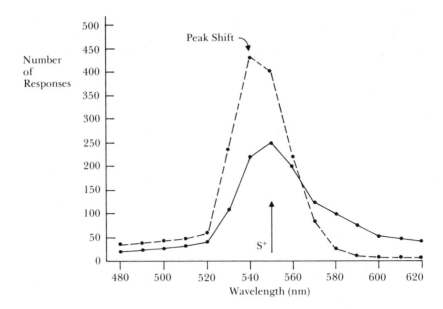

Figure 8–11. The Phenomenon of Peak Shift. *Results of generalization tests for two groups of pigeons trained to peck a key illuminated
with 550-nm light. For one group (solid line) there was no S⁻. The peak
of the gradient is at S⁺. For the second group (broken line), S⁻ was 590
nm. The peak of the gradient is shifted away from S⁻. (After Hanson,
1959.)*

for that group displays both the asymmetry and the peak shift which
the Spence theory predicts.[21] In addition, it provides clear evidence
that operant discrimination learning produces inhibition.[22]

Transposition

The phenomenon of peak shift provides impressive support for
the Spence theory of discrimination learning. However, it is possible
to suggest an alternative account of peak shift which has nothing to do
with the interaction of excitation and inhibition. This account derives

21. Hanson, 1959. It should be noted that while the shape of the gradients in Figure
8–11 conforms to Spence's predictions, the magnitude of responding does not. For the
group exposed to a 590-nm S⁻, there should be a gradient of inhibition which subtracts from the gradient of excitation, lowering response rate. Yet we see that this
group responds substantially more than the group trained with no S⁻, and thus with
no inhibitory gradient.

22. The peak shift is only one of many possible indications that operant discrimination
training involves the development of excitation and inhibition. For others, see Rilling,
1977.

from another phenomenon, known as *transposition,* initially studied some 60 years ago by the Gestalt psychologist Wolfgang Köhler.[23] In addition to providing an alternative to the Spence account of peak shift, transposition puts the more general issue of identifying the effective stimulus in *any* discrimination-learning situation in a new perspective.

Köhler argued that stimuli are judged not in absolute terms, but relative to one another. Throughout this chapter, even in discussing the difficulties attached to the specification of which stimuli control an animal's behavior, we have been treating stimuli as if they were absolute, independent entities. We label the brightness of the key or the intensity of a tone as a stimulus, without regard to the other lights and noises which are present in the chamber. This approach, while convenient and simple, does not square well with what is known about perception. Stimuli do not exist as absolute entities in a vacuum; they are a part of situations, and they are perceived as part of situations. If one looks at a burning candle at midnight, one perceives the candle to be very bright indeed. However, if the same candle is lit at noon on a sunny day, it appears dim. The brightness of the candle is evaluated against a background of illumination. When we describe the candlelight as bright, what we really mean is that it is bright relative to its background. If the background changes, the brightness of the candle will also change.

The relative nature of perceptual judgment bears upon discriminative control in the following way: a pigeon may be exposed to a discrimination procedure in which S$^+$ is a key illuminated with a 20-watt bulb and S$^-$ is a key illuminated with a 10-watt bulb. When the pigeon learns the discrimination, what has it actually learned? Has it learned that the 20-watt stimulus signals food, as we have been assuming throughout this chapter, or has it learned that the *brighter* stimulus signals food, as the facts of perception suggest? If it learns the latter, consider how it will respond to the stimuli presented during a generalization test. If a 40-watt stimulus is presented, it will be even brighter than the S$^+$. Having learned to respond to the brighter of two stimuli, the pigeon may make more responses to the 40-watt stimulus than it does to the 20-watt stimulus. But this is precisely the phenomenon we have labeled as peak shift above. In short, it may be that peak shift has nothing to do with the interaction between excitatory and inhibitory gradients, but rather that it is a reflection of the fact that animals evaluate stimuli in terms of their relation to one another.

In studies of chickens and chimpanzees, Köhler observed that

23. Köhler, 1939.

when they were trained with the brighter of two stimuli as S⁺, then tested with the S⁺ paired with a still-brighter stimulus, they would reliably choose the new, brighter stimulus. Köhler called this phenomenon *transposition,* by analogy to the fact that the notes which comprise musical melodies do not change their relation to each other when the melodies are transposed to a different key.

Tests of transposition typically involve, first, the training of a discrimination between two stimuli and, second, presenting test trials in which a choice is offered between new stimuli which are on the same dimension as the training stimuli. A transposition or relational choice is one in which the stimulus chosen has the same relation to the other stimulus as the S⁺ does to the S⁻. A nontranspositional, or absolute choice, is one in which the stimulus chosen is the one which is closer or more similar to the S⁺. A typical transposition test is diagrammed in Figure 8–12. In the most impressive demonstrations of transposition, a new stimulus is presented along with the S⁺ and the new stimulus is chosen because it bears the same relation to the S⁺ as the S⁺ did to the S⁻.

Thus, the methods used to study transposition differ from those used to study peak shift. Transposition tests involve choices between two stimuli which are both present (simultaneous discrimination), while generalization tests record the number of responses to stimuli which are presented one at a time. Nevertheless, the fact that peak shift is consistent with transposition suggests the possibility that it may be transposition.

Experimental Tests of Transposition • Is there a way to distinguish empirically these two accounts of peak shift? The answer is yes. What

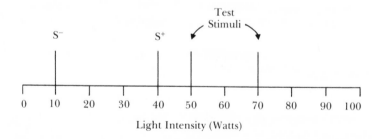

Light Intensity (Watts)

Figure 8–12. Schematic of a Typical Transposition Test. *Transposition Test: Phase 1: 10 watts, S⁻; 40 watts, S⁺. Animals learn to choose the S⁺. Phase 2: 50 and 70 watts presented. Animal's choice is a test of transposition. Possible outcomes: (1) Choice of 50 watts is an* absolute *choice, a choice of the stimulus closest to S⁺. (2) Choice of 70 watts is a* relational *choice, a choice of the brighter stimulus.*

effect, if any, should the degree of difference between the test and training stimuli have on transposition/peak shift? The relational account would certainly suggest that it should make no difference. If S^+ is a square of 100 cm² area, and S^- is a square of 60 cm² area, the animal learns to choose the larger square. If then confronted with 150- and 250-cm² squares, or 250- and 500-cm² squares, or 500- and 1,000-cm² squares, the animal should in all cases choose the larger square.

The Spence account makes a different prediction. As is clear from Figure 8–10, there comes a point on the stimulus continuum where the inhibitory gradient contributes little to the overall generalization gradient. At this point, the excitation will be greater for a stimulus closer to S^+ than one further from it even though the closer stimulus is smaller than the far one. The Spence theory would predict that at this point transposition will not be observed. Thus the two theories differ clearly in their predictions about the effect of the distance between test and training stimuli in transposition tests: the relational theory predicts no effect and the Spence theory predicts a switch from transposition to choice of the stimulus nearest S^+ as the distance increases.

The experimental evidence supports neither theory. As the distance between test and training stimuli increases, the likelihood of transposition decreases, a finding which supports Spence's theory. However, choices do not really reverse; rather, animals seem to respond randomly to the test stimuli, not consistently choosing one or the other.[24] It is clear that these data do not support the relational view, but they do not quite support the Spence view either. On the other hand, in generalization tests, rather than choice tests between two stimuli, the reversal predicted by Spence's theory is the rule. In Figure 8–11, the fact that more responses occur to the 540-nm stimulus than to the 550-nm stimulus (peak shift) supports the relational theory as well as the Spence theory. However, the fact that there is less responding to the 530-nm stimulus than to the 540-nm stimulus supports only Spence.

This evidence would seem decisive. However, there is evidence from a different type of discrimination study, known as the *intermediate size problem*, which provides strong support for relational theory. Suppose animals are trained with a 150-cm² square as S^+, and 100- and 200-cm² squares as S^-, as diagrammed in Figure 8–13. Since gradients of inhibition will develop symmetrically on both sides of the S^+, the Spence theory would predict no peak shift or transposition. The likely effect of this procedure in a generalization test is that the

24. See Riley, 1968.

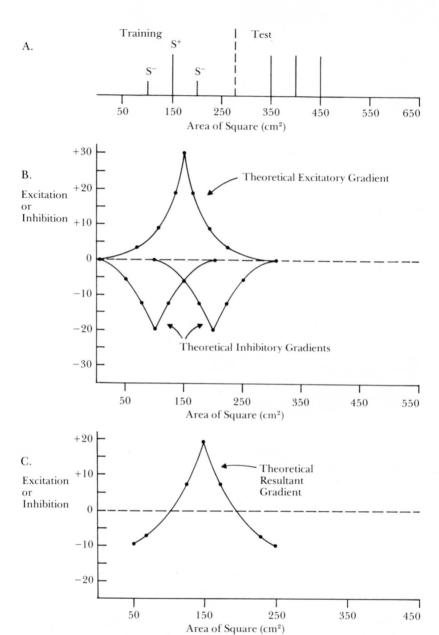

Figure 8–13. The Intermediate Size Problem. *The procedure is depicted in A; an S*$^+$ *is sandwiched between two S*$^-$*s. Theoretical gradients of excitation and inhibition consistent with Spence's theory are depicted in B and the resultant gradient is depicted in C. The expected gradient in C is not shifted at all. It remains symmetrical with a peak at S*$^+$*. Thus Spence's theory would predict a choice of the stimulus closest to S*$^+$ *in any test with three new stimuli.*

generalization gradient will be narrowed, as depicted in Figure 8–13C. According to the relational theory, animals exposed to this type of problem learn to choose the stimulus of intermediate size. If given three new stimuli, transposition will occur and the intermediate stimulus will be chosen, though it is further from S^+ than one of the outside stimuli. This is what occurs in such experiments.[25] On the other hand, tests of generalization after training of this type produce gradients like those predicted by Spence's theory.

Another experimental test of the relational theory is the following: rats were exposed to cards which were divided in half. The bottom half of the cards were an intermediate shade of gray. The top half of the cards were either one of three lighter shades or one of three darker shades. The animals had to learn to make a left turn when the top of the card was darker than the bottom and a right turn when the top of the card was lighter than the bottom. The procedure is diagrammed in Figure 8–14. After they learned, they experienced a number of test trials. On these trials, the bottom of the card was no longer an intermediate gray, but one of the other six shades. Sometimes, for example, two of the darker stimuli were arranged with the lighter of the two on top. The animals had learned to make a left turn in the presence of each of these stimuli. However, they had learned to make a right turn when confronted with the pattern light above dark. Which response did they make? One response would indicate that their responding was controlled by absolute stimulus properties and the other would indicate that their responding was controlled by relations among stimuli. In the overwhelming majority of such test trials, the animals' responses were appropriate to the relation between the stimuli and not their absolute characteristics.[26]

What is one to make of all this contradictory evidence? Tests for transposition itself tend to confirm the relational view. Studies of generalization gradients tend to confirm the Spence view. Perhaps both views are correct some of the time. In transposition tests, animals are given a choice between stimuli. It is perhaps not surprising that under these conditions they respond to the relation between them. In generalization tests, animals are presented with one stimulus at a time. It is not surprising that relational control is less likely under these conditions. Thus transposition and the peak shift may actually be different phenomena, the first being the product of the perception of stimulus relations and the second being the product of the interaction between gradients of excitation and gradients of inhibition. It is even logically

25. Gonzalez, Gentry, and Bitterman, 1954.
26. Lawrence and DeRivera, 1954.

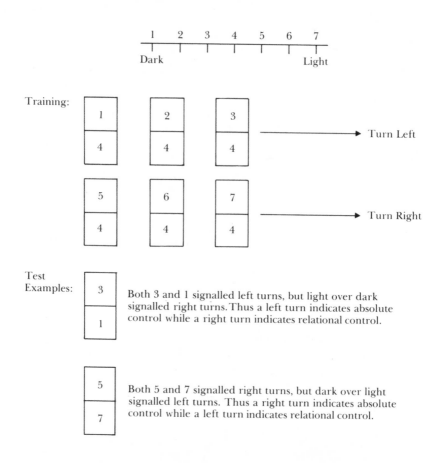

Figure 8–14. A Test of Control of Responding by Stimulus Relations. *A procedure studied by Lawrence and DeRivera, 1954, which provided support for the relational view of discrimination learning is diagrammed schematically.*

possible that animals respond to relational properties of stimuli in general, and that discrimination training produces gradients of excitation and inhibition.

For example, it might be that an animal in a discrimination experiment learns that the S⁺ is the "brighter" stimulus and not that it is the "40-watt" stimulus. Nevertheless, reinforcement might produce a gradient of excitation about relatively bright stimuli and a gradient of inhibition about relatively dim ones. The controversy we have discussed between the theories of Spence and of Köhler may actually be a reflection of the different kinds of questions researchers ask about stimuli and behavior. Köhler and others who have argued for the relational view seem primarily concerned with discovering what the stimulus is. Spence and his followers seem primarily concerned with discovering how the stimulus, whatever it is, controls operant behavior.[27]

DISCRIMINATIVE CONTROL AND
BEHAVIORAL ENGINEERING

We have now concluded our discussion of discriminative control of operant behavior. It is clear that the issues involved are complex and that most problems are still unresolved. The practical significance of resolving these issues is enormous, since the most serious obstacles to successful behavioral engineering involve problems of discrimination and generalization. Modification or elimination of maladaptive behavior can often be accomplished easily enough; the problem comes when the step from therapy to the natural environment must be made. A therapy program which produces therapeutic change in the therapy situation and no change outside it is no use whatever. Somehow, behavior in therapy situations must be appropriately generalized to the natural environment.

Behavior engineers have long been sensitive to the problems involved in producing appropriate discriminative control of behavior. In one case study in which the therapists attempted to produce classroom-appropriate behavior in a child, training began in a special room with a single therapist. After the appropriate behavior was occurring reliably, the experimenters gradually introduced distractions into the situation. Each new distraction produced a disruption of the child's behavior. However, the disruptive behavior was quickly extinguished. Ultimately, the training was shifted to a regular classroom situation. When therapy was terminated, the child was able to behave appropriately in a natural classroom setting. What these therapists did was not depend upon, or hope for, natural generalization. Rather, they built up to a situation in which training actually occurred under the stimulus conditions which would be relevant when therapy ceased.[28]

Though this sort of program is ideal, it is time-consuming and not always practical. When circumstances demand compromise, a good strategy is to extend training conditions as much as possible in the

---

27. Zeiler, 1963, presents an interesting argument which clearly articulates the difference between these two problems and attempts to provide a theoretical framework which incorporates the research findings which support each point of view.
28. Goocher and Ebner, 1968.

hope that as the variety of conditions under which appropriate behavior is maintained increases, the likelihood of generalization to all situations will increase. An example of this strategy is a case of a retarded child who engaged in self-mutilation. The therapist eliminated the mutilation by delivering painful shocks each time it occurred. This effectively eliminated self-mutilation in the presence of the therapist, but mutilation continued to occur in the presence of other people. Another therapist substituted for the original one and also delivered shock for self-mutilation. The behavior ceased in the presence of this individual as well. Now, however, the treatment generalized to all individuals.[29] The view which underlies this strategy is that the more there are stimulus elements in common between therapeutic and natural environments, the greater will be the likelihood that behavior change in therapy will be generalized to nontherapy situations.

Still another strategy for promoting generalization which is gaining increasing popularity is not to depend on generalization at all. Instead, behavioral engineering techniques are taught to relevant members of the community and the family. Now, the same contingencies which successfully modified behavior in the therapy situation can be instituted in the natural environment.

The problem of discriminative control is not always centered on insuring generalization. Sometimes generalization is too extensive and the problem is to limit it. This is especially true in education. When one attempts to shape a behavioral repertoire, one's goal is that behavior will occur in all (sufficient generalization), and only (sufficient discrimination), those situations in which it is appropriate. Thus, the behavioral engineer must walk a fine line to insure that discriminative control will be neither too broad nor too narrow. The best way to limit generalization is to institute explicit discrimination training. In training students to write, it is important to distinguish the style appropriate for technical writing from the style appropriate to creative writing. The way to do it is to train students explicitly in the two styles and in the stimulus conditions appropriate to each of them.

What does the laboratory have to teach us about discriminative control? How are studies of discriminative control in the restricted experimental environment applicable to problems of discriminative control in complex, natural settings? In some ways, applicability is quite limited. Laboratory studies of generalization teach us that an animal is more likely to emit a response in the presence of a stimulus which is similar to the training stimulus than in the presence of a stimulus which is quite distinct from the training stimulus. This is an im-

29. Lovaas and Simmons, 1969.

portant principle with enormous predictive power. The problem is this: in the laboratory, it is easy to specify whether a stimulus is similar to a training stimulus or not; training stimuli are chosen specifically to lie on a continuum which provides the means of judging similarity. Stimuli in the natural environment are not so neat. Is the classroom similar to the library? Is it more similar to the home? Is the hospital ward with a token economy similar to the local community? If not, on what dimensions is it different and how can it be made more similar? Without knowing what dimension of a stimulus situation is relevant for comparison, it is impossible to assess stimulus similarity.

However, studies of generalization in the laboratory may provide a means for assessing stimulus similarity in the natural environment. If one assumes the general shape of generalization gradients as a given, then one can use the probability of responding in situations which differ from the training situation as an index of stimulus similarity. If the probability of responding is low, then the situation is judged as different from the training situation. If the probability of responding is high, then the situation is judged as similar to the training situation. The logic of this kind of analysis is exactly the reverse of what is done in the laboratory. There, the degree of stimulus similarity is known and the shape of the generalization function must be determined. Once this is done, however, the generalization function itself may be used as an index of stimulus similarity in the natural environment. If such a strategy proves reliable, it will represent an enormous contribution to our understanding of behavior in the natural environment.

There is another very clear lesson to be learned from the laboratory. In the absence of explicit discrimination training, discriminative control is left to chance. Any of a host of different stimuli which stand in the same relation to reinforcement may control responding. To insure control of responding by a particular stimulus, one must arrange the situation so that that stimulus is the best predictor of reinforcement. The way to do this is to establish a discrimination, with the target stimulus as S^+ and its absence or some other stimulus as S^-. In this way, the control of behavior by incidental stimuli will be minimized, and the likelihood of overgeneralization will be reduced.

Before concluding our discussion of the relevance of principles of discriminative control developed in the laboratory to the application of behavioral engineering principles outside the laboratory, there is one particularly puzzling thing which should be discussed. The typical problem in application seems to be assuring generalization. Without some device to promote generalization, it will not occur. In contrast, in the laboratory generalization occurs routinely. The problem, if there is one, is to limit it. Why should the laboratory situation be so different from the engineering situation?

One can only speculate about the answer to this question. A major difference between the laboratory study of generalization and the pursuit of generalization in applied settings is that in the laboratory generalization testing is performed in the same situation in which training occurs, while in application what is desired is generalization to situations which are radically different from the training situation. It could well be that background stimulus conditions exert control on behavior even when there is another stimulus present which is a better predictor of reinforcement than any of the background stimuli. A second possible explanation is that, in the laboratory, typically only one stimulus dimension at a time is varied. In the natural environment, many aspects of the situation change simultaneously. That natural situations differ from one another in so many respects may significantly reduce the likelihood of generalization. Furthermore, when many aspects of a situation change together, the development of discriminative control by a particular feature of the environment becomes more difficult. Finally, in applied settings, the goal of engineering is to change behavior which is already being reinforced in the natural environment. Thus, for the therapy to be successfully generalized, explicit reinforcement must be overcome. There is nothing analogous to this problem in laboratory studies of generalization.

SUMMARY

This chapter has focused on a few central points. They may be summarized as follows:

1. The study of discrimination and generalization is primarily concerned with uncovering the processes by which operant behavior comes under the *control* of environmental objects and events.

2. In any situation, there are a large number of stimuli which may control responding, many of which are only incidental to the specific experimental task.

3. When a number of stimuli are equally predictive of reinforcer availability, they may share control over the operant. Alternatively, one stimulus may be more salient than the others and overshadow them in controlling responding.

4. In any situation, that stimulus which is the best predictor of reinforcer availability can be expected to control responding. Explicit discrimination training allows the experimenter to determine

which stimulus will control responding by insuring that the most informative relation is between that stimulus and reinforcement.

5. Discrimination learning involves learning to pay attention to relevant (predictive) aspects of the situation and learning to ignore irrelevant (unpredictive) aspects of the situation.

6. Responding which is under the control of a particular stimulus will also occur in the presence of other, similar stimuli. This phenomenon of generalization, and the reliable observation of peaked, orderly generalization gradients, indicates that discrimination learning involves the development of excitation to S^+ and inhibition to S^-.

7. The phenomenon of transposition and related phenomena indicate that animals do not evaluate stimuli absolutely, independent of context. Rather, at least under some circumstances, a stimulus is evaluated in relation to other available stimuli. Lights are not "bright" or "dim" but "brighter" or "dimmer."

8. Many of the problems encountered by behavioral engineers center on discrimination and generalization. Behavior change in therapy must be generalized, but not overgeneralized, to appropriate conditions in the natural environment to be really effective. While some techniques for promoting generalization have been explored, the area remains largely uninvestigated.

9

Aversive Control

Punishment and Avoidance

In the first chapter of this book we suggested that the control of behavior by environmental events is a fact and that the analysis of behavior and behavioral engineering are not efforts to *invent* techniques of control so much as they are efforts to *understand* and *describe* behavior control as an existing characteristic of the natural environment. In that chapter, we argued that individuals routinely manipulate the behavior of others using the same techniques (though perhaps without the same understanding or efficiency) that behavioral engineers use.

For some aspects of human life this claim can hardly be denied: the use of punishment and the threat of punishment are salient characteristics of everyone's upbringing; they are the main constituents of most legal and penal systems; they are significant components of most educational programs. There is no one whose behavior has not been influenced by anticipated aversive or unpleasant consequences. While one may deny having studied hard in order to get good grades, or having worked hard in order to receive a promotion, one cannot deny having eased off the accelerator as a police car came into view to avoid a traffic ticket, or having cleaned up one's room to avoid a parental lecture. In short, there seems to be an asymmetry in people's willingness to acknowledge the sources of control of their behavior. Control of behavior by aversive consequences is readily acknowledged while control of behavior by positive consequences is not.

It is therefore surprising that to this point our discussion of the principles of behavior control has focused almost exclusively on positive consequences. The last four chapters have discussed the role of positive reinforcement in shaping and maintaining behavior; no mention has been made of punishment or the threat of punishment. What does the analysis of behavior have to tell us about punishment? What can the laboratory teach us about the kind of behavior control which is most obvious in the ordinary environment?

AVERSIVE STIMULI AND BEHAVIOR

There are at least four different ways that the relation between aversive stimuli and behavior can be arranged, and each type of arrangement has a different effect on behavior. First, an aversive stimulus can be delivered independently of an organism's behavior. That is, nothing the organism does influences its occurrence. This arrangement between aversive stimuli and behavior is characteristic of Pavlovian conditioning and is typically referred to as *Pavlovian fear conditioning* (see Chapter 4); it has a profound influence on behavior. Second, aversive stimuli may be presented as a consequence of a particular response. For example, each time the rat presses a lever it receives a painful electric shock to the paws. This type of relation between aversive stimuli and behavior is called *punishment.* Third, aversive stimuli may be presented independently of the organism's behavior, but be terminated or eliminated by a particular response. Thus, a rat may occasionally receive a painful shock which remains on until it presses the lever. This relation between aversive stimuli and behavior is called *escape.* Finally, an aversive stimulus may be presented if the organism fails to make a particular response. For example, a rat may receive a brief electric shock every 30 seconds unless it presses the lever during that time. This type of relation is known as *avoidance.*

It is not difficult to find instances of each of these relations between aversive stimuli and behavior in the everyday experience of most people. Response-independent aversive stimuli are an all-too-common feature of modern life. Air pollution and noise have become routine aspects of urban existence. The occurrence of each of these stimuli is independent of the individual's responses, and the individual can typically do nothing to terminate them. Punishment is so commonplace that no examples are necessary. Escape is also common; one escapes from bad television programs by turning off the set, and from bad movies and lectures by leaving the auditorium. One escapes hot summer weather by going north and cold winter weather by going south. Most natural instances of escape involve actually leaving the scene, while in the laboratory, escape often involves making a response which changes the scene. Finally, one avoids interest charges by paying bills when they are due, one avoids being stranded on the highway by filling the gas tank before it is empty, and one avoids long lines by purchasing concert tickets in advance.

In this chapter, we will first discuss some of the facts of fear conditioning, punishment, escape, and avoidance. We will discuss the procedures with which they are studied, and the phenomena which characterize them. We will occasionally illustrate the use of these techniques of aversive control in therapy and education. Second, we will discuss some of the theories which have been developed to account for the phenomena of aversive control.

CONDITIONED SUPPRESSION

If a rat is trained to press a lever for food, and after lever pressing is well established the rat is subjected to periodic pairings of a stimulus (tone) and a painful electric shock, the rat will eventually press the lever much less when the tone is present than when it is absent. The tone–shock pairings have the effect of suppressing lever pressing for food, a phenomenon which is typically referred to as *conditioned suppression*. [1]

The degree of suppression which results from a particular procedure is usually measured by a number known as the *suppression ratio*. If we call response rate during the conditioned stimulus (CS) *B*, and response rate in the absence of the CS, *A*, then suppression can be assessed with the ratio

$$\frac{B}{A+B} \tag{1}$$

If the CS has no effect on responding, the ratio will be 0.5; if the CS completely suppresses responding, the ratio will be 0.0.

To illustrate the phenomenon of conditioned suppression, let us consider the following demonstration. Pigeons were trained to peck a key for food which was available on a VI schedule. Periodically, a tone was presented for 2-minute periods. After a number of sessions like this, the tone was followed by shock delivered to the pigeon's wings. Figure 9–1 presents cumulative records of responding both during the tone and in its absence in a session before shock was introduced, in the 8th session of tone–shock pairings, in the 20th session, and in the 32nd session. As the figure shows, during the preshock session the tone had no effect on key pecking. The suppression ratio was about 0.5. By the 8th session of tone-shock pairings, there was consider-

---

1. Conditioned suppression was initially observed by Estes and Skinner, 1941. The phenomenon is also referred to as the "conditioned emotional response" or CER.

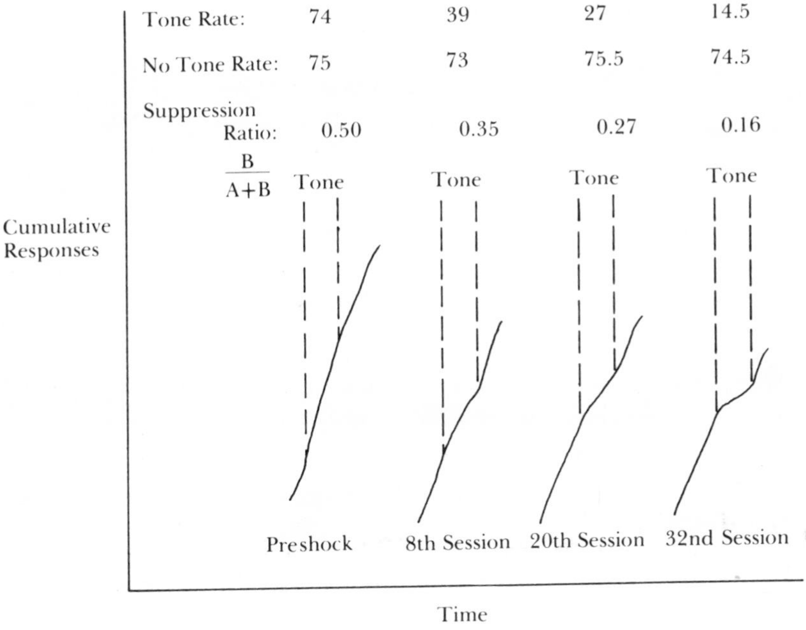

Tone Rate:	74	39	27	14.5
No Tone Rate:	75	73	75.5	74.5
Suppression Ratio: $\dfrac{B}{A+B}$	0.50	0.35	0.27	0.16

Figure 9–1. Development of Conditioned Suppression in the Pigeon. *Cumulative records of key pecking are taken from a number of different sessions of a conditioned suppression procedure. At the top of the figure, response rates (in responses per minute) and suppression ratios [rate during tone/(rate during tone + rate without tone)] for each of the sessions depicted are presented. (Adapted from Hoffman, 1969, p. 187.)*

able suppression of responding during the tone. The cumulative record during the tone was flatter than at other times and the suppression ratio was 0.35. The degree of suppression increased over the course of further sessions and was 0.27 in the 20th session and 0.16 in the 32nd session.

Thus, if an electric shock is delivered to an organism without regard to its behavior but reliably preceded by a signal or CS, responding for food reward during the CS is suppressed. A Pavlovian conditioned fear procedure can substantially reduce the frequency of occurrence of operant behavior.[2]

2. The development of conditioned suppression does not always take the form depicted in Figure 9–1. First, it is often much more rapid. With rats as subjects, food-reinforced lever presses may be substantially suppressed in just a few trials (e.g., Kamin, 1969). Second, sometimes the effect of early trials, before the CS has been well established as a signal, is that responding is suppressed in both the presence and the absence of the CS (e.g., Seligman, 1968). Only when the CS is well established as a signal for shock, and conversely, when the absence of the CS is established as a signal for safety, is suppression restricted to the presence of the CS.

Variables Influencing Conditioned Suppression

One of the most significant variables in determining how much suppression the CS will ultimately produce at the end of training is the intensity of the shock. The more intense the shock is, the greater the suppression will be. However, even with very intense shock, suppression is rarely complete. Animals will continue to respond at some rate during the CS.

What about the relation between the conditioned stimulus and the unconditioned stimulus? How important is the CS as a signal for shock to the phenomenon of suppression? We discussed this matter in Chapter 5 in distinguishing between fear and anxiety. If an animal experiences occasional presentations of unsignaled painful electric shock, it may suppress responding throughout the session.[3] Rather than having fear (and suppression) controlled by the presence of a particular stimulus, this procedure seems to produce fear and suppression controlled by the entire apparatus. Not only is suppression of responding nearly complete, but this procedure can also produce stomach ulceration in rats. Thus, response suppression may result simply from the presentation of painful shock; that suppression is restricted to particular periods of time is the result of the signaling relation between a CS and shock.

An important point to notice about conditioned-suppression experiments is that if the baseline schedule of reinforcement is a VI, as it typically is in studies of conditioned suppression, response rate can decrease substantially and have only a small effect on the number of reinforcements the animal receives. We saw in Chapter 7 that response rate can be reduced by more than half and add only a few seconds to the average time between reinforcements. Thus, suppression like that in Figure 9–1 costs the animal little in the way of reinforcement frequency. The same is true if the baseline schedule is an FI. The first demonstration of conditioned suppression used an FI baseline and obtained substantial suppression.[4] On the other hand, if the baseline reinforcement schedule is a ratio schedule, reductions in responding produce a large reduction in the frequency of reinforcement. Interestingly, if ratio schedules are the baseline, conditioned suppression does not reliably occur. With variable-ratio schedules, no suppression is observed, at least when the shocks are only moderately intense.[5] With fixed-ratio schedules the occurrence of suppression

3. Seligman, 1968.
4. Estes and Skinner, 1941.
5. Lyon and Felton, 1966.

depends upon when in the ratio the CS occurs: if it comes early in the ratio, suppression occurs reliably, and if it comes late in the ratio, suppression does not occur.[6]

The phenomenon of conditioned suppression shows us that an aversive Pavlovian contingency generally has massive effects on ongoing, appetitively reinforced operant behavior. Pavlovian conditioning affects not only reflexes; a Pavlovian CS can also have a substantial influence on goal-directed, voluntary activity. Let us examine now the operant analog of conditioned suppression. What are the effects on ongoing, appetitive, operant behavior of the imposition of a contingency between responses and aversive stimuli?

PUNISHMENT

If, instead of being presented independently of responding, a painful electric shock depends upon the occurrence of the response (punishment), substantial suppression of responding occurs. The extent to which punishment suppresses responding seems to be influenced by the same variables which influence the magnitude of conditioned suppression.

Factors Influencing the Effectiveness of Punishment

As the intensity of the punishing stimulus increases, the degree of suppression increases. If very intense shock is used, suppression may often be virtually complete. The effect of shock intensity on suppression can be seen in Figure 9–2. Rats that had been trained to press a lever for food on a VI schedule were divided into different groups. For each group but one, responses were punished, with the intensity of the shock varying from group to group. A suppression ratio was calculated, with *B* representing response rate during sessions which included punishment and *A* representing response rate during sessions before the introduction of punishment. All groups of rats showed suppression relative to a control group which received no punishment. However, suppression when shock was intense was much greater than suppression when shock was mild.

As in the case of conditioned suppression, the schedule of reinforcement which is maintaining responding influences the degree to which responding is suppressed by punishment. In general, responding on interval schedules is suppressed more than responding on ratio schedules, presumably for the same reason that conditioned

6. Lyon, 1964.

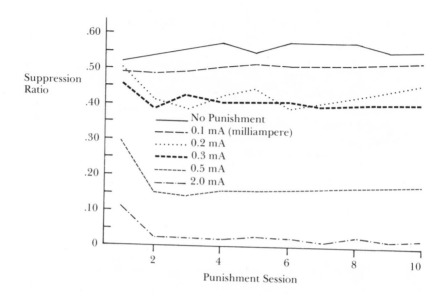

Figure 9–2. Effects of Shocks of Different Intensity as Punishers of Lever Pressing in Rats. *Each curve presents a suppression ratio over 10 sessions for a different group of rats. The groups differed in the intensity of the electric shock used to punish responding. (After Camp, Raymond, & Church, 1967.)*

suppression procedures have larger effects on interval- than on ratio-maintained responding. The cost of response rate reductions is much less on interval than on ratio schedules. On fixed-ratio schedules, the effect of even intense punishment appears to be that the pause after reinforcement is lengthened; once responding begins, it occurs at virtually the same high rate as without punishment.[7]

Thus, as with conditioned suppression, both the intensity of the punisher and the baseline reinforcement schedule which is maintaining responding influence the degree of suppression which a punishment procedure produces. In addition, there are other factors which influence the effectiveness of punishment which are not relevant to conditioned suppression.

One such factor is the temporal relation between the response and the punishing stimulus. We saw in Chapter 6 (see Figure 6–2) that if reinforcement is delayed, its ability to increase response rate is diminished in proportion to the amount of delay. Delay of punishment reduces its effectiveness in the same way. As the interval between

7. Azrin, 1959; Fantino, 1973.

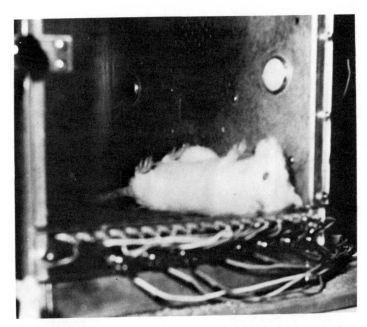

A way to solve the problem of punishment. This rat's lever-presses produce both food pellets and shock through the grid floor. The rat lies on its back so that its fur insulates it against the shock, and presses the lever with its hind foot to produce food. (Courtesy of Nathan Azrin.)

response and punishment increases, the amount of suppression produced by the punishing stimulus decreases. In one of many experiments which have obtained this effect, two groups of rats whose lever pressing was maintained on a VI schedule were scheduled to receive punishing shocks for lever presses on a VI 2-min schedule. For one group, the shock was delivered immediately; for a second group, the shock was delivered 30 seconds after the lever press which produced it had occurred. Notice that this second group could, and did, continue pressing the lever during the 30-second delay interval, so that some shocks might have occurred almost immediately after a lever press; all that the procedure specified was that the shock would come 30 seconds after the response which produced it. Despite the possibility that Group 2 might often experience shock just after a response, the difference in suppression between the two groups was striking. Figure 9–3 presents suppression ratios for both groups over the course of training. Suppression was almost complete for the no-delay group, while it hovered between 0.3 and 0.4 for the 30-second delay group.

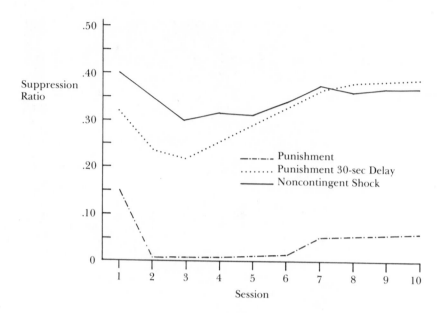

Figure 9–3. Effects of Delay of Punishment. *This figure depicts suppression of responding by immediate punishment, delayed punishment, and noncontingent shock. For the three groups of animals, the intensity of the shock and the frequency of the shock were the same. Only the relation between responses and shock differed among the groups. (The two punishment curves are adapted from Camp, Raymond, & Church, 1967. The noncontingent shock curve is from Church, 1969, Figure 10.)*

There is a third curve in Figure 9–3. This is from a group of rats which received response-independent shocks at a rate of one every 2 minutes on the average, analogous to a conditioned suppression procedure but without a warning signal. The degree of suppression in this group is virtually identical to the degree of suppression in the delayed punishment group. Thus, at least with delays as long as 30 seconds, punishment procedures seem no more effective in suppressing responding than procedures in which shock is independent of responses. For punishment to be maximally effective, it must be immediate.

If we ask ourselves why it is that an organism responds at all when its responses are punished, we can deduce another factor which is likely to influence the effectiveness of punishment. Organisms respond because responses produce food as well as shock, and because they are food-deprived. If one were to provide an alternative means of obtaining food, the effectiveness of the shock ought to be greatly enhanced. And indeed it is. A number of experiments have shown that punishment suppresses responding much more when an alternative route to reinforcement exists than when it does not. In one such study, human subjects were engaged in a button-pushing task for reinforcement. When there was only one button to push, the subjects pushed the button 500 times in only a few minutes. When each button push produced a loud, annoying buzz (the punishing stimulus), the rate of button pushing was moderately suppressed; subjects still pushed the button 500 times, but now it required about 18 minutes. Finally, when each button push produced the buzz, but another button was present on which responses produced reinforcement but no buzz, there was virtually immediate and complete suppression of responding on the first button.[8]

We have thus identified four variables which influence the effectiveness of punishment: the intensity of the punishing stimulus; the schedule of reinforcement which is maintaining responding; the delay between responses and punishment; and the availability of an alternative route to reinforcement.[9] In all the research we have described, however, the punishing stimulus was electric shock. While shock is certainly the most often used aversive stimulus, it is not the only one.

Types of Punishing Stimuli

Stimuli other than electric shock are occasionally used in research on punishment, especially with human subjects. Though these stimuli tend to be less effective than electric shock, they do suppress responding noticeably.

One such stimulus is temperature. Blasts of extreme cold or warm air may effectively suppress responses on which they depend. Indeed, blasts of room-temperature air, if they are powerful, are effective aversive stimuli. Also, loud noise can be used effectively to punish responding. Noise is a commonly used stimulus in experiments with human subjects.

Another commonly used aversive stimulus is not a stimulus at all, but the removal of one. It is called *time-out* and it can be illustrated by reference to the standard pigeon-conditioning situation. Suppose a pigeon has been trained to peck a lit key for food on a VI schedule. After pecking is firmly established, a punishment dependency is introduced; every 10th key peck turns out the key light for 10 seconds.

8. Herman and Azrin, 1964.
9. Azrin and Holz, 1966; Church, 1969; Fantino, 1973.

During this time, key pecks have no effect. The punishment, in short, consists of a period in which food is not available. Time-outs of this sort are sometimes effective in suppressing the responses which produce them.[10] The effectiveness of a time-out depends, of course, on what it is that the time-out is making inaccessible. In Chapter 7, we reported evidence that pigeons would peck a key to produce a time-out from a high fixed-ratio (FR) schedule. The ratio is apparently sufficiently aversive that, given the opportunity, an animal will escape for brief periods of rest. Thus, the same objective event—time-out—may punish responses or reinforce them.

Time-out is frequently used in research with human subjects. It is also used in behavioral engineering situations. In addition, time-out is perhaps the most common form of punishment employed in the home. Withdrawal of the opportunity to watch television, or play with a favorite toy, or withdrawal of the opportunity for parental contact and affection are often far more effective as punishers than spanking.

There is one final type of punishing stimulus which is commonly used, especially with humans. It is called a *conditioned punisher*. If a stimulus like a tone has been arranged to signal reliably an aversive stimulus like shock (as in conditioned suppression procedures) and subsequently responses produce the tone, the tone will suppress responding. There is nothing aversive about the tone before it is used to signal shock; it is the contingent relation between tone and shock which results in the tone's coming to suppress responding. For this reason it is called a *conditioned* punisher.

Parents employ conditioned punishment commonly in the home. The tone of voice or facial expression which typically precedes a spanking or banishment to one's room will effectively come to punish behavior by itself. A major virtue of the use of conditioned punishment in engineering situations is that it is usually much easier to arrange and deliver than unconditioned aversive stimuli. In addition, it can be used with some frequency without concern for possible physical injury, unlike electric shock or loud noise.

Punishment in the Natural Environment

There are few aspects of childrearing and education which arouse as much controversy as the use of punishment. For generations, punishment was the major tool of both parent and teacher. However, in the last few decades, influenced in part by conclusions drawn (sometimes erroneously) from laboratory research, punishment has been

10. Leitenberg, 1965.

losing favor. Some argue against the use of punishment on ethical grounds; others argue that punishment simply does not work. Still others are concerned that it works all too well. Finally, some express concern that it has harmful side effects. We will take up some of these concerns now, and see what the laboratory can tell us about the effectiveness and the drawbacks of punishment as a technique of behavior control.

Does Punishment Work?

In light of all the evidence discussed in the preceding pages, it seems odd that one should ask this question at all. If the experiments we have been discussing show anything at all, surely it must be that punishment works. Yet the question continues to be asked. This is due in part to the writings of E. L. Thorndike. When Thorndike initially put forth the law of effect, it had two facets: rewards increased the likelihood of responses which preceded them, and punishments decreased the likelihood of responses which preceded them. In later work, on the basis of the evidence available at that time, Thorndike revised the law of effect: rewards worked but punishments did not.[11] In 1944, this later view of Thorndike's was buttressed by an extensive series of experiments on punishment conducted by W. K. Estes. Estes's experiments seemed to show that while punishment did suppress behavior, its effects were temporary and hardly more pronounced than the effects of the same aversive stimuli delivered independently of the animal's behavior. In short, Estes's experiments seemed to suggest that aversive stimuli produced a temporary suppression of operant responses, whether or not they actually depended upon those responses. The effect of punishment, that is, an explicit relation between responses and aversive stimuli, over and above the effect of the aversive stimuli themselves, seemed negligible.

Thus, the question "Does punishment work?" is not as straightforward as it might appear. A more relevant question is this: Does a *dependency* between responses and aversive stimuli result in greater suppression of those responses than occurs when the aversive stimuli are merely presented independently of responses? With the techniques available to Estes when he did his experiments, the answer to this question seemed to be no. As years of research have revealed techniques which increased the effectiveness of punishment, the an-

11. Thorndike, 1931, 1932, came to this conclusion on the basis of experiments which employed punishing stimuli which, by standards of current research, are extremely mild.

swer to this question has changed. There is no doubt that punishment can suppress responding more effectively than noncontingent presentation of aversive stimuli. A glance at Figure 9–3 reveals the very large difference in suppression between electric shock which is dependent on responses and electric shock which is independent of responses.[12] Thus punishment does work. Yet it does not always work—in Estes's experiments, punishment did not have impressive effects like those in Figure 9–3. Thus, we must ask a second question: Under what conditions does punishment work?

Maximizing the Effects of Punishment

The reader may be able to guess from the preceding discussion what some of the operations are which can maximize the effectiveness of punishment. We have already seen that the effectiveness of punishment is a function of the intensity of the punishing stimulus and of the delay between response and punishment. It follows from those experiments that to maximize the effectiveness of punishment:

1. The punishing stimulus should be as intense as possible, and
2. The delay between between response and punishment should be as short as possible.

Both of these points require comment. It is perhaps not difficult to use an extremely intense punisher when the recipients of the stimulus are rats. When children's responses are being punished, however, factors aside from the potential effectiveness of punishment enter into consideration. One's goal in punishing the responses of one's children is to maximize the effectiveness of punishment without injuring the child or being unnecessarily cruel. How does one determine the point at which punishment becomes cruel? Obviously, the analysis of behavior has little to say about this problem. There is certainly no consensus on what constitutes cruelty, either. The best the analysis of behavior can do is offer the following recommendation:

3. The punishing stimulus should not be introduced in mild form and gradually increased in intensity. It should be introduced at whatever intensity one has determined will be the maximum. Individuals will differ in deciding what the maximum punishment in-

---

12. The effects are not always as large as Figure 9–3 suggests, however. See a study by Church, Wooten, and Matthews, 1970, for a much smaller effect of the response–shock dependency.

tensity they use will be. Having made this decision, however, they should use that punishment from the outset.

Why is this the case? Evidence from the laboratory suggests that when animals receive mild electric shock, they adapt to it. After a while, it does not seem to hurt much. If the intensity of the shock is gradually increased, the animals continue to adapt to each change in intensity. An extremely intense level of shock can be reached in this gradual fashion, with surprisingly little effect on behavior. If the same level of shock is introduced right from the start of punishment, it will often produce complete suppression of the punished response.[13]

Let us see how common practice with punishment conforms to principles (2) and (3). Is punishment typically immediate? Sometimes it is, but often remarks like "Just wait until your father gets home," or "Because of what you did, you cannot go to the movies on Saturday," are the immediate consequences of the response to be punished while the actual punishment is deferred for hours or even days. Also, sometimes an attempt is made to reason with the child after a transgression. The parent patiently explains why the response which just occurred was undesirable, looking for signs of comprehension, and perhaps remorse. If these responses are not forthcoming. then perhaps punishment will follow. It is likely that what is being punished under these conditions is not the transgression at all but the child's response to the parental lecture.

Now, what about the intensity of punishment? It seems that common practice is to attempt to affect behavior with the mildest possible punishment. If a mild punishment fails, then the punishment is escalated. If it still fails, it is escalated once again. The process continues until an effective level of punishment is found. Parents adopt this strategy presumably in the desire to be humane. Yet, it may have the opposite effect. If the child continues to adapt to the punishment as its intensity is gradually increased, the level of punishment ultimately reached may be much higher than what would have been effective if it had been used from the first. The parent who catches a young child stealing pennies may begin with a stern lecture. If the stealing persists, punishment may move from there to mild spankings, severe spankings, elimination of some of the child's pleasurable activities, withdrawal of affection, and so on. Another parent, who punished the very first instance of stealing with a spanking may not have occasion to punish stealing again. It would, of course, be desirable to eliminate behavior with the mildest punishment possible. However,

13. Azrin and Holz, 1966, for example.

since one does not know in advance what this optimal punishment is, one runs the risk when following this strategy of ultimately using punishment which is far more severe than would otherwise have been necessary.

4. Punishment should be certain. When responses are punished intermittently, the effectiveness of the punishment procedure is reduced.[14]

What else can be done to maximize the effectiveness of punishment? Since the behavior to be punished is presumably occurring because it is producing reinforcement, any operation which weakens the relation between response and reinforcement at the same time that punishment is being delivered should enhance the effectiveness of the punishment. A variety of such operations can be identified.

5. Have the delivery of punishment serve as a signal (S⁻) that reinforcement is not available for the punished response. If this is not possible, then

6. Decrease the frequency with which the reinforcer is available as a consequence of the response, or

7. Arrange a dependency between the reinforcer and an alternative response. Establish alternative routes to the goal which are not undesirable. Complete suppression of a response with only mild punishment is possible if an alternative response which produces the same reinforcement is available. If one's child continues to steal pennies in the face of intense punishment, then establishing a set of little jobs for earning pennies may successfully eliminate stealing.

Punishment works and there are rules for maximizing its effectiveness. We turn now to a final question: Should punishment be used to control behavior? This amounts to a question about the drawbacks of punishment. Does punishment have harmful or undesirable side effects and, if so, what are they?

Side Effects of Punishment

It has long been claimed that punishment has a variety of undesirable effects in addition to suppressing behavior. We may categorize these effects as members of a single class which we will call *emotional*

14. See Azrin, 1956; Azrin, Holz, and Hake, 1963.

behavior. There are some instances in which the emotional effect of punishment must be inferred from what the organism is doing (or not doing) and there are other instances in which the emotional effect *is* what the organism is doing. In describing these emotional effects, we will address the following questions:

1. Are these emotional effects produced by punishment or is the mere presentation of aversive stimuli enough to produce them?

2. Are these emotional effects produced by punishment or does any method of eliminating behavior produce them?

Any decision about the ultimate desirability of punishment as a technique of behavior control depends upon the answers to these questions.

The emotional effects of punishment are of two general types. One type is thought to be a kind of general arousal of part of the nervous system. Its behavioral effect is complete suppression of all food-motivated behavior. In short, it has been claimed that punishment results not in suppression of the specific response which produces it, but in general suppression of all operant behavior. If this were true, the use of punishment to control behavior would be undesirable. However, experimental evidence suggests that it is not true.

In one experiment, rats were trained to both press a lever and pull a chain to produce food. After training, only one of these responses was made available to each rat; for some it was the chain and for some it was the lever. Under these conditions, the rats were exposed to either punishment (electric shock for each response) or noncontingent shock. After these procedures had been in effect for a while, the animals were tested for suppression with the opportunity for both responses available. Recall that, for each rat, shock had only occurred when one of the response alternatives was available. If the suppressive effects of punishment are general, then we should expect suppression of both responses during the test. On the other hand, if the suppressive effects of punishment are specific, then we should expect to observe no suppression of responding on the alternative which was not available during punishment training.

Figure 9–4 indicates that punishment resulted in a suppression ratio of 0.2 for the punished response and of 0.4 for the unpunished response. Thus, punishment does appear to suppress behavior generally, though admittedly the target behavior is suppressed more than other responses. But is punishment responsible for the suppression? The right-hand portion of Figure 9–4 suggests not; for animals that received noncontingent shock, the suppression ratio for both re-

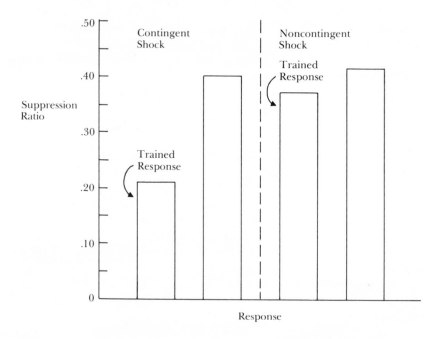

Figure 9–4. Effects of Punishment on Unpunished Responses. *This figure depicts the effects of punishment and noncontingent shock on responses which occurred during the shock procedure and on responses which did not occur during the shock procedure. The bars labeled "Trained Response" depict the suppression ratio of responses which were available to the animals during shock sessions. The other bars are suppression ratios for responses which the animals had previously been trained to make, but which were not available during shock. The large suppressive effect of punishment is specific to the punished response. Its effect on the other response is equivalent to the effects of noncontingent shock. (After Church, Wooten, & Matthews, 1970.)*

sponses was about 0.4. Thus, punishment produces no more suppression of unpunished behavior than does noncontingent shock. It is the presentation of an aversive stimulus, and not punishment, which produces general suppression.[15] Indeed, there is even evidence that shock used as punishment has less of an emotional effect than the same shock delivered independently of responding.[16] This may be a

15. This experiment suggests a parallel to our discussion of positive reinforcement in Chapter 6. Recall that we endorsed Staddon's and Simmelhag's view that reinforcement selects behavior rather than strengthening it. The mere presentation of food may be responsible for increasing an animal's total output. Punishment seems like a mirror image. The mere presentation of shock suppresses responding. Punishment *selectively suppresses* responding.
16. Hearst, 1965.

manifestation of the difference between fear and anxiety, which was discussed in Chapter 5 and reviewed briefly earlier in this chapter. Fear, which results when shock is predictable, seems to produce a less general and pronounced disruption of behavior than anxiety, which results when shock is unpredictable. The relation between responses and shock in a punishment procedure means that the shocks are predictable.

Punishment and Aggression • Another important emotional side effect of punishment is that it reliably produces reflexive aggression. Rats that receive punishment will attack another rat; monkeys will attack another monkey; pigeons will attack another pigeon.[17] If it is true that punishment reliably produces aggression, there is good reason to avoid the use of punishment as a means of behavior control. As before, the question is not whether punishment produces aggression, but whether it *uniquely* produces aggression. And the answer to this question is quite clearly no. First, the mere presentation of aversive stimuli, whether or not they depend upon responses, produces aggression, which typically occurs as an immediate consequence of the aversive stimulation. Second, aggression results from the use of other procedures which eliminate responding. Extinction procedures have produced aggression in both pigeons and monkeys.[18] When reinforcement is made available again, the aggressive behavior stops. Finally, aggression may be observed when reinforcement is available on schedules which seem aversive. Both pigeons and monkeys will attack restrained targets when working for food on FR schedules.[19]

It therefore seems undeniable that while punishment does produce aggression, it shares that characteristic with a wide variety of other procedures. Aggressive by-products of punishment do not amount to a unique indictment of punishment as a technique of behavior control.

Negativity of Punishment • B. F. Skinner offers another criticism of punishment. It is that punishment makes a negative contribution to the behavioral repertoire. It eliminates behavior which, for one reason or another, is undesirable; it does not substitute a response which provides an acceptable means to the reinforcer. The aim of behavioral engineering in the long run is to establish reasonably complete and effective behavioral repertoires. Punishment does little in the ser-

17. See Ulrich and Azrin, 1962; Azrin, Huchinson, and Sallery, 1964; Azrin, Huchinson, and Hake, 1967.
18. Azrin, Huchinson, and Hake, 1966; Huchinson, Azrin, and Hunt, 1968.
19. Huchinson, Azrin, and Hunt, 1968; Gentry, 1968.

vice of this goal. Skinner's proposed alternative is the reinforcement of some other response which is both acceptable and effective. Indeed, such a strategy substantially enhances the effectiveness of punishment in suppressing a target response. However, if reinforcement of an alternative response, coupled with extinction of the undesirable response, is an effective way to alter the behavioral repertoire, why bother with punishment at all? The answer is that, unlike extinction coupled with reinforcement of another response, punishment works almost immediately. A single presentation of a punishing stimulus may be sufficient to suppress completely the target response. Some situations require rapid effects, and there is no substitute for punishment.

A particularly dramatic example comes from research on schizophrenic children. One of the more striking symptoms often displayed by some schizophrenic children is self-destructive behavior. Such children will repeatedly claw at themselves until they bleed, punch themselves in the head, or hit their heads against the wall. To prevent serious injury, such children must often be kept restrained and sedated. In dealing with a problem of this sort, speed is of the essence. For this reason, painful electric shocks are often administered. In the case of one boy who would hit his head up to 2,000 times in an hour if unrestrained, twelve shocks contingent upon this self-mutilation were sufficient to eliminate the behavior permanently. While most of these children's problems cannot be solved with punishment, a necessary first step to more complete therapy is the elimination of self-mutilation.[20]

This concludes our discussion of punishment phenomena. It seems as though the mere presentation of an aversive stimulus suppresses responding. A punishment contingency primarily works to suppress responding *selectively*. Thus, punishment seems like a mirror image of food reinforcement. Food presentation enhances behavior and a reinforcement contingency enhances behavior *selectively* (see Chapter 6).

ESCAPE AND AVOIDANCE

Escape refers to a procedure in which responses eliminate an aversive stimulus which is otherwise present. The onset of that stimulus is not under the organism's control. One escapes cold winter weather by going south. Avoidance, on the other hand, refers to a procedure in which responses prevent the occurrence of an aversive stimulus. One avoids interest charges by paying bills when they are due.

20. Bucher and Lovaas, 1968; Lovaas and Simmons, 1969.

Escape procedures are sometimes referred to as *negative reinforcement* procedures—negative because the removal rather than the presentation of something is the reinforcer. The pattern of behavior maintained by an escape or negative reinforcement contingency bears a striking qualitative resemblance to the pattern of behavior maintained by positive reinforcement. When responses are reinforced by escape according to one or another schedule of reinforcement, behavior patterns appropriate to the schedule emerge. When the magnitude of the negative reinforcer is varied (e.g., the amount of time free from shock as a consequence of an escape response), the frequency of escape responses varies directly with reinforcement magnitude. This phenomenon has a direct parallel when food reinforcement is used to maintain responding.[21]

Discrete-Trial Avoidance

In the case of avoidance, both the procedures and the phenomena are more complicated. There are two standard procedures for studying avoidance, and many variants on each of them. In the oldest type of avoidance procedure, animals are exposed to discrete trials. Periodically, a stimulus (say a tone) is presented. If the animal makes the required response while the tone is on, it prevents shock from occurring at the end of the tone. If the animal does not make the required response, when the tone goes off it is followed by prolonged electric shock. If the animal now makes the required response, it turns off, that is, escapes, the shock. Thus, avoidance procedures of this type are actually escape–avoidance procedures. Figure 9–5 presents a schematic diagram of the standard escape–avoidance procedure.

In one of the more common types of avoidance experiment, animals are placed in a chamber which is divided in half by a barrier. The animal is placed on one side of the chamber, or *shuttle box,* and is required to jump over the barrier to the other side of the box to escape or avoid shock. Dogs exposed to such a procedure will learn to avoid shock in 20 trials or so.[22] Rats exposed to the same procedure will learn to avoid shock in 40 or 50 trials.[23]

The development of avoidance responses often follows a reliable pattern. Early in training, animals do not avoid shock at all; when the shock comes on, they suffer through it for a while, jumping about in

21. See Catania, 1963, for data on magnitude of food reinforcement and Fantino, 1973, pp. 262–265, for data on the magnitude of negative reinforcement, or shock-free time.
22. Solomon and Wynne, 1953.
23. Kamin, 1956.

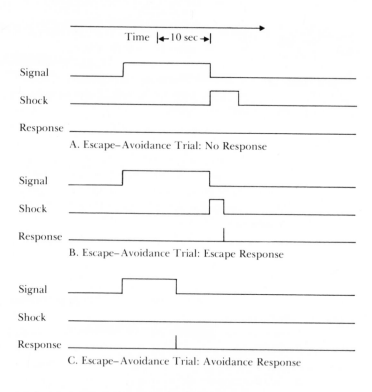

Figure 9–5. Schematic Diagram of the Standard Escape–Avoidance Procedure. *Depicted are a trial in which no response occurs (A), a trial in which an escape response occurs (B), and a trial in which an avoidance response occurs (C). A response is indicated by a vertical line.*

the box, and eventually jump over the hurdle. In other words, they escape the shock but do not avoid it. As trials proceed, animals continue to escape and not avoid; however, the latency of their escape responses grows shorter and shorter.[24] There comes a point at which they escape the shock virtually at the moment it begins. When finally they begin to avoid, the avoidance responses come at the onset of the stimulus which signals shock; the animals do not wait until just before the shock is due to arrive. A pattern of avoidance development like this suggests that avoidance responses are not simply escape responses which occur prematurely. If this were the case, one would expect that when an animal begins to make avoidance responses, they will occur near the end of the signal. However, since the earliest avoidance responses come near the beginning of a trial, it appears

24. See Bolles, Moot, and Nelson, 1976, for some recent, contradictory evidence.

that the onset of avoidance reflects a change in the animal's sensitivity to the contingencies which are operative in the situation.

Shock Postponement

The second standard type of avoidance procedure, which we will call a shock-postponement procedure, includes neither discrete trials nor signals. The animal is placed in the chamber and the session begins. A timer is set, let us say, to time a 5-second interval. When the timer has timed 5 seconds, a brief, inescapable electric shock is delivered; then the timer begins again. Each 5 seconds another brief shock will occur. If the animal makes a response (lever press or hurdle jump), the first timer is deactivated and another timer begins to operate. It is set, let us say, to time 30-second intervals. After 30 seconds, the same brief shock will occur. Timer 2 will be deactivated and Timer 1 will be reactivated. However, if the animal makes another response before 30 seconds has elapsed, Timer 2 will reset to the beginning, and start timing 30 seconds all over again. Every time the animal responds, Timer 2 will reset and start again. If ever the animal fails to respond within 30 seconds, and a shock occurs, Timer 1 will become active and stay active, delivering shocks every 5 seconds until the animal responds again.

This shock-postponement procedure (also known as *free-operant avoidance* or *Sidman avoidance,* after the researcher who developed it) has two important variables: the two time intervals.[25] Timer 1 in the example above times the interval between two shocks, or the *shock–shock (S–S) interval.* Timer 2 times the interval between response and shock or the *response–shock (R–S) interval.* In the example, the S–S interval is 5 seconds and the R–S interval is 30 seconds. If the animal could tell time, it could respond exactly once every 30 seconds and never receive a shock. Though animals are not this efficient, a well-trained dog may respond only five or six times a minute, and virtually never receive a shock. Rats respond more frequently than dogs and typically receive some shocks no matter how well trained they are, but at the peak of their performance rats may only receive a few shocks an hour instead of the 720 shocks per hour they would receive by not responding.

By varying the R–S and S–S intervals, one can influence the rate at which an animal responds. If the R–S interval is short, say 5 seconds, response rate is high; if the R–S interval is long, say 60 seconds, response rate is low. Similarly, if the S–S interval is 5 seconds, response

---

25. See Sidman, 1953, 1966.

rate will be high; if it is 60 seconds, response rate will be low. In all cases, the responding of animals on this type of procedure moves in the direction of maximum efficiency without ever reaching it as the R–S and S–S intervals are varied.

These then are the two most common avoidance procedures: discrete-trial, signaled avoidance, in which a stimulus periodically signals an impending shock and a response during the signal avoids the shock; and free-operant, unsignaled avoidance, in which shocks are arranged to occur repeatedly and an animal must respond steadily to prevent them. Organisms learn to avoid shock effectively when exposed to either procedure. What is the nature of this learning process? What part of the avoidance procedure is crucial for learning to occur? The very same questions can and have been asked about punishment. How does it work and what aspects of it are crucial? As we discuss different theories which have been proposed in the domain of aversive control, we will see that for each theory of avoidance learning there is a companion theory of punishment. We will begin our discussion of the different theories by attempting to identify those aspects of aversive control which seem to make it particularly difficult to understand.

THEORIES OF AVERSIVE CONTROL

If one were to describe the phenomena of avoidance and punishment to an individual who knew nothing about the analysis of behavior, that individual would probably have no trouble providing an explanation. It seems obvious and intuitive that if an animal knows a response will be punished, it will not make the response. Similarly, if an animal knows that the only way to avoid pain is by making the response, it will surely learn to make it.

Let us attempt to make this intuitive explanation a bit more rigorous. What it means to "know" about punishment and avoidance contingencies is that, in the case of punishment, a response leads to shock and no response leads to no shock; in the case of avoidance, it is that a response leads to no shock and no response leads to shock. In symbols, we may write:

Punishment	Avoidance
$R \rightarrow Sh$	$R \rightarrow \overline{Sh}$
$\overline{R} \rightarrow \overline{Sh}$	$\overline{R} \rightarrow Sh$

This seems enough to explain both punishment and avoidance. Actually, however, a bit more is contained in the intuitive explanation. It also assumes that an animal will prefer no shock to shock; if not, even with the knowledge described above, there would be nothing to make the animal follow the contingencies.

Despite the simplicity and appeal of our intuitive explanation of punishment and avoidance, these phenomena have posed substantial theoretical difficulty for behavior theory. The feature of our intuitive account which makes it problematic for the behavior theorist is the nature of the reinforcing event. What event maintains avoidance? What event keeps the organism from responding under punishment contingencies? Our intuitive account suggests that the absence of shock is the crucial event. But how can the absence of something be an event? When does it start? How long does it last? An organism that has never received a shock will not press a lever to avoid shock. What most of the different theories of avoidance and punishment have in common is the search for an event, other than the absence of shock, which can be said to maintain responding.

The theories offered to explain avoidance and punishment fall into five classes. Efforts have been made to account for avoidance (1) strictly in terms of Pavlovian conditioning (Pavlovian theory), (2) in terms of the joint action of Pavlovian and operant conditioning (two-factor theory), (3) strictly in terms of operant conditioning (operant theory), (4) in cognitive terms, that is, based upon what an organism expects to happen in such procedures (cognitive theory), and (5) in biological terms, that is, based upon built-in responses to danger which characterize different species (biological theory). We will take up each of these theories in turn and discuss the problems they encounter.

Pavlovian Theory

A Pavlovian account of punishment and avoidance must begin by identifying the stimuli and the reflexes which occur in these aversive situations. The reflex is assumed to be produced by the aversive stimulus itself. Shock, for example, elicits a host of skeletal movements, including attack, and a variety of autonomic responses like heart rate change, urination, and blood pressure change, all of which are taken as indices of fear. A Pavlovian account of punishment takes the following form: when shock occurs, it elicits fear and a variety of skeletal movements. Each shock is paired with a set of movements leading up to and including the response which is punished (see Figure 9–6). As the pairings between these movements and shock continue, the stimulation produced by the muscles becomes a CS for fear. As a result, when the organism begins to make a response, its early movements produce stimuli which are CSs for fear. The fear response elicited by the CS is thought to be incompatible with the punished response, that

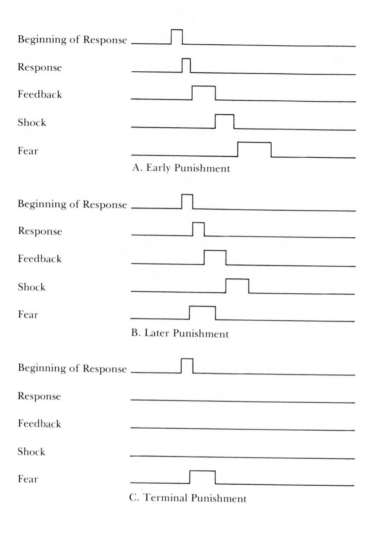

Figure 9–6. Pavlovian Theory of Punishment. *Schematic drawing of the development of response suppression according to Pavlovian theory. In early punishment, shock elicits fear. In later punishment, the beginning of the response is established as a CS for fear, which now occurs before the response. Ultimately, the beginning of the response reliably elicits fear, which is incompatible with the response to be punished. That response is therefore suppressed.*

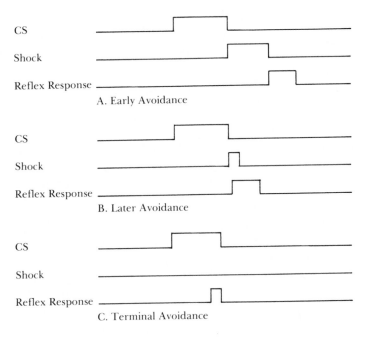

CS

Shock

Reflex Response

A. Early Avoidance

CS

Shock

Reflex Response

B. Later Avoidance

CS

Shock

Reflex Response

C. Terminal Avoidance

Figure 9–7. Pavlovian Theory of Avoidance. *Schematic drawing of the development of avoidance responding according to Pavlovian theory. Early in training, shock elicits a response which happens to escape shock. Later in training, as the CS is paired with shock the CS elicits the reflex, with the result that the animal avoids the shock rather than escaping it.*

is, it is impossible for the organism to make the punished response at the same time it is making the Pavlovian fear CRs.

A Pavlovian account of avoidance is similar (see Figure 9–7). When shock occurs, it elicits a response which successfully escapes the shock. This response might be jumping (over the hurdle in a shuttle box), or attacking (biting the lever), or simply becoming agitated and active (thereby increasing the chances that the escape response will occur). These responses, initially elicited by shock, eventually are elicited by the stimulus which precedes shock. As a result, the reflexive escape response ultimately becomes a reflexive avoidance response.

According to the Pavlovian theory of avoidance and punishment, the consequences of the response do not exert control over responding. It is just the Pavlovian contingency which matters and the fact that shock can be avoided is only incidental. It would seem, on the face of it, that this theory cannot successfully account for what we know about punishment. Consider the comparison we made earlier between punishment and noncontingent shock which occurs, for example, in studies of conditioned suppression. Punishment is much more effective in suppressing behavior than noncontingent shock (see Figures 9–3 and 9–4). The only difference between the two procedures would seem to be the relation between response and shock, which, according to the Pavlovian theory, should not matter. Yet, clearly, it does matter.

Can Pavlovian theory accommodate this fact? The answer is yes. Consider just the relation between stimuli and shock in punishment and noncontingent shock procedures. In punishment procedures, shock only occurs when a response occurs. As a result, the feedback from the beginning of the response will be a perfect predictor of shock. Shock will always and only occur after that stimulus has occurred. In contrast, in a noncontingent shock procedure, feedback from the response will only occasionally precede shock; sometimes shock will occur in the absence of the response. Thus, response feedback will be just one of many stimuli which occasionally precede shock and it will therefore be less likely to become the CS for fear. And even if it does eventually elicit fear, it will do so less reliably than in a punishment procedure. Thus, one could explain the difference between punishment and noncontingent shock strictly on the basis of the quality of the signaling relation between response-produced stimuli and shock.[26]

There are other facts about punishment which Pavlovian theory cannot explain so easily, however. Consider what the organism experiences in the chamber when it is successfully avoiding shock or has stopped receiving punishment. Now when the CSs occur, they are not followed by shock. Each successful avoidance response is a Pavlovian extinction trial. The CS produced by the response occurs, but is not followed by shock since the response is not fully executed. Thus, Pavlovian theory would lead one to expect that avoidance responding would at some point stop, and punished responding at some point resume when conditioned fear extinguished. Once this occurred, pairings of CS and shock would resume and fear would presumably be reestablished. Appropriate behavior would then reappear. However, this would again lead to extinction. If one follows this argument through, it becomes apparent that Pavlovian theory predicts a kind of cycle of conditioning, extinction, reconditioning, reextinction, and so on, with the result that avoidance and suppression should come and go. This is not typically what happens. Avoidance, once acquired, is

26. See Mackintosh, 1974, p. 295.

often virtually permanent. Animals will respond on hundreds and hundreds of trials without receiving shock. Similarly, punishment, if the shock is intense, often produces complete response suppression. The inability to account for the permanence of punishment and avoidance behavior is a serious problem for Pavlovian theory.[27]

There are other problems with Pavlovian theory. Suppose in a discrete-trial avoidance procedure an organism is required to make one response to escape shock but a different response to avoid it. According to Pavlovian theory, avoidance responses are merely reflexive escape responses moved forward in time. If this is so, organisms should be unable to learn to avoid when the required avoidance response differs from the required escape response. It has been known for some years that although it is relatively difficult to learn to avoid under these conditions, organisms do learn.[28] It is not clear how Pavlovian theory can account for this fact.

Does Pavlovian theory have any interesting implications about what we might expect to observe in punishment and avoidance experiments? The theory depends for its account of both avoidance and punishment on responses elicited by the aversive stimulus. However, the role of these reflex responses is quite different in the two cases. In the account of punishment, reflex responses compete with the response being punished and make it less likely. In the account of avoidance, reflex responses facilitate the occurrence of escape, and ultimately avoidance responses.

Suppose we chose a single response, like lever pressing in rats or key pecking in pigeons, and explored its sensitivity to both punishment and avoidance procedures. Presumably, shock will elicit the same reflexes whether it is used as a punisher or as a stimulus to be escaped and avoided. This being the case, we would expect, on the basis of Pavlovian theory, that if shock was effective in punishing key pecks, key pecking would be difficult to learn as an avoidance response. Conversely, if key pecking was easily learned as an avoidance response, it would be difficult to suppress with punishment. In general, according to Pavlovian theory, responses easily learned in avoidance will be difficult to suppress with punishment and responses easily suppressed by

27. Just how persistent avoidance responding is, is somewhat controversial. While there are many demonstrations of persistent avoidance (see Seligman and Johnston, 1973, for a review) there are also demonstrations in which avoidance responding waxes and wanes in much the way Pavlovian theory would predict (see McAllister and McAllister, 1971, and Denny, 1971, for examples). It may be that persistent avoidance is more likely in dogs than in rats, though it has been observed in rats also (e.g., Seligman and Campbell, 1965).

28. Mowrer and Lamoreaux, 1946.

punishment will be difficult to learn in avoidance. This prediction follows, as we saw, from the fact that Pavlovian theory claims that shock elicits responses which compete with the punished response and facilitate the avoidance response.

It turns out that responses easily controlled with one type of procedure are difficult to control with the other. There is not much systematic evidence on this point, but informal evidence is very suggestive. Key pecking in pigeons is readily suppressed by shock as a punisher but extremely difficult to maintain in avoidance experiments.[29] Moreover, it happens that close inspection of the pigeon's behavior when shock occurs reveals a pattern of movement of the neck muscles which is exactly the opposite of that required for pecking.[30] Thus, not only does Pavlovian theory predict the relation between punishment and avoidance, but the elicited response to shock which has been identified is also consistent with a Pavlovian account. To complete the argument, it would be necessary to show that a response which a pigeon will easily learn in an avoidance situation will not be effectively suppressed by punishment.

A similar story can be told of rats: lever pressing is easily suppressed by punishment but difficult to acquire as an avoidance response. Whether responses easily learned in avoidance are difficult to suppress with punishment remains to be determined. Thus, while a strictly Pavlovian account of punishment and avoidance is not able to accommodate all of the facts, it leads to interesting and, as yet, unexplored predictions about the relation between punishment and avoidance.

Two-Factor Theory

Perhaps the most influential theory of aversive control views punishment and avoidance as the product of both Pavlovian and operant influences. It is therefore usually called *two-factor theory*. Most of the attention devoted to two-factor theory has been in explaining escape and avoidance, so we will focus on those phenomena in this discussion.[31]

---

29. There is ample evidence that it is exceedingly difficult to train pigeons to peck a key to avoid shock (Hineline and Rachlin, 1969; Schwartz, 1973). For a general discussion, see Bolles, 1970.

30. Smith, Gustavson, and Gregor, 1972.

31. Two-factor theory probably began with a classic paper by O. H. Mowrer, 1947. Early contributors to the development of two-factor theory include N. E. Miller, 1948. More recently, two-factor theory has been developed largely by R. L. Solomon and his collaborators (e.g., Rescorla and Solomon, 1967).

Consider a discrete-trial, escape–avoidance procedure. A tone is presented and followed by shock. First, the animal learns to escape the shock. While escape is occurring, however, Pavlovian conditioning is also occurring; on each trial, tone (CS) is paired with shock (US). After a number of trials, the tone should elicit fear just as the shock does. The animal may now make the escape response to escape from the fearful CS. But escape from the CS is avoidance of the US. Thus the two-factor theory of avoidance suggests that avoidance is not really avoidance at all. It is escape from a stimulus which, through pairing with shock, has become fear-provoking. Notice how elegantly two-factor theory solves the problem mentioned earlier of having a non-event (the absence of shock) maintain avoidance; it is not the absence of shock at all, but the elimination of the CS, which maintains avoidance. Similarly, since escape is crucial to successful avoidance behavior, the theory maintains that both Pavlovian and operant factors influence and maintain avoidance.

Two-factor theory seems a sensible and straightforward account of discrete-trial avoidance learning. But what of the shock-postponement procedure mentioned earlier? Recall that in this procedure there is no stimulus which signals shock. What can the CS be under these conditions? We saw in Chapter 4 that Pavlovian conditioning can occur when there is no CS other than the passage of time. If the US occurs at regular intervals, then the passage of a certain amount of time can become a CS and elicit responses. This temporal conditioning may well be occurring in shock-postponement procedures. Time between a response and shock is constant, and one could easily imagine that fear could be conditioned to a period of time after the last response. When the organism made a response, fear would be low or nonexistent. As time passed without a response, fear would grow. When it became sufficiently intense, the response would occur, escaping the fear and as a by-product avoiding the shock. There is ample evidence that animals that learn to avoid shocks on shock-postponement procedures do not distribute their resonses randomly in time; rather, the likelihood of a response increases as the time since the last response increases.[32] This seems to provide elegant support for a two-factor interpretation of avoidance learning in shock-postponement procedures.

The two-factor theory of punishment is similar. The stimulus properties of the response which is punished come, via Pavlovian conditioning, to elicit fear. When the animal begins to make the punished response, fear occurs, and any response other than the punished one

32. Anger, 1963.

will succeed in escaping fear. Thus, two-factor theory implies that when punishment works it is because some response other than the punished response is strengthened by the successful elimination of fear.[33]

What evidence is required to support the two-factor theory of punishment and avoidance? To begin with, it is clear that when avoidance is being learned, the signal should be fear-evoking. There is no doubt that it is. There are a number of experiments which are variants on the following procedure: animals are first trained to escape and avoid shock in a standard discrete-trial procedure. After they have learned to avoid shock, they are put in a new situation, in the presence of the signal for shock. Now if they learn to make a response which is completely different from the previous avoidance response, they can escape the signal. Shock never occurs in this new situation. Animals reliably learn to make the response which escapes the signal. What could possibly be maintaining the response if the signal is not fear-evoking?[34]

There is other evidence in support of two-factor theory. This evidence shows that if a CS which has been made to elicit fear through a standard Pavlovian conditioning procedure is presented to an animal while it is responding to avoid shock, the CS will increase the animal's rate of responding. Consider, as a concrete example, a dog that has been trained to jump over a hurdle to avoid shock on a shock-postponement procedure. After it has learned to avoid reliably, it is placed in a new situation and exposed to pairings of tone and shock. These Pavlovian conditioning trials presumably make the CS a conditioned elicitor of fear. Now the animal is returned to the avoidance procedure. It responds, say, six times a minute. Occasionally, the tone is presented. It turns out that presentations of the tone reliably produce increases in the rate at which the animal makes avoidance responses—sometimes to double the rate without the tone.[35] Moreover, if the animal is exposed to a Pavlovian conditioning procedure which includes a CS⁻ or safety signal (an inhibitor of fear), and that stimulus is then occasionally presented while the animal is making avoidance responses, the rate of avoidance responding decreases significantly, often to half the rate which occurs in the absence of the CS⁻.[36]

What these experiments show is that stimuli known to produce or

33. Solomon, 1964.
34. See Miller, 1948; McAllister and McAllister, 1962.
35. Rescorla, 1967b.
36. Rescorla and LoLordo, 1965.

inhibit fear can alter the rate of avoidance responding. By itself, this fact does not necessarily support two-factor theory. Support comes from the inference that since Pavlovian conditioned fear *can* affect the rate of avoidance responding, it is therefore a necessary component of all avoidance responding. In an ordinary avoidance experiment, escape and avoidance develop at the same time that conditioned fear is presumed to develop. As a result, one cannot isolate conditioned fear from the operant consequences of responses and attribute á significant causal role to fear itself. The virtue of the experiments described above is that conditioned fear is produced in one situation and the operant consequences of responses occur in a different situation. When the CS is then presented, and it influences responding, this effect can be attributed to fear alone. The drawback of these experiments is that it can never be proven that because a CS for fear *can* influence avoidance, it *does* influence avoidance in an ordinary discrete-trial procedure. Nevertheless, these experiments certainly suggest that the two-factor account of avoidance may be accurate.

There is another side to the story, however. Just because two-factor theory has been so influential and successful in generating further research, a great many facts have been revealed which point persuasively to its inadequacy as an account of avoidance. We will review some of these facts and the problems they pose below.

Locating the Conditioned Stimulus (CS) • We have seen that it is easy to identify the CS in discrete-trial procedures and difficult, but not impossible, in shock-postponement procedures. There is another type of avoidance procedure in which the difficulty in specifying the CS grows substantially. In this procedure, shocks are programmed to be delivered so many times per hour, but, unlike the shock-postponement procedure, they are distributed randomly in time. One shock may follow another by a few seconds or by many minutes; there is no fixed time between shocks which might serve as a temporal CS. This type of procedure is analogous to a VI schedule while the shock-postponement procedure is analogous to an FI schedule. Rats will learn to press a lever on this procedure if the consequence of lever pressing is a reduction (not necessarily to zero) in the overall frequency of shocks.[37] We will discuss this experiment in greater detail below. For now, it is sufficient to note that while one might be able to make an *ad hoc* argument which hypothesized a CS in a procedure

---

37. Herrnstein and Hineline, 1966.

of this type, it would not resemble CSs which have been used in experiments on Pavlovian conditioning. In addition, if one can find a CS in this situation, in which there is neither an external stimulus nor a regular temporal pattern to shock delivery, one might begin to wonder whether there is any situation in which one could not identify a possible CS.

Locating the Conditioned Response (CR) • Pavlovian fear conditioning presumably produces conditioned fear responses. A wide variety of different responses have been used at different times as indices of conditioned fear. If conditioned fear is a crucial component of avoidance responding, we should expect to observe conditioned fear responses in avoidance procedures. Moreover, we should expect fear CRs to terminate abruptly when the avoidance response occurs. The evidence on this matter points clearly to the conclusion that fear CRs are not reliably observed in avoidance experiments.[38] Sometimes they are observed, sometimes they are not. Sometimes when they are observed, they occur at the wrong time. There is no set of fear responses of which it can be said that at least one was observed each time an investigator looked for it.

There is additional evidence that fear does not reliably occur in avoidance situations, especially not when avoidance responding has been well maintained for some time. When dogs are used as subjects, one can observe signs of fear manifested in their facial expressions and in their posture and gait. Pet owners have little difficulty in determining whether their dogs are afraid. If one watches dogs that have been successfully avoiding for some time, one sees no external sign of fear at all. On the contrary, the dogs appear quite nonchalant and relaxed as they make their avoidance responses.[39] Finally, if one trains animals to avoid shock until they are avoiding successfully most of the time, then puts them in a new situation in which they respond to produce food and occasionally presents the avoidance signal, if the signal is fear-provoking one ought to observe conditioned suppression. Typically, one does not.[40] There is little indication that the shock signal is sufficiently fear-provoking that it will suppress responding when presented in a conditioned suppression experiment.

In summary, there are a number of different lines of evidence to suggest that fear is not present in avoidance situations, at least not in animals that have already learned to respond. It is difficult to main-

38. See Rescorla and Solomon, 1967.
39. Solomon and Wynne, 1954.
40. Kamin, Brimer, and Black, 1963.

tain that escape from fear is what sustains avoidance responding in light of this evidence.

Extinction of Avoidance • Let us examine closely what happens during an avoidance trial in which the animal successfully avoids shock. The CS occurs and is followed by a response. As a result, the US does not occur. Thus each successful avoidance trial is a Pavlovian extinction trial: CS followed by no US. From what we have already seen in Chapter 4, extinction of Pavlovian conditioning should be relatively rapid: probably within 50 trials, and certainly within a few hundred trials, the CS should stop eliciting fear. Thus, two-factor theory of avoidance might lead one to expect the course of avoidance learning to look something like the following:

1. Trials 1–30: Escape but no avoidance; acquisition of conditioned fear.
2. Trials 31–100: Reliable avoidance and concomitant extinction of conditioned fear. As a result of extinction of fear, extinction of avoidance.
3. Trials 101–130: Return to escape but no avoidance. As each trial occurs, the CS is again paired with shock and conditioned fear is re-established.
4. Trials 131–200: Reliable avoidance returns. This, of course, carries with it extinction of fear and extinction of avoidance.
5. Trials 201–220: Escape but not avoidance.

The cycling of periods of escape with periods of avoidance ought to continue indefinitely as fear alternately undergoes extinction and reconditioning. If one disconnects the shocker so that shock never occurs, avoidance responding should continue until fear is extinguished; then it should cease entirely.

Thus, two-factor theory implies an interesting and detailed set of predictions both about trial-by-trial avoidance behavior and the course of extinction, an account which parallels the account which Pavlovian theory would yield. None of these predictions is confirmed by available evidence. First of all, once avoidance responding is acquired, it typically occurs reliably. The predicted cycling of escape and avoidance over blocks of trials does not occur. More significantly, when the shocker is disconnected, animals often continue to make avoidance responses for hundreds and hundreds of trials. Typically, the experimenter's patience wears out before the animal's responses do. Whereas complete extinction of fear in a conditioned suppression procedure may occur within 12 trials if the shock is mild, and within 50 if the shock is extremely intense, no sign of extinction of avoidance responding may be seen even after 200 trials.[41]

It might be argued that avoidance situations are sufficiently traumatic that once responding develops it can never be extinguished; responses once learned are irreversible. As it turns out, there are at least two methods one can use to produce very rapid extinction. The first method is simply to have the shock occur whether or not the avoidance response occurs. This sort of procedure, in which the response has no reinforcing consequence, is more analogous to extinction of appetitive responding than is turning off the shocker. When shock is delivered whether or not the animal jumps over the hurdle or presses the lever, extinction is rapid.[42]

The second method for producing rapid extinction is known as *response blocking*. To take a typical example, an animal that has been trained to jump across a barrier from one side of a box to the other to avoid shock is placed on the side in which the trials begin as normally. The CS is presented. When the animal attempts to make the avoidance response, it encounters a floor-to-ceiling obstruction which makes it impossible to get to the other side of the box. The animal is thus forced to remain in the presence of the CS. Shock is not delivered. When the avoidance response is blocked in this way, avoidance responding is rapidly extinguished.[43]

Thus, avoidance responding can be extinguished, but not by performing the operations which one would expect to produce extinction of conditioned fear. All the data taken together show that while fear, when present, may influence avoidance responding, it is not necessary for the occurrence of avoidance and its elimination does not result in the cessation of avoidance. It seems clear that an alternative to two-factor theory must be found.

Operant Theory

Since the Pavlovian and two-factor theories are both unable to explain many of the phenomena characteristic of aversive control, it is necessary to look elsewhere for a satisfactory account. A question which immediately arises under these circumstances is why the simple and straightforward principles used to account for the appetitive control of behavior cannot be applied with facility to the aversive control

41. Annau and Kamin, 1961; Solomon and Wynne, 1954.
42. Davenport and Olson, 1968.
43. Baum, 1970.

of behavior. The crucial element in the maintenance of a response by food reinforcement is the consquence of the response—food. Why can't one argue that the crucial event in studies of aversive control is similarly the consequence of responding—reduction in frequency of shocks? And why can't one argue that just as reinforcement increases the frequency of responding, punishment decreases the frequency of responding?

Proponents of this operant account of punishment and avoidance have attempted to develop their case by demonstrating that punishment and avoidance contingencies can successfully control responding in situations in which the imputation of conditioned fear is extremely unlikely.[44] In one experiment, two timers were set to run independently of each other. One timer was programmed to deliver shocks at a rate of 6 per minute on the average; the other timer was programmed to deliver shocks at a rate of 3 per minute on the average. In the case of both timers, however, the interval between shocks was random; a shock was just as likely 2 seconds after the last shock as it was 2 minutes after the last shock. As a result, the amount of time that elapsed after a shock was not a good predictor of when the next shock would come. Only one timer ran at any given time, and the animal's responding determined which one it was. If the animal did not press the lever, the timer which delivered 6 shocks per minute ran; if the animal did press the lever, the timer which delivered 3 shocks per minute ran. Thus, the reinforcer for lever pressing was a shift in control of shock delivery from a timer which delivered shocks at high frequency to one which delivered shocks at lower frequency. Each response activated the low-frequency timer until the next shock occurred.

There are a number of things to notice about this procedure. First, no escape from shock was possible. Second, it is hard to imagine what a CS for fear could be; there was no external stimulus, and unlike shock-postponement procedures, the passage of time was not a reliable predictor of shock. Finally, it was entirely possible in this procedure that a lever press would occur and be followed immediately by shock; the lever press activated the low-frequency timer, and if a shock was imminent, it would be delivered. Thus, occasional pairings of response and shock which are characteristic of punishment procedures were an inevitable part of this avoidance procedure. The only positive consequence of responding was a long-term one. On the average, if rats responded reliably they would receive half as many

44. See Herrnstein, 1969; Herrnstein and Hineline, 1966; Rachlin and Herrnstein, 1969.

shocks than if they did not respond reliably. In short, responses did nothing but reduce shock frequency. Despite these difficult, almost impoverished consequences of responding, when the experiment was done, 19 of 20 rats learned to respond reliably.[45] This result is impressive evidence that a sufficient condition for avoidance learning is reduction in shock frequency.

To evaluate the operant account of avoidance, we must ask whether it can explain known facts of aversive control. As it turns out, most facts about aversive control do not contradict operant theory; rather, operant theory seems to have nothing to say about them one way or another. Why, for example, is avoidance responding so difficult to extinguish when the extinction procedure involves disconnection of the shocker. One could argue from the operant account that responses continue to decrease shock frequency during extinction, and thus they continue to be maintained. But this account reintroduces the very problem which led to so many theoretical accounts of avoidance in the first place: How can a nonevent maintain behavior? It is clear that sometimes nonevents can be stimuli. If one is accustomed to the regular beat of a metronome, a missed beat will certainly be noticed, but if the metronome winds down, will the missed beats continue to be noticed as stimuli indefinitely? The operant account of avoidance implies that missed shocks are noticed as stimuli essentially indefinitely.

Another problem is posed by the rapid extinction produced by response blocking. If the animal cannot even make the avoidance response, why should the response extinguish? Operant theory simply has nothing to tell us about this phenomenon. Finally, if shock-frequency reduction, without conditioned fear, is both necessary and sufficient to explain avoidance, why does avoidance responding increase when a stimulus which has been made a CS for fear in a different situation is introduced to the avoidance procedure? These phenomena seem too central to an understanding of avoidance to be left out of any reasonably complete account of aversive control. Our quest for a satisfactory theory must go further.

Cognitive Theory

We have seen that each of the theoretical attempts to circumvent the problems inherent in an intuitive account of aversive control have met with problems of their own. It is time now to come full circle and return to the intuitive account. Perhaps if the intuitive account, based

45. Herrnstein and Hineline, 1966.

upon what an organism knows, expects, and desires, can be made more rigorous, the problems connected with it will disappear.[46]

The postulates of the cognitive theory are simple and direct. These are:

1. An animal prefers no shock to shock.

2. An animal expects that if it responds, no shock, rather than shock, will occur.

3. An animal expects that if it does not respond, shock will occur.

4. Expectancies are strengthened when they are confirmed and weakened when they are disconfirmed. The expectancy that a response leads to no shock is confirmed whenever a response occurs and is not followed by shock. It is disconfirmed whenever a response occurs and is followed by shock. Similarly, the expectancy that no response leads to shock is confirmed whenever shock occurs in the absence of a response and disconfirmed whenever shock does not occur in the absence of a response.

5. Finally, the probability of an avoidance response increases as the degree of confirmation of the two expectancies (2 and 3 above) increases.[47]

In addition to these cognitive characteristics of theory, there is also an emotional component. It contains just two principles:

1. Fear is conditioned to a CS paired with shock.

2. Fear is extinguished when a CS is not paired with shock.

It is important to note that these principles merely state that ordinary Pavlovian conditioning and extinction may occur in avoidance procedures. We shall see that according to the theory, while Pavlovian conditioned fear may play an important role in the initial occurrence of avoidance responses, it has no role at all in the maintenance of avoidance responses.

Let us now apply the theory to what is known about avoidance. First, how are avoidance responses initially acquired? An inspection of the cognitive part of the theory reveals that expectancies can play

46. For early cognitive theories, see Hilgard and Marquis, 1940; Richie, 1951. The theory we will present was formulated by Seligman and Johnston, 1973.
47. For rigorous definitions of the terms "preference" and "expectancy," see Irwin, 1971.

no role in response acquisition. How is the animal to develop the expectancy that responding leads to no shock if it does not already make the response? It is the emotional, Pavlovian component of the theory which explains the initial occurrence of responses. The theory contends that responses elicited by either shock or the CS provide the basis for early avoidance responses. If the response required by the experimenter resembles responses elicited by shock or the CS, learning of expectancies will begin rapidly; if, on the other hand, the response required by the experimenter does not closely resemble elicited responses, the learning of expectancies will be slow; indeed, they may not be learned at all. This aspect of the theory has much in common with the Pavlovian theory discussed earlier, and there is much evidence to support it.

Once avoidance responses begin to occur and expectancies begin to develop, the cognitive component of the theory takes over. Let us see how it accounts for a number of avoidance phenomena which have posed problems for other theories. First, consider the major stumbling block, extinction. Why is extinction by disconnecting the shocker slow, while extinction by response blocking and by presenting shock whether or not the response occurs is fast? Each time the animal makes the response and shock does not occur, the expectancy that responding leads to no shock is confirmed, and, according to the theory, strengthened, with the result that the probability of the response increases. Thus, extinction by turning off the shocker does nothing to alter one of the critical expectancies. The other expectancy, that no responding leads to shock, would be disconfirmed if the animal did not respond; however, the extinction procedure usually does not begin until the probability of a response is so high that the animal responds on virtually every trial. Thus, there is no effective opportunity for disconfirmation of this expectancy. Here is where response blocking comes in. When the animal is not allowed to make the response, it is forced to experience disconfirmations of the expectancy that not responding leads to shock. Ultimately, it develops the expectancy that not responding leads to no shock and stops responding. Thus, even though the other expectancy, that responding leads to no shock, is never disconfirmed, response blocking can produce extinction.

Note that extinction of the avoidance response in this way has no implications about the status of conditioned fear. It is logically possible for fear to be present even after the avoidance response has extinguished. The determinants of fear are different from the determinants of avoidance. There is in fact evidence that fear is often present in very dramatic form during response-blocking procedures.[48]

Now, what of extinction by presentation of shock whether or not the response occurs? With this procedure, the expectancy that not responding leads to shock is unaltered. However, the expectancy that responding leads to no shock is disconfirmed. Disconfirmation reduces the strength of the expectancy and the probability of the response. Thus, the two effective extinction procedures are effective for different reasons; each operates on and weakens a different expectancy.

The theory does an impressive job of explaining much of what we know about aversive control. It cannot, however, explain everything. There are still a number of aspects of aversive control which resist explanation by the cognitive theory:

Why does a CS for fear which is taken from a different situation and imposed on an avoidance procedure increase responding even in animals whose behavior has been maintained on the avoidance procedure for many, many sessions? Presumably, in these animals the relevant expectancies are as strong as they can be. Moreover, consider what expectancies might have developed to the CS during fear conditioning. Here, shock occurred whether or not the animal responded. Thus, the CS might well evoke the expectancies that responding *and* not responding lead to shock. If these expectancies had any effect, it would be to decrease the likelihood of a response rather than increase it.

Why is it that some responses are never learned as avoidance responses even though they occur frequently enough for both relevant expectancies to develop? It has been shown that some particularly reflexive types of responses can be reliably trained as escape responses, but not as avoidance responses.[49]

Thus, there is still much work to be done before a resonably complete account of avoidance is available. The cognitive theory does manage to account for some of what is known about avoidance, but not all. Before turning to a final view of avoidance learning, in comparing cognitive theory to earlier ones, it should be noted that it was developed when the facts were in. This gave it the advantage that it could be tailored to suit the facts. Other theories, especially two-factor

---

48. See Baum, 1970.
49. Turner and Solomon, 1962. It should be noted that when he developed his framework for the study of expectancy and preference, Irwin, 1971, explicitly intended that it apply only to voluntary behavior. It may be that expectancies do not play a role in determining the occurrence of reflexive behavior.

theory, did not have all the information in hand when they were developed. This does not imply that there is something wrong with the cognitive theory; however, a true test of its utility will be its ability to predict new phenomena, and to explain new phenomena which arise in future years.

Biological Theory

The biological approach to avoidance learning is not really incompatible with the earlier ones; indeed, the ideas of this approach are an important part of both the Pavlovian theory of avoidance and the cognitive theory. What distinguishes this approach from the others is primarily emphasis.

Imagine an animal living its life in a relatively hostile natural environment. Among the most important things it must learn is a set of responses which protect it from danger; it must learn to avoid its predators. On the basis of any of the theories we have discussed so far, we might expect avoidance of a predator to develop after a substantial number of trials in which the animal first escapes from the predator, or learns what stimuli (CSs) reliably signal the arrival of a predator so that these stimuli can be escaped and the predator avoided. Animals that learn to avoid in this way in the wild are likely to wind up inside another animal before they learn to avoid it. It seems clear that if animals are to survive in the natural environment, they must learn to escape danger quickly.

Robert Bolles pointed this out and went on from there to outline an approach to avoidance learning which focused upon the repertoire of defensive responses with which members of different species are endowed and the relation between those responses and the ones required in the laboratory.[50] Bolles contended that each species has a set of built-in defensive responses—called *species-specific defense reactions* or *SSDRs*. Common SSDRs include freezing, attack, and flight. When a danger situation develops, an organism will make one of its SSDRs. If this response eliminates the danger, all is well; if not, the animal will make another SSDR; and another, and another, until one of them succeeds. Only when all of the animal's defensive repertoire has been sampled and proven ineffective will non-SSDRs occur. The order in which SSDRs are tried may be random or, more likely, SSDRs may be arranged on a hierarchial scale, with some reliably tried before others.

What are the implications of this account of avoidance in nature for

50. Bolles, 1970.

our understanding of avoidance in the laboratory? It follows from this account that the single most important determinant of avoidance will not be whether a CS is present, whether a response turns off the CS, whether a response can escape shock, or any of the other variables we have considered in this chapter. Rather, what will largely determine the rapidity of acquisition of avoidance responses is the response the animal is required to make. If the response resembles an SSDR, the animal will learn quickly; if the response does not resemble an SSDR, the animal will learn slowly or not at all. It is Bolles's contention that while other variables may influence the rate at which avoidance is learned, their influence is insignificant in comparison to the influence exerted by the relation between the required response and the animal's SSDR repertoire.

Consider the relation between the biological theory and other theories. Both the Pavlovian and cognitive accounts of avoidance explicitly acknowledge the importance of responses elicited by the aversive stimulus. For Pavlovian theory, the avoidance response arises out of these elicited responses; it can come from nowhere else. This view is quite similar to the biological view. However, developers of Pavlovian theory chose to focus upon how aspects of an avoidance situation facilitated or retarded the development of Pavlovian CRs; that is the domain from which an account of avoidance was expected to come. On the other hand, Bolles focused on the relation between the elicited responses and the required response, and relegated Pavlovian conditioning variables to a secondary position. Similarly, the cognitive theory of avoidance explicitly acknowledged (1) that expectancies cannot develop until the avoidance response is occurring and (2) that it is likely that the avoidance response will arise from those responses elicited by the aversive stimulus. Cognitive theory then focused on what happens after the response is occurring. The biological theory focused instead on what determines the early occurrences of the responses; what happens later is of lesser importance. Thus, the difference between the biological view of avoidance and other views is a difference in emphasis rather than a confrontation between logically incompatible formulations.

According to the biological theory, what reinforcement does in avoidance situations is *select* one response from a set of available responses; it does not shape a new response or strengthen an old one. Ineffective responses drop out and effective ones remain. This view is an exact parallel of the view of positive reinforcement proposed by Staddon and Simmelhag (see Chapter 6). You will recall their contention that reinforcement or the law of effect was the major principle of behavior *selection*, but that the *principles of behavioral variation,* which determined what the set of responses was on which reinforcement would operate, did not themselves include the law of effect. In the biological account of avoidance, it is the determinants of the set of SSDRs themselves which are the principles of variation, and avoidance and escape contingencies serve to select a particular SSDR from the set.

What is the evidence for the biological theory? Is there reason to believe that the response one requires in an avoidance experiment has a major influence on avoidance learning? The answer is unequivocally yes. In the case of the rat, some avoidance responses may be learned in one or two trials; an example is jumping out of a box. Other avoidance responses may require many hundreds of trials for acquisition; an example is the familiar lever press. Bolles suggests that the reason lever-press avoidance is learned at all is that the animal may accidentally make an SSDR (such as freezing or attacking) on the lever. If this does not happen, the rat may never learn to lever press, and, indeed, many rats do not learn.

It is important that a response which is difficult to acquire as an avoidance response is easily learned under other circumstances. Otherwise, it would be neither interesting nor surprising that organisms learn some responses only with great difficulty. It would surprise no one if 10,000 trials were required to train a rat to stand on its head—in any situation. One could argue that lever pressing was similarly difficult to learn if it were not for the fact that it is easily learned under conditions of appetitive reinforcement

The same pattern of data characterizes the pigeon. Pigeons learn to lift their heads, flap their wings, hop on a foot switch, and fly very rapidly in avoidance situations. However, they learn to peck a key to avoid with the greatest difficulty. It may take up to 20 hours of painstaking training to develop key-peck avoidance responding. Obviously, the key peck is acquired with great ease under conditions of food reinforcement.

These two examples are sufficient to make a case that the response one chooses to require has a major effect on the results of one's experiment. This is because some responses (non-SSDRs) will not occur in danger situations. Ideally, with the biological theory in hand, one can study the behavior of a particular species in nature, catalogue the defense reactions of that species, and then make detailed predictions about which avoidance responses will be rapidly learned in the laboratory and which will be slowly learned. If one could do this, the biological account of avoidance would have enormous power.

It is not so simple a task, however. Consider, for example, the response of running around in an exercise wheel. It has occasionally been studied in research with rats. Running (fleeing a situation) is an SSDR for the rat. However, in nature, when the rat runs, it escapes the situation. In the laboratory, when the rat runs in a wheel, it remains in the situation. In contrast, when the rat runs from one side of a shuttle box to the other, it escapes. Should wheel running be easily learned or not? Should it be learned more rapidly or less rapidly than shuttle box running? There is no easy way to answer these questions, even if one knows the rat's SSDRs in detail. As a result, what one does is first discover how rapidly avoidance is acquired with one response or another, then rank the different responses in terms of difficulty, and then look for a coherent justification of this ranking in terms of what is known of the organism's SSDRs. This kind of working backward is less powerful and appealing than being able to specify in advance the responses that an organism will learn quickly and the responses that an organism will learn slowly. Nevertheless, it is the state of the science at present.

We have outlined and discussed a number of different accounts of aversive control in the preceding pages, and we have seen that no single account can be used to explain all that is known. While fear is not a necessary concomitant of avoidance responding, it has a dramatic influence on it, and may have an especially important role in the early development of avoidance. While avoidance cannot be explained solely on the basis of reflexes, it is clear that reflexive responses to the aversive stimulus play an important role. Finally, while there is no doubt that the prevention of the aversive stimulus is crucial to avoidance learning, there is some controversy as to whether avoidance reflects strengthened responses or strengthened expectancies. Each theory, though unable to explain all of what is known about avoidance, has led to interesting predictions and discoveries. As a result, the number of facts which any future theory will be required to explain continues to grow. In this way, we continue to learn more and more about aversive control without quite being able to understand all that we know.

10

Interactions Between Pavlovian and Operant Conditioning

In our discussion of theories of avoidance and punishment in the last chapter, we identified two-factor theory as the most influential and thoroughly tested account of aversive control. Though it cannot explain all that we know about punishment and avoidance, it does explain many phenomena. And it does so by using the two sets of conditioning principles to which we have devoted so much attention—those of Pavlovian and operant conditioning—as conceptual tools in analyzing a single situation.

Avoidance and punishment procedures are not the only ones in which Pavlovian and operant principles are both operative. Almost any experimental situation allows the possibility that both Pavlovian and operant conditioning will occur. And if both kinds of conditioning do occur, they may interact in some way to produce the phenomena we observe in the experiment. In this chapter, we will discuss some experimental situations in which both kinds of conditioning occur and identify some phenomena which seem to result from their interaction.

First, under what conditions do both Pavlovian and operant conditioning occur? Consider an animal undergoing operant discrimination training. A dog is trained to push a panel with its nose. When a tone is on, panel pushes produce food; when the tone is off, panel pushes produce nothing. Is this operant procedure free of Pavlovian influence? Is the tone simply a discriminative stimulus or is it also a Pavlovian conditioned stimulus? Panel pushing is an operant and it is presumably controlled by its past consequences. However, the tone is a signal for food, and if one records the dog's salivation, one will observe conditioned salivation to the tone.[1] Thus, the operant discrimination procedure includes both Pavlovian and operant contingencies, and whether one calls the procedure Pavlovian or operant depends upon what response one is measuring. If one measures salivation the procedure is Pavlovian, and if one measures panel pushing the procedure is operant.

The same sort of complication is present in most procedures which are putatively studies of Pavlovian conditioning. A tone sounds and is followed by the delivery of a food pellet. The dog approaches the pellet and ingests it. One measures salivation to the tone. But the dog's approach to the pellet is operant behavior. Thus we see that the joint occurrence of Pavlovian and operant conditioning is more likely the norm than the exception in common experimental situations. Faced with this fact, researchers have come increasingly to study the role played by both kinds of conditioning in experimental settings with which we are already familiar.

PAVLOVIAN RESPONSES DURING OPERANT CONDITIONING

One way to study the joint occurrence of Pavlovian and operant conditioning is to impose an operant contingency on responding and simultaneously record both operant responses and Pavlovian responses. Imagine entering a bakery, examining the pastries, choosing one, paying for it, taking it home, unwrapping it, and eating it. This is an operant sequence. Presumably, during this sequence you will also be salivating. What is the relation between conditioned salivation and components of the operant sequence?

A number of experiments involving concurrent measurement of Pavlovian and operant responses have shown that they are related in complex ways. In one, dogs were trained to press a panel for food; some dogs received food on a fixed-ratio (FR) schedule, and some on a fixed-interval (FI) schedule. Figure 10–1 presents second-by-second rates of salivation and panel pressing for one dog exposed to each schedule. For the dog exposed to the FI schedule, both panel pressing and salivation began and grew together. For the dog on the FR schedule, salivation did not occur reliably until an appreciable number of panel presses had occurred.

What can be said about the relation between Pavlovian and operant conditioning on the basis of these data? It seems clear that conditioned salivation has no causal role in the maintenance of panel press-

1. See Konorski, 1967; Shapiro, Miller, and Bresnahan, 1966; and Williams, 1965.

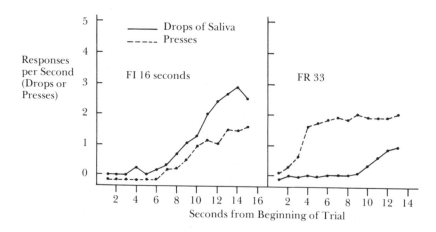

Figure 10–1. Concurrent Measurement of an Operant and a Pavlovian Conditioned Response. *Panel pushing and salivation are plotted over the course of a trial for one dog whose panel pressing was reinforced on an FI schedule and one dog whose panel pressing was reinforced on an FR schedule. For the first dog, pressing and salivation began and grew together; for the second dog, panel pressing preceded salivation. (After Williams, 1965.)*

ing. Panel pressing *precedes* salivation in the case of the FR schedule and cooriginates with salivation in the case of the FI. In neither case does salivation precede panel pressing.

What about the possibility that panel pressing has some causal role in the occurrence of salivation? To examine this possibility, the dogs were exposed on alternate days to schedules of food delivery which were independent of responses; the panel was not even present. One can assess the role of panel pressing in the control of salivation by comparing salivation on these days with salivation on days in which panel presses were required to produce food. The results of this comparison are in Figure 10–2. It is apparent that the observed pattern of salivation was completely independent of the actual concomitant occurrence of operant responses.

If salivation does not exert a causal influence on panel pressing, and panel pressing does not exert a causal influence on salivation, what is the nature of their relation in these experiments? An answer to this question may be found by examining the relation between responses and the imminence of food on FI and FR schedules. On FI schedules, food is available at regular intervals. It is the passage of time and not the occurrence of responses which marks the impending delivery of food. If we ignore the fact that panel presses are occur-

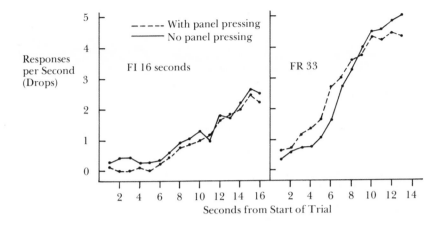

Figure 10–2. Effects of the Occurrence of an Operant on the Occurrence of a Pavlovian Conditioned Response. *The figure depicts the occurrence of salivation over the course of trials in which panel pressing also occurs and in trials in which no panel pressing is possible. For one dog, panel pressing was reinforced on an FI schedule; for the second dog, pressing was reinforced on an FR schedule. (After Williams, 1965.)*

ring, the procedure is an instance of Pavlovian delay conditioning, with the passage of time as the CS. In studies of delay conditioning, one observes a gradual increase in salivation like that depicted in Figure 10–1. Similarly, in studies of FI schedules, one observes the gradual increase (scallop) in operant responses depicted in Figure 10–1. Thus, both salivation and panel pressing increase as the likelihood of food (or the animal's expectation that food is likely) increases.

The situation is different on the FR schedule. Now it is the occurrence of responses and not the passage of time which signals the imminent availability of food. If conditioned salivation depends upon the animal's expectation that food is near, and if that expectation in turn depends upon the occurrence of operant responses, we would expect the beginning of salivation to lag behind the beginning of panel pressing, as indeed it does. To translate these relations into a more familiar context, we would expect that if one ate dinner regularly at the school cafeteria at the same time each day, initiation of the operant (walking to the cafeteria) and initiation of conditioned salivation would co-occur. Both would begin as a function of the passage of time since the last meal. If, on the other hand, one purchased pastries, as in the example above, one would not expect salivation to begin until a number of responses (choosing, purchasing, walking home, etc.) had occurred. Here, as in the FR schedule, the expectation of food availability is largely a function of the number of operant responses which have occurred.

In summary, concurrent measurement of operant and Pavlovian conditioned responses seems to reveal little direct interaction. Both kinds of responses can be conditioned by the same procedure in the same situation, but they seem to exert minimal influence on each other. If the conditioned responses themselves do not interact, perhaps the *contingencies* do. Perhaps a Pavlovian contingency affects operant responding directly.

PAVLOVIAN CONTINGENCIES DURING OPERANT CONDITIONING

One way to examine the possibility that Pavlovian contingencies have a direct effect on operant responding is to train animals to make an operant response and, when that response is well established, to expose the animals to Pavlovian conditioning. Then, while the animal is engaged in the operant response, the Pavlovian CS may occasionally be presented and the effects of that CS on the ongoing operant behavior may be assessed. Consider, for example, the case in which operant responding is maintained by food reinforcement, and Pavlovian conditioning is then conducted with shock as the US. When the Pavlovian CS is then presented while the animal is engaged in the operant behavior, a dramatic reduction in responding occurs. This phenomenon is called conditioned suppression (see Chapters 4 and 9). In contrast, when a Pavlovian CS for shock is superimposed on a baseline of operant *avoidance* responding, the result is an increase in the rate of operant responding.[2]

How is one to account for these interactions? One possible account assumes that Pavlovian conditioning produces a motivational state in the animal. We have already discussed this type of account in our discussion of two-factor theory in Chapter 9. That is, if shock is the US, fear is conditioned; if food is the US, some sort of appetitive motivation is conditioned. In addition, it is assumed that the ongoing operant responding is controlled in part by the motivational state of the organism, fear in the case of avoidance and hunger in the case of food-maintained responding. If we further assume that appetitive and aversive motivational states are antagonistic, we can see how a signal for shock suppresses food-reinforced responding while it accelerates responding which avoids shock. A signal for fear reduces

2. Rescorla and LoLordo, 1965.

hunger and, as a result, responding for food is suppressed. A signal for fear enhances fear and, as a result, avoidance responding is enhanced.[3] This account has intuitive appeal. If, in walking across the street to the bake shop, we hear the squeal of brakes, the honking of automobile horns, and the crush of metal against metal, we are likely to lose our appetite for pastries. On the other hand, if the same frightening sounds occur as we are crossing the street to avoid a large German shepherd, our fear will probably increase and we will cross the street faster.[4]

This account of Pavlovian–operant interactions in terms of motivational states induced by Pavlovian conditioning which influence operant responding has difficulty explaining the results of studies in which Pavlovian appetitive conditioning is superimposed on operant appetitive responding. Experiments in which signals for food are presented while the animal is making operant responses for food have yielded both dramatic increases and dramatic decreases in operant responding during the Pavlovian signal. Let us consider some examples.

A dog is trained to press a panel for food and then exposed to Pavlovian conditioning trials in which a CS is followed by food. Later, the dog is returned to the panel-pressing situation and occasionally presented with the CS. On the basis of our analysis of the effects of Pavlovian signals for shock, we would expect panel pressing to increase when the CS is present. It is as if one were walking toward a bakery to purchase pastries and a clock chimed 6:00 as one walked. The clock chime (CS for dinner) might increase the speed at which one walked to the bakery. However, the results of such an experiment are precisely the opposite of what one would expect: a CS for food decreases panel pressing while it elicits profuse salivation.[5]

Now consider a second example. A pigeon that has been trained to peck a white key for food is then exposed to Pavlovian conditioning trials in which illumination of a key with red light is followed by food. The pigeon comes to peck at the red key. Now the pigeon is returned to the operant procedure, pecking at the white key for food, and the color of the key occasionally changes from white to red, signaling

3. LoLordo, 1967, has shown that this summation of fear occurs even when the Pavlovian US and the operant reinforcer are different aversive events. In his study, the operant aversive stimulus was shock and the Pavlovian US was a loud noise. Presentation of the CS increased avoidance responding.
4. See Rescorla and Solomon, 1967, for a detailed discussion of experiments of this type.
5. This experiment, done in 1936, is reported by Konorski, 1967.

food delivery. The pigeon pecks the key at a substantially higher rate when it is red than when it is white, the opposite of the results just described for dogs.[6]

What can account for these contradictory results? In the study with dogs, and many other studies with rats or monkeys which also found suppression of responding, the CS for food was displaced away from the operant lever. In the study with pigeons, the CS was located on the operant key. In addition, in the pigeon, the response produced by a Pavlovian CS for food was pecking—the very same response as the required operant. This identity of operant and Pavlovian responses is not true of lever pressing in dogs, rats, or monkeys. We could imagine that, for the pigeon, Pavlovian key pecks simply add to operant key pecks, resulting in an overall increase in key pecking. That the rate of operant responses *decreases* during the CS in the studies with dogs, rats, and monkeys suggests the possibility that some Pavlovian response which is directed at the CS is conditioned in those animals as well. However, since the CS is away from the lever, the occurrence of CRs during the CS would compete with and reduce the frequency of operant responses.

A way to test these speculations is to try to turn the pigeon into a rat. For example, one could train a pigeon to engage in an operant other than key pecking, pair a lit key with food, and observe the frequency of the operant during the CS. The results of such a study are presented in Figure 10–3. The pigeons were trained to hop on a treadle for food and exposed to pairings of key light and food. The solid lines in Figure 10–3 depict day-to-day rates of treadle hopping when the CS was absent; the broken lines depict rates of treadle hopping when the CS was present. It is clear from the figure that not only was treadle hopping suppressed during the CS, it was virtually eliminated. What was the pigeon doing if it was not hopping on the treadle? The answer to this question appears in the bottom of Figure 10–3, which presents rates of key pecking during the CS (broken lines) and in its absence. This particular pigeon pecked the key between 90 and 150 times a minute when the CS was on. Thus, separating the operant and Pavlovian responses makes the pigeon's performance on this type of procedure look like the rat's.

There is another way to turn the pigeon into a rat. If we train pigeons to peck a key for food but have the CS for food in Pavlovian conditioning trials displaced away from the key, we should observe suppression of key pecking during the CS instead of facilitation; the pigeons presumably will spend some time during the CS directing be-

6. See LoLordo, 1971; Schwartz, 1976.

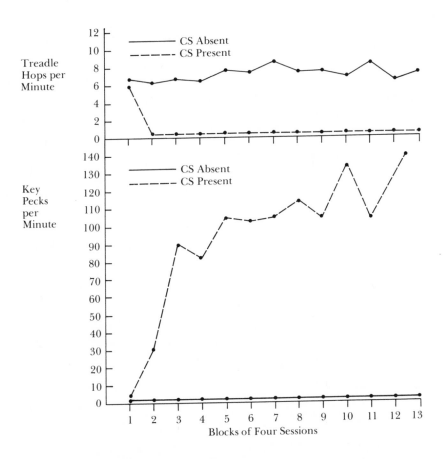

Figure 10–3. Effects of a Conditioned Stimulus for Food on Operant Treadle Pressing for Food. *The top of the figure presents treadle pressing, and the bottom, key pecking in the absence of and in the presence of the CS, a lit key. (After LoLordo, McMillan, & Riley, 1974.)*

havior toward the CS instead of the key. This is what has been observed in a number of experiments of this type.[7]

In one such experiment, pigeons trained to peck a key for food were then exposed to pairings of CS and food. In some phases of the experiment, the CS was a change in the color of the key. In other phases, it was the illumination of a second key. Here, both keys would be lit simultaneously during the CS. The results of this experiment, for two pigeons, are presented in Figure 10–4. The first pair of bars is from the phase in which the CS was a change in the color of the key.

7. LoLordo, McMillan, and Riley, 1974; Farthing, 1971; Schwartz, 1976.

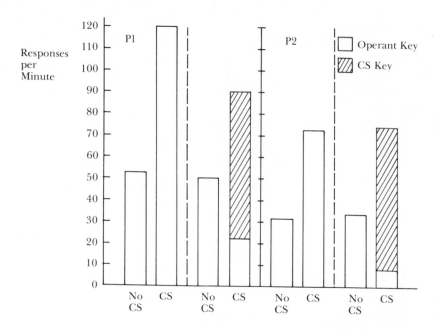

Figure 10–4. Effects of the Locus of a Conditoned Stimulus for Food on the Rate of Operant Responding for Food. *The left bar in each pair depicts rate of key pecking in the absence of a CS for food. The right bar depicts rate of key pecking in the presence of a CS for food. When the CS was on the operant key, the rate of operant key pecking was* higher *during the CS than in its absence. When the CS for food was on a separate signal key, the rate of operant key pecking was* lower *during the CS than in its absence. However, the sum of CS key rate and operant key rate was greater than operant key rate alone in the absence of the CS. (After Schwartz, 1976.)*

The first bar in the pair presents response rate in the absence of the CS and the second presents response rate in the presence of the CS. Both pigeons showed very substantial enhancement of key pecking while the CS was on.

The second pair of bars is from the second phase of the experiment in which the CS was illumination of a second key. Again, the first bar in the pair presents response rate in the absence of the CS. The second bar presents response rate, summed on both keys, during the CS. The open part of that bar is responding on the operant key and the striped part is responding on the CS key. If we look only at behavior on the operant key, the pigeons in this experiment behave like dogs, monkeys, rats, and pigeons hopping on treadles in similar experiments: the CS suppresses operant responding. If, on the other hand, we look at responding on both keys, we observe enhancement and not suppression. What happens in this procedure in which the operant key and the CS key are spatially separated is that operant and Pavlovian pecking are also spatially separated. In this way, the factors responsible for the difference between pigeons and other animals on procedures of this type become apparent. That is, in the standard pigeon experiment, the CS is on the operant key and the Pavlovian response is the same as the operant, while in standard rat, dog, and monkey experiments, the CS is not located in the place where the operant must occur, and Pavlovian and operant responses are different.

The resolution of the contradictory outcomes of these experiments poses a problem for the view that Pavlovian contingencies influence operant responding by altering the animal's motivational state. A signal for food should have the same effect on the animal's motivation whether it is located on the response key or elsewhere. It should have the same effect whether the animal is key pecking for food or treadle hopping. We have seen that it does not. The effect of a Pavlovian contingency on operant responding will depend in part on whether the responses produced by the Pavlovian CS compete with or blend with the operant response.[8]

Notice, however, that an account of operant–Pavlovian interaction solely in terms of competition or blending of responses cannot explain the results of the studies employing CSs for shock. A CS for shock suppresses lever pressing for food but enhances lever pressing to avoid shock. The required operant and the location of the CS are the same in both cases. An account based on Pavlovian alteration of motivational states does a much better job than an account based on response competition in these cases. Thus, while we can be sure that Pavlovian and operant contingencies interact, we cannot specify a single mechanism which underlies all such interactions.

---

8. There is another line of research on the interactions between Pavlovian and operant conditioning which also poses problems for the view that Pavlovian contingencies have a motivational influence on operant responding. In these studies, a stimulus which has been established as a Pavlovian CS is then used for the same subjects as an operant discriminative stimulus. The typical findings in these studies is that Pavlovian experience with the stimulus facilitates learning the operant discrimination. However, this seems to be the result not of the motivational state produced by the CS, but of the information carried by the CS. If a tone has been paired with food pellets during Pavlovian conditioning and is then used as an S[+] for lever pressing for food pellets, an animal quickly learns to lever press when the tone is present. However, if the tone is used as an S[+] for lever pressing for sucrose, the previous Pavlovian conditioning has no effect (Trapold, 1970). The *motivational* properties of the tone are the same in both cases but its properties as a *signal* are relevant only in the first case. See Trapold and Overmeier, 1972, for a discussion of experiments of this type.

PAVLOVIAN CONDITIONING DURING OPERANT DISCRIMINATION TRAINING

The fact that explicit Pavlovian contingencies superimposed on operant contingencies can influence the occurrence of operant responses raises a question about whether Pavlovian contingencies which are a concomitant of operant conditioning procedures have similar effects. Stated in another way, some operant conditioning procedures have Pavlovian contingencies built into them. To what extent do these Pavlovian contingencies contribute to experimental outcomes?

One such procedure is an operant discrimination. If pigeons are exposed to a multiple schedule (Chapter 7) in which periods of VI reinforcement availability signaled by, for example, a green key light, alternate with periods of extinction, signaled by a red key light, the green key light is effectively a CS for food. If we ignore for a moment the fact that key pecks are required for food and focus only on the relation between the green and red keys and food, it is clear that the green key signals food while the red key does not. Thus the green key, as a predictive stimulus, should elicit Pavlovian conditioned responses, and the form of the conditioned responses should be pecks at the CS. If the schedule associated with the red key is changed to a VI identical to that which operates when the key is green, then the predictiveness of the green key is eliminated; food is just as likely when the key is red as when the key is green. Such a procedure, as we saw in Chapter 5, should result in the extinction of Pavlovian conditioned responses.

In a study which confirmed this expectation, pigeons were exposed to a multiple schedule in which the key color alternated between red and green for 30-second periods. Food was delivered at irregular intervals and it was *independent* of responding (such schedules are called *variable-time* or VT schedules). Sometimes food was presented with the same frequency whether the key was red or green. Here we would expect no Pavlovian conditioned pecking since neither red nor green was predictive with respect to food. Sometimes food was presented only in the presence of one of the stimuli; in this case, that stimulus was predictive and Pavlovian key pecking should have occurred. Some results of that experiment are presented in Figure 10–5. It is clear from the figure that high rates of key pecking were maintained by a stimulus which differentially predicted food. When the likelihood of food was independent of the color of the key, key pecking decreased dramatically.

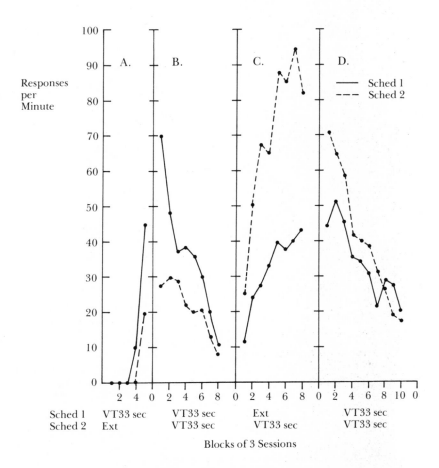

Figure 10–5. Maintenance of Key Pecking by Response-Independent Food Presentation. *Responses per minute are plotted during each component of a multiple schedule when food was presented during both components (B) and (D) or when food was presented only during one component (A) and (C). Key pecking occurred at high rates only in the latter case. (After Gamzu & Schwartz, 1973.)*

Behavioral Contrast

The experiment just described was one in which pecks were not required to produce food. What should happen when pecks are required? An example of what we might expect is depicted in Figure 10–6. On the left are responses per minute during red and green when pecks in the presence of either color are being reinforced on a VI 3-min schedule. The operant contingency between response and

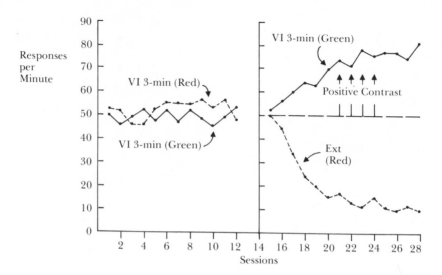

Figure 10–6. An Example of Positive Behavioral Contrast. *A pigeon is first exposed to a multiple VI 3-min VI 3-min reinforcement schedule. The color of the response key alternates between red and green, and key pecks in the presence of either color are reinforced on a VI 3-min schedule. As depicted in the left side of the figure, the pigeon pecks at about the same rate in red and green. Then, reinforcement is discontinued in red (Ext). Response rate in red goes down. At the same time, response rate in green goes up. This increase in response rate in green, despite no change in the schedule or rate of reinforcement, is known as positive behavioral contrast.*

reinforcer maintains responding at an appreciable rate even though there is no predictive Pavlovian contingency between either stimulus and the reinforcer. Thus, when red and green signal the same VI schedule, key pecking, rather than being eliminated as in Figure 10–5, is maintained at a reasonably high rate. However, when food is subsequently made available for responding only during green, as in the right portion of Figure 10–6, responding during green, though reinforced on the same VI 3-min schedule as before, is significantly elevated. This phenomenon is reliably observed in operant discrimination experiments and it is called *positive behavioral contrast*. The word "contrast" is used because response rate in green (S$^+$) changes in a direction opposite to the change in red (S$^-$) response rate, and it is "positive" contrast because S$^+$ response rate increases.

The phenomenon of behavioral contrast has been extensively researched and a number of different theoretical explanations have been proposed.[9] We will focus on a recent account which views contrast as the product of an interaction between operant and Pavlovian contingencies. The account is known as the "additivity theory" of contrast.[10] When the pigeon is shifted from the VI–VI procedure to the VI–EXT procedure, the green key becomes a differential predictor of food. As such, it generates Pavlovian key pecking like that depicted in Figures 10–5*A* and 10–5*C*. If Pavlovian key pecking simply adds to the operant key pecking already being maintained by the dependency between key pecks and food (left side of Figure 10–6) the net result will be an increase in overall key pecking—positive behavioral contrast. Thus, the additivity theory accounts for positive contrast in terms of the addition of pecks controlled by a Pavlovian contingency (Figure 10–5) to pecks already controlled by an operant contingency.

This account of contrast parallels the account offered above of the effects of a Pavlovian CS for food on operant responding for food, and the reader may be able to guess at procedures one could use to substantiate the account of contrast. They parallel procedures just described in the study of the effects of Pavlovian appetitive conditioning on food-reinforced responding and, in general, provide support for additivity theory:

1. If a pigeon is trained to hop on a foot treadle instead of pecking the key, behavioral contrast does not occur. The reason for this is that the Pavlovian CR of pecking does not sum with the operant of hopping.[11]

2. If the stimuli signaling the components of the multiple schedule are not on the key, contrast often does not occur. The reason for this is that Pavlovian CRs are directed at the signal and not at the key. Thus, as in (1), they do not sum with key pecks. In an experiment of this type, pigeons were exposed to a series of multiple schedules in which food was available on a VI 1-min schedule in either one or both components. The stimuli used to signal the components were varied from one procedure to the next; they were sometimes different key colors, sometimes the presence or absence of another light located away from the key, and sometimes the presence or absence of a tone. Positive behavioral contrast was only

9. See Reynolds, 1961a; Terrace, 1971; Rachlin, 1973; Mackintosh, 1974; Schwartz and Gamzu, 1977.
10. See Schwartz and Gamzu, 1977.
11. Westbrook, 1973; Hemmes, 1973.

observed when the stimuli signaling the components of the multiple schedule were located on the response key.[12]

3. In standard procedures employed with rats as subjects, in which the discriminative stimuli are not on the lever, contrast often does not occur. This may be because, as in (1), lever pressing is not a Pavlovian CR or, as in (2), CRs are directed at the signal, which is not on the lever. In either case, there is not summation of CRs and lever presses.[13]

PAVLOVIAN CONTINGENCIES AND OPERANT BEHAVIOR: SUMMARY

The evidence we have reviewed makes it clear that when both Pavlovian and operant contingencies are present in a situation, either by design or by accident, they will both exert control over behavior:

1. A CS for shock suppresses operant responding for food.

2. A CS for shock enhances operant responding which avoids shock.

3. A CS for food suppresses operant responding for food when the CR and the operant are incompatible.

4. A CS for food enhances operant responding for food when the CR and the operant are compatible.

5. Positive behavioral contrast generally occurs in an operant discrimination under conditions which would produce (4), and generally does not occur under conditions which would produce (3).

There is presently no account of the mechanism which underlies Pavlovian–operant interaction which can explain all of these effects. An account based upon the creation of motivational states by Pavlovian contingencies can comfortably explain 1 and 2, but not 3–5. An account based upon competition or blending of Pavlovian CRs and operant responses can comfortably explain 3–5, but not 1 and 2. It may be that not all instances of Pavlovian–operant interaction can be traced to a single, underlying mechanism.

12. Schwartz, 1974a. Contradictory evidence may be found in Hemmes, 1973.
13. In opposition to the additivity theory of contrast, there are some demonstrations of contrast in rats. A most impressive one is reported by Gutman, Sutterer, and Brush, 1975.

CONDITIONED REINFORCEMENT

The first part of this chapter clearly established that a Pavlovian CS for food or shock can be a powerful source of discriminative control over operant behavior. Now we will see whether such a stimulus can also be a source of reinforcement. Can a stimulus of no particular biological significance be transformed through Pavlovian conditioning into a reinforcer? Can a tone which reliably signals a reinforcer like food become a *conditioned reinforcer* itself?

The concept of conditioned reinforcement is enormously significant if one is to entertain seriously the possibility that what one finds in the laboratory mirrors what goes on in the natural environment. Pigeons, rats, and dogs work in experimental settings to produce food or water or avoid shock. People rarely engage in behavior which produces or avoids biologically significant stimuli directly. Many people are virtually never deprived of food and water. If one is to account for human behavior in terms of reinforcement principles one must look elsewhere for the reinforcers. Likely reinforcers in the natural environment are money, social approval, status, and power. How do such stimuli or states come to be reinforcers? It is possible that the reinforcing character of these stimuli is the result of some sort of conditioning. The obvious influence of stimuli like money on human behavior challenges the behavior theorist to develop an account of how money might reinforce behavior. Thus, the applicability of the principles of behavior control may depend upon our understanding of conditioned reinforcement.

Demonstrating Conditioned Reinforcement

How do we know that a stimulus is a conditioned reinforcer? What effect should a conditioned reinforcer have on behavior? Before we identify a stimulus as a conditioned reinforcer, we might insist that it do everything that an unconditioned reinforcer can do. If the pairing of a tone and food endows the tone with foodlike properties, we should be able to substitute tone for food in any experimental situation and gain the same degree of control over behavior as we would with food. Operationally, this stringent criterion has been reflected in experiments in which putative conditioned reinforcers are used to train new responses—responses which the animal has not previously made. Thus, for example, a rat trained to run down an alley for tone-food pairings might be placed in an operant conditioning chamber and trained to press a lever for tone presentations. The lever pressing of this rat might be compared with that of a second rat, also trained to press a lever for tone presentations but without previous experience of tone–food pairings. If the first rat learned faster and pressed more than the second rat, we would conclude that by Pavlovian conditioning the tone had become a conditioned reinforcer. We may call this criterion a *new learning* criterion.

A second, less stringent criterion is that a conditioned reinforcer should have the power to maintain behavior which has already been learned. Thus, for example, a pigeon might be trained to peck a key for tone–food pairings. After key pecking is well established, food presentations are discontinued and pecks produce only the tone. The experimental question is whether pigeons whose pecks produce the tone continue pecking longer than pigeons whose pecks produce neither food nor tone. This criterion we shall call the *maintenance* criterion.

A final, still less stringent criterion for labeling a stimulus a conditioned reinforcer requires that responding be influenced by variations in the contingency between responses and stimulus presentations in the same way that responding is influenced by variations in the contingency between responses and food presentations. For example, it is well established that response rate is a function of the frequency and schedule of food reinforcement (Chapter 7). We can ask whether response rate is a similar function of the frequency and schedule of conditioned reinforcement. Also, we know that different schedules of food reinforcement maintain different temporal patterns of responding. Do schedules of conditioned reinforcement affect responding in the same way? We will call this criterion the *parametric sensitivity* criterion since it asks whether responding is influenced by parametric variations in conditioned reinforcement in the same way that it is influenced by parametric variations in unconditioned reinforcement.

The earliest experiments on conditioned reinforcement established a conditioned reinforcer by pairing a click with the presentation of food. In one experiment, a click was paired with food while rats were being trained to eat from a feeder. Subsequently, lever presses produced the click. The rats made a substantial number of lever presses, presumably an indication of the reinforcing power of the click. Lever presses decreased over time, an indication that the click was extinguishing as a conditioned reinforcer.[14]

In another experiment, rats were trained to press a lever for click plus food and then lever pressing was observed when presses produced only a click. These animals pressed the lever more than animals

14. Skinner, 1938.

for which lever presses did not produce clicks.[15] Thus, we have paradigmatic instances of both the new-response and maintained-response tests of conditioned reinforcement. What is there about the relation between click and food which seems to make the click a conditioned reinforcer?

Establishing a Conditioned Reinforcer

A conditioned reinforcer looks procedurally like a Pavlovian CS. A neutral stimulus reliably precedes a US but instead of evaluating whether the neutral stimulus evokes Pavlovian conditioned responses, we evaluate its power to maintain operant responses. Thus, it is not surprising that issues we discussed in the chapters on Pavlovian conditioning reappear in a discussion of conditioned reinforcement. Our earliest interpretation of the conditions necessary for Pavlovian conditioning isolated temporal contiguity between CS and US. Subsequent research and theoretical analysis led to a revision of our understanding. Informativeness or predictiveness of the CS was also necessary; temporal contiguity was not sufficient in itself. The same controversy between the temporal contiguity and predictive contingency views has characterized research on conditioned reinforcement.

Consider the following experiment. Rats already trained to press a lever for food experienced trials with the lever absent in which food presentation was preceded by two stimuli, S_1 and S_2 as depicted in Figure 10–7A. For one group of rats, (Group B) S_1 was also occasionally presented alone, without S_2 or food, as in Figure 10–7B. After this training, the rats were placed in an extinction situation in which lever presses produced only S_1 for some animals and only S_2 for others. Based upon research on predictiveness of stimuli discussed in Chapter 5, what would we expect the results of such an experiment to be? Let us consider first the rats (Group A) who experienced only the stimulus sequences depicted in Figure 10–7A. S_1 and S_2 both reliably preceded food. However, since S_1 appeared a half-second before S_2, the appearance of S_2 was redundant; all the information available regarding food was carried by S_1. If the predictiveness of a stimulus is essential to its conditioned reinforcing power, we would expect these rats to have responded more when responses produced S_1 than when responses produced S_2.

Now, consider the second group of rats (Group B). When S_1, S_2, and food occurred in sequence, S_2 was again redundant. However,

15. Bugelski, 1938.

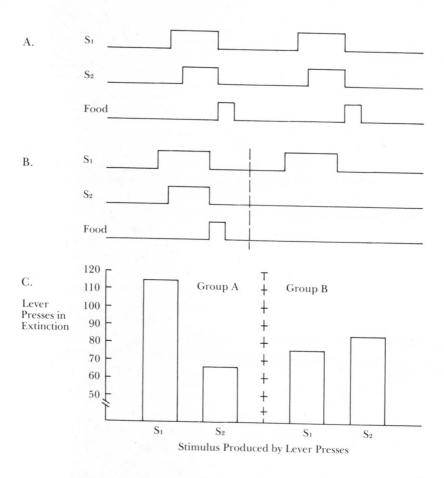

Figure 10–7. Effects of the Informative Value of Stimuli on Their Effectiveness as Conditioned Reinforcers. A *depicts the* S_1–S_2–*food sequence received by Group A.* B *depicts the two types of sequence received by Group B.* C *depicts responses in extinction for both groups when lever presses produced either* S_1 *or* S_2 *(After Egger & Miller, 1962.)*

some of the time only S_1 occurred. As a result of these extra trials, S_1 no longer made S_2 redundant; sometimes S_1 was followed by food but sometimes it was not. Now, S_2 was the best predictor of food. On the basis of an information hypothesis, we would expect these rats to have responded more in extinction for S_2 than for S_1.

As can be seen in Figure 10–7C, the predictions based upon an information hypothesis were confirmed experimentally. Rats in Group A, which experienced only S_1–S_2–food trials, pressed more for S_1 than S_2 in extinction. Rats in Group B, which sometimes experienced S_1

alone, pressed more for S_2 than S_1.[16] Note that this experiment cannot be taken to show that informativeness is *necessary* for a stimulus to become a conditioned reinforcer. What it does show is that the more informative a stimulus is, the more effective it is.[17]

Having found that the predictiveness of a stimulus contributes significantly to its conditioned reinforcing power, we are left with a difficult and subtle question: What is it about predictiveness of a stimulus which makes the stimulus reinforcing? Is it predictiveness per se, or is it the event that the stimulus predicts?[18] Attempts to answer this question have centered on research on what are called *observing responses.*[19]

Observing Responses

Imagine a pigeon pecking a white key for food. Sometimes food is available on an FI schedule and sometimes food is available on an FR schedule. In either case, the key remains white. If the pigeon pecks a second key (observing key), it will change the color of the light on the operant key to red if the FI is in effect and to green if the FR is in effect. By pecking the observing key, the pigeon can find out what pattern of responding is appropriate on the operant key. Pecks on the observing key are called *observing responses* because they yield information without having any effect on the delivery of food itself. If observing responses are maintained, they are presumably reinforced by the information they provide about food availability on the operant key.

There is now abundant evidence that animals will make observing responses to get information about the availability of food or the likelihood of shock. For example, in one experiment pigeons were faced with a choice. Pecks on either of two keys were reinforced on either an FI 10-sec or an FI 40-sec schedule. Which schedule was in effect was determined by the experimenter. If the subject pecked one of the keys, that key would turn red if the FI 10-sec schedule was in effect and green if the FI 40-sec schedule was in effect. If the pigeon pecked the other key, the key would turn yellow no matter what schedule was in effect. Pecks on either key served equally well to

---

16. Egger and Miller, 1962.
17. See Egger and Miller, 1963, and Seligman, 1966, for similar results. Thomas, Berman, Serednesky, and Lyons, 1968, have shown that these effects only appear if an intermediate amount of training is done. Borgealt, Donahoe, and Weinstein, 1972, have suggested that the duration of S_1 and S_2 as well as their overlap may be crucial. Thus, it may be that results consistent with the information hypothesis are obtained only under a limited set of training and test conditions.
18. See Hendry, 1969a, especially the chapters by Schuster, Wyckoff, Hendry, and Dinsmoor and collaborators.
19. Wyckoff, 1952.

satisfy the FI requirement and produce food. The only consequence of key selection was information about what schedule was in effect. The pigeons showed a very strong preference for the key which provided information.[20] The same effects have been obtained when the reinforcement schedule was either FR 10 or FR 90.[21] In each case, the occurrence of the reinforcer was unaffected by the animal's choice; the only consequence of choice was information. It seems on the surface that the reduction of uncertainty is sufficient to make a stimulus a conditioned reinforcer.

However, there are alternative explanations of animals' apparent preferences for predictive stimuli. It is possible that predictive stimuli will be reinforcing only if the news provided by the stimuli is relatively good. Stimuli which provide information may derive reinforcing value not solely from the information they provide but also from their association with the events they predict. If they predict relatively undesirable events, they may not be reinforcing. Imagine turning in assignments to a teacher who provides no feedback when the assignments are satisfactory and lots of feedback, on request, when they are unsatisfactory. The only news you can get from your teacher is bad news. It is possible that, given the choice between no information and bad information, you will choose no information. This is the essence of the view we are presently exploring.

There is some evidence to support the view that stimuli are reinforcing only when they provide good news—that is, only when they predict events which are positive. In one experiment, pigeons were exposed to a VI schedule of food reinforcement for pecking. During a random, unsignaled proportion of the time, pecks produced electric shock on an FR schedule. When observing responses produced signals for both shock-free periods and shock periods, high rates of observing responses were recorded. However, when observing responses only produced signals for shock periods, many pigeons did not make observing responses, and those that did did not sustain them.[22] Note that a procedure which only signals shock periods provides just as much information as a procedure which signals both shock and shock-free periods. The absence of the signal for shock when an observing response occurs is itself a signal for no shock. Nevertheless, observing responses were not maintained on this procedure. This failure is presumably the result of the fact that the only

20. Bower, McLean, and Meachem, 1966.
21. Hendry, 1969b.
22. Dinsmoor, Flint, Smith, and Viemeister, 1969.

stimulus actually produced by the observing response was correlated with an aversive situation.

Thus, it appears that pure information may not be sufficient to endow a stimulus with reinforcing power and maintain observing responses. A crucial component of the control of observing responses may be that the stimuli which they produce be associated with something positive.

Chained Schedules of Reinforcement

There is another class of experimental procedures which has been used to study conditioned reinforcement. These procedures involve the use of *chained schedules of reinforcement.* Consider a pigeon exposed to a multiple schedule of reinforcement. Periods of green key illumination during which pecks are reinforced on a VI schedule alternate with periods of red key illumination, during which pecks are not reinforced. After some training, the pigeon learns the discrimination and pecks the green key frequently and the red key very infrequently. At this point the procedure is changed; red is still correlated with extinction and green with VI, but now the pigeons must peck the red key to turn it green. In other words, pecks on the red key are required to produce periods of green key, VI reinforcement. This procedure is called a *chained schedule.* When a pigeon is exposed to it, its response rate in red increases dramatically.[23]

What maintains responses in red? Presumably, responding is maintained by the presentation of the green stimulus which is itself associated with food. Thus, green is a conditioned reinforcer of red key responding. If an animal is exposed, for example, to a chained FR 50/FI 60-sec schedule, one observes an FR pattern of responding in the first link of the chain and an FI pattern in the second link. If the chain is FI 1-min/FI 1-min, one observes two separate FI scallops (see Figure 7–2); production of the stimulus correlated with the final link of the chain maintains responding in just the same way that food maintains responding. This result is taken as evidence that stimuli of this sort are conditioned reinforcers.

The study of chained schedules is of considerable importance for an understanding of behavior sequences. Even in simple situations, the path to reinforcement requires a number of different responses in sequence; the pigeon must peck the key, walk to the feeder, put its beak in the feeder, and ingest grain. As the complexity of a situation

23. Ferster and Skinner, 1957.

increases, the number of links in a chain to reinforcement must increase dramatically. The possibility that stimuli along the way help organize chains and keep behavior in the direction of reinforcement has had a prominent role in a number of accounts of complex behavior.[24] What is the evidence that stimuli associated with different links of a chain are important?

Consider a chain in which a pigeon must complete five FI 1-min schedules to obtain food. To evaluate the significance of the stimuli on the key which change from link to link of the chain, we need a comparison procedure. One possibility is to compare the chain to an FI 5-min schedule. The temporal pattern of reinforcement should be the same on an FI 5 as it is on the chain. The problem is that the response requirement is different; the FI 5 requires only one response for reinforcement while the chain requires five responses— one to terminate each FI link. Thus, we need a different comparison procedure. The procedure of choice is called a *tandem schedule*. The relation between responses and reinforcements on a tandem are the same as on a corresponding chain; the difference is that as the animal moves from link to link on a tandem schedule, there is no correlated change in the exteroceptive stimulus. Comparable chain and tandem procedures are depicted in Figure 10–8.

Animals exposed to a tandem schedule of this sort do not reliably develop a set of FI scallops. They respond at moderate rates and responding increases as the 5-minute interreinforcement interval progresses, but there is no clear sign of temporal patterning appropriate to an FI schedule within each FI link. In marked contrast, on the chained schedule animals stop responding. Pigeons will refrain from pecking the key to move from the first to the second link of the chain often for hours. Though responding is well maintained on the tandem, and obviously is well maintained on an FI 5-min schedule, it is not maintained on the chain. This is impressive evidence for the importance of the stimuli associated with the different links of the chain, though not of the sort one might have expected.

Why should responding cease on this procedure? Let us consult Figure 10–8 for a moment. The yellow key is paired with food and should be a conditioned reinforcer. Thus, pecks on orange should be

---

24. This notion has been central in almost all theories of behavior. It figures prominently in Skinner's thinking (Skinner, 1938) and just as prominently in C. L. Hull's (Hull, 1952). In contrast, many critics of behavior theory have focused their criticism explicitly on chaining as a model of how complex behavior is organized (Lashley, 1951; Chomsky, 1957, 1959). The view of these critics is that complex sequences of behavior reflect a hierachically organized plan of action in which sequencing of acts is controlled by a central plan which rests above the acts themselves.

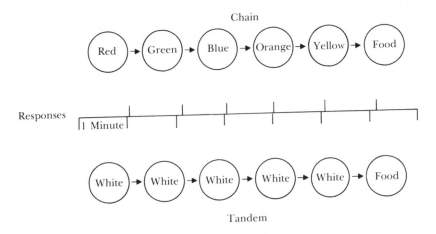

Figure 10–8. Diagram of Chain and Tandem Schedules. *On a chain schedule, responses are required to move the animal from one link to the next, and each link is correlated with a different stimulus. A tandem schedule has the same response requirement as a chain but the stimulus does not change from link to link.*

maintained by the production of yellow. Orange, however, is not paired with food; it is paired with yellow. In a Pavlovian conditioning context, conditioning of orange would be called higher order conditioning. As we saw in Chapter 4, higher order conditioning is an elusive phenomenon. While second-order conditioning (as with orange the CS and yellow the US) does occur, third- and fourth-order conditioning (as with blue the CS and orange the US, or green the CS and blue the US) do not occur.[25] Viewed from this perspective, it is not surprising that the chain does not maintain responding.

There is a way to program multiple-link chains so that responding will be maintained. If the key remains white from link to link but the termination of each link, including the last, produces a brief change in the stimulus (let us say, from white to red), responding will be maintained. Now the chain of five FI 1-min schedules will produce five fixed-interval scallops. This result should not be surprising. Red is associated with food and the consequence of responding in each link of the chain is production of red. The red stimulus is an ordinary, first-order conditioned reinforcer, and its occurrence maintains schedule-appropriate behavior in chains with as many as 15 separate links.[26]

25. See Rizley and Rescorla, 1972.
26. Kelleher, 1966.

All of this evidence offers support for the view that stimuli become conditioned reinforcers by being paired with unconditioned reinforcers. In the chain depicted in Figure 10–8, stimulus change from one link to the next provides information; yet this information is insufficient in the absence of pairing to maintain responding. When the stimuli signaling the movement from link to link of the chain are all paired with food, responding is maintained.

However, there is evidence which complicates matters by suggesting that predictiveness is sufficient to make a stimulus a conditioned reinforcer on a chained schedule. Pigeons were exposed to a chained schedule in which completion of each link was signaled by a brief stimulus change. The only exception was the terminal link. Completion of the terminal link produced food but no stimulus change. Thus, the brief stimuli which signaled the completion of earlier links were never paired with food, though they provided information about the animal's progress. Nevertheless, schedule-appropriate behavior was maintained through all the links of the chain. Behavior on this procedure was indistinguishable from behavior on procedures in which the brief stimuli were paired with food. This last finding suggests that a stimulus can be a conditioned reinforcer if it provides information about progress toward the goal, whether or not it is directly associated with the goal itself.[27]

Concurrent-Chain Schedules

The section of this chapter on conditioned reinforcement began with a discussion of some of the different procedures investigators have used to test for conditioned reinforcing effects and some of the criteria which have been adopted for evaluating those effects. In studies of chained schedules, the criterion of *parametric sensitivity* is usually employed. If the rate and pattern of responding which produces a stimulus is appropriate to the schedule on which the stimulus is delivered, we may identify that stimulus as a conditioned reinforcer. There is a significant variant of the chained schedule procedure which permits further exploration of parametric sensivity. It is called a *concurrent-chain schedule*.

Consider a commonly studied example. A pigeon is confronted with three response keys. The left key is red and the right key is green while the center key is dark. The pigeon pecks the two side keys and pecks on each key are reinforced according to identical VI schedules. As shown in Figure 10–9, the reinforcer is not food; rather, when a

27. Stubbs and Cohen, 1972.

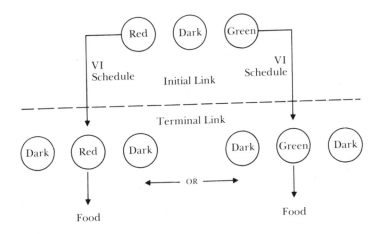

Figure 10–9. Diagram of a Concurrent-Chain Procedure. *Typi-cally, conditions of reinforcement in the two terminal links differ while the requirements for getting to the terminal links are the same for each choice key. Preference for one choice key or the other is taken as an indication of the relative effectiveness of each of the conditioned reinforcers (red or green on center key). This effectiveness is correlated with the conditions of reinforcement which prevail on the center key.*

side key peck is reinforced, both side keys go out and the center key is lit with either red or green, depending upon which side key peck was reinforced. Now, pecks on the center key produce food reinforcement.[28]

It may be, for example, that pecks on the red center key produce food on a ratio schedule, while pecks on the green center key produce food on an interval schedule. If we were interested in whether animals prefer ratio schedules to interval schedules, how would we find out? We might record response rates when the center key was red and when it was green and take the higher of the two to be an indication of preference. However, we know from Chapter 7 that such a strategy would be inappropriate. Ratio schedules select higher response rates than interval schedules and an animal might well prefer the interval schedule though it responds faster on the ratio schedule. We can avoid this problem by evaluating responding on the two side keys during the initial link of the chain. The schedules of reinforcement here are identical. The reinforcers themselves are red center key and green center key. If an animal pecks the red side key more than the green side key, it must be because the red center key is a more potent

28. This procedure was initially developed by Autor, 1969.

reinforcer than the green center key. If this is the case, it must be because the red center key is associated with a ratio schedule while the green one is associated with an interval schedule. Thus, preference in the initial link of the chain is taken as a measure of the relative effectiveness of conditions in the two possible terminal links of the chain. By varying conditions associated with the terminal links, we can get an idea of how those conditions affect the conditioned reinforcing power of a stimulus.

Let us consider some examples of research with concurrent-chain schedules. One experiment was very much like the hypothetical one described above. Pigeons' pecks during the initial, choice link of the chain produced terminal links associated with either VR or VI schedules of food reinforcement. There was no indication of preference for either ratio or interval schedules; rather, pigeons preferred the schedule which produced more frequent reinforcement. More specifically, the relative rate of responding on the two choice keys was directly proportional to the relative rate of reinforcement provided in the terminal links of the chain. Mathematically, the findings can be summarized by the equation:

$$\frac{R_{left\ initial}}{R_{left\ initial} + R_{right\ initial}} = \frac{r_{left\ terminal}}{r_{left\ terminal} + r_{right\ terminal}}$$

where R = responses and r = reinforcements. This equation is an instance of the matching law (see Chapter 7). Thus, the effectiveness of conditioned reinforcers in controlling behavior may be described by the same quantitative relation that describes the effectiveness of unconditioned reinforcers in controlling behavior.[29]

In a similar experiment, the schedules of reinforcement in the terminal links of the chain were identical. The links differed in the magnitude of reinforcement available. It was found that relative rate of responding in the initial links of the chain matched relative magnitude of reinforcement in the terminal links.[30] Similarly, it has been shown that delay of reinforcement in terminal links affects responding in initial links in accordance with the matching law.[31] Thus, procedures involving concurrent chain schedules have provided a useful tool for evaluating the effect on the power of conditioned reinforcers of a diverse set of variables. The general conclusion is that the effectiveness of a conditioned reinforcer is an orderly function of the

29. Herrnstein, 1964.
30. Neuringer, 1967.
31. Killeen, 1970.

frequency, magnitude, and delay of the unconditioned reinforcer with which it is associated.[32]

Token Reinforcers

We suggested earlier that any account of human behavior based upon operant conditioning principles would have to depend heavily upon the role of conditioned reinforcement. Most human behavior does not produce food or water or avoid noxious stimuli directly. Human behavior produces money, social approval or scorn, and so on. Why does money sustain behavior? It is tempting to argue that it is the association of money with things like food, clothing, and shelter which gives money its power, that money is simply a conditioned reinforcer. However, in many respects, the relation between money and the things it buys is very indirect; the delay between obtaining money and obtaining food may be days or weeks long. Animal studies of conditioned reinforcement provide no hint that it is sufficiently powerful to bridge such long delays. Indeed, conditioned reinforcing effects in the laboratory are remarkably fragile. Thus, we will need some direct evidence that money can be established as a conditioned reinforcer by virtue of its association with unconditioned reinforcers before any arguments about the role of conditioned reinforcers in the control of human behavior can be taken seriously. Such evidence is available.

Some of the earliest investigations of conditioned reinforcement involved procedures in which chimpanzees responded for tokens (poker chips) which could subsequently be exchanged for food. It was assumed that if responding was maintained by token reinforcement, this would be evidence that tokens acquire reinforcing value by virtue of their association with food. Among the interesting findings which came out of these studies were the following:

1. Some chimpanzees worked as hard for tokens (exchangeable for grapes) as they did for grapes.

2. Chimpanzees would work for tokens even if a delay of one hour was imposed between obtaining the token and exchanging it for

---

32. As with nearly all conclusions drawn in this chapter, this one must be qualified. Whether or not concurrent chains produce the quantitative effects described in this section depends upon the relative duration of the initial link. If the initial link is too short, pigeons "overmatch"; they prefer the richer of two terminal links more than the matching law says they should. If the initial links are too long, pigeons "undermatch." These findings were reported by Fantino, 1969, and he suggested that preference was mostly determined by the relative overall time to reinforcement when the duration of initial and terminal links were added together.

food, provided they could hold onto the tokens during the delay period.

3. Chimps would learn a new response for token reinforcement, even if a delay was imposed between obtaining the token and exchanging it. With no delay, the chimps learned as rapidly with token reinforcement as with food reinforcement.

4. When chimps housed in pairs were simply given tokens, struggles for dominance, begging, and even stealing of tokens were observed.[33]

More recent research has shown that when responses produce tokens according to some schedule of reinforcement, a pattern of responding appropriate to the schedule develops.[34] Responding in chimps can be maintained on an FR 125 for tokens, even when 50 tokens must be accumulated (6,250 responses) before exchange for food is permitted.[35] Results of this sort make plausible the claim that conditioned reinforcement, at least in the form of tokens, maintains behavior in the same way as does money.

What makes the case particularly convincing, however, is research that has been carried out in applied settings. Token reinforcement is becoming an increasingly popular instrument of behavior control in both mental hospitals and schools, as for example in the case history described in Chapter 1. In these settings, tokens have the status of money. They can be exchanged for a variety of different reinforcers and some reinforcers "cost" more than others so that tokens sometimes need to be saved, and so on.[36]

Token Reinforcement and Psychopathology • The case history described in Chapter 1 was an idealized description of a token economy in operation. You will recall that we left the patients functioning relatively normally and efficiently, caring for themselves, and engaged in productive social interaction. However, they were still in the hospital. A more recent effort produced more dramatic results. A ward which housed 60 schizophrenic patients was converted into a token economy. In the 11 months of the program, there was a significant change in the conduct of patients on the ward, much as described in Chapter 1. Moreover, twice as many patients were discharged during that time as during the preceding 11 months. Thus, it appears that a system of

33. Wolfe, 1936; Cowles, 1937.
34. Kelleher, 1957.
35. Kelleher, 1958.
36. Some of the pioneering work with token economies has been done by Ayllon and Azrin, 1968, and by Staats, 1975.

A chimp trained to deposit tokens to produce food reinforcement.
(Courtesy of Yerkes Primate Center.)

token reinforcements can effect enough improvement in some patients to get them out of the hospital.[37] Token reinforcement is also
effective in mediating the transition of patients from hospital to community. The use of tokens in supervised community residences (often
a first stop for patients discharged from a hospital) seems to increase
the chances that the patients will adjust to being on their own in the
community.[38]

37. Atthowe and Krasner, 1968.
38. Henderson, 1969.

Tokens are not only effective in treating hospitalized patients with severe disturbances. They have also been a valuable component of marriage counseling. In one instance, couples spent some time identifying their problems, determining the needs of each member which were unsatisfied by the other, and subsequently delivered token reinforcement to each other for responses which corrected the previous deficiencies in the relationship. This procedure succeeded in improving the marriages.[39]

These examples only scratch the surface. The successes of token reinforcement in treating psychopathology are many and varied. However, these cases leave a number of difficult questions. How important were the tokens themselves? How permanent were the behavioral improvements? What made the tokens reinforcing? We can be reasonably sure that the tokens were crucial; in most attempts to use token reinforcement, token availability is discontinued for a time, and, in general, the pathological responses which have been eliminated return. The other two questions cannot at present be answered. Of particular relevance to this chapter is determining what endows tokens with reinforcing power. Is it their pairing with unconditioned reinforcers, their informational value, or both? The research which might answer this question has not been done.

Token Reinforcement in Education • The use of token reinforcement in the classroom has been so successful in the last few years that we may be witnessing the beginning of a major change in education. While operant principles in general are being employed at all levels of the educational system, token reinforcements have thus far been used almost exclusively in early education.

In one experiment, 4-year-old children were given reading training either with token reinforcement or without tokens but with the normal social approval which accompanies reading. The children reliably paid attention, worked, and read only when they were receiving tokens.[40] In a second study, children received tokens for reading which could either be immediately exchanged (for trinkets or peanuts) or accumulated in plastic containers and subsequently exchanged in large numbers for toys. The 4-year-old children worked steadily and enthusiastically for the tokens (which they could see accumulating in the plastic containers) for up to 40 minutes at a time.[41] This result is especially dramatic if one considers how unlikely it is

39. Stuart, 1969.
40. Staats, Staats, Schutz, and Wolf, 1962.
41. Staats, Finley, Minke, and Wolf, 1964.

that a 4-year-old will spend more than 10 consecutive minutes at any activity. A third experiment provides evidence that token reinforcement may even be an improvement on other operant conditioning methods. Teachers attempted to strengthen effective study behavior by reinforcing such behavior with approval and attention and by extinguishing (ignoring) nonproductive or counterproductive behavior. These methods met with little success. A token system was then introduced and it resulted in a marked improvement in effective study and in cooperation.[42]

The effectiveness of token reinforcement is even more dramatic in classrooms for retarded, emotionally disturbed, or culturally deprived children. In one study with emotionally disturbed children, three different procedures were compared: structuring the classroom situation and stating explicit rules of conduct; providing rules and structure and, in addition, social approval for appropriate behavior; and, finally, providing rules, social approval, and tokens. Only the last of these procedures was effective in eliminating classroom disturbance.[43] In another study, tokens were provided to retarded adolescents for attentiveness and study. This procedure increased the proportion of the school day spent studying from 30% to 80%.[44] Finally, in a preschool for culturally deprived children, tokens were provided to sustain behavior during three 5-minute study sessions each day. One study session dealt with reading the alphabet, one dealt with writing the alphabet, and one dealt with counting. Less than 8 months after the program began, the children were better advanced in these skills than children from nondeprived backgrounds. In addition, their average score on an intelligence test increased by 12 points. These effects were produced with a total of about 50 hours of training per child.[45]

As in the case of treatment of psychopathology, these studies do not tell us how tokens work. They do not provide us with an analysis of conditioned reinforcement. What they do provide is a clear and powerful demonstration that conditioned reinforcement can be used to maintain already established responses and to train new ones in the natural environment. Such a demonstration should increase our confidence in the relevance of the analysis of behavior in the laboratory to an account of behavior outside it.

These studies raise another issue which is far more general and sig-

---

42. Bijou, Birnbrauer, Kidder, and Tague, 1967.
43. O'Leary, Becker, Evans, and Saudargas, 1969.
44. Broden, Hall, Dunlap, and Clark, 1970.
45. Staats, 1968.

nificant than a demonstration of the power of conditioned reinforcers. Are these educational methods desirable? Is the product of
these techniques the kind of educational system we need or want?
There is a long tradition of criticism by educators of methods of education which depend upon external goals or bribes instead of rewards
intrinsic to the task itself. Learning "for its own sake" has always been
preferable to learning for extrinsic rewards. Obviously, a system of
extrinsic rewards is at the heart of token reinforcement procedures—
indeed, it is at the heart of operant principles generally. Moreover,
the developing technology of behavior will allow us to employ these
extrinsic rewards with maximum effectiveness. The view of one of the
leading proponents of the use of token reinforcement is this:

> *However, the behavior involved in acquiring a complex repertoire such as
> reading is in the beginning not intrinsically reinforcing; it is work. Thus,
> some type of extrinsic reinforcement must be introduced to maintain the be-
> haviors required for learning. Schools rely upon coercive attendance for
> most children . . . in conjunction with such reinforcers as teacher and peer
> social approval, competition, learning for its own reward, parental ap-
> proval, negative reinforcement (relief from disapproval), and so on. . . .
> They may be considered to be natural reinforcers, because of our traditional
> practices, but they are extrinsic reinforcers like any others.*
> *. . .For many children, the reinforcers are not adequate, and their learn-
> ing behaviors are not maintained; from that point on, they cease to learn. In
> fact, they will usually learn behaviors that are anti-learning skills.* [46]

How are we to evaluate this view? Criticism of the use of token reinforcement in educational settings has taken two general forms. The
first is that our major educational goal is to develop the ability to find
creative, novel solutions to novel problems and that token reinforcement, while perhaps facilitating the acquisition of specific skills, does
nothing to develop those more general skills. [47] It is even possible that
token reinforcement interferes with the development of creative problem-solving ability. We suggested, in discussing the views of Staddon
and Simmelhag in Chapter 6, that contingent reinforcement may
work primarily to establish efficient and stereotyped behavior—the
antithesis of creative problem-solving.

The second criticism of token reinforcement in education is that
the use of reinforcers which are extrinsic to the task at hand will undermine intrinsic interest in the task. One might imagine children

46. Staats, 1975, p. 406.
47. See Levine and Fasnacht, 1974.

reading because reading is fun. When they receive tokens for reading, the control of reading shifts from its intrinsic consequences to the extrinsic tokens. If this shift occurs, the child will no longer read when token reinforcement is unavailable. There is some experimental evidence that such a shift from intrinsic to extrinsic control over behavior occurs. Nursery school children reinforced with "good player" awards for drawing were less likely to draw at another time, in the absence of "good player" awards, than children whose initial drawing had not been reinforced.[48] When a token reinforcement system was instituted during part of the schoolday for adolescent, female delinquents, classroom performance improved. However, this improvement was cancelled by an equivalent deterioration in peformance during the parts of the day in which tokens were unavailable.[49] These deleterious effects were so pronounced that the researchers involved with the token system suggested, in evaluating the 5-year-long project, that "an operant regimen, though it may be effective in managing behavior in the institution, actually has a deleterious effect on the persistence of post-treatment, pro-social behavior."[50]

The evidence is certainly not conclusive on this matter and it is a problem of substantial significance. However, in the face of strikingly impressive evidence that token reinforcement in combination with other procedures of behavior technology produces significant acquisition of a wide variety of disparate skills, it is inappropriate to reject this technology simply because it is not one's ideal of education. It may work better than anything that has gone before it, and its adoption by school systems is likely to be reinforced by better scores on a host of achievement tests. It is therefore incumbent upon critics of the technology to support their criticism with evidence that it is undesirable.

INTERACTION OF PAVLOVIAN AND OPERANT CONDITIONING: CONCLUSIONS

We began this chapter by reviewing a variety of situations in which Pavlovian and operant contingencies interact in controlling responding. We concluded that whenever a Pavlovian contingency is present, it will influence ongoing operant behavior, though the precise nature of this influence will depend upon details of the procedure and the situation. We turned next to a discussion of conditioned reinforce-

48. Lepper, Greene, and Nisbett, 1973.
49. Meichenbaum, Bowers, and Ross, 1968.
50. Ross, Meichenbaum, and Bowers, 1974, p. 3.

ment as an instance of interaction between Pavlovian and operant contingencies. The discussion of conditioned reinforcement suggested these conclusions:

1. A neutral stimulus will become a conditioned reinforcer if it bears a predictive or informative relation to the unconditioned reinforcer.

2. Conditioned reinforcers may be used to produce new learning or to maintain already acquired responses.

3. Conditioned reinforcers are sensitive to parametric manipulations in the same way that unconditioned reinforcers are.

4. Most evidence from studies of observing responses and of chained schedules of reinforcement suggests that the reinforcing power of conditioned reinforcers comes not solely from their predictiveness, but also from the value of the stimuli they predict. That is, stimuli are conditioned reinforcers by virtue of their association with unconditioned reinforcers.

5. When tokens are established as conditioned reinforcers by virtue of their association with a variety of unconditioned reinforcers, they may be used to sustain large repertoires of behavior for long periods of time in the absence of unconditioned reinforcement. Token reinforcers of this sort have been used with great effectiveness in both therapeutic and educational settings. They provide some convincing evidence that the reinforcing power of money in society is related to principles of conditioned reinforcement.

This discussion of the interactions between Pavlovian and operant conditioning concludes our presentation of the principles of conditioning. We have presented those principles sympathetically, and perhaps implied that a complete understanding of behavior in terms of conditioning principles and widespread application of those principles to the full range of human affairs awaits only the working out of some minor details in the laboratory.

This vision of a future in which conditioning principles are sufficiently developed to explain everything may be accurate. However, there are a number of major challenges which conditioning theory must address. There is reason to believe that the applicability of conditioning principles may be extremely limited, that behavior theory may never tell us about aspects of human behavior which are of central importance. In the final chapters of the book we discuss some of these challenges to behavior theory, and attempt to put its contribution to our knowledge in perspective.

11
Misbehavior of Organisms

Throughout the book, we have presented behavior theory as a rapidly developing science which is moving toward a systematic understanding of the behavior of animals and people. To be sure, we have indicated problems in the various subareas of behavior theory which seem extremely resistant to solution. The current status of research and theory on schedules of reinforcement (Chapter 7), on discrimination learning (Chapter 8), on avoidance learning (Chapter 9), and on the relation between Pavlovian and operant conditioning (Chapter 10) is marked by unanswered questions. Clearly, there is still much work to be done.

However, none of the unsolved problems or unanswered questions we have identified has threatened the central assumptions and formulations of behavior theory. Behavior theorists continue to search for laws of behavior which are general from situation to situation and from species to species. They continue to search for the simple elements of experience which, when combined, will yield the complex behavior which characteristically occurs in the natural environment. And they continue to emphasize the role of experience in determining what organisms do.[1]

In this and the next chapter, we will discuss some phenomena

1. T. S. Kuhn, 1962, argues that a science normally progresses when its practitioners work on rather small, focused problems. What allows them to do so is the existence of a shared theoretical framework which addresses broader issues. By adopting the theoretical framework, one is free to concentrate on minor problems which would be unintelligible without the framework but which are perfectly natural within it. Consistent with Kuhn's analysis, the rather specific controversies which occupy the attention of be-

which challenge the very core of behavior theory. We will discuss instances of the "misbehavior of organisms."[2] What it means to say that organisms "misbehave" is that under certain conditions, they do things which contradict or violate the central principles of behavior theory. These instances of misbehavior suggest that there may be significant biological constraints on what organisms learn and do. Such constraints imply not only that behavior theory may have failed in its effort to develop general principles, but, more seriously, that the search for such general principles may be misguided.

In this chapter, we will first review the fundamental assumptions and definitions which have guided the analysis of behavior. We will then discuss some research findings, examples of misbehavior, which challenge these assumptions. Some of the research comes from outside the standard laboratory setting. However, some of it comes from the very situations which have embodied the assumptions of behavior theory and yielded its most powerful principles. After identifying the empirical phenomena and the problems they raise, we will turn in the next chapter to a discussion of theoretical alternatives to behavior theory which may be able to incorporate the phenomena.

DISCOVERING GENERAL LAWS OF BEHAVIOR

Imagine a visitor from another planet about to embark on the study of human behavior. Having no preconceptions about the nature of the human organism, his first step in the investigation might be careful observation. The observation would reveal a host of physical and behavioral characteristics which distinguish people from other organisms. It would quickly become clear to this visitor that if one is to find out about people, one must study them directly. Though it would certainly be more convenient to do research with smaller, more docile, more easily cared for organisms, the differences among different

---

havior theorists may reflect their general agreement on broader issues. Kuhn also argues that some problems are very difficult—almost impossible—even to identify from within a theoretical framework. In the history of science, it has often been the case that problems are recognized and explored by outsiders, people who do not work from within the perspective of the particular framework in question. It is the insights of these outsiders which frequently lead to revolutionary breakthroughs in scientific development. Kuhn's general account seems again to apply in the case of behavior theory. Many of the key observations we will discuss in this chapter originated in research which was not a part of the framework which has governed behavior analysis.

2. Breland and Breland, 1961, coined this expression, a parody on Skinner's seminal *Behavior of Organisms* (1938).

types of organisms would seem so pronounced that it would be hazardous to study one organism to find out about another.

This attitude is shared by most nonpsychologists. While many people believe that one can learn about some aspects of humans through the study of nonhumans (for example, the structure and function of a large number of body organs), their confidence in species continuity stops short at the level of thought, feeling, and action. Current practice in behavior theory belies popular belief. Much of what we think we know about human behavior comes from the study of the behavior of nonhumans. We are confident that the behavior of pigeons in the laboratory is an accurate representation of the behavior of both pigeons and people outside the laboratory. Why?

From the outset, the experimental analysis of behavior has been guided by the assumption that general, that is, transspecies and transsituational, laws of behavior exist. Just as one can learn about the human eye by studying the eye of a horseshoe crab, so one can learn about human behavior by studying the behavior of the pigeon or the rat. However, while adopting the assumption of species similarity, behavior analysis has always been mindful of the fact of species difference. Many of the things that pigeons do reflect behavior processes unique to the pigeon and its close relatives. If one merely observes the pigeon in its natural environment and expects one's observations to provide general principles of behavior, one is likely to be disappointed. While part of what the pigeon does may be a reflection of general principles of behavior, another part will reflect systems of action which are specific to the species. The difficult problem is to separate the species-specific characteristics from the general ones. The best way to do this is to bring the pigeon into an artificial, laboratory environment which prevents species-specific behavior patterns from exerting their influence. In other words, behavior analysis should employ research methods which neutralize the unique biological contributions to the behavior of a species. If one successfully eliminates these biological influences, what remain to be observed are principles of behavior which will generalize across species.

Arbitrariness

How does one eliminate these biological influences? What methods will yield general principles of behavior control? Studies of evolution and natural selection teach us that the force which shapes a species is selection pressure from the environment. Though changes in the genetic constitution of members of a species may occur at random, they are not passed on at random. Some genetic alterations yield organisms poorly suited to survive in the natural environment while others yield organisms especially well suited for survival and reproduction. Thus, pressure from the environment ultimately yields organisms whose central characteristics are particularly well attuned to that environment. Therefore, if one studies the behavior of organisms in the natural environment, one is likely to observe a great many species-specific responses which are specifically adapted to that environment. If one's interest is in general (transspecies) principles of behavior rather than principles unique to the pigeon or the rat, one's task is greatly simplified when the animals are studied in an environment in which species-specific behavior patterns are irrelevant. In short, to maximize the chances of obtaining principles of behavior control which are true for all organisms, one should study behavior in an artificial and arbitrary experimental environment. If the environment is artificial and arbitrary, it will not call forth specially adapted, species-specific patterns of behavior.

What does it mean to say that the experimental environment is artificial and arbitrary? How can we define arbitrariness? Consider an historical example. The earliest research of B. F. Skinner was concerned with hunger and its effects on reflexes. To study this problem, Skinner and others attempted to measure general activity levels and the frequency and form of responses which were specific components of the feeding system. Such measurements were difficult to make, partly because it was difficult to quantify changes in the state of these activities over time. What was needed was a reliable measuring instrument. Skinner's search for such an instrument led to what is commonly known as the Skinner box, in which rats are trained to press a lever for food. He was not at this time particularly interested in the acquisition or control of lever pressing; he was interested in hunger. Lever presses were easy to count, and by counting them one could tag changes in the strength of the animal's feeding-related behaviors.[3]

There was nothing about lever presses which made them especially appropriate to measure hunger. One could as well count chain pulls or paw swipes or a host of other things. All that was special was that the response produced food. By measuring the frequency of the response, one could measure the animal's need for food and, in this way, one could learn about hunger. More significantly, one could compare hunger to other states of need in the animal. Suppose one wanted to assess the relative impact of hunger and thirst on an animal's behavior. If one were measuring specific feeding and drinking activities, a comparison of hunger and thirst would be impossible.

3. Skinner, 1932. Also, see Herrnstein, 1974.

Since feeding and drinking activities are different, an attempt to compare them would present the proverbial problem of comparing apples and oranges. How many bites of food, for example, are equivalent to how many licks of water? If one were, instead, measuring neither feeding nor drinking but some third activity, like lever pressing, a direct comparison of the two different need states would be possible. Since lever pressing bears no intrinsic relation to either feeding or drinking, we can take it to be an unbiased estimator of both. This is precisely what it means to describe one's experimental situation as arbitrary.

To further emphasize this point, consider an analogy. The chemist needs to know about the weight of the reagents he is using. He puts them on a scale and takes the reading of the scale to determine their weight. In performing this operation, the chemist is assuming, quite reasonably, that the behavior of the scale is independent of any of the properties of the reagents except their weight, that the scale will provide an *unbiased* estimate of the weight of any substance. If it turned out that a particular scale was influenced not only by the weight of a substance, but also by its acidity, the scale would be useless to the chemist. Instead, the behavior of the scale is assumed to be independent of the chemical characteristics of the substances being weighed. In analogous fashion, Skinner, in his earliest work, took the frequency of lever pressing to be an unbiased, or arbitrary, indicator of the strength of various biological needs.

With this example in hand, let us extend the notion of arbitrariness to aspects of the experimental environment other than the response one is measuring. Suppose one is interested in Pavlovian conditioning or operant discrimination learning. What should one use as a CS or discriminative stimulus? While the stimulus one uses must be something the animal is able to detect, it should not be something intrinsically related to the US or to the reflex. Thus, if one is studying conditioned fear, with shock as the US, it might well be a bad idea to use as a CS a picture of one of the organism's natural enemies. There is little doubt that such a stimulus will produce fear, but fear may result from the fact that the predator bears an intrinsic relation to danger situations. If so, such an experiment will tell us little about conditioned fear in general. It will tell us about fear responses as a built-in characteristic of the species we are studying. Instead of using a picture of a predator as a CS, we use a light, or a tone, a stimulus which, it seems, can hardly be intrinsically related to danger. That the relation between CS (tone) and US (shock) is arbitrary insures that the conditioning phenomenon one observes will not be specific to either the species or the situation being studied.

Tests for Arbitrariness

Let us make this notion of arbitrariness more concrete. Figure 11-1 depicts a limited characterization of the world of the rat, divided into the classes "stimuli," "operants," and "reinforcers." Suppose one does Experiment 1: in the presence of a bright light, lever presses produce food. The rat learns to press the lever at a high rate. Does this fact reflect a general principle or is there something special about the situation which taps a built-in, species-specific characteristic of rats? To begin to answer this question, we do Experiment 2: a dim light is substituted for the bright one. Suppose it turns out that while rats still press the lever in Experiment 2, they do so at much lower rates than in Experiment 1. What are we to conclude from this result?

Two possibilities are apparent. First, it is possible that there is an intrinsic relation between brightness and lever pressing. If so, we would

Stimuli	Operants	Reinforcers
Lights 　Bright 　Dim 　Colored Tones 　Soft 　Loud Buzzers Clicks Temperature Air puffs Tastes Etc.	Lever Pressing Wheel Running Alley Running Biting Licking Rearing Tail Flicking Etc.	Food Water Sex Temperature Shock Poison Loud Noise Etc.

Experiment 1:	Bright Light —— Lever Press —— Food
Experiment 2:	Dim Light —— Lever Press —— Food
Experiment 3:	Dim Light —— Wheel Run —— Food
Experiment 4:	Bright Light —— Wheel Run —— Food
Experiment 5:	Bright Light —— Wheel Run —— Water
Experiment 6:	Dim Light —— Wheel Run —— Water
Experiment 7:	Bright Light —— Lever Press —— Water
Experiment 8:	Dim Light —— Lever Press —— Water

Figure 11-1. Outline of Concrete Procedures an Experimenter might use to Determine the Arbitrariness of an Experimental Situation. *The eight listed experiments serve to highlight the meaning of "arbitrary." It does not mean that all stimuli (or operants or rewards) are interchangeable. It does mean that the difference between any two stimuli (for example, bright and dim light) will be the same regardless of the operant or reward being used.*

be forced to conclude that Experiment 1 did not yield general principles, that is, that the situation was not arbitrary. Second, it is possible that a bright light will maintain higher rates of *any* operant than will a dim light. To test this possibility, we do Experiments 3 and 4. Wheel running is reinforced by food in the presence of either a dim light (Experiment 3) or a bright one (Experiment 4). Suppose the results of these experiments parallel the results of Experiments 1 and 2; wheel running occurs at a higher rate in the presence of a bright light than in the presence of a dim one. Now, we can conclude that the relation between brightness of a light and the frequency of an operant is general; bright lights are more effective as discriminative stimuli in maintaining behavior than are dim ones. If, on the other hand, it turned out that rats ran more in wheels in the presence of dim lights than in the presence of bright ones, we would have to conclude that there was a significant interaction between members of the category "stimuli" and members of the category "operant"; in short, we would have to conclude that our experiments were permitting the intrusion of non-arbitrary, biologically influenced characteristics of the organism and were not yielding general principles.

But again, assume that Experiments 3 and 4 confirm the principle suggested by Experiments 1 and 2, that bright lights control higher rates of responding than dim ones. Can we conclude at this point that our experimental situation is arbitrary and that the principles derived from it are general? Not quite yet. It is possible that the results of all four experiments are unique to situations in which food is the reward. Thus, we do Experiments 5–8. If it turns out that substituting water for food does not change the effect of brightness on responding, we may then reasonably conclude that all eight experiments involved learning arbitrary relations and yielded general principles. It may seem that the procedures required to determine the arbitrariness of a situation are unnecessarily cumbersome. What must be considered, however, is what such a set of experiments accomplishes. If one does Experiments 1–8, and they work in the manner stipulated, one can then use just this set of experimental situations to uncover principles of learning and behavior control which should characterize virtually all situations, or at least all situations involving stimuli, operants, and rewards which are arbitrarily related.[4]

There is also something else to be said for the program of experiments just described; these experiments point out precisely what fea-

---

4. One would also have to perform a similar series of experiments on a different species to be sure that the principles derived from the first series extend to animals other than rats.

ture of experiments must be arbitrary in order for the principles derived from these experiments to be general. To uncover this feature, let us first consider what it is not. Arbitrariness does not mean that the set of effective stimuli, operants, and rewards must be the same for all organisms. If this had to be the case in order for our principles to be general, there would be no hope of uncovering general principles. Different species possess different sensory systems. They receive and interpret different aspects of the physical world. As a consequence, the set of possible effective stimuli will differ from one species to another. The same is obviously true of operants. Pigeons fly and peck, and rats never will. Finally, reinforcers are also likely to differ from species to species. Food and water will presumably act as reinforcers for any species, but other stimuli may serve as reinforcers for rats but not for pigeons.

This discussion may only be stating the obvious. It may have been apparent to the reader that "arbitrariness" and generality cannot depend on identity of the members of the categories stimuli, operants, and reinforcers for all species. Rather, arbitrariness might simply require that once the members of each category have been identified for a species, they can be chosen at random and yield the same experimental outcomes. In short, any stimulus, for a particular species, must be equivalent to any other stimulus in its ability to control behavior and, similarly, any operant must be equivalent to any other in its susceptibility to control. But this principle is violated by the stipulated results of Experiments 1 and 2 in Figure 11–1. Bright and dim lights are not interchangeable; they have different effects.

If arbitrariness does not require stimulus equivalence and operant equivalence, what does it require? The answer to this question comes from focusing not on the three classes of events—stimuli, operants, and reinforcers—but from focusing on *relations* between the classes. Consider the example of Experiments 1 and 2. From those experiments, we conclude that bright lights are more effective than dim ones in controlling lever pressing. The two types of stimuli are not equivalent. What a claim of arbitrariness and generality requires is that bright lights will be more effective than dim ones no matter what operant we are measuring and no matter what reinforcer we are providing. Similarly, wheel running may be more easily trained than lever pressing. As long as this difference obtains no matter what stimuli and reinforcers are used, we can treat our experimental situation as arbitrary. In general, if we rank stimuli and reinforcers on the basis of their effectiveness in controlling one operant, the rankings should be the same when tested with a different operant. If we rank operants on the basis of the ease with which they can be controlled by one reinforcer, the rankings should be the same when tested with a different reinforcer. Arbitrariness demands that there be no intrinsic relation between members of the three categories such that rankings change from one situation to the next.

Having established what "arbitrariness" means, and why it is important to behavior theory, we turn now to a consideration of the evidence. Have the methods of behavior analysis succeeded in creating an artificial environment which neutralizes the biological characteristics peculiar to each species? Is there evidence that what goes on in the conditioning chamber sometimes reflects these species-specific characteristics rather than neutralizing them. As we shall see, there is reason to believe that the methods of behavior analysis have not entirely succeeded.

THE "MISBEHAVIOR OF ORGANISMS"

Two former associates of B. F. Skinner's, Keller and Marion Breland, used their training in behavior analysis to establish a prosperous animal training business. In 1961, they published a whimsical but startling paper, "The Misbehavior of Organisms," which recorded their occasional failures, in which organisms "misbehaved." What they meant by "misbehavior" was that contingencies of reinforcement did not entirely succeed in controlling what the animals did. Let us consider a few of their examples:

The Dancing Chicken

The chicken walks over about 3 feet, pulls a rubber loop on a small box which starts a repeated auditory stimulus pattern (a four-note tune). The chicken then steps up onto an 18-inch, slightly raised disc, thereby closing a timer switch, and scratches vigorously, round and round, over the disc for 15 seconds, at the rate of about two scratches per second until the automatic feeder fires in the retaining compartment. The chicken goes into the compartment to eat, thereby automatically shutting the door. The popular interpretation of this behavior pattern is that the chicken has turned on the "juke box" and "dances."

The development of this behavioral exhibit was wholly unplanned. In the attempt to create quite another type of demonstration which required a chicken simply to stand on a platform for 12–15 seconds, we found that over 50% developed a very strong and pronounced scratch pattern, which tended to increase in persistence as the time interval was lengthened. (Another 25% or so developed other behaviors—pecking at spots, etc.) However, we were

A chicken trained to "dance" after pulling on a string which turns on the music. (Courtesy of Animal Behavior Enterprises.)

able to change our plans so as to make use of the scratch pattern, and the result was the "dancing chicken" exhibit described above.

In this exhibit the only real contingency for reinforcement is that the chicken must depress the platform for 15 seconds. In the course of a performing day (about 3 hours for each chicken) a chicken may turn out over 10,000 unnecessary, virtually identical responses.[5]

The Miserly Raccoon

The response concerned the manipulation of money by the raccoon (who has "hands" rather similar to those of the primates). The contingency for reinforcement was picking up the coins and depositing them in a 5-inch metal box.

5. Breland and Breland, 1961, pp. 681–682.

Raccoons condition readily, have good appetites, and this one was quite tame and an eager subject. We anticipated no trouble. Conditioning him to pick up the first coin was simple. We started out by reinforcing him for pick-ing up a single coin. Then the metal container was introduced, with the requirement that he drop the coin into the container. Here we ran into the first bit of difficulty: he seemed to have a great deal of trouble letting go of the coin. He would rub it up against the inside of the container, pull it back out, and clutch it firmly for several seconds. However, he would finally turn it loose and receive his food reinforcement. Then the final contingency: we put him on a ratio of 2, requiring that he pick up both coins and put them in the container.

Now the raccoon really had problems (and so did we). Not only could he not let go of the coins, but he spent seconds, even minutes, rubbing them together (in a most miserly fashion), and dipping them into the container. He carried on the behavior to such an extent that the practical demon-stration we had in mind—a display featuring a raccoon putting money in a piggy bank—simply was not feasible. The rubbing behavior became worse and worse as time went on, in spite of nonreinforcement. [6]

The "dancing chicken" danced though it was not trained to do so. As the Brelands point out, the chicken expended substantial unneces-sary effort. The reinforcement contingency was not responsible for this activity, and one suspects that a reinforcement contingency would not eliminate it. The coin rubbing of the racoon was not merely un-necessary: it interfered with responses which would have produced food. Nevertheless, the racoon continued to manipulate the coins until the Brelands abandoned the project.

These examples and others reported by the Brelands are perplex-ing because they demonstrate the failure of reinforcement contin-gencies to control behavior. Why do the reinforcement contingencies fail? What other than contingent reinforcement could be responsible for the "misbehavior" of the chicken and the racoon? The Brelands suggested a possibility:

Here we have animals, after having been conditioned to a specific learned response, gradually drifting into behaviors that are entirely different from those which were conditioned. Moreover, it can easily be seen that these par-ticular behaviors to which the animals drift are clear-cut examples of in-stinctive behaviors having to do with the natural food-getting behaviors of the particular species. [7]

6. Breland and Breland, 1961, p. 682.
7. Breland and Breland, 1961, p. 683.

The Brelands labeled their observation *instinctive drift*. In their view, whenever a situation permitted the intrusion of species-specific behavior patterns, these patterns would occur. If circumstances were right, these instinctive behaviors would compete with the conditioned behaviors. As a result, animals would substantially reduce the frequency with which they obtained reinforcement.

There are a few things to notice about the Brelands' observations. First, loss of control over behavior was not random; it was a clear reflection of species-specific behavior patterns. Second, these behavior patterns occurred in extraordinarily artificial environments. So powerful were these responses that they occurred under nonoptimal conditions at the cost of food to hungry animals. What are we to make of this? The conditioning chamber seems to prevent the occurrence of responses like this; hence, the claim for general principles. However, one must wonder about whether any situation which prevents the occurrence of responses as powerful as these is not fundamentally distorting our understanding of the principles of behavior control. If the conditioning chamber in fact prevents these sorts of species-specific behavior patterns, it cannot be telling us anything very important about the control of behavior in the natural environment.

The Brelands' paper was widely read and cited. Yet, it seemed to have rather little influence on the course of research done in conditioning laboratories. No one was moved to develop a research program like the one depicted in Figure 11–1. Investigators seemed to be impressed by the examples, but not by their implications. What seems to have stirred up inquiry into the arbitrariness of learning in general and of the methods of behavior analysis in particular was a quite different sort of phenomenon, a phenomenon researchers have known about for years but attended to only recently. It is the phenomenon of taste aversion learning, or poisoning.[8]

TASTE AVERSION LEARNING

A rat is permitted access to a flavored solution, say vanilla. After drinking the solution for a few minutes, the rat is sublethally poisoned. The poison makes the rat sick, and it takes 20 minutes or so for the poison to act. A day or so later, the rat, now fully recovered, is again given access to the vanilla-flavored solution. The rat avoids the solution. Apparently the rat has learned, in one trial, to associate a

---

8. For early findings, see Richter, 1953; Rzoska, 1953; Garcia, Kimmeldorf, and Hunt, 1961. For recent reviews, see Revusky and Garcia, 1970, and Rozin and Kalat, 1971.

flavor (vanilla) with poison. Not only has the rat learned in one trial, but it has learned when the interval between taste and illness was 20 minutes long. In fact, rats can learn to avoid a flavor when the interval between taste and illness is 12 hours long.[9] This is the basic taste aversion learning phenomenon.

What makes taste aversion learning seem special? To evaluate taste aversion learning as special or problematic, we must know with what familiar phenomena it should be compared. What kind of learning is taste aversion learning? At first glance, it looks like an example of Pavlovian conditioning: the taste (vanilla) is the conditioned stimulus (CS), and the illness is the unconditioned stimulus (US). Compared with, say, Pavlovian conditioned fear, taste aversion seems special for at least two reasons: first, it is acquired on one or a few trials while conditioned fear typically requires a number of trials; second, it is acquired even when the interval between CS and US is quite long (up to 12 hours), while in most Pavlovian conditioning studies, the CS–US interval is a matter of seconds.

Thus, taste aversion learning seems like extremely rapid and powerful Pavlovian conditioning. Does this fact present behavior analysis with a problem? It seems not. In discussing arbitrariness above, we stressed the fact that arbitrariness referred to relations—between CSs and USs or between operants and reinforcers. Taste aversion learning may be rapid because tastes are very effective CSs, or it may be rapid because illness is a much more potent US than electric shock. If either or both of these possibilities is borne out, then taste aversion can be treated as an instance of Pavlovian conditioning.

How might we test whether the rapidity of taste aversion learning is the result of the unusual potency of taste as a CS or poison as a US? A research program along the lines outlined in Figure 11–2 would serve us well. Combine taste with shock (*A*), and tone with poison (*B*), and tone with shock (*C*), as well as taste with poison (*D*). If poison is more potent than shock, we would expect faster conditioning in *D* than in *A*. If taste is more potent than tone, we would expect faster conditioning in *A* than in *C*. If either tastes or poisons are more potent than more common CSs, we would expect the slowest conditioning in *C*. Finally, if both taste and poison are especially potent, we would expect the fastest conditioning in *D*.

But is taste aversion learning appropriately viewed as Pavlovian conditioning? What is the conditioned response? Is the taste appropriately viewed as a CS? After all, the animal must ingest the flavored

9. See Revusky and Garcia, 1970.

Pavlovian conditioning	Punishment
A. Taste — Shock B. Tone — Poison C. Tone — Shock D. Taste — Poison	A'. Lick— Taste— Shock B' Lick— Tone— Poison C'. Lick— Tone— Shock D'. Lick— Taste — Poison

1. If taste is an especially potent CS, then
   A faster than C
   D faster than B
2. If poison is an especially potent US, then
   B faster than C
   D faster than A
3. If both taste and poison are especially effective, then
   D faster than A or B
   A or B faster than C

Figure 11–2. Hypothetical Test of the Arbitrariness of Taste Aversion Learning. *If the outcomes of experiments A–D confirm any of the predictions 1–3, then taste aversion might justifiably be viewed as a conventional conditioning phenomenon. Whether taste aversion is viewed as Pavlovian conditioning (A–D) or punishment of licking (A'–D') has no bearing on the predicted outcomes of the experiments.*

solution. One might view taste aversion as a discriminated punishment procedure. The animal emits a response (licking) which produces a discriminable taste, and the response is punished with poison (illness). What the animal might be learning is to suppress the punished response of licking.

We seem to be at an impasse. It is clear that we cannot decide whether taste aversion learning is special without first deciding with what it should be compared. But how are we to decide whether it should be compared with studies of Pavlovian conditioning or with studies of punishment? With careful analysis, we can find our way out of the impasse. Return to the right side of Figure 11–2. Listed under the heading "Punishment" are four hypothetical experiments in which licks produce either distinctive flavors or tones, and either poison or shock. Whether we view taste aversion learning as Pavlovian conditioning or as punishment, we can do essentially the same experiments to decide whether it is special. The predictions outlined in Figure 11–2 are the same whether we do Experiments *A–D* or Experiments *A'–D'*. As long as those predictions are confirmed, we

can be confident that taste aversion learning poses no special problems, no matter what category of conditioning it is placed in. Similarly, if those predictions are not confirmed, taste aversion learning
does pose a problem, again independent of whether it is classed as
punishment or Pavlovian conditioning.[10]

What then are the results of such a series of experiments? Precisely
this series of experiments has not been done. However, research very
much like it strongly suggests that the predictions in Figure 11–2
would not be confirmed. Rats were exposed to the following procedure: whenever they licked at a tube containing a flavored solution,
the lick produced both a click and a light flash. Thus, at the same instant, the rats experienced a taste, a light, and a noise. Some of the
rats were subsequently poisoned; other rats received painful shock to
the feet. After a number of such trials, the drinking of the rats was
evaluated in a procedure in which the light and noise were separated
from the taste. On one day licks at a tube produced the flavored solution, but no light or noise, while on the next day licks at a tube produced light and noise but tap water instead of the flavored solution.
Based upon the predictions outlined in Figure 11–2, we might expect
roughly the following results:

1. Since taste is a more powerful CS than light or noise, it should
overshadow the other two stimuli when all three are combined (see
Chapter 4). As a result, rats should avoid the flavored solution but
not the bright and noisy one.

2. Since poison is a more potent US than shock, rats given poison
should evidence a larger aversion to the CS than rats given shock.

The results of this experiment are presented in Figure 11–3. The
number of licks at the tube per minute are presented for both pretests
with audio-visual and taste cues separated and posttests (after conditioning) with audio-visual and taste cues separated. The top part of
Figure 11–3 presents data for rats that experienced poison as a US;
the bottom part presents data for rats that experienced shock. It is
clear that, with poison as a US, taste dominated noise and light as a
CS. The rats showed no change in drinking from the bright, noisy
tube between pre- and posttests and a substantial decrease in drinking
from the taste tube. On the other hand, with shock as the US, exactly
the reverse was true. There was no decrease at all in drinking the
flavored water, and a substantial decrease in drinking the bright,

10. See Schwartz, 1974b.

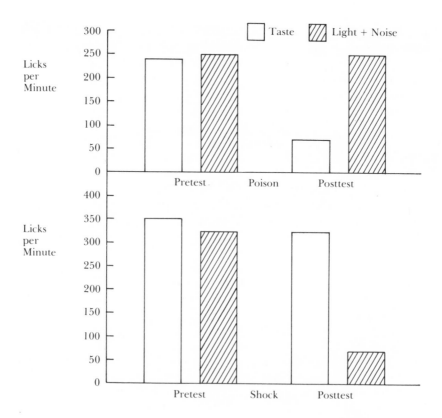

Figure 11–3. The Relation of Cue to Consequence. *With poison as a US (top figure), rats associate the poison with taste and not with light or noise. With shock as the US (bottom figure), the reverse is true. (After Garcia & Koelling, 1966.)*

noisy water. Moreover, shock was just as effective in suppressing drinking as was poison.[11] Thus, the experiment fails to support either of the predictions derived from Figure 11–2. We must conclude that taste aversion learning reflects neither the power of taste as a CS, nor the power of poison as a US, but the power of the two in combination. When the combination is broken (as when shock is the US), we find almost no conditioning to the taste. Thus, the phenomenon of taste aversion learning violates the assumption of arbitrariness outlined in detail above, because its most striking characteristics depend upon the interaction between a particular type of CS (taste) and a particular type of US (poison).

11. Garcia and Koelling, 1966.

Belongingness

Rather than being arbitrary, taste aversion seems to point to a different principle, one we will call *belongingness*.[12] Taste and stomach illness seem to go together. Taste and pain to the feet do not, nor, for that matter, do audio-visual stimuli and stomach illness. The notion of belongingness should strike an intuitive chord. If, after eating a fine dinner out, you go home and get sick to your stomach, it is likely that you will associate the illness with something you ate. You will not associate illness with the color of the wallpaper in the restaurant, or with the music played by the violinist, or with the floral pattern on the china you ate from, or with the people who accompanied you, or with the ride home. Each of these other stimuli bears the same temporal relation to your illness as does the food, yet surely it will be the food, and not any of the other cues, which you will subsequently avoid.[13] As it turns out, what the rat learns from the taste aversion experiment is similar to what you might learn from the restaurant. The rat seems built to behave as if "It must have been something I ate."

In judging the significance of taste aversion learning it is appropriate to inquire first about its generality. Is the belongingness relation between taste and illness a biological adaptation peculiar to the rat or is it a more general phenomenon? If it is more general, we should find it in other species. But what should we find? If we consider the adaptive value of a built-in taste aversion learning mechanism, it becomes clear that what we should look for is not a special relation between *taste* and illness which cuts across species boundaries, but a special relation between whatever property of food the organism uses to identify it and illness. In species which identify food by properties other than taste, a special *taste* aversion mechanism would not be very useful. The point of such a mechanism, after all, is to steer the organism away from toxic foods on the basis of only minimal experience. What, for example, should be the result of poisoning experiments when the subjects are birds that depend primarily on visual cues for food identification? We might expect a reversal of the results depicted

---

12. Initially coined by E. L. Thorndike many years ago, the term belongingness is now sometimes used to refer to nonarbitrary relations among stimuli, or responses and stimuli (see Schwartz, 1974b).

13. We can speculate, in addition, that it would not be all of the food you ate at the restaurant, or even a random subset of what you ate. In all likelihood, you would associate your illness with *novel* foods that you ate. After all, you may have eaten coq au vin and Caesar salad and chocolate mousse many times before without getting sick. But you may never have eaten snails before. As it turns out, rats also seem primed to associate novel foods with illness. As they become accustomed to a food, they seem to learn that it is safe. See Revusky and Bedarf, 1967.

in the top of Figure 11–3. If these birds were poisoned after ingesting a colored tasty solution, and then given a choice between a colored tasteless solution and a colorless tasty one, they should avoid the color and not the taste. If they did, this contradiction of the results obtained with rats would provide elegant support for the principle that organisms are built to associate stimuli they use to identify food with gastrointestinal consequences.

Such an experiment was done with bobwhite quail (*Colinus virginianus*). The quail drank blue sour water and were then poisoned. One group was then tested with sour water while the other group was tested with blue water. The quail given blue water drank only about one-fifth as much as they had before poisoning. For rats exposed to the same procedure, the reverse was true; they avoided the sour water but not the blue water.[14] Thus, the general lesson to be learned seems to be that learned food aversions reflect a built-in predisposition to associate the properties of food relevant to its identification with gastrointestinal distress. The phenomenon of food aversion learning is both general (transspecies) and nonarbitrary.[15]

What is the import of the nonarbitrariness of taste aversion learning for behavior analysis? In what way should the assumption of arbitrariness be reevaluated or modified? One might first ask whether similar nonarbitrary relations contribute to any of the familiar phenomena investigators have been studying with conventional experimental methods over the years. In short, is the box arbitrary?

IS THE BOX ARBITRARY?

In attempting to evaluate whether the box is arbitrary or not, we will focus on the two most common sets of experimental conditions: the rat pressing a lever and the pigeon pecking a key. While these are not the only situations investigated by researchers, they are the most common ones. Thus, evidence about possible nonarbitrary influences occurring in these situations would have rather broad implications.

---

14. Wilcoxin, Dragoin, and Kral, 1971.
15. During the above discussion, we did not distinguish between learning and maintenance of behavior. Taste aversion seems to reflect nonarbitrary *learning*. On the other hand, most of the Brelands' observations have nothing to do with learning. The "misbehavior" they described did not begin to appear until the contingencies were well learned. Many of the examples of "misbehavior" we will discuss in the remainder of this chapter similarly focus on the *maintenance* of behavior rather than learning. How many instances of "misbehavior" may be found in learning situations remains an open question. So far as the implications of these kinds of phenomena for behavior analysis are concerned, it hardly matters whether the biological characteristics of a particular species influence the acquisition of responses, or their maintenance, or both.

There have been intimations in each of the preceding chapters that the phenomena one observes in the box reflect nonarbitrary relations between behavior and environmental events. What we will do here is bring much of this evidence together. Let us begin by examining the simplest of situations: What happens when a pigeon is placed in an operant conditioning chamber and periodically presented with food?

Superstition Revisited

In Chapter 6, we discussed the phenomenon of "superstition." In 1948, Skinner delivered food to hungry pigeons and watched them. He found that almost every pigeon developed a stereotyped behavior pattern.[16] When Staddon and Simmelhag repeated Skinner's experiment, they also found that pigeons ended up with stereotyped response patterns. Unlike Skinner, they found that all pigeons did the same thing. As time to feed grew near, the pigeons reliably pecked. This uniformity in behavior appeared despite the fact that food presentations early in the experiment rarely followed pecking. Food presentations followed other kinds of responses, and by Skinner's account of the law of effect, these other responses should have been strengthened. Instead, these other responses dropped out over time and were replaced by pecks. Why should all pigeons be pecking? It turns out that pecking is a species-characteristic consummatory response in the pigeon. Hungry pigeons peck at food and in feeding situations. The occurrence of pecking in the superstition experiment reflects not the operation of the law of effect, but the operation of a biological program.[17]

It is tempting to draw from this example the conclusion that "superstition" must be ruled out of an operant analysis, but that all other principles may remain unchanged. What makes this conclusion unacceptable, however, is that the biologically determined response that pigeons end up making is precisely the same as the response researchers have treated as an arbitrary operant for 40 years or so. Studies of schedules of reinforcement, or discrimination learning, with pigeons as subjects record pecks (at a key) as the dependent variable. How can we be sure that these pecks are in fact under the control of the reinforcement contingencies operating in the experiment and not the pigeon's biological program? The discovery by Staddon and Simmelhag demands a careful reevaluation of the phenomena observed in pigeon operant conditioning experiments.

16. Skinner, 1948.
17. Staddon and Simmelhag, 1971.

Autoshaping

Suppose we place hungry pigeons in a conditioning chamber and periodically present them with food. Suppose, in addition, that a few seconds prior to each food delivery, we light up a response key. Pigeons exposed to this kind of procedure reliably end up pecking just before food is delivered. In addition, they all end up pecking at the same place—the response key. This phenomenon has come to be called "autoshaping" (automatic shaping). Instead of training pigeons to peck a key, one can simply expose them to an autoshaping procedure. Pairings of key light and food will typically have pigeons pecking the key within 50 trials (see Chapter 6, pp. 147–149).[18]

What is this autoshaping phenomenon? It seems to be a straightforward instance of Pavlovian conditioning. The lit key is the CS and food is the US. But what is the conditioned response? The conditioned response, pecking, is precisely the same as the response investigators have taken to be a prototypic, arbitrary operant. This is where the problem lies. Recall what arbitrary means. For a response to be arbitrary, it must bear no intrinsic relation to the reinforcer being used. One operant can be substituted for another, or one reinforcer substituted for another, without materially affecting the functions one obtains. But Pavlovian CRs are not arbitrarily related to the reinforcer. Rather, the form of the CR is directly influenced by the reinforcer. Dogs salivate when food is a US, but they increase heart rate when shock is a US. There is a special relation between CR and US (or reinforcer) which characterizes Pavlovian conditioning. If autoshaping is an instance of Pavlovian conditioning, there must be a special relation between pecking and food. If so, the key peck operant cannot be viewed as arbitrary. The crux of the matter, then, is whether autoshaping should appropriately be viewed as Pavlovian conditioning.

The evidence on this matter is almost wholly positive. First, the form of the autoshaped response seems generally to match the form of the consummatory response. Thus, when food is the US pigeons "eat" the key, while when water is the US they "drink" the key.[19] When access to a sexually receptive mate is the US, pigeons "court" the lit key and "coo" at it just as they do their prospective mate.[20] Similar consummatory responses have been observed in other species exposed to autoshaping procedures. Most central to our concerns, when

18. Brown and Jenkins, 1968.
19. Jenkins and Moore, 1973.
20. Rackham, cited by Hearst and Jenkins, 1974.

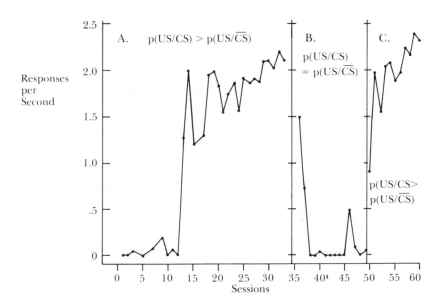

Figure 11–4. Informativeness as a Necessary Condition for Autoshaping. *Key pecking began and was maintained when the lit key was an informative signal for food* (A). *When food was as likely when the key was off as when it was on* (B), *key pecking ceased. Pecking reappeared* (C) *when the informativeness of the key was reestablished. (After Gamzu & Williams, 1971.)*

rats receive food signaled by the insertion of a lever into the box, or by illumination of tiny lights in the lever, they sniff, lick, and chew on the lever.[21]

Second, the development of autoshaped key pecking seems governed by the same aspects of the stimulus–reinforcer relation that govern more traditional occurrences of Pavlovian conditioning. We saw in Chapter 5 that the key to Pavlovian conditioning was an informative relation between CS and US; the CS must be a differential predictor of the US for conditioning to occur. The same is true of autoshaping. If one arranges a procedure which contains key–food pairings, but also contains food presentations in the absence of the lit key so that food is just as likely when the key is off as when it is lit, pigeons do not learn to peck the key. If they have already learned to peck the key and this procedure is introduced, they stop pecking, as

21. Peterson, Ackil, Frommer, and Hearst, 1972; Stiers and Silberberg, 1974. For reviews, see Hearst and Jenkins, 1974, and Schwartz and Gamzu, 1977.

evidenced in Figure 11–4. Thus, the necessary condition for autoshaping is that $p(US/CS) > p(US/\overline{CS})$.[22]

These data are certainly impressive support for the view that autoshaping reflects Pavlovian conditioning in operation. However, as regards the larger issue of the arbitrariness of the key peck, it seems possible that pecking is *both* a Pavlovian CR and an arbitrary operant. That one can generate and maintain pecking with Pavlovian procedures does not necessarily mean that the pecking which occurs on operant procedures is attributable to Pavlovian influence, or even that the pecking which occurs on Pavlovian procedures will not be susceptible to operant influence. In other words, the autoshaping phenomenon does not necessarily tell us anything about the arbitrariness of the key peck *as an operant*.

There is, however, a phenomenon which makes it clear that the key peck is special. Suppose one wanted to make the following argument: the first key peck which occurs on an autoshaping procedure is generated by a Pavlovian, stimulus–reinforcer (CS–US) contingency. Once that peck occurs, however, it is followed closely in time by food. Temporal contiguity between pecks and food (the law of effect) quickly exerts control over the response. This kind of argument could be made for any instance of Pavlovian conditioning in which the US is a known positive reinforcer. Once the first CR occurs, it is necessarily close in time to the US, and this accidental response–reinforcer relation could contribute to the maintenance of the CR. What gives the argument special force in connection with autoshaping is that the autoshaped response, the key peck, is demonstrably sensitive to operant contingencies in a host of situations.

The Omission Effect

How could one test this argument? Some years ago, in a test of similar arguments with regard to conditioned salivation, Pavlovian conditioning trials were arranged which were standard but for the fact that if the dog salivated during the CS, food (the US) was not delivered. Every CR prevented food. If the pairing of salivation and food was responsible for the occurrence of salivation, dogs would quickly stop salivating on this procedure. They did not. The dogs continued salivating on 50 percent or more of the trials for session after session; they could not withhold salivation in order to obtain food. This phenomenon has come to be known as the *omission effect*.[23]

22. Gamzu and Williams, 1971, 1973.
23. Sheffield, 1965.

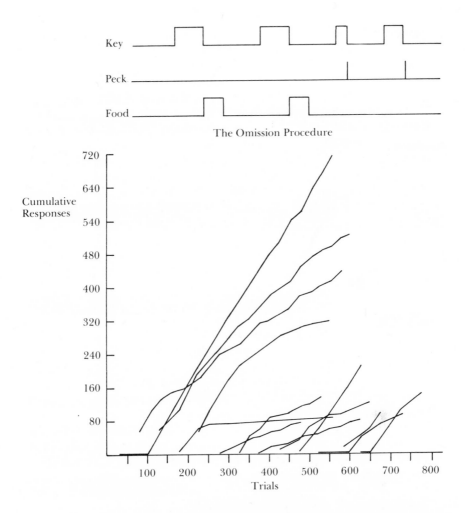

Figure 11–5. The Omission Phenomenon: Maintenance of Key Pecking in the Face of Negative Consequences. *The omission procedure is diagrammed at the top of the figure, and cumulative responses of pigeons exposed to the procedure are presented at the bottom.* (After Williams & Williams, 1969.)

More recently, an analogous experiment was performed in an autoshaping context. The procedure is depicted at the top of Figure 11–5. The key was periodically illuminated for 6 seconds. If no peck occurred during this time, the key was extinguished and food was presented. A peck on the lit key turned out the light, ending the trial, and prevented food. As with salivation, pecking persisted over many sessions under these conditions. The bottom portion of Figure 11–5 presents cumulative totals of responses over 800 trials for 13 different subjects. All subjects responded on at least 10 percent of the trials, some responded on more than 50 percent of the trials, and one responded on 90 percent of the trials. The contingencies operative in the experiment were such that any response other than key pecking could be followed immediately by food and key pecks could *never* be followed by food. If an accidental correlation between response and reinforcer was contributing to the maintenance of responses, we would expect stereotyped responses other than key pecks to develop.

The fact that key pecking reliably occurred under these conditions makes it clear that operant contingencies play no critical role in the maintenance of key pecking on autoshaping procedures. Indeed, the demonstrated *insensitivity* of key pecks to their consequences on the omission procedure makes one wonder how the same response (key peck) could be so sensitive to its consequences in standard operant procedures.[24] This omission phenomenon is what provided the crucial evidence that key pecking cannot be viewed as an arbitrary operant, and it has been primarily responsible for generating enormous research interest in autoshaping. It has been reproduced a number of times in different laboratories, and with different species, most notably the rat.[25]

The determination that key pecking is not an arbitrary operant raises more questions than it answers. We can conclude that the box is not arbitrary. This is the question we set out to answer at the beginning of this section. The standard pigeon-conditioning environment (and probably the rat-conditioning environment as well) permits the intrusion of species-specific behavior patterns. Moreover, the species-specific behavior which occurs is the very one that investigators have characterized as an arbitrary operant. But does it make a difference that key pecks are not arbitrary responses? Are any of the phenomena we have discussed in earlier chapters dependent upon the nonarbitrariness of the key peck? If we revised our methods and studied a different, truly arbitrary response, would any of the principles we

24. There is accumulating evidence that autoshaped key pecks are not "the same response" as operant key pecks. Schwartz and Williams, 1972, found evidence that operant and autoshaped pecks differ in duration, the latter being substantially shorter than the former, and that operant pecks are primarily sensitive to their consequences, while autoshaped pecks are primarily sensitive to Pavlovian, stimulus–reinforcer relations. This difference in the two kinds of pecks has been confirmed in other research as well. See Gamzu, 1971; Schwartz, Hamilton, and Silberberg, 1975; and Schwartz, 1977a and 1977b. However, there is still some uncertainty surrounding both the reliability of these findings and their proper interpretation.
25. Stiers and Silberberg, 1974.

have developed thus far require revision? We pointed out at the beginning of the chapter that the strategy of creating an arbitrary environment was adopted to maximize the generality of one's findings. The fact that the experimental environment is not arbitrary does not imply that one's findings are not general. It is possible that whether or not a situation is arbitrary, the phenomena one observes in operant conditioning experiments will be the same. This is the issue we must now address: Is there evidence that the nonarbitrary nature of the key-peck operant makes a critical contribution to operant conditioning phenomena? To answer this question, we will review some findings which have already been discussed in other contexts.

Operant Discrimination

We made the argument in Chapter 10 that any operant discrimination procedure includes relations between stimuli and reinforcers which are sufficient to produce Pavlovian conditioning. We have just seen that in the pigeon, Pavlovian contingencies can produce key pecks as conditioned responses (autoshaping). If we put these two facts together, we might expect that an operant discrimination procedure will yield Pavlovian conditioned key pecks. The phenomenon of positive behavioral contrast (see Chapter 10) confirms our expectation.

If a pigeon is exposed to a multiple schedule, with the color of the response key alternating, say, between red and green, and with pecks reinforced according to the same variable-interval (VI) schedule in the presence of both stimuli, the pigeon will peck at roughly the same rate at both red and green lights. When food is discontinued in one of the components of the schedule (extinction), as response rate decreases in extinction, there is a concomitant, substantial increase in responding during the unchanged VI schedule. This increase is called positive behavioral contrast. Historically, a determination of the variables affecting contrast has seemed central to an understanding of the mechanisms underlying discriminative control in general. Recently, however, an account of contrast has been advanced which views it not as the key to understanding discriminative control, but as a result of the nonarbitrary nature of the key-peck operant. This account explains contrast as an instance of autoshaping.[26]

When the same VI schedule is operating in both red and green, the Pavlovian relation between each of the stimuli and food is noninformative. Food is as likely in the presence of red as in the presence of

26. See Schwartz and Gamzu, 1977.

green. As we saw in Figure 11–4, such conditions do not produce autoshaped responding. When food is discontinued in the presence of one of the stimuli, the other one becomes a differential predictor of food. For example, if extinction is introduced when the key is green, then p(food/red) > p(food/red̄). This differential contingency is sufficient to produce autoshaped pecking. According to the account of contrast based on autoshaping, these autoshaped pecks add to the already maintained operant pecks with the net result that overall pecking increases. In sum, the phenomenon of positive behavioral contrast is viewed as the result of Pavlovian conditioning of key pecking. As we saw in Chapter 10, there is substantial evidence to support this account of contrast. It may not be a complete account of the phenomenon, but it is certainly at least a partial account.

Why does contrast, seen in these terms, raise problems about the arbitrariness assumption? Perhaps all operant discrimination phenomena can be at least partially attributed to the occurrence of Pavlovian conditioning. We must remind ourselves of what gets conditioned in a Pavlovian conditioning experiment. In general, the nature of the US determines the nature of the CR. Thus, with food as the US, the CR is a component of the animal's feeding repertoire. For the pigeon, the CR turns out to be pecking, which also happens to be the recorded operant. Thus, operant and Pavlovian responses may add together. For the rat, the CR may well be some form of licking or gnawing. It is certainly not lever pressing. Thus, on the standard multiple-schedule procedure employed with rats, contrast should not, and in general does not, occur. One can eliminate contrast in the pigeon by training pigeons to hop on a treadle rather than peck a key for food. Thus contrast reflects not a general principle of conditioning, but the accidental fact that for the pigeon both operants and CRs take the same, nonarbitrary form, and are directed at the same place—the lit key.

We do not intend to suggest here that, since behavioral contrast results from nonarbitrary relations between response and reinforcer in the conditioning chamber, all operant discrimination phenomena result from similar relations. Rather, the demonstration that these nonarbitrary relations influence some aspects of discrimination requires that we reevaluate the phenomena of operant discriminative control generally. It may turn out that most of the phenomena of discriminative control do not depend upon nonarbitrary relations between the response and the reinforcer. The point is that the observed relation between autoshaping and behavioral contrast transforms this possibility from the status of assumption to the status of empirical issue.

Avoidance Learning

Consider the following experiment. Pigeons are exposed to a series of trials in which a green light appears on a key for 6 seconds and is followed by food. If they peck the key while it is lit, the trial immediately ends without food. This is the omission procedure discussed above. After the pigeons have come to peck the key reliably (and prevent food), the procedure is changed. Now, after 6 seconds of key illumination, the pigeons receive a painful electric shock. Pecks on the key have the same consequence as before; they prevent delivery of the US. This is an avoidance procedure of the type described in Chapter 9. The only difference between omission and avoidance procedures is the US. If the US is food, it is an omission procedure, and if the US is shock, it is an avoidance procedure. When pigeons are shifted to avoidance from omission, they stop pecking the key. If the procedure is changed so that some trials (when a the key is green) are omission and others (when the key is red) are avoidance, pigeons peck reliably to avoid food but not to avoid shock.[27] This experiment provides a rather clear indication that there is something special and nonarbitrary about the relation between pecking and food. Not only does pecking occur in a feeding situation even when it costs the pigeon food, but pecking does not occur in a danger situation when it will save the animal from shock.

We have already discussed the possibility that avoidance learning in general is nonarbitrary in Chapter 9, where we suggested that the single most important variable in determining the outcome of avoidance experiments is the nature of the required operant. If the required operant is a part of the species-specific defense repertoire, avoidance responding will develop slowly. If the response is a part of a different system, let us say, the feeding system, avoidance responding may not develop at all.[28] Thus, pigeons may learn to flap their wings, hop, stretch their necks, or fly to avoid shock without great difficulty, while learning to peck a key only with extensive, careful training, if at all.[29] Similarly, rats may rapidly learn to avoid shock by jumping out of boxes or running down alleys, but learn to press a lever very slowly. It seems clear that while other variables will influence the acqusition of avoidance responding, the key variable is the relation of the required response to the built-in defensive repertoire. Thus, the entire area of avoidance learning may be seen as evidence

27. Schwartz, 1973.
28. Bolles, 1970.
29. See Bedford and Anger, 1968; MacPhail, 1968; Hineline and Rachlin, 1969.

against the assumption of arbitrariness. Since pigeons can learn responses other than key pecking to avoid shock, we know that the problem with key-peck avoidance is not that avoidance is too difficult. Since pigeons can readily learn to key peck for food, we know that the problem with key-peck avoidance is not that pecking is too difficult. The problem must lie in the relation between key pecking and shock.

Pavlovian Conditioning

As a final instance of nonarbitrariness within the standard methods of behavior analysis, we will consider some Pavlovian conditioning phenomena. As we discussed above, taste aversion may be viewed as an example of nonarbitrary Pavlovian conditioning. However, since it differs so substantially from the traditional laboratory preparation, it is tempting to treat taste aversion as an isolated anomaly. Therefore, our present concern will be with indications of nonarbitrariness within the domain of familiar Pavlovian conditioning studies.

To begin, let us review what nonarbitrary Pavlovian conditioning should look like. We know that the conditioned response is not arbitrary; it is intimately related to the US. What is traditionally viewed as arbitrary is the relation between the CS and the US. Thus, the fact that pigeons peck in autoshaping experiments poses no particular problem for the view that autoshaping is arbitrary Pavlovian conditioning. What would pose a problem would be evidence that the key light, a visual stimulus, is critical to autoshaping. The available evidence on this issue is thin. While there is some indication that pigeons can be autoshaped with an auditory CS, the effects are much less reliable than with a visual CS.[30] In addition, since discriminative control is *generally* achieved faster and to a higher degree of accuracy with visual than with auditory stimuli in the pigeon, it may be that the superiority of visual over auditory stimuli in autoshaping merely reflects a general characteristic of the pigeon's sensory apparatus. In keeping with the procedures needed for demonstrating nonarbitrariness outlined in Figure 11-1, we would need to show that, under some conditions, tones or noises are more effective controlling stimuli than lights.

A number of experiments, with both pigeons and chicks as subjects, indicate that visual stimuli dominate auditory ones when food is the US, and the reverse is true when shock is the US.[31] In one such ex-

---

30. Hearst and Jenkins, 1974.
31. See Foree and LoLordo, 1973; Shettleworth, 1972b. The story is actually a bit complicated, however. Both Shettleworth, and Foree and LoLordo in a later publication (1975) found that as long as food or water is present in a situation, light will dominate tone, even when aversive stimuli are also present.

periment, pigeons were trained to hop on a treadle in the presence of a tone and a red light. For some pigeons, treadle hops produced food, while for others they avoided shock. Subsequently, pigeons were tested with the red light alone or with the tone alone. For pigeons that had been obtaining food, the red light almost totally overshadowed the tone in controlling responding. For pigeons that had been avoiding shock, the tone overshadowed the red light. Thus, under some conditions at least, a tone can be more effective than a light in controlling the behavior of pigeons.[32] This suggests that the superiority of light over tone in autoshaping may, in fact, be an instance of nonarbitrariness in Pavlovian conditioning.[33]

IS BEHAVIOR ARBITRARY?

We have just reviewed evidence that many familiar conditioning phenomena are at least partly the result of nonarbitrary relations between behavior and environmental events which standard experimental methods have failed to eliminate. Efforts to establish arbitrary or unbiased experimental situations have not been entirely successful. In the light of such evidence, what should the behavior analyst do?

One possibility is that better methods, which eliminate species-characteristic bias, can be developed. Such a strategy is consistent with the view that the goal of the analysis of behavior—to discover laws which generalize across species and across situations—is a reasonable one, but that the means to the goal must be improved. Alternatively, one could take the evidence for nonarbitrariness to indicate that the search for general laws is a mistake. Since much of the behavior of animals seems powerfully controlled by species-specific characteristics, one might decide to study the specialized behavioral characteristics of each species. Underlying this choice is the view that most interesting behavior in the natural environment is not arbitrarily related to environmental events.

The issue we are confronting is this: *Is behavior arbitrary?* As one researcher has put it:

Psychologists had hoped that in the simple, controlled world of levers and mechanical feeders, of metronomes and meat powder, something quite general would emerge. If we took an arbitrary action such as pressing a lever, and an arbitrary organism such as an albino rat, and set it to work pressing

---

32. Foree and LoLordo, 1973.
33. Note that the treadle-hopping experiment is not properly an instance of Pavlovian conditioning at all; tone and light are discriminative stimuli for the operant of treadle hopping. It seems reasonable to infer, however, that the presence of an operant requirement does not alter the special stimulus–reinforcer relations observed.

a lever for an arbitrary foodstuff, by virtue *of the very arbitrariness of this contingency, we would find features of the rat's behavior general to real life instrumental learning. . . . the very arbitrariness and unnaturalness of the experiment(s) was assumed to guarantee generality, since the situation would be uncontaminated by past experience the organism might have had and by special biological propensities he might bring to it.*[34]

Inherent in the emphasis on arbitrary events, however, is a danger: the laws may not be general, but peculiar to arbitrary events.[35]

The validity of the above passage seems undeniable. However, we are left with an unanswered question: How important are arbitrary associations? If most of the behavior of organisms is arbitrary, then there is no particular difficulty in claiming that the "laws of behavior," while not universal, are still quite general. The view suggested by the above quote seems to differ. It suggests a rather broad domain (in terms of both situations and species) in which nonarbitrary behavior is the rule. In attempting to reconcile arbitrary and nonarbitrary kinds of behavior, M. E. P. Seligman defined a continuum of *preparedness of association.* Some associations, like the one between taste and poison, are *prepared,* that is, they are easily and quickly learned, even under nonoptimal conditions. Some associations, like the one between noise and poison or between pecking and shock avoidance are *contraprepared,* that is, they are learned with the greatest difficulty, even under optimal conditions. Finally, some associations, like the one between noise and shock, are *unprepared,* that is, they are learned with moderate difficulty under ideal circumstances. The arbitrary associations which have been the traditional source of behavior analysis fall into this category.

Seligman suggests that much of what simple organisms do is prepared. He also suggests that such phenomena as language learning and the development of certain psychopathologies in humans are prepared. Thus, in his view, any research program which fails to capture prepared association is missing a substantial and central portion of the domain of learning.

The concept of preparedness, as an attempt to relate arbitrary and nonarbitrary learning, is problematic.[36] The important point for present purposes, however, is the emphasis which is placed upon the significance of nonarbitrary learning in the natural environment.

There is the alternative point of view, mentioned above. One could

34. Seligman and Hager, 1972, p. 2. See also Seligman, 1970.
35. Seligman and Hager, 1972, p. 3.
36. See Schwartz, 1974b.

acknowledge the existence of nonarbitrary kinds of learning, and of "misbehavior," and take these phenomena as a forceful and dramatic *justification* for attempting to create an artificial environment in the laboratory. If one views arbitrary learning as playing a significant role in shaping the behavior of organisms, especially complex organisms, then phenomena like taste aversion, rather than vitiating the effort to create arbitrary, experimental situations, only point out how important it is to make one's experimental situation arbitrary. If one is interested in general principles of behavior and not in principles peculiar to the rat or pigeon, and if one believes that significant general principles can be identified, then, unless one studies behavior in arbitrary situations, one will never be able to separate the general principles from the species-specific ones. This point of view was explicitly expressed by Skinner even before the assumption of arbitrariness had been seriously challenged:

> *In any case, behavior in a natural habitat would have no special claim to genuineness. What an organism does is a fact about that organism regardless of the conditions under which it does it. A behavior process is none-the-less real for being exhibited in an arbitrary setting.* [37]

Skinner's view and Seligman's do not differ in acknowledging the existence of nonarbitrary behavior; they differ in evaluating its significance. The question again is this: How much of behavior in nature is arbitrary?

Let us assume for the moment that most of what an organism does is nonarbitrary, that is, constrained by the organism's biological character. This assumption has characterized a branch of biology known as *ethology*. An implication of this view is that one can hardly hope to learn about people by studying pigeons. Indeed, if one studies the behavior of pigeons in a sufficiently artificial environment, one will not even learn very much about them. It is apparent that this view is an explicit contradiction of the views which have dominated behavior theory. If it turns out, as evidence presented in this chapter suggests, that the conditioning chamber is not nearly as artificial and arbitrary as investigators had hoped, then at least one will learn about pigeons.

Now let us make a slightly different assumption. Suppose that while the behavior of relatively simple organisms, like rats and pigeons, is largely nonarbitrary, the behavior of more complex organisms, like human adults, is striking in its arbitrariness. This view approximates the view which has characterized behavior theory. On this

37. Skinner, 1966, p. 1208.

view, if the conditioning chamber is nonarbitrary, we can learn about pigeons and rats from it, but not about people. However, if the chamber is arbitrary, we find ourselves in the paradoxical position of learning rather little about the organisms we are studying (since their behavior is largely nonarbitrary) but learning a great deal about people. It seems critical, therefore, to address the question: Is behavior arbitrary? A proper evaluation of the phenomena observed in the conditioning chamber will depend upon how we answer that question.

12

Constraints on Behavior

In the last chapter we discussed evidence that standard experimental situations are not arbitrary. At least some of the phenomena we observe in the box are the product not of general principles of behavior, but of characteristics of behavior which are specific to the species being studied. Efforts to create arbitrary or unbiased experimental environments which would lead to general principles of behavior have not entirely succeeded.

Is it appropriate to try to create an arbitrary environment? Is there reason to believe that an appreciable proportion of what an organism learns and does in the natural environment is arbitrary? Or, in contrast, is it possible that most of what organisms learn and do is largely influenced by characteristics of organisms which are unique to members of their species, or unique to the specific function being served (e.g., feeding, defense, reproduction)?

Let us begin by reconsidering a hypothetical event. Suppose you go to a restaurant for the first time. You are impressed right away by the fresh flowers, the delicate china, the ornate chandeliers, and the colorful landscapes that hang on the walls. You enjoy a number of courses, some familiar and some novel. In all, you have a thoroughly delightful experience. Later that night, you become sick to your stomach.

To what will you attribute your illness? Of course, you will conclude that it was something you ate. It would not occur to you to attribute your illness to the paintings on the wall or to the chandeliers. Moreover, it is likely that you will associate your illness neither with any random part of your meal nor with all of it. Instead, something novel will get the blame. Despite the fact that a host of different stimuli share the same temporal relation to your illness, you will be biased to form an association between the illness and only one or a few of those stimuli. The key word in this example is *bias*.

ASSOCIATIVE BIAS

That you will be biased in forming an association is not controversial. It is a fact of behavior. Indeed, the existence of biases may be the surest sign that an organism learns. Bias can be a reflection that one's response to a current set of events is influenced by one's experience with similar events in the past. Thus you might associate a novel food with illness because past experience with familiar foods (not followed by illness) rules them out of consideration. An account of present associative bias based upon past learning experience would pose no special problem for behavior theory. Principles of generalization, attention, and discrimination could be used to provide a reasonably complete and coherent picture. If a pigeon is trained to peck a green key for food and is subsequently given a choice between a green key and a key illuminated with a white triangle, it will peck the green key. If a rat which has been exposed to pairings of light and shock is then exposed to pairings of the same light coupled with a tone prior to shock, the rat will show associative bias and associate the shock exclusively with the light. The light and tone bear identical relations to the shock, just as the food and the plate on which it is served bear identical relations to illness. Nevertheless, light and noise will not share equally in the association with shock.[1] This kind of bias is what behavior theory is substantially about.

The problem posed by the phenomenon of taste aversion is not that it demonstrates associative bias, but that it may demonstrate a bias which does not depend upon past experience. That is, the bias may be built into the rat, and perhaps into the person. It is a kind of bias which behavior theory has systematically avoided. It is a bias whose underlying mechanisms will not be revealed by the methods of behavior theory.

CONSTRAINTS ON LEARNING

The systematic exploration of built-in associative bias is known as the study of "constraints on learning."[2] At first glance, this may seem

1. Kamin, 1968. See the discussion of this experiment in Chapter 5, pp. 89–91.
2. See Shettleworth, 1972a; Hinde and Hinde, 1973.

a strange title. Constraint implies limitation or restriction. Constrained learning is somehow less adaptable, less flexible, than unconstrained or arbitrary learning. Yet what seems so dramatic about the taste aversion learning phenomenon is its superiority over unconstrained, or arbitrary learning. Taste aversions are learned in one trial, and they are learned over long delays between taste and illness. Such characteristics make taste aversion strikingly different from most instances of learning about tones and shocks, or lights and food.

However, a careful analysis will reveal that "constrained" is just the right description for taste aversion learning. Imagine a wild rat that habitually feeds on a particular kind of food in a particular garbage dump. One day someone tosses some mildly poisonous, tasteless, odorless dye into the garbage. The dye coats the rat's food supply, changing its color. The rat eats its diet and subsequently gets sick. By virtue of its associative bias, the rat will be unable to associate its illness with the new color of the food. It may return to the dump repeatedly and eat the tainted food repeatedly and become sick repeatedly. The very selectivity which allows the rat to learn rapidly and effectively about something vitally important under ordinary circumstances (the relation between taste and illness) will, under these unusual circumstances, prevent the rat from learning. If the association of taste and illness were an arbitrary one, like the association of tone and shock, the rat might learn much more slowly to avoid dangerous foods under most circumstances than it ordinarily does. However, it would learn just about as well to avoid foods on the basis of their color as on the basis of their taste. Thus, the phenomenon of taste aversion does reveal a constraint on learning. It may be that anytime one finds a specialized ability in an organism to learn a particular thing, one will find in the same organism a specialized *inability* to learn other, similar things.

Consider a second example rather far removed from taste aversion. A number of theorists, led by Noam Chomsky, have suggested that people are constructed so that they develop the ability to speak and understand natural language in accordance with extremely complex grammatical rules with extraordinary speed.[3] If this is the case, then the specialization which makes it easy to learn a natural language may make it difficult to learn an artificial language, like a computer language, whose rules are significantly different from those of a natural language. The label "constraints on learning" suggests an emphasis not on the remarkable ability of young children to speak after minimal and nonoptimal exposure to the language, but on the kinds

3. See, for example, Chomsky, 1975.

of learning that the mechanism underlying this ability rules out. The word "constraint" also points us to what may be the most significant difference between built-in associative bias and bias which is based upon past learning experience. What is the product of past experience can presumably, within limits, be undone by future experience. We can eliminate the pigeon's bias for green over triangles by extinguishing key pecks to green. We can eliminate the rat's bias for light over tone by presenting tone alone and following it with shock. We may not be able to eliminate the rat's bias for tastes over colors as signals for stomach illness.

Why has behavior theory systematically avoided the study of built-in associative bias over the years? Recall the philosophical tradition from which behavior theory grew (Chapter 2). The focus of the British Empiricists was on the *flexibility* of the human mind. All knowledge came from experience, and people began life without predispositions or biases which made the assimilation of some experiences more likely than the assimilation of other experiences. In short, a complete understanding of what human adults knew and did would come from an analysis of the experiences they had had.

Behavior theory has taken as its task an analysis of the flexibility of organisms. There are important respects in which all dogs are alike, and all people are alike; and dogs are different from people not as a result of experience, but as a result of built-in, biological characteristics of different species which set limits on the effects experience can produce. But behavior theory has not been interested in these limits on the effects of experience. It has been interested in understanding what, within these limits, makes one dog different from another, or one person different from another. It has taken as its task the explanation of the enormous variety of human knowledge, actions, and goals. Such variety, it is assumed, must result from the diversity of individual experience.

It is hardly a startling claim that there are biological limits on what an organism perceives and what it does. The external environment appears to your pet dog fundamentally different than it does to you. Similarly, you and your dog are capable of quite different movement patterns. The structure of your muscles, joints, and motor nervous system simply permits you to do things which dogs cannot, and conversely. But behavior theory has focused its attention elsewhere. One can see this in the definitions and methods which have guided behavior theory. By defining the stimulus in terms of its ability to control behavior and by choosing stimuli which are clearly within the organism's perceptual capacity, one forecloses the possibility of an analysis of the biological limits on perception and focuses instead on an analysis of how experience with a stimulus determines its effect on behavior.[4] Similarly, by defining the response class in terms of its effect on the environment, and by choosing a response class on the basis of ease of execution and measurement, one forecloses an analysis of the biological constraints on action. Finally, by insisting upon an arbitrary combination of stimulus, operant, and reinforcer, one forecloses the possibility of analysis of biological constraints on learning.[5]

For the behavior theorist, it is not the built-in constraints on perception and action which tell us much about what organisms do. Of course, the structure of the human nervous system and musculature imposes limits on human action. However, the biological limits of human action are broad. Individual muscle movements can be organized into larger units of activity, or operants, in many different ways.

4. Though this general characterization is accurate, there are some notable exceptions. See, for example, Blough and Blough, 1977; Wright and Cumming, 1971.

5. There is an interesting parallel between the approach of behavior theory to its subject and its attitude toward theory as a part of science. Just as a constraint on learning will make some things easy to learn and some things nearly impossible, a powerful theory will make some facts easy to find and some facts almost undiscoverable. In an important sense, a theory is a kind of collective constraint on learning. It tells the investigators what to look for in nature and it tells them how to interpret and evaluate phenomena once they are observed. A theory imposes order on the mass of events occurring in any experiment, and allows one to separate the important events from the trivial ones. Indeed, a theory often tells the investigator what an event is. As T. S. Kuhn, 1962, has noted, when an area of inquiry undergoes a revolutionary conceptual change, the newly resulting theory does not simply account for the old facts. The facts themselves change. Significantly (and this is the sense in which theories represent constraints on learning), the new theory may point to the importance of events which were there to be observed in all the old experiments, but which were ignored or treated as trivial because the old theory dictated that view.

Many students of behavior theory have been critical of theoretically oriented approaches to the study of behavior precisely because a powerful theory introduces a bias which prevents one from noting important events (see, for example, Sidman, 1960, and Skinner, 1950). According to this view, instead of allowing theory to dictate one's observations, one should allow past experience to be the guide. One should look for certain things in Experiment 2 because one observed those things in Experiment 1. One *induces* principles of behavior (if event *x* occurred in the last three experiments, it should occur in the next one) from observation, rather than *deducing* them from theory. The inevitable bias in observation should come from past observation, not from theoretical structure. Similarly, from the point of view of behavior theory, the associative bias we are discussing in this chapter comes to organisms not from built-in constraints but from past experience. It is significant that Skinner's views about how organisms come to know and do things are meant by him to apply to the behavior of the scientist, Skinner, just as they apply to the behavior of the pigeon. Some who are critical of this inductive approach to science, in contrast to a theory-based, deductive approach, liken the atheoretical scientist to a person who jumps off the roof of a 30-story building. As the person passes each floor on the way down, he observes, "So far, so good." To critics of Skinner's views of science, this metaphor captures the limits of the inductive approach.

For the behavior theorist, what determines which units of behavior will be formed is their function—their effect on the environment. Units of activity are the result not of biological constraints on movement, but of experience with the consequences of movement.

In the next part of the chapter, we will examine the tradition of behavior theory for some implicit ideas about how behavioral units are organized by experience. We will then turn to a different tradition—the ethological one. Ethology has been concerned from its inception with the biological constraints on perception, action, and learning, with constraints on units of activity which are built into the members of a species. The discussion of ethological concepts will be oriented to highlight the contrast between ethological views and the views which characterize behavior theory. Next, we will discuss notions of constraint which characterize some students of human language, again with the aim of highlighting the contrast between those notions and the views of behavior theory. It will turn out that ethology and modern linguistics have much in common when viewed from the perspective of behavior theory. Finally, we will look for some resolution of the differences between the views that the organization of behavior is the product of experience and that the organization of behavior is a part of the built-in biological character of organisms by looking at the issue from a developmental and a phylogenetic perspective.

THE CREATION OF BEHAVIORAL UNITS

Consider a rat which is about to undergo its first experience in an experiment. While in its cage, the rat has engaged in a variety of different activities: it has eaten, licked from a water spout, groomed, sniffed about the cage, poked its nose through the openings in the cage, reared on its hind legs, and so on. It has never done anything like lever pressing. Then, the rat is placed in the experimental chamber. After an initial fear reaction to being handled, and to being in a novel environment, the rat begins to do the same kinds of things it does in its cage: it sniffs, rears, explores, and grooms. The feeder operates and the rat approaches it hesitantly, picks up the food pellet, and chews it. The feeder operates a few more times until the rat shows no hesitancy in approaching it and ingesting the food. Now the rat spends most of its time around the feeder—sniffing at it, poking its nose at it, rearing on its hind legs, and so on.

The experimenter now introduces a contingency. To operate the feeder, the rat must press the lever which is located a few inches away from the feeder. The rat eventually leaves the area of the feeder and continues exploring—sniffing, rearing, and poking its nose. At last it rears right near the lever, and when it comes down its front paws brush against the lever and depress it. The feeder operates and the rat scurries over to get the food pellet. It returns to the area around the lever and sniffs around. This time, while sniffing at the lever, the rat's nose inadvertently depresses it. Again the feeder operates. Now the rat returns to the lever and begins exploring it with its paws. Again the lever is depressed and again the feeder operates. At this point, the rat's behavior is extremely inefficient. Most of its activity around the lever—its pawing and sniffing and rearing—does not depress the lever and close the switch. However, occasionally the switch is closed and the feeder operates. The rat comes to spend all of its time around the lever. It has clearly learned something. But what has it learned?

Careful observation would reveal that the rat has not learned to do anything new and different. It has learned to do the same things it has been doing for months in its cage, but to do them in a particular place. With continued experience, the rat's behavior changes. It learns that rearing is unnecessary to produce food; only landing on the lever is necessary. It learns that sniffing at the corners of the lever is unnecessary to produce food; only depressing the lever with the nose is necessary. The rat seems to identify the single feature which each of its different activities with respect to the lever share, and that is the downward deflection of the lever. Once this information is acquired, the efficiency of the rat's behavior increases dramatically. The rat may end up lying down with its mouth poised at the feeder, reaching one paw over to the lever to depress it smoothly and economically.

One could tell a similar story about pigeons learning to peck keys. Adult pigeons do not have to learn to peck. What they have to learn is to peck at a particular place. Early in training, the pigeon's behavior is erratic; it bobs up and down, stretches its neck, pecks around the lit key, and so on. Later in training, the pigeon has eliminated virtually all of the unnecessary behavior and it stands by the key, striking it efficiently and accurately, again and again.

What these examples are intended to suggest is that an operant contingency creates a new unit of behavior. Before training, lever pressing and key pecking do not exist as integral units of activity in the animal's repertoire. If we drew up an exhaustive list of the rat's activities in the experimental chamber after the first few reinforcements, it might include eating, grooming, sniffing, rearing, and pawing. Most of these activities would be directed at the lever. By the end of training, a new category of activity—lever pressing—has been created and added to the others. The rat continues to rear, sniff, groom, and paw as before. However, when it is around the lever, it lever presses.

The Form of the Behavioral Unit

What determines the form which this new unit of activity takes? It is precisely the contingency of reinforcement. Recall that the operant is defined on the basis of those characteristics necessary to produce reinforcement. The lever press is defined not by the way the rat moves the lever, but by the way the lever must be moved in order to close the switch. The rule relating lever movement to feeder operation is what defines the response class. Thus, if the contingency required not merely switch closure but switch closure which lasted for 5 seconds, the rat would develop a different behavioral unit. Instead of making brief, discrete lever presses, the rat would hold the lever down. The particular muscle movements in this lever-holding situation might look very different from the movements which occurred in lever-pressing situations. Alternatively, the rat might be required to exert a substantial force on the lever, so that reinforcement depended upon lever presses of at least 100 grams of force (customarily, 10 or 15 grams of force are required). Again, the resulting behavioral unit would look very different from what one would observe with a more straightforward lever-pressing requirement. The rat might have to throw its whole body into each response.

The claim is that an operant contingency results in the development of new behavioral units. What is meant by "new" and by "unit"? Clearly, the muscle movements of the rat are not new. Each of them has occurred countless times before as part of one activity or another. Thus what is new is the sequence of old and familiar muscle movements. What is new is the organization of those old movements. It is much like the practiced pianist learning a new piece. The particular movements involved in playing the piano are old and familiar. Yet, when the pianist learns a new piece, he or she is learning something new. It is a new combination of old and well-practiced movements. Once the piece is well learned, the pianist will play it not as a sequence of individual movements but as a single, well-integrated act. This is what is meant by a "unit." Once the sequence of movements, be it a lever press or a sonata, is well established, it is a permanent part of the behavioral repertoire. The rat will stop pressing the lever if lever presses stop producing food. However, if a few months later the rat is returned to the experimental chamber, it will press the lever—not as a by-product of rearing or sniffing, but in its smooth and efficient form.

If the lever press produces food, the rat will continue pressing. If the lever press does not produce food, the rat will stop. In either case, the rat will provide clear evidence that its behavioral repertoire has been permanently altered, for, along with eating, drinking, grooming, sniffing, and so on, there now exists a behavioral category of lever pressing. Operations which suppress the response, like extinction or punishment, may work to keep the lever press from occurring. They will not, however, break it apart as a behavioral unit. It is in this sense that an operant contingency creates new and permanent units.

It is not startling to come to the insight that practice develops skill.[6] However, the development of behavioral units by operant shaping implies something more. If you keep doing the same thing again and again, you will learn to do it better and faster. But what determines what this "thing" will be? The important inference to be drawn from operant shaping is that these "things" or behavioral units are organized precisely on the basis of that property or those properties on which reinforcement depends. Thus, just as one can create the lever press unit in any of a large number of different ways by specifying what must occur to produce food, perhaps one can create the piano-playing unit or the golf-club swinging unit in any of a large number of ways by similarly specifying what must occur to produce reinforcement. The strategy of functional definition of response classes, adopted largely as a convenience, may be telling us something important about the development and organization of behavioral units. Hidden in this definitional strategy may be the germ of a theory of how experience determines behavioral units.

Consider as an example of how operant contingencies may shape units of behavior a case in which the rule relating reinforcement to responses specifies in detail the form of the response. Rats were required to press a lever for water. The degree of displacement of the lever on each press was measured, and counted in one of eight categories. Initially, any displacement at all produced reinforcement. After two sessions, lever displacements which fell in the first category were not reinforced; all other displacements were. After two more sessions, only displacements in categories 2–7 were reinforced. Then, only displacements in categories 3–7, then 3–6, then 4–6, then 4–5, and finally, only displacements in category 5 were reinforced. Figure 12–1 presents distributions of responses across the eight displacement categories throughout this sequence of procedures, for one rat. The striped bars represent categories which were reinforced. It is clear

6. For discussions of skill development, see Bilodeau, 1966, and Schmidt, 1975a and 1975b.

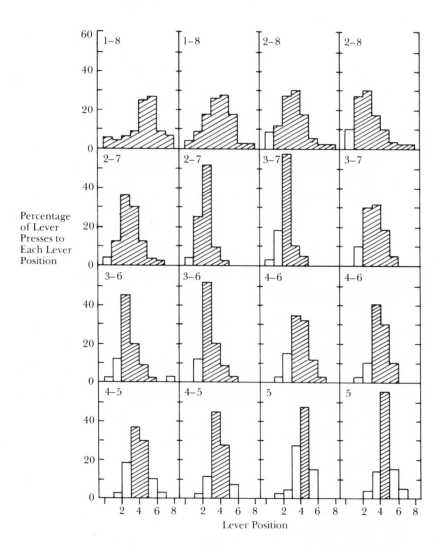

Figure 12–1. Shaping the Form of the Lever Press. *These graphs present data for a rat exposed to a series of procedures in which lever presses produced water reinforcement. The amount of lever displacement fell into one of eight categories. Initially, displacements in any category produced water (panels labeled 1–8 in the figure). Ultimately, only displacements in category 5 were reinforced. In between, the range of acceptable categories was gradually narrowed. The graphs present the percentage of total lever presses which fell in each category over each procedure. The striped bars represent responses which were reinforced, that is, fell within the required categories. (From Herrick, 1964.)*

from Figure 12–1 that as the required response was redefined, becoming progressively more stringent from day to day, the rat quickly learned to make responses of the appropriate form. What began as an operant class "lever press" ended as an operant class "lever press of a particular displacement." As the operant definition changed, the response form changed to match it. Research which has required responses of a particular force, or of a particular duration, has found a similar matching of response form to the reinforcement contingency.[7]

What happens to the form of the response when the animal is not required by the reinforcement contingency to modify it? One study which recorded the force of each lever press early in training found that force differed enormously from press to press prior to any reinforcement and also for the first 10–20 reinforced presses. However, before the first session was over, a stereotyped and efficient response force developed. The rats pressed the lever with about the same force each time, and it was typically the minimum amount necessary for reinforcement. When, after four conditioning sessions, reinforcement was discontinued, the variability of response force from press to press increased, though many of the lever presses were of the same force as those which had come to dominate during sessions which included reinforcement.[8] This finding, that extinction increases response variability, has been confirmed in a number of different experimental contexts.[9] Thus, reinforcement produces stereotypy, with the precise form of the response largely determined by the rule for production of reinforcement, and extinction reduces some of the stereotypy.

Adaptability and Response Selection

If one reflects on these phenomena, they make very good adaptive sense. One would want an organism to continue to perform, in as rigid a manner as possible, those responses which produce rewards. However, when rewards stop coming, before the animal stops the response altogether it is sensible to first perform variations on the theme. Suppose an animal was accustomed to going to a particular spot along a riverbank to catch its food (say, insects) every day. One day, when it made its trip to its familiar place, it found no food. It went back the next day and again found no food. If extinction eliminated responses, after a few more days the animal might abandon the

7. Notterman and Mintz, 1965; Schwartz and Williams, 1972.
8. Notterman, 1959.
9. Antonitis, 1951; Guthrie and Horton, 1946; Warden and Lubow, 1942.

riverbank altogether. If, however, extinction increased variability before it eliminated the response, the animal might wander up and down the bank a little way and might discover a new, rich feeding place just a short distance from the old one.

These phenomena suggest an understanding of the reinforcement process which fits nicely with the theoretical framework proposed by Staddon and Simmelhag (see Chapter 6). In brief, they proposed that behavior must be understood in terms of processes of variation (processes which generate a wide variety of response forms) and processes of selection (processes which select from the broad set of response forms the ones which are effective). The law of effect, or the principle of reinforcement, was for Staddon and Simmelhag the principal selector of responses. The data on development of stereotyped responses support that view. What the data also suggest is that one of the principles of variation should be extinction. The discontinuation of reinforcement serves, at least temporarily, to increase the range of response forms from which subsequent reinforcement will select.

The evidence for operant shaping of stereotyped behavioral units is impressive. However, the features of behavior which have been studied are somewhat disappointing. Lever presses and key pecks are, after all, simple responses. That one can make the response occur in one way rather than another by changing the reinforcement rule does suggest that an operant contingency can determine the character of simple behavioral units. But what do such simple units have to do with complex human activities like playing a piano? Is one to assume that the principles of organization of complex human acts can be induced from the principles of organization of a lever press or a key peck? One could not be faulted for withholding judgment on the relation between the key peck as a behavioral unit and piano playing as a behavioral unit. Since the development of behavioral units has not been the primary focus of the analysis of behavior, there has not been much research on the formation of operants more complicated than lever presses and key pecks.

One such investigation has recently been reported. In that study, pigeons were confronted with a 4 × 4 matrix of lights, located between two response keys. Each trial began with the response keys lit, and with the upper left light in the matrix lit, as in Figure 12–2*A*. A peck on one of the side keys moved the light down one position in the matrix. A peck on the other key moved the light across one position in the matrix. When the light reached the bottom right corner of the matrix, as in Figure 12–2*D*, the feeder operated.

What did this situation require? All that the pigeon had to do was peck each key three times. The pecks could occur in any order. If the pigeon pecked either key a fourth time, the trial ended without rein-

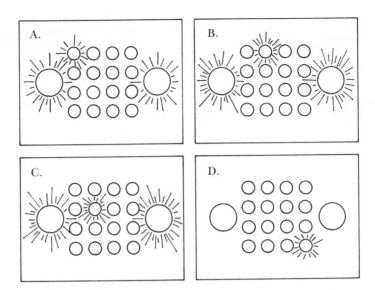

Figure 12–2. Schematic Drawing of Apparatus for a Response-Sequencing Experiment. *In* A, *a trial begins with keys lit and upper left light of the matrix lit. In* B, *a peck on one of the side keys has moved the light one position to the right in the matrix. In* C, *a peck on the other side key has moved the light one position down. Finally, in* D, *three pecks on each key have moved the light to the bottom right and ended the trial with food.*

forcement. In all, there were 20 different possible sequences of left and right key pecks which would have produced food. Thus, we have a situation which requires a moderately complex operant (three pecks on each of two keys) but which permits flexibility in the form (sequence of pecks) which the operant can take. A situation of this sort seems well suited to the study of the development of behavioral units.

When pigeons were exposed to the procedure, they started out engaging in a wide variety of different sequences. However what began as a variable collection of individual responses ended as an efficient and stereotyped behavioral unit. The pigeons engaged in the same sequence in nearly every trial. Moreover, the unit which emerged—three pecks on one key followed by three pecks on the second key—was one which satisfied the reinforcement contingency with minimal effort.[10] This shaping in the direction of minimal effort is also observed when other properties of responses, like force, are re-

10. Vogel and Annau, 1973.

corded. Such findings suggest a general hypothesis about the formation of behavioral units by experience: a contingency of reinforcement will establish units of behavior which satisfy the contingency requirements with minimal effort and maximal efficiency. One could imagine such unit formation occurring in stages. First, a class of responses which satisfies the reinforcement rule develops. Second, the members of that class are refined so that unnecessary effort is eliminated. The elimination of extra effort produces both greater efficiency and greater stereotypy of the members of the response class.

In this section, we suggested that behavioral units are defined by the operant contingency, and training produces a class of responses which satisfy the criterion for reinforcement with minimal effort expenditure and maximal efficiency. We also suggested that the principles which underlie the formation of simple behavioral units may be relevant to the formation of more complex units. This account suggests a picture of an organism of almost limitless adaptability. Only the imagination of the experimenter limits the range of possible behavioral units. But we know that such a picture is inaccurate because there are constraints on what an organism can do or learn which come with the organism and do not depend upon experience. It was just the existence of such constraints which led us to a discussion of behavioral units in the first place. It is, therefore, appropriate to turn now to a discussion of some of the central principles of ethology, the branch of behavioral science which has focused on a detailed analysis of the built-in constraints on action and learning which characterize different species.

CONSTRAINED LEARNING: AN EXAMPLE

Imagine yourself resting by a lake on a quiet, warm day. You notice a wasp (*Ammophila campestris*) carrying a dead caterpillar. The wasp carries the caterpillar a bit further and then drops it near a small mound of dirt. The wasp then goes to the mound, scratches away the dirt, and disappears into a hole. Soon after, its head pops up, it grasps the caterpillar and pulls it into the hole. Then it climbs out of the hole, rebuilds the dirt mound, and leaves.

As it turns out, what you saw is only a small part of an amazing collection of caretaking activities which occupy the wasp (called the digger wasp) throughout the reproductive season.[11] The beginning of summer brings the wasp into a reproductive "mood." This mood gen-

11. Baerends, 1941 (discussed in English by Eibl-Eibesfeldt, 1970).

erates a set of complex activities, including selection of nest sites, building nests, hunting for caterpillars, laying eggs, feeding larvae, and repeatedly opening, inspecting, and closing the nests. Each of these individual activities is in turn composed of a set of rather specific movements, and is triggered by rather specific stimuli. Thus, the wasp begins its reproductive sequence by searching for a suitable nest location. Then it scratches and bites in order to build the nest. When this is done, it meticulously carries away the loose dirt which was displaced during nest building. This done, the nest is closed off with a clump of dirt and the search for a caterpillar begins. The nest-building "mood" is replaced by a hunting "mood."

When the caterpillar is caught and killed, retrieval supplants hunting and the caterpillar is brought back to the nest. The nest is opened; the wasp climbs in and turns around, grasps the caterpillar, and pulls it in. Now, retrieval is replaced by egg laying; the wasp lays an egg, climbs out of the nest, and covers it up. But this is just the beginning. The wasp will repeatedly visit the nest with more caterpillars—small ones at first and larger ones as the larva grows—opening the nest, inspecting it, depositing the food, and closing it on each visit. Finally, when the larva pupates, the digger wasp closes the nest for the last time and pays it no more attention. More amazing still is the fact that the wasp supervises a large number of nests at the same time. Every morning, each nest is inspected. The rest of the day is spent satisfying the requirements of each nest. There are small caterpillars to be placed in nests containing small larvae, or nests containing a supply of unconsumed caterpillars, and there are large caterpillars to be placed in nests with large larvae or with no surplus of caterpillars. The digger wasp is able to keep track of the location of all nests and of their individual needs.

How does the wasp learn such a complex set of activities? How is it able to remember late in the day what it saw in each of the nests early in the morning? It would seem that an organism capable of all this would have to be remarkably intelligent, and able to master any of the simple tasks we have discussed throughout this book. In fact, quite the contrary is true. Though the wasp's care of its young is intelligent, the wasp is not. It would find even the simplest operant conditioning task a problem.

Suppose that after watching the wasp drag the caterpillar to the nest and then enter it, you pulled the caterpillar a distance away. The wasp would emerge from the nest to pull in the caterpillar, not find it, and leave the nest to search for it. When it found the caterpillar, it would drag it to the nest again and reenter the nest to inspect it. If you pulled the caterpillar away again, the wasp would again retrieve it, replace it, and enter and inspect the nest. You might have to pull the caterpillar away 30 or 40 times before the wasp finally learned to retrieve it and bring it directly into the nest without first dropping it alongside the nest and entering and inspecting it. This behavior hardly seems intelligent.

Or suppose you tampered with the contents of a nest, either by adding caterpillars to those already present or by removing all the caterpillars. If you did this before the wasp's morning inspection, the wasp would modify its behavior accordingly. If it discovered an empty nest it would bring more caterpillars than usual, and if it discovered a very full nest it would bring fewer caterpillars. However, if you raided or stuffed the nest *after* the morning visit, the changed nest conditions would have no effect on the wasp's behavior. If the wasp's morning inspection of a particular nest revealed no surplus caterpillars, it would return to the nest repeatedly during the day to supply food. If, on its first return, it encountered the same nest, filled (by you) with caterpillars, it would not adjust its plan. It would spend the day filling that nest with caterpillars as if it were still empty.

Thus, the caring for offspring displayed by the digger wasp is a contradiction. On the one hand, it is extremely complex, efficient, and sensitive to changes in what is required from day to day or from nest to nest. On the other hand, it is resistant to adaptive modification in the face of the simplest challenges of an unusual sort. In this respect, it is a perfect example of constrained learning. Most of what the wasp does is not learned. The movements involved in searching for a nest site and building a nest, in hunting for and killing caterpillars, in opening, inspecting, and closing nests do not require specific experience. In addition, the order in which these different acts occur does not need to be learned. The successful completion of one act automatically sets the stage for the next. Yet some parts of the sequence do depend upon experience; the wasp determines how each nest is to be serviced by inspection, and its behavior subsequent to the inspection is clearly influenced by the results of the inspection. Once that inspection is complete, however, the wasp's course is determined. Later, contradictory evidence about the state of a particular nest cannot alter the wasp's course of action. We are left with a sense that the caretaking behavior of the wasp is certainly not an arbitrary operant, or a set of arbitrary operants. Neither is it an inflexible reflex, like a knee jerk or an eyeblink. What then is it?

THE ETHOLOGICAL APPROACH TO BEHAVIOR

The business of ethology has been the analysis of behavior sequences, much like the behavior of the wasp, in different species and in different situations. By careful observation of the behavior of the members of these different species, ethologists have uncovered many behavior patterns as complex, efficient, and dramatically intelligent as that of the wasp. They have also developed a set of concepts with which to describe these behavior patterns.[12]

A view which rests historically at the heart of ethology is that just as anatomical structures are built into an organism—genetically programmed—so are behavioral structures, or, more accurately, so are the physiological underpinnings of behavioral structures. To understand these structures, one must first be able to identify them. This requires careful observation of the behavior of an organism in the natural environment and detailed description of that behavior. Once the behavior has been described, one can begin to trace its evolutionary history, determine its significance for the survival of the species, and isolate the factors which control it. Controlling factors include, first, conditions internal to the organism which are necessary antecedents of a particular pattern and, second, environmental stimuli or events which are necessary to produce the different components of that behavior pattern. In the case of the digger wasp, aspects of the terrain determine the suitability of a particular place for nesting and the presence of such a suitable place produces nest building. The completed nest, in turn, produces hunting. The dead prey produces return to the nest which, in turn, produces digging, entering, and so on. The state of the nest during morning inspection produces the appropriate hunting behavior. However, none of these different activities will occur if the wasp is not in a state of caretaking readiness. The elaborate set of caretaking activities of the wasp is conditional upon internal changes in the organism brought on by the onset of the mating season. Without these internal changes, none of the crucial environmental stimuli will have significance. Attractive nest sites and caterpillars only produce the appropriate behavior when the wasp is in a caretaking "mood."

Since early ethologists had the view that the capacity for most patterns of behavior is laid down in the genetic constitution of members of a species, it is not surprising that a cornerstone of ethology has been a focus on the adaptiveness of behavior. Evolution, through

12. See Eibl-Eibesfeldt, 1970; Hinde, 1970; Tinbergen, 1951; von Frisch, 1967. The brief discussion of ethology which follows is a description of "classical" ethology as articulated by its major early figures, Konrad Lorenz and Niko Tinbergen. The contrasts between behavior theory and classical ethology are clear and dramatic, the former focusing on the flexibility of behavior and on the role of experience in shaping it, and the latter focusing on the rigidity of behavior and on its genetic determinants. Modern ethologists hold much less extreme views. They acknowledge and study flexible experientially based behavior, just as behavior theorists are coming to acknowledge and study inflexible, genetically based behavior.

natural selection, selects behavior patterns in the same way it selects features of the anatomy. Species members whose behavior is particularly well suited to environmental conditions will have the most offspring, and pass on the capacity for the adaptive behavior pattern. Over many generations, the adaptive behavior pattern will become characteristic of all members of a species. In general, the behavior one observes to be characteristic of the members of a given species will be the product of fine tuning, over thousands of years, of that species to the environmental conditions in which it evolved.

How are these genetically programmed, well-adapted behavior patterns to be understood? The ethological analysis of behavior classically centered on two concepts: the fixed-action pattern (FAP) and the sign stimulus. The FAP *is* the behavior: one characterizes it by means of careful and detailed observation. The sign stimulus is that aspect of the environment which produces the FAP: one identifies it both by careful observation and by experiment. Finally, since the effectiveness of the sign stimulus is conditional upon the internal state of the organism, ethologists have also attempted to characterize these different internal states and the variables which determine them.

The Fixed-Action Pattern (FAP)

The fixed-action pattern is a complex sequence of movements which is extremely stereotyped. However, not all stereotyped movement sequences are fixed-action patterns. Acts like shoe tying or car starting or the sequencing of pecks to move a light around in a matrix are stereotyped and complex. They are not fixed-action patterns because their formation depends upon experience; fixed-action patterns do not. They are also not fixed-action patterns because their continued occurrence depends upon their consequences. If the pigeon which pecks left three times and then right three times is only paid off for sequences beginning on the right, its behavior will change. In contrast, a fixed-action pattern depends only on the presence of a triggering antecedent stimulus; the consequences of the FAP are irrelevant to its occurrence. Thus, for example, a dog hiding a bone in the house will make movements to cover the bone with dirt, movements which are triggered by the presence of the bone, though no dirt is available.

A most impressive example of the fixedness of the FAP comes from research on the spider *Cuprennius salei*.[13] The spider constructs a cocoon in which it deposits eggs. It begins by spinning the bottom, and

13. This research, done by M. Melchers, is reported by Eibl-Eibesfeldt, 1970.

then spins the sides. The eggs are deposited and the cocoon is then closed. If the spider is disrupted after spinning the bottom and the bottom is destroyed, it will continue spinning as if the bottom were still present and eventually lay eggs which fall through the cocoon to the ground. The spider will then close the top of the cocoon. If the glands which provide the material for cocoon construction are dried up, the spider will nevertheless go through the motions of spinning and at the appropriate point lay its eggs, even though no structure has been built. Finally, if the spider is placed on a half-finished cocoon, it will go through the identical spinning sequence, as if nothing were there. The resulting cocoon is often unsuitable for receiving the eggs. In each of these cases, the spider goes through virtually the same number of spinning movements—about 6,400—although the resulting structure is either useless or nonexistent. It is this insensitivity to consequences which perhaps best distinguishes an FAP from well-practiced stereotypies like shoe tying.

Even when some components of the FAP are modifiable or sensitive to consequences, the general character of the activity is not. A famous example is the egg retrieval of the greylag goose.[14] If an egg is displaced from the nest, the goose will extend its bill beyond the egg and pull it in, tucked carefully in the underside of the bill. This retrieval has two components: one is a direct movement out of, and back into, the nest, and the other is a side-to-side balancing movement performed while the egg is tucked under the bill. If one removes the egg from the bill in the middle of a retrieval sequence, the side-to-side balancing movements will cease. They seem to depend upon the presence of the egg. However, the rest of the action pattern—the pulling back into the nest—will occur just as if the egg were present.

It seems as though the FAP is just a chain of simplex reflexes: the execution of reflex 1 is the trigger for reflex 2 whose execution is the trigger for reflex 3, and so on. The fixedness and the insensitivity to consequences of the FAP certainly reminds one of reflexes. The FAP and the reflex seem to differ only in complexity. However, ethologists explicitly reject this view. Instead of conceiving the organization of an FAP as a chain of reflexes as depicted, hypothetically, in Figure 12–3*A*, ethologists view the organization of the FAP as central. Somewhere in the nervous system there exists a plan for the entire sequence. Once this plan is activated, it runs through, and it does not depend upon feedback from completion of one movement for the beginning of the next movement. A diagram like that in Figure 12–3*B* might conform to the ethological view of FAP organization.

14. Lorenz and Tinbergen, 1957.

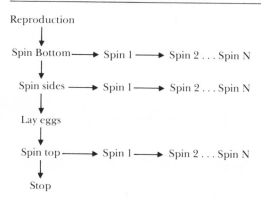

Stim 1 ⟶ Spin 1 ⟶ Feedback (Stim 2) ⟶ Spin 2 ⟶

Feedback (Stim 3) ⟶ Spin 3 ⟶ Feedback (Stim 4) ⟶ Spin N–1 ⟶

Feedback (Stim N) ⟶ Spin N ⟶ Feedback (Stim N+1) ⟶

Lay Eggs ⟶ Feedback ⟶ Spin top of cocoon ⟶ Feedback ⟶

Stop

A. The Cocoon Spinning of the Spider as a Reflex Chain

Reproduction
↓
Spin Bottom ⟶ Spin 1 ⟶ Spin 2 ... Spin N
↓
Spin sides ⟶ Spin 1 ⟶ Spin 2 ... Spin N
↓
Lay eggs
↓
Spin top ⟶ Spin 1 ⟶ Spin 2 ... Spin N
↓
Stop

B. The Cocoon Spinning of the Spider as a Centrally Organized Activity

Figure 12–3. Two Models of the Organization of Fixed-Action Patterns. *A depicts an organizational scheme in which the completion of one movement provides the stimulus for the next one. This scheme would typify a behavior theory account of the spider's behavior. B depicts an organizational scheme in which the full sequence is triggered, as a motor plan, from the beginning. This scheme is characteristic of the ethological orientation.*

Attempts to evaluate the two views experimentally have provided clear support for the ethological view. What should happen if an FAP is interrupted for a while in midstream? On the reflex-chain view, when the animal is allowed to continue the sequence, the necessary stimulus (feedback from an earlier movement) will be gone. On the ethological view, the animal should pick up where it left off. We saw in the case of the spider that interrupting cocoon building does not destroy the sequence of movements, or even alter it appreciably. It is as though those 6,400 movements are represented as a single unit in the spider which will run off inevitably once begun.

Similar results occur if a movement sequence is permanently interrupted structurally. For example, the eel moves by means of an undulating wave which starts at its head end and progresses backward. Viewed as a reflex chain, this movement pattern would be explained in terms of one muscle contraction which provides feedback which triggers the next muscle contraction in the next segment of the eel's body which in turn provides feedback which triggers contraction in the next segment and so on. One can surgically eliminate all of the nerve fibers providing sensory information about muscle contraction without disturbing the eel's movement pattern. If one then mechanically restrains movement of the middle third of the eel's body, one observes the movement of the front third followed by movement of the posterior third at exactly the time such movement would have begun if the middle third had been unrestrained. Thus, the movement rhythm of the eel does not depend upon either neural or mechanical chains of individual muscle responses.[15]

Thus, the fixed-action pattern is conceived by ethologists as a centrally organized, built-in, stereotyped sequence of activities which is controlled not by its consequences, but by antecedent triggering or sign stimuli. Modern ethologists view fixed-action patterns as comprising a much smaller portion of the animal's behavioral repertoire than classical ethologists did. That is, modern ethologists recognize much more flexibility in the behavior of animals than did their predecessors. However, modern views on the determinants and organization of fixed-action patterns, where they exist, are not radically different from earlier views.

The Sign Stimulus

The occurrence of fixed-action patterns depends upon the presence in the environment of specific triggering or *sign* stimuli, whose power to produce the fixed-action pattern does not depend, in any obvious way, on the animal's experience. As an example, consider the prey-catching behavior of the frog *Xenepis laevis*. Small, moving visual stimuli and local vibrations in the water produce turning toward the stimulus, moving toward it, and snapping. If the frog spots a small moving insect, it will pursue it and snap at it. If the insect stops moving, the frog will continue to stare at the spot where the insect last moved, but will not approach it or snap at it. After a while, if the insect remains motionless, the frog will ignore it. If one takes frogs before metamorphosis, as tadpoles which have never snapped at prey, and isolates them, after metamorphosis they will snap at a moving

15. E. von Holst, discussed in Eibl-Eibesfeldt, 1970. See also Bullock and Horridge, 1965, or Roeder, 1963.

spot of light. Also, a gentle touch of the legs will produce turning toward the stimulus followed by snapping.[16]

Careful observation will usually allow one to get a rough idea about what the sign stimulus is for a particular behavior. If one observes the behavior of a male stickleback fish which is maintaining and defending a territory during mating, one will notice that when another male approaches, the first one engages in a series of threatening and aggressive activities. From such an observation, one could infer that the stimulus "intruding male" produces aggression. It turns out, however, that only a small part of the intruding male is necessary for the production of aggression. The male must have a red belly. If one presents a model to a stickleback which is in all respects like an intruding male except that it does not have a red belly, no aggression will occur. If, on the other hand, one presents a model which bears no resemblance to the fish but is red on the bottom, aggression will occur. If the model is turned upside down, so that the red is on top, again there will be no aggression.[17] Thus, while observation will provide an approximate specification of the sign stimulus, experimentation is necessary for its precise identification.

This fact should not surprise us. To begin to attempt a really precise account of what the animal is doing, one needs to know what the world looks like to the animal. One needs to map out the animal's perceptual world, or *Umwelt.*

The *Umwelt*

One of the early ethologists, Jakob von Uexküll, provided an elegant and entertaining description of the *Umwelt* concept many years ago.[18] Uexküll distinguished between the objective, physical world in which all organisms lived and the personal, perceptual world, *Umwelt,* which characterized each species. If a species does not possess color receptors, then color is not a part of the perceptual world (*Umwelt*) of that species. To map out the *Umwelt* of a species requires detailed and imaginative experimentation.

Consider a forest. For people, it is an environment full of sensory stimulation. There are multiple odors, colors, shapes, and sounds: an almost endless variety of sense experience. One of the creatures of the forest is the tick. The female tick, after mating, climbs onto a twig or branch and waits. She waits for a mammal to pass by. When one

16. Eibl-Eibesfeldt, 1970.
17. Tinbergen, 1951.
18. von Uexküll, 1957 (originally published in 1938).

Discovering an animal's Umwelt. *The herring gull broods its eggs. When one investigates what cues the gull uses to identify the eggs of its species, one finds that size is critical—the bigger the eggs, the better. Here, a gull attempts to brood an enormous model egg in preference to a real one.* (Photo by Thomas McAvoy—Time-Life Inc.)

comes, she drops off the twig and onto the mammal. She then burrows down to a hairless spot on the mammal, penetrates its skin, and pumps herself full of blood. Having done this, she falls to the ground, lays her eggs, and dies.

How does the tick manage this feat in the midst of a teeming forest? It seems a remarkable achievement to be able to pick out a scurrying mammal in the midst of other animals, sights, sounds, and smells of the forest. In fact, for the tick it is quite simple. The world of the tick does not contain all these sights, sounds, and smells. The *Umwelt* of the tick is so bare that a mammal could scarcely go undetected. The tick is sensitive to butyric acid, which is secreted by the skin glands of mammals, and to heat, and to virtually nothing else. Thus, when a mammal passes by, the tick does not have to pick the scent out of a myriad of other scents. The others do not exist for the tick; butyric acid does. Thus, the tick drops. Once on the mammal, it moves toward warmth. In this way, it gets under the fur to the surface of the skin to have its last supper. That all the tick "knows" about mammals is butyric acid is clear from the fact that a tick will drop onto a warm rock which smells from a mammal and destroy its probiscus as it burrows into the "skin" of the rock. Thus, the forest of the tick is very different from the forest of the squirrel, the bear, or the human.

Thus, each species organizes and filters events in the environment

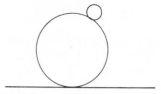

A.   Model of an Adult Blackbird

B.   Two-Headed Model of an Adult Blackbird

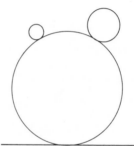

C.   Two-Headed Model of an Adult Blackbird Which
      Differs from B Only in the Size of the "Body"

Figure 12–4. Models Used to Determine the Releaser of Gaping in
the Blackbird. *The bird gapes at head 1 in* B *and at head 2 in* C, *indicating that the releaser is the relative size of the head and not its absolute
size.* (*After Tinbergen and Kuenen, 1957.*)

in its own unique way. While the human observer sees a piece of red
cardboard approach, the stickleback sees a male rival with a red belly.
To avoid the trap of imposing human perceptual categories on the
nonhumans under observation, it is essential to manipulate the putative sign stimulus to discover precisely which feature or features is significant to the animal being observed.

Research like this has revealed that sign stimuli are often quite
subtle. For example, the blackbird (*Turdus merula*) chick gapes at a
model of the adult which consists of two black disks, the larger one

representing the body and the smaller representing the head, as in Figure 12–4*A*. The gaping is directed at the smaller of the two disks. However, the sign stimulus is not the absolute size of the smaller disk, but the ratio between it and the larger disk. This can be shown by presenting the chick with models like those in Figures 12–4*B* and 12–4*C*. These models have two "heads," one larger than the other. The larger head in *B* is the same size as the larger head in *C,* and the same is true of the small heads. Figures 12–4*B* and 12–4*C* differ in the size of the body; it is much bigger in *C* than in *B*. If the chick is presented with model 12–4*B,* it gapes at the smaller head; if it is presented with 12–4*C,* it gapes at the larger one.[19] It seems clear that the sign stimulus is a relation of head to body, and not the absolute size of either.

Thus, careful observation, coupled with systematic experiment, allows one to penetrate the *Umwelt* of a particular species to discover the sign stimulus for particular fixed-action patterns. This simple and elegant general research strategy requires a caveat, however. A sign stimulus is not always an *effective* sign stimulus. The red belly of a stickleback produces aggression only when the other male is in the appropriate "mood," that is, when it is internally ready to respond to the intruder with aggressive display. The female ring dove will build a nest for its eggs only when it is ready, and getting ready requires an elaborate interaction between the male and the female.[20] The bee seems quite colorblind unless it is searching for food, in which case it is well attuned to color.[21] Thus, research with these organisms while they are in a "food-seeking mood" will reveal sign stimuli which may not even be detected under other conditions. To get a more complete and accurate picture of fixed-action patterns and their controlling stimuli, we must consider the internal or motivational factors which act as necessary preconditions for the lock-and-key relation between environmental events and the actions they trigger.

The Ethological View of Motivation

The likelihood of occurrence of a fixed-action pattern depends upon a set of influences internal to the organism. If a frog has just eaten a number of insects and an ideal sign stimulus (small moving object) appears, the frog may not snap at it. If, on the other hand, the

19. Tinbergen and Kuenan, 1957.
20. See Lehrman, 1955, 1961.
21. von Frisch, 1967; Tinbergen, 1951.

frog has gone without food for some time, the same object will reliably produce snapping. Moreover, the frog will actively explore its environment to get itself in the presence of a sign stimulus for snapping. This exploration has been referred to as *appetitive behavior,* to distinguish it from the snapping, which is called *consummatory.* [22] In the operant conditioning chamber, the lever press may be viewed as appetitive behavior while ingestion of the reinforcer is consummatory. If the rat is placed in the conditioning chamber when neither severely deprived nor satiated, the presentation of food may produce the appropriate fixed-action pattern of ingestion, but the rat may not engage in the appetitive (operant) behavior of lever pressing in order to be presented with the sign stimulus for feeding. Thus deprivation activates a search for sign stimuli by the animal.

For a severely deprived animal, a stimulus which is far from the optimal sign stimulus may nevertheless produce the fixed-action pattern. Thus, there seems to be a trade-off between internal and external factors in determining whether a fixed-action pattern will occur. When internal factors are optimal, almost any stimulus will produce the FAP. When internal factors are at their worst, not even the perfect sign stimulus will produce an FAP. Between these two extremes, the quality of the stimulus necessary to produce an FAP seems to be an inverse function of the internal readiness for execution of that FAP.

Classical ethology focused attention on the FAP and its organization, on sign stimuli and their control over fixed-action patterns, and on the role played by internal, motivational conditions in determining the sign-stimulus/fixed-action-pattern interaction. Response systems are ready to go. Recognition of significant stimuli and the connections between these stimuli and action are preestablished. Not only does it seem unnecessary for the organism to profit from experience, but we have encountered evidence (in the cocoon-spinning spider and the caterpillar-catching wasp) that it is impossible, or at least very difficult, for the organism to do so. In contrast, modern ethology views organisms as much more flexible and affords experience a much greater role in determining what animals do. Thus, we must ask now what is the role of experiences like those which are studied in conditioning laboratories? Do they have no significant role in the natural environment? Do the "general laws of behavior" generalize only from one conditioning chamber to the next? Or do they have a circumscribed, modest role in the natural environment? Let us turn then to an assessment of the importance of experience in the life of an organism from the ethological point of view.

22. Craig, 1918.

THE ETHOLOGICAL PERSPECTIVE ON LEARNING

Ethologists are quick to acknowledge that organisms are influenced by experience. Learning is responsible for at least a small portion of the behavior of many species, and a substantial portion of the behavior of some. However, many ethologists contend that how, when, and what an organism will learn is constrained by the genetic endowment of the species. Organisms inherit a kind of genetic blueprint or master plan. The blueprint completely specifies some aspects of the organism's behavior. For other parts of the repertoire, behavior is more loosely specified by the blueprint. Room is left for experience to influence the final, adult character of the behavior. But the blueprint permits learning only under a limited set of conditions and only about a limited set of things, so that even when experience can influence an organism, the range of its effects will be relatively small. Perhaps most important, the process by which an organism gains from experience will be specialized. Different species will learn different things in different ways.

We can compare the ethological notion of a behavioral blueprint to the blueprint of a building. The blueprint divides a building into rooms in an inflexible way. The "categories" of the building are specified in advance. Within each category, or room, experience can have its influence. The room can be furnished in a large number of ways. But the structure of the room—its size, its shape, its location in the building—imposes constraints on how it will be furnished. Some rooms, like bathrooms and kitchens, have their ultimate character even more rigidly specified by the blueprint than other rooms. The locations of sinks, ovens, toilets, and so on, impose major limitations on how the room will look when it is furnished.

Nearly 300 years ago, one of the intellectual predecessors of behavior theory, British Empiricist John Locke, spoke of how a mind is furnished:

> *Let us then suppose the Mind to be, as we say, white Paper, void of all Characters, without any* Ideas; *How comes it to be furnished? Whence comes it by that vast store, which the busie and boundless Fancy of Man has painted on it, with an almost endless variety? Whence has it all the materials of Reason and Knowledge? To this I answer, in one word, from* Experience.[23]

23. Locke, 1690.

The Empiricist tradition following Locke differs from the ethologists in that, for the ethologists, the mind or the behavior of organisms is a building divided into rooms. How the rooms are furnished has something to do with experience, but it has much more to do with the structure imposed on the rooms, prior to any experience, by the form of the building. Thus, if one really wants to understand the major determinants of the character of a building or the behavior of an organism, one studies the structure which determines what the rooms are, and not the experience which determines how they are furnished. For the ethologist, Pavlovian and operant conditioning processes certainly play a role in determining the behavior of an organism and, as such, they should be understood. However, entirely different kinds of learning also play a role in determining adult behavior, and the blueprint can tell us what kinds of learning will occur under what kinds of conditions. The analysis of behavior may tell us about some of the ways in which organisms learn when they do learn, but an understanding of the blueprint will tell us when they learn and what they will learn about.

This ethological approach to learning would criticize the tradition of behavior theory not only for its emphasis upon experience as a determinant of behavior, but for the methods used to study the effects of experience. One can attempt to isolate the learning experiences of organisms from the other determinants of their behavior by placing them in artificial and arbitrary situations which, of course, is precisely what the methods of behavior analysis set out to accomplish. For the ethologist, such a strategy will lead to substantial distortion. The blueprint is the product of the evolutionary history of a species. Its character is shaped by natural selection so that the organism is well adapted to the environment in which it evolved. To understand learning, one must study it under the conditions in which the blueprint has been shaped to allow it to occur.[24] Thus, studies of learning within the ethological tradition almost always take account of the variables which

---

24. The most pointed and thorough criticism of the tradition of behavior analysis and its relation to the principal assumptions of ethology has been written by Konrad Lorenz, 1965. Lorenz says:

"The more complicated an adapted process, the less chance there is that a random change will improve its adaptedness. There are no life processes more complicated than those which take place in the central nervous system and control behavior. Random change must, with an overpowering probability, result in their disintegration. Blithely assuming that 'learning' (whatever that may be) automatically achieves adaptive improvement of behavior mechanisms implies neither more nor less than the belief in a preestablished harmony between organisms and environment. The amazing and never-to-be forgotten fact is that learning does, in the majority of cases, increase the survival value of the behavior mechanisms which it modified" (p. 12).

would be relevant within the naturalistic setting. The questions about learning which ethologists ask focus on how learning and fixed-action patterns are interwoven in the development of adult organisms.

One example illustrates nicely how learning represents a small but significant contribution to the overall behavior pattern. A finch found on the Galapagos Islands (*Cactospiza pallida*) uses straight, thin pieces of wood to pry insects out of their burrows in the bark of trees. A male of the species raised in captivity searched for sticks and poked them in crevices and holes but only *after* feeding. When it spotted an insect in a crevice, it dropped the stick and tried to get at the insect with its bill. The bird eventually learned to use the stick as a tool.[25] The important point here is that the fixed-action pattern of poking already existed as a part of the animal's repertoire. The eventual occurrence of that action pattern in the service of feeding represents a learned variation on an already established theme.

An example which makes a similar point is the attack behavior of the polecat (*Putorius putorius*). Polecats attack and kill small rodents by grasping them at the neck and biting them there. This efficient form of attack requires practice, however. Unpracticed polecats bite at whatever body part they can reach. If the prey fights back, the polecat retreats and tries again. Eventually, the polecat learns to grasp the rodent by the neck so it cannot bite back.[26]

Still other examples can be found in the development of species-characteristic songs by various birds. One particularly elegant set of experiments has been done on the song development of the white-crowned sparrow.[27] In the ordinary course of events, the sparrow (especially the adult male) develops a long and elaborate call. While most features of the song are common to all members of the species, in all locales, there are some features idiosyncratic to the immediate environment, that is, there are local dialects. The developing sparrow will learn the dialect of its locale. However, in order to learn, the sparrow must be exposed to the song during the period between its 10th and 50th day of life. If it hears the song between 10 and 50 days of age, it displays its own song normally as an adult. If it hears the song after 50 days of age, or never hears it, it comes to sing a crude, white-crowned sparrow song, with minimal detail. Thus, the sparrow learns the song, but only during a tightly constrained period in its development. Indeed, the learning is more constrained than that. If the sparrows are exposed to the songs of other birds between 10 and 50 days

25. Eibl-Eibesfeldt, 1970.
26. Eibl-Eibesfeldt, 1970.
27. Marler, 1970.

of age, this exposure has no effect on song development. Their adult song matches neither the songs they heard nor the songs of normally raised white-crowned sparrows. Thus, it seems that white-crowned sparrows are constrained to learn only their dialect of white-crowned sparrow song, and only if they hear it in the first 50 days of life. While the fact that they do learn it is undeniable, the fact that the learning process is so tightly constrained is equally undeniable, and perhaps more significant.

Imprinting

One final, very well-known example of naturalistic learning which has a number of features in common with song learning is the phenomenon of *imprinting*.[28] If a newly hatched duckling is allowed to observe a member of its species briefly within the first day of its life, and follows that species member around, it will develop a permanent attachment to organisms or objects which have critical features in common with the imprinting object. It may be that species recognition, for many species, is learned through imprinting and not built into the newborn organism. The baby opens its eyes, sees something moving around (in all likelihood, one of its parents), and follows that object. Subsequently, the baby is permanently attached to the class of objects like the one it followed around.

A little reflection will reveal that leaving the recognition of members of one's species to learning is a bit chancy. The young duckling might observe a hawk in the vicinity and follow it around. The consequences of such learning would not be pleasant for the duckling. This is where the constraining, built-in blueprint comes in. As it turns out, there is a very brief period, a *sensitive period* shortly after birth, when the young organism is extremely likely to be imprinted. Imprinting will occur to the appropriate object if it appears during this period, but the likelihood of imprinting falls rapidly to nearly zero after this sensitive period has passed. Since it is overwhelmingly likely that the objects in the immediate environment of the newly hatched ducklings will be its parents, and since the imprinting period lasts only for a brief time after hatching, the likelihood that the duckling will imprint on its parents is extremely high. Nevertheless, under unusual circumstances, one can get ducklings imprinted on wooden models, people, people's shoes, and a host of other inappropriate stimuli.

In addition to the temporal constraint on imprinting which makes

28. See Lorenz, 1937; Rajecki, 1973; Hoffman and Ratner, 1973; Sluckin, 1965.

appropriate species identification likely, there are constraints on the characteristics which an imprinting object must have which also serve appropriate species identification. What these characteristics are vary from species to species but they are often sufficiently specific to eliminate many possible inappropriate contenders for the imprinting object. Again, despite this additional constraint, the imprinting process can occasionally miscarry. However, except under experimentally contrived conditions, this is unlikely.

The discovery of imprinting in birds has led investigators to look for similar processes of social attachment in other species. In the dog, for example, there seems to be a sensitive period between 4 and 6 weeks of age during which a permanent attachment is formed to whatever organism (dog or human) is usually around.[29] The formation of this attachment seems independent of how the puppy is treated by the other organism. Some investigators have argued that the development of attachments in humans is imprinting-like and characterized by a sensitive period in the first half of the first year.[30] While these attempts to generalize the imprinting process across species are by no means universally accepted, the evidence seems clear that, in at least some species, this very specialized, constrained kind of learning plays a crucial role in development.

ETHOLOGY AND BEHAVIOR THEORY

For the ethologist, kinds of learning like the ones just described are the norm. They are special, perhaps even unique. They are often species-specific, that is, characteristic of all and only the members of a particular species, or function-specific, that is, characteristic of many species but only in the service of a particular function, like feeding. What would be extraordinary to the ethologist would be a demonstration of laws of behavior which were both species-general and trans-situational. The only general principle of learning is that learning is not characterized by a set of completely general principles. Consider how the ethologist might characterize the kind of research done within the tradition of behavior theory. The experimenter creates an artificial environment in order to neutralize the possible role played by species-specific or function-specific characteristics. Suppose he succeeds. The result for the behavior theorist will be general principles of behavior. The result for the ethologist will be the elimination of any possible chance of discovering real principles of behavior. If

29. Scott and Fuller, 1965.
30. Gray, 1958.

the organism is programmed to fit adaptively into its natural environment and you place it in an environment unlike its natural one, you will effectively be studying a handicapped organism—a misfit. What can such studies possibly tell you about the behavior of that organism in the environment for which it was designed. The phenomenon of taste aversion learning, discussed in Chapter 11, which has created such a stir among behavior theorists, hardly seems surprising to the ethologist. One observes it, and learning phenomena like it, all over the natural world. For example, the snapping frog, whose fixed-action pattern of staring and snapping at small objects seems rigid and unmodifiable, learns on one trial to stop snapping at foul-tasting objects. For the ethologist, what is special or unusual is learning to lever press when the light is green but not when it is red.

We saw in the last chapter numerous instances in which seemingly well-established principles of behavior control failed to hold because of the intrusion of species-specific characteristics. There are many other instances, in addition to instances in which, while operant control remains present and effective, nonoperant control can also be detected.[31] For example, pigeons trained to peck another pigeon to obtain food will do so. However, what begins as a discrete, efficient peck ends up as a full-blown, lengthy sequence of aggressive behavior.[32] This transformation in response form costs the pigeon food. If pigeons are trained to press a lever with their breasts for food, they tend to peck at it. If they must attack another pigeon before pressing the lever, they tend to shake the lever violently with their beaks.[33] If a male stickleback is trained to bite a rod or to swim through a ring for the opportunity to display at a sexually receptive female, it will learn to do so, though it will make the biting response at a much lower rate than the swimming response. However, if extinction conditions are introduced, the rate of biting will increase to match the rate of swimming through the ring. This peculiar set of facts has a ready explanation if one knows something about the determinants of the various activities in the natural environment. It turns out that, for the stickleback, sexual and aggressive response systems are mutually inhibitory. The more the stickleback consumes the reinforcer (displays at the female), the more sexually aroused it becomes. But the more sexually aroused it becomes, the less likely it is to engage in aggressive behavior. Thus, it bites the rod (aggressive behavior) at a low rate. When

31. For a review, see Shettleworth, 1972a.
32. Azrin and Huchinson, 1967.
33. Reynolds, Catania, and Skinner, 1963.

the reinforcer is discontinued, the inhibition of aggressive tendencies by sexual arousal is removed and bar biting increases.[34] It is an open question how many other seemingly peculiar outcomes of conditioning experiments might be understood if placed in an appropriate, naturalistic framework.

Our brief review of ethology is intended to provide a sense of the conflict between the ethological approach and the approach of behavior theory. Ethology is largely concerned with uncovering principles of behavioral organization which are the product of the fine tuning of a species to its environment in evolution. This organization, while it facilitates adaptation to the natural environment, constrains the organism's reception of information from the environment, the organism's possible alternatives of action on this information, and the ways in which the organism can profit from experience. Behavior theory studies the organization and control of behavior as a result of conditioning experience. The behavior theorist is not insensitive to the concerns of ethology. Indeed, it is a sign of sensitivity that such pains were taken to create artificial, biologically neutral, experimental situations. It is just that the interests of the behavior theorist lie elsewhere.

Where should one's interests lie? If one is concerned with understanding human behavior, should one adopt the ethological orientation or the orientation of behavior theory? Our review of ethology, while suggestive, was by no means conclusive. It is time now to make a similar exploration in the domain of human behavior. We will not be exploring "human ethology," though one could.[35] Instead, we will briefly explore some recent arguments about the nature of human language. Many of these arguments stand in the same relation to behavior theory as ethology does, though they come from very different historical origins and focus on a very different subject matter.

THE TALKING ANIMAL:
LANGUAGE AND VERBAL BEHAVIOR

Ethologists are critical of behavior theory for its neglect of the innate predispositions of the behaving organism. Modern students of language have articulated precisely the same objection. The following statement made by Noam Chomsky, a dominant figure in modern linguistics, could as well have been made by an ethologist:

34. Sevenster, 1968.
35. See Eibl-Eibesfeldt, 1970, and McGrew, 1972, for examples.

Suppose that in investigating organisms, we decide, perversely, to restrict ourselves to tasks and problems that lie outside their cognitive capacity. We might then expect to discover simple "laws of learning" of some generality. Suppose further that we define a "good experiment" as one that provides smooth learning curves. . . . Then there will be "good experiments" only in domains that lie outside of O's [the organism's] cognitive capacity. For example, there will be no good experiments in the study of human language learning, though there may be if we concentrate attention on memorization of nonsense syllables, verbal association, and other tasks for which humans have no special abilities.

. . . This discipline may, indeed, develop laws of learning that do not vary too greatly across cognitive domains for a particular organism and that have some cross-species validity. It will, of necessity, avoid these domains in which an organism is specially designed to acquire rich cognitive structures that enter into its life in an intimate fashion. The discipline will be of virtually no intellectual interest, it seems to me, since it is restricting itself in principle to those questions that are guaranteed to tell us little about the nature of organisms. [36]

For Chomsky, the orientation of behavior analysis is especially misguided when applied to language:

By studying language we may discover abstract principles that govern its structure and use, principles that are universal by biological necessity and not mere historical accident, that derive from mental characteristics of the species. . . . To come to know a human language would be an extraordinary intellectual achievement for a creature not specifically designed to accomplish this task. A normal child acquires this knowledge on relatively slight exposure and without specific training. He can then quite effortlessly make use of an intricate structure of specific rules and guiding principles to convey his thoughts and feelings to others. . . . For the conscious mind, not specially designed for the purpose, it remains a distant goal to reconstruct and comprehend what the child has done intuitively and with minimal effort. [37]

Chomsky's claim here is that just as it is unlikely that a spider, in its short life, could come to learn the rules of web spinning in arbitrary fashion, so it is unlikely that the child, in just a few years, could come to learn the complex rules which govern its language. Rather, the

36. Chomsky, 1975, p. 26.
37. Chomsky, 1975, p. 4.

child must be equipped with a specialized learning capacity which is tuned to the rules of natural languages. This capacity would be responsible for the ease of language learning. On the basis of this view, it is clear that any attempt to study language learning which neglects the assumed specialized learning capacity would necessarily miss many of the essential attributes of the learning process.

Chomsky's point is that the specialized language-learning capacity is as universal a characteristic of the species as is the heart. On the face of it this claim seems rather unlikely. How does one reconcile a species-universal language-learning capacity with the myriad of different languages which people speak and understand? The vocabularies of different languages are obviously quite different and so are the grammatical rules of different languages. If there are characteristics which all languages share, they must certainly be more abstract than the characteristics of language one studies in a foreign language class. But, what are they?

This question is by no means answered and a substantial amount of study is being directed by modern linguists at attempts to uncover universal characteristics of language. A few possibilities which may be suggested are these:

1. The child seems constrained to learn to communicate via spoken language. There is evidence that babbling is the precursor in the child of language, that babbling sounds are universal, and that as the child is exposed only to the sounds of its native language, the babbling sounds appropriate to that language continue, while other sounds which may be appropriate to other languages, drop out.[38]

2. The child seems constrained to look for certain kinds of regularities in the incoming speech flow and to ignore others. This involves, first, an ability to segment continuous, unbroken auditory experience into discrete speech sound categories.[39] Second, this involves the ability to identify certain classes of words—for example, nouns, verbs, adverbs—and to treat the members of these classes in common with respect to the rules which govern the ways in which they can be related. In short, the child seems to learn a kind of code for talking about its world. The particular characteristics of the code may vary from one language to another, but the child may still start out with knowledge of the general properties of all natural codes—with a knowledge of the *kinds* of combinations of words which are acceptable in any language. For example, in all languages there are rules which

38. Lenneberg, 1967.
39. See Eimas, Siqueland, Juscyk, and Vigorito, 1971.

specify the order in which words may appear, that is, all languages have grammars. The child learning language may be tuned in advance to pick out regularities in the ordering of words.[40]

Even in the absence of clearly agreed upon universal properties of language, there are aspects of the language-development process itself which strongly suggest that it is a biological universal having much in common with the kinds of action patterns studied by ethologists. Let us review a few of these features of language development briefly:

1. There is the simple fact that virtually all children, whether brilliant or feeble, in all cultures, whether industrial or primitive, learn the extraordinarily complex rules of their native languages in about the same brief period of time with no apparent difficulty.[41]

2. There seems to be a sensitive period for language learning, much as we observed with imprinting and bird-song learning. At around puberty, the ability to learn language is dramatically reduced. Thus, it is easier for children to learn a second language than for adults. In addition, if one examines patients who have suffered brain damage which resulted in language loss (aphasia), one observes that virtually all children under the age of 12 recover complete language ability, while for older patients recovery is much less likely.[42] Also, if one examines language development in retarded children, one discovers that it parallels language development in normal children. It is only slower. However, when retardates reach puberty, language development essentially stops, or, if it continues, it is the result of specific, painstaking instruction. In normal children, language development is complete long before puberty. With intellectual development slowed in retardates, complete acquisition has often not occurred by puberty.

40. See Fodor, Bever, and Garrett, 1974, especially Chapter 3.
41. For a detailed treatment of the voluminous literature on language development, see Brown, 1973; Fodor, Bever, and Garrett, 1974. It should be noted that many arguments against an account of language learning based upon conditioning principles have focused on the speed of language learning and the ease of acquisition. The arguments are basically of the form that there is no way a language could be learned so rapidly on the basis of specific conditioning experiences. The argument has been quite influential, but it should not be. By what criteria is language learning rapid? The child requires about 2 years of exposure to learn the language. In this time, the child certainly experiences about as much input as all the rats and pigeons in the collective history of behavior analysis. The child is surrounded by language for 12 or more hours a day, every day, for 2 years. Perhaps this still can be called rapid acquisition. However, to make the argument meaningful, we must specify criteria for identifying learning as rapid.
42. Lenneberg, 1967.

3. Attempts to identify shaping of language by reinforcement in the natural environment have generally met with failure. Parents tend to provide reinforcement on the basis of the meaning of a child's utterance and not its form, despite the fact that the utterances of young children do not conform to the rules of adult grammar. Nevertheless, the child masters the adult grammar and does not continue to use its primitive language form despite reinforcement.[43]

The above outline is just that, and it barely scratches the surface of recent work in linguistics and psycholinguistics. It does, however, provide the flavor of the evidence adduced by linguists and psycholinguists for a specialized language-learning capacity. What has the behavior theorist to offer in the face of arguments of this type?

Skinner and Verbal Behavior

Language has concerned the students of the analysis of behavior from the beginning. Both Pavlov and Watson attempted to extrapolate the conditioning principles they were developing to the domain of language. However, perhaps the most ambitious effort, and the one most in the spirit of the guiding principles of behavior analysis we have articulated in this book, was provided by Skinner.[44] Skinner wrote not about language, but about verbal behavior. Verbal behavior is defined by Skinner as behavior reinforced through the mediation of other persons. Thus, the behavior of walking to the sink and getting a glass of water is reinforced by the ingestion of water. The behavior "Please get me some water" is also reinforced by the ingestion of water. Each behavior is part of an operant class. The difference is that, in the latter case, reinforcement depends upon, or is mediated by, another person—the listener.

Skinner suggests that verbal behavior is shaped by the reinforcing community. Children begin to speak by imitation. They learn correspondence between words and objects and learn to make requests, demands, ask questions, and so on because the consequences of these responses are that the items requested are provided, and the questions asked are answered. Children learn to ask rather than demand as they get older because the "audience" establishes a discriminative contingency. "Please pass the water" is reinforced while "Give me some water" is not. Children learn to describe the world accurately

---

43. Brown, 1973.
44. Skinner, 1957.

(e.g., "The water is on the table") because accurate descriptions are reinforced (with praise or approval) while inaccurate ones are not. Children learn to speak in accordance with rules of grammar ("They went to the park" instead of "They goed to the park") because grammatical utterances are reinforced while nongrammatical ones are not. Once the verbal repertoire is established, the person's verbal behavior is controlled by a complex, often subtle set of discriminative stimuli in the environment, and by similarly subtle and complex reinforcement contingencies established by the verbal community. The shaping and subsequent control of verbal behavior is not different in principle from the shaping and control of lever pressing. The differences are only in complexity.

Linguistics versus Behavior Theory

Skinner's treatment of verbal behavior has been subjected to heavy criticism.[45] Much of the criticism is directed at Skinner's neglect of the specialized learning capacities which occupy the linguists. It is not that conditioning principles play no role in language learning, nor is it that the audience does not establish contingencies which influence what a speaker will say. Rather, the claim is that the contribution made by conditioning to language is the tip of an iceberg. Far more significant is the existence of the specialized learning capacity. In this form, the linguistic criticism of Skinner and behavior theory is identical to that of the ethologists.

There is also a second line of criticism which does not focus on what Skinner's account leaves out. Instead, it attempts to show that Skinner's account is wrong, that it is in principle impossible for conditioning principles to explain the development of language. Suppose language is the result of conditioning. What is it that is conditioned? Do specific sentences get conditioned? A bit of reflection will reveal that this is impossible. Even the young child is able to understand more sentences than it could possibly learn and to produce sentences which it has never heard—indeed, which no one has ever uttered. Perhaps the vocabulary gets conditioned. While this may be true, vocabulary is perhaps the least interesting aspect of language. It is the ability to *order* particular elements of vocabulary in regular and comprehensible ways which concerns the linquist.

As children grow and their language proficiency increases, the likelihood that any utterance will be a repetition of something already heard or said gets smaller and smaller. It is not inconceivable that in

45. Chomsky, 1959.

an hour or so from now you will encounter a friend and utter: "I just finished Chapter 12 of Schwartz's book. Boy, was it hard to understand!" Though you have never said precisely that before, and chances are you have never heard it said, it is obvious that you would have no difficulty saying it. Nor would you have difficulty interpreting utterances which neither you nor anyone else has ever heard before, like "John feeds his pet walrus sandwiches of tuna fish and watermelon."

The problem is that almost all adult utterances are unique; language is creative. In contrast, behavior analysis seems to be concerned with the principles which determine when an organism will emit an already acquired response again. The main dependent variable used by behavior analysis is frequency of occurrence. One counts lever presses or key pecks which occur again and again and one depends upon measures of frequency to provide an indication of the significance of the variables being manipulated. But of what value is frequency of occurrence as a dependent variable when one is dealing with phenomena (utterances) which in general do not occur more than once?

The response of the behavior theorist to this problem might be the suggestion that it is not unique to language. No two lever presses are exactly the same. The probability of a lever press of a particular force and duration made by a particular part of the rat's anatomy contacting a particular part of the lever is effectively zero. What we do to overcome the essential uniqueness of each lever press is to collapse all lever presses into a single class, defined by a common property, and ignore the differences among individual members of the class. This is what the definition of the operant is all about. One could attempt to establish similar equivalence classes in the domain of language. This, indeed, was one of Skinner's major aims in his book. One major issue between Skinner and his critics is whether the units of language or verbal behavior which come out of Skinner's analysis are the right ones. His strategy in defining units of verbal behavior is the same as his strategy in defining other operants: units are defined on the basis of those properties on which reinforcement depends. The alternative view is that the units are not created by experience with reinforcement contingencies, but instead are a part of the person's intellectual blueprint, like the unfurnished rooms of a house. It is this blueprint which allows one to classify words into abstract categories and to speak in accordance with linguistic rules.

It must be that in learning a language one learns not specific strings of words, but a set of rules which allow one to impose order on the utterances of others and to utter sentences which will in turn he interpretable by others. Somehow, when the developing child is being exposed to its language, it is able to abstract from the stream of speech the rules which govern the language. We have not had occasion to describe conditioning phenomena in terms of "abstraction" and "rule learning" until now. Perhaps these are the features of language which distinguish it from the phenomena which have occupied us previously. Careful analysis will reveal, however, that one could use "abstraction" and "rule learning" to characterize many of the activities of rats and pigeons which we have discussed throughout the book.

Suppose a pigeon is exposed to a procedure in which key pecks at a red triangle are reinforced. The pigeon learns to peck the red triangle. We might say that the pigeon has learned a rule relating key pecking to food. What makes the pigeon's behavior "rule-governed" is our confidence (borne out, of course, by empirical fact) that if the pigeon finds itself in a quite novel situation which includes a response key illuminated with a similar stimulus, it will peck the key. Thus, the pigeon has learned not a specific response controlled by a specific stimulus situation, but a class of responses which will be controlled by a class of stimulus situations. Let us ask next what defines the response class and the stimulus class which are related to each other by the reinforcement rule. We have just reviewed how the response class is defined. The operant is defined on the basis of those properties on which reinforcement depends. But this definition of the operant is an abstraction. The response class is clearly defined by a single property or a small set of properties which all of its members have in common. However, every instance of the operant will also possess features which are not a part of the definition. These features, the experimenter and, presumably, the pigeon ignore. The point is that the definition of the operant does not provide a complete description of any single instance. In this sense, it is abstract.

Now, what of the stimulus class? How is it defined? What makes a particular novel situation more or less similar to the training situation? That the stimulus was described above as a red triangle already represents an abstraction. Red and triangle are only two of an essentially inexhaustibly large set of stimuli which might be controlling the pigeon's behavior. The temperature in the box, the brightness of the houselight, the roughness of the floor surface, the screws located in the walls, and so on, might each be controlling key pecking. We eliminated these features of the stimulus situation from our initial description because intuition and a substantial body of research indicate that the controlling stimulus is likely to be on the key. But even if we restrict our attention to the key, there is still an extremely large set of possible controlling stimuli: color, size, shape, texture, temperature, and brightness are but a few possible factors. Which one of these properties in fact defines the stimulus class and tells us whether any new situation will be similar to the old one?

We cannot answer this question. As research on discrimination learning indicates (Chapter 8), for one pigeon the controlling stimulus might be color; for another, shape; for a third, brightness. However, we do know how to make the organism define the stimulus class in a particular way. If we establish a rule relating only one property of the stimulus to reinforcement, so that pecks at a red triangle produce food while pecks at an otherwise identical red square do not, we can be reasonably sure that the pigeon will abstract just that relevant property as the definition of the stimulus class. In this example, the stimulus will be "triangle." As in the case of operants, this definition abstracts a single property which many stimuli may have in common. It does not provide a complete description of any individual member of the stimulus class. Since differential reinforcement can effectively influence the pigeon's definition of the stimulus class, one might argue that if pigeons not exposed to differential reinforcement in the chamber define their stimulus classes idiosyncratically, for example, shape for one, size for another, color for a third, these idiosyncrasies will reflect differential reinforcement in the past history of each animal.

Thus, some familiar phenomena of operant conditioning can be redescribed with a terminology which includes "abstraction" and "rule learning." The fact that language entails these processes does not necessarily rule it out of the domain of behavior analysis.[46] There is more that the behavior analyst might argue. One may want to make a distinction between language ability and language use. Even if language ability does depend upon a specialized learning capacity, and knowing about this capacity can tell us what a person *can* say, it cannot tell us what a person *will* say. What a person will say may well be under the control of reinforcement contingencies established by the audience. Thus, in the terms of Staddon and Simmelhag (Chapter 6), the

46. The debate does not end here. Suppose we grant that abstraction and rule learning have a place in the analysis of behavior and focus on more specific questions like what feature or features will define the categories of a language. What are the defining properties of nouns and verbs and so on? One cannot point to aspects of the environment, like red or square, to define these classes. Rather, these classes are defined in terms of grammatical features—constraints upon what can be substituted for what, or what can be transformed into what, which are specified by the rules of language. Since one cannot point to these grammatical features as properties of the environment, it is unclear that the formation of language units can properly be related to "discriminative control" as it is ordinarily studied and understood.

language-learning capacity may tell us about principles of variation, but reinforcement contingencies may tell us which bits of verbal behavior get selected.

Finally, the behavior analyst may inquire about just how uniquely human the language-learning capacity is. The force behind this inquiry comes from recent demonstrations that rather impressive language abilities can be established in chimps through rigorous application of conditioning principles.[47] The training goes slowly, in striking contrast to the language learning of the child, and the finished product is far less complex and subtle than the language of an ordinary 4-year-old, especially with respect to syntax, which poses the central problem for conditioning-theory accounts of language. Nevertheless, the possibility is open that the language-learning capacity is not nearly as specialized as most linguists would claim.

For those maintaining the view that language learning represents a specialized human ability, the chimp-training studies are a confirmation. That chimps learn with difficulty under seemingly ideal conditions only highlights the ease with which children learn under nonoptimal ones. As a dramatic example of this point, the training techniques which have succeeded with chimps have been used to reestablish language in adults who suffered brain damage which resulted in almost complete loss of language ability, or aphasia.[48] Recall from our earlier discussion that spontaneous recovery in such patients is unlikely. Yet, these training procedures seem successful. As with the chimps, however, the learning is slow. Thus, it might be argued that language learning in the chimp is like language learning in the person whose specialized capacity for language learning has been destroyed. As such, it has rather little to do with accounting for the initial acquisition of language by human children.

This example of the treatment of aphasic patients seems to capture the essence of the linguistic criticism of the methods of behavior theory. The aphasic patient, by virtue of brain damage, is not quite a complete person. The destruction of a part of the brain specialized for language function has taken away that person's language-learning advantage; it has neutralized a species-specific learning capacity. But the methods of behavior theory are *designed* to accomplish precisely the same effect. By studying organisms in arbitrary, biologically neutral situations, behavior theory takes away the learning advantages peculiar to each species. What remains is a kind of least common denominator, a set of learning principles which may characterize all

47. See Gardner and Gardner, 1969; Premack, 1971.
48. Glass, Gazzaniga, and Premack, 1973.

species. One must wonder how accurate a picture of the behavior of any species one gets by studying its members under conditions in which they are handicapped, conditions for which they did not specifically evolve.

RECONCILING BEHAVIOR THEORY
WITH ETHOLOGY AND LINGUISTICS

In this chapter, we have presented a point of view which contrasts sharply with the point of view represented in the rest of the book. The tradition of behavior theory treats organisms as if they were utterly malleable and adaptable. By studying the behavior of these organisms in arbitrary situations, under the influence of arbitrary contingencies, behavior theory hopes to uncover the principles which underlie this adaptability. Ethology treats organisms as rigidly constrained by a genetic blueprint. Most adaptations to the environment are built into the organism. Those which depend upon experience depend upon very specific kinds of experience and the blueprint insures the organism's sensitivity to just those kinds of experience. The same view seems to characterize much of linguistics.

The debate among individuals who hold these views is a peculiar one. The behavior analyst does not deny the existence and importance of species-specific determinants of behavior. Skinner has acknowledged the significance of what he calls "phylogenetic contingencies," and has even suggested a parallel between the shaping of behavior by the law of effect and the shaping of behavior by natural selection which is similar to the selection process articulated by Staddon and Simmelhag (Chapter 6).[49] Similarly, neither the ethologist nor the linguist denies the influence of reinforcement contingencies on behavior. The disagreement between the ethologist and the behavior theorist seems to center on what would be the most important thing to know about organisms—the processes which determine those characteristics which all members of a species share, or the processes which determine those characteristics which make members of a species different from one another. By attempting to understand the genetic blueprint, the ethologist is focusing on aspects of the organism which it shares with all members of its species. In the domain of language, one might find a set of rules common to all languages which people are especially prepared to learn. By attempting to understand the effects of reinforcement contingencies, the behavior theorist is focusing on aspects of the organism which differentiate it from other

49. Skinner, 1966; 1974, Chapter 3.

members of its species. In the domain of language, one might find the principles by which the idiosyncrasies of particular languages (like their vocabularies) are learned, and which account for individual differences in language skill, and even situation-to-situation differences in language use within a single individual. The questions we must face are: (1) How do these two different orientations fit together and (2) which of them should we choose to pursue?

It is a truism that increasing phylogenetic complexity carries with it increasing flexibility and increasing individual variation. If one takes this seriously, it would seem that in studying animals with many constraints on behavior, like pigeons, one should focus on the genetic blueprint, while in studying unusually complex and plastic organisms, like people, one should focus on the influence of experience. This would imply that behavior theory has adopted a sensible and important strategy for an attempt to understand human behavior. Note, however, that this strategy has been employed primarily in the study of pigeons, not people. This suggests that for the study of pigeons, the methods of behavior analysis may be the wrong ones. If so, we are left with a peculiar paradox that behavior theory may tell us rather little about the behavior of the organisms it actually studies, while telling us much about the behavior of people.

But, if the striking thing about human behavior is its interindividual variety, what are we to make of the linguistic effort to find species universals, and how are we to assess the importance of ethological principles to our own lives? A recent paper by Paul Rozin offers some interesting speculations on this matter.[50] Rozin is concerned with relating the "intelligence" of simple organisms to the "intelligence" of more complex ones. His view is that the behavior of simple organisms is guided by specialized learning capacities. Though these capacities may be extraordinarily complex and sophisticated, they are rigidly tied to a particular behavioral system, and cannot be used in the service of other systems. These very same, or similar, learning capacities may be present in more complex organisms also. The difference between the simple and the complex organism is that the complex one can access these strategies in the service of a great variety of different behavioral systems. While the specialized learning capacity of the simple organism is present and makes learning possible, it cannot be used freely by the organism. In the complex organism, these capacities become generally available so that they can be manipulated and used in contexts quite removed from the ones for which they were evolved.

Let us consider a few examples. One is the food-selection (or food-

50. Rozin, 1976.

avoidance) system of the rat. Another is the song learning of the sparrow. Both of these systems require a learning capacity far more sophisticated than that required for simple Pavlovian conditioning. The animal must remember the stimulus input for a long time, the learned response is often quite complicated, and so on. Yet, as we have seen, the sophistication is actually superficial precisely because the learning capacity is tightly tied to feeding or song learning and cannot be employed in other contexts. Most instances of Pavlovian conditioning, in contrast, are quite flexible.

An even more striking example is the "language" of honey bees.[51] A foraging bee communicates information about the location of food sources to other bees. The bee calculates both the distance and the direction of the food source from the hive and communicates this information with a series of dancing movements. It gauges direction with respect to the sun's position. But the sun's position in the sky changes during the day. Thus, if the bee communicates information about direction on the basis of where the sun was when it found food, and not where it presently is, its fellows will be misled. The bee does not do this. Instead, it communicates direction on the basis of the sun's present position. What this means is that the bee has both an accurate clock and a computer of astronomical data (sun position) in its head. In a sense, the bee knows as much as the navigator of an airplane. The difference between them is that the airplane navigator knows what he or she knows and the bee does not. As a result, the navigator can use the astronomical information to serve a variety of ends, like avoiding storms, and the bee cannot. This is the sense in which, for the bee, astronomy is a part of what Rozin calls the "cognitive unconscious" while it is quite conscious and accessible to the navigator.

Rozin's notion is that in people many of these learning capacities are accessible and hence can be used with great flexibility. One can see accessibility grow during the early development of the child. If a young child (before the age of six or so) is confronted with two rows of marbles, as in Figure 12–5*A*, and asked whether the two rows have the same number of marbles, the child will say yes. If one of the rows is then transformed, as in Figure 12–5*B*, in front of the child's eyes, the child will now say that the longer row has more marbles. By about the age six, the child learns that changing the spacing of an array of objects does not change their number. That is, the child learns to *conserve* number.[52] However, this ability to conserve is very specific. If

---

51. von Frisch, 1967.
52. The tracing of the child's ability to conserve is perhaps the most well known and most heavily researched aspect of the broad and influential theory of development of Jean Piaget. For a review, see Flavell, 1963.

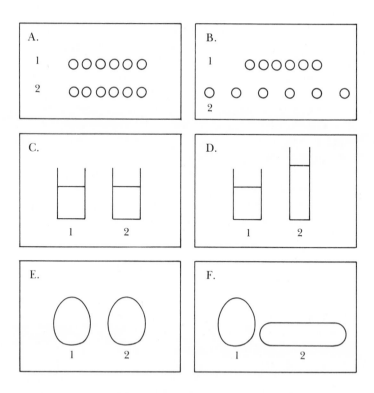

Figure 12–5. Schematic of Three Different Conservation Tasks. A *and* B *depict a conservation of number task,* C *and* D, *conservation of liquid quantity, and* E *and* F, *conservation of weight. In each case, the transformation of one of the objects (A to* B, C *to* D, *or* E *to* F) *is done while the child watches.*

one pours liquid from vessels of one shape into vessels of another shape, as in Figures 12–5C and 12–5D, or flattens clay balls into pancakes, as in Figures 12–5E and 12–5F, the child will not conserve liquid quantity or weight, and will say that the taller vessel contains more water and the flatter clay ball contains less clay. Ultimately, the child learns to apply the same reasoning which produces number conservation to these other situations. Accessibility has increased. More significantly, the child comes to describe accurately the reasoning process which is necessary for conservation. At this point, the learning capacity is fully accessible. In contrast, no matter how old the bee gets and how much experience it has as a navigator, it will never be able to use its ability in the general way that a child can.

Some learning capacities may never become universally accessible. The capacity to learn a language may be one. Children learn the rules of grammar rather effortlessly and speak grammatically, though they may never have access to those rules—even as adults. Indeed, the great difficulty linguists have had in even describing the rules of grammar, which presumably everyone knows, may be a testimony to the inaccessibility of these rules. Rozin has suggested that many of the problems teachers encounter in teaching reading may stem from attempting to teach in units (phonemes) which are inaccessible to the child.[53] Consider how easy a task learning to read should be. The child already knows the spoken language. All that is required is a mapping of 26 symbols (letters) onto already familiar sounds. Yet, many children learn to read only with great difficulty. Consider the child who has learned to say the letters. The child says "duh" when it sees *d* and "guh" when it sees *g*. It is then asked to read "dog" by blending the individual sounds. But there is no "duh" in dog; the *d* sound (and necessary mouth movements) is different before an *o* than it is in "duh," and no matter how fast "duh-o-guh" are blended, they will not make "dog."[54] What Rozin suggests is that while individual speech sounds are certainly represented in the child, they are, as are the rules of grammar, inaccessible; that is, they are not easy to teach explicitly. A unit of reading which may be more accessible is the syllable, since unlike the letter sounds syllables can be pronounced separately in isolation. Children learn at least some basic reading skills much more rapidly if syllable-size units are employed (for example, can-dy) rather than letter sounds (cuh, a, en, duh, y).[55]

Unlike language, with rules which are generally inaccessible, and conservation, with rules which are generally accessible, some capacities may become fully accessible, but only to a select few. We all learn early to behave in accordance with physical principles. We learn to anticipate the landing point of a thrown ball, to balance on a bicycle, and so on. Just as all bees are navigators, we are all physicists. But for a small number of us, the physical principles in accordance with which we operate become fully accessible and manipulable. It may be that scientific development frequently is a reflection of the increase in accessibility of principles which we have "known" all along.[56]

These examples suggest the ways in which Rozin's notion of accessibility may help us to coordinate behavior theory with the ethological and linguistic perspectives on human behavior. On some levels, at

53. See Gleitman and Rozin, 1973.
54. See Liberman, 1970; Liberman, Cooper, Shankweiler, and Studdert-Kennedy, 1967.
55. Gleitman and Rozin, 1973.
56. This is not a new idea. It is the central aspect of Plato's theory of knowledge, articulated, for example, in *The Republic,* in the fourth century B.C.

which learning capacities are inaccessible, the behavior theoretic framework may not apply; learning may not be arbitrary. On other levels, at which accessibility is present and flexibility is maximal, the arbitrary learning principles of behavior theory may tell us a great deal.

CONCLUSION

In assessing the extent to which behavior in the natural environment is arbitrary, we encountered two disciplines—ethology and linguistics—both of which differ radically from behavior theory in their fundamental assumptions, in their theoretical conceptions, and in their empirical orientation. Behavior theory emphasizes the flexibility of organisms, and focuses on the role of experience in shaping the behavioral repertoire of the adult. Both ethology and linguistics emphasize the role played by the biological character of the species in constraining the ways in which experience can affect organisms.

The point of this chapter has been to articulate the differences between these approaches, and not to choose among them. The differences which we uncovered tended to revolve more around what it would be most important to find out than around matters of actual theoretical dispute. By choosing to pursue one or another of these approaches, one is essentially making a bet on the future. So long as both approaches are pursued, there will be no losers.

Bibliography

[*The numbers in brackets at the end of each reference refer to the pages of the text on which each reference is cited.*]

Amsel, A. The role of frustrative non-reward in non-continuous reward situations. *Psychological Bulletin*, 1958, *55*, 102–119. [178]

Amsel, A. Frustrative non-reward in partial reinforcement and discrimination learning. *Psychological Review*, 1962, *69*, 306–328. [178]

Amsel, A. Partial reinforcement effects on vigor and persistence. In K. W. Spence & J. T. Spence (Eds.), *The psychology of learning and motivation* (Vol. 1). New York: Academic Press, 1967. [178]

Amsel, A. Inhibition and mediation in classical, Pavlovian and instrumental conditioning. In R. A. Boakes & M. S. Halliday (Eds.), *Inhibition and learning*. New York: Academic Press, 1972. [178]

Anger, D. The role of temporal discrimination in the reinforcement of Sidman avoidance behavior. *Journal of the Experimental Analysis of Behavior*, 1963, *6*, 477–506. [251]

Annau, Z., & Kamin, L. J. The conditioned emotional response as a function of the intensity of the US. *Journal of Comparative and Physiological Psychology*, 1961, *54*, 428–432. [256]

Antonitis, J. J. Response variability in the white rat during conditioning, extinction, and reconditioning. *Journal of Experimental Psychology*, 1951, *42*, 273–281. [135, 343]

Appel, J. Aversive effects of a schedule of positive reinforcement. *Journal of the Experimental Analysis of Behavior*, 1963, *6*, 423–428. [158]

Atthowe, J. M., & Krasner, L. A preliminary report on the application of contingent reinforcement procedures (token economy) in a "chronic" psychiatric ward. *Journal of Abnormal Psychology*, 1968, *73*, 37–43. [10, 295]

Autor, S. M. The strength of conditioned reinforcers as a function of frequency and probability of reinforcement. In D. P. Hendry (Ed.), *Conditioned reinforcement*. Homeward, Ill.: The Dorsey Press, 1969. [291]

Ayllon, T., & Azrin, N. H. *The token economy: A motivational system for therapy and rehabilitation.* New York: Appleton-Century-Crofts, 1968. [10, 294]

Azrin, N. H. Some effects of two intermittent schedules of immediate and non-immediate punishment. *Journal of Psychology*, 1956, *42*, 3–21. [236]

Azrin, N. H. Punishment and recovery during fixed ratio performance. *Journal of the Experimental Analysis of Behavior*, 1959, *2*, 301–305. [228]

Azrin, N. H., & Holz, W. C. Punishment. In W. K. Honig (Ed.), *Operant behavior: Areas of research and application*. New York: Appleton-Century-Crofts, 1966. [231, 235]

Azrin, N. H., Holz, W. C., & Hake, D. F. Fixed-ratio punishment. *Journal of the Experimental Analysis of Behavior*, 1963, *6*, 141–148. [236]

Azrin, N. H., & Huchinson, R. R. Conditioning of the aggressive behavior of pigeons by a fixed-interval schedule of reinforcement. *Journal of the Experimental Analysis of Behavior*, 1967, *10*, 395–402. [364]

Azrin, N. H., Huchinson, R. R., & Hake, D. F. Extinction-induced aggression. *Journal of the Experimental Analysis of Behavior*, 1966, *9*, 191–204. [239]

Azrin, N. H., Huchinson, R. R., & Hake, D. F. Attack, avoidance and escape reactions to aversive shock. *Journal of the Experimental Analysis of Behavior*, 1967, *10*, 131–148. [239]

Azrin, N. H., Huchinson, R. R., & Sallery, R. D. Pain-aggression toward inanimate objects. *Journal of the Experimental Analysis of Behavior*, 1964, *7*, 223–228. [239]

Azzi, R., Fix, D. S. R., Keller, F. S., & Rocha e Silva, M. I. Exteroceptive control of response under delayed reinforcement. *Journal of the Experimental Analysis of Behavior*, 1964, *7*, 159–162. [118]

Baerends, G. P. Fortpflanzungsuerhalten und orientierung der grab-wespe, *Ammphila campestris*. *Tijdschrift Voor Entemologie*, 1941, *84*, 68–275. [346]

Baerends, G. P. The contribution of ethology to the study of the causation of behavior. *Acta Physiologica Pharmacalogia Neerlandia*, 1958, *7*, 466–499. [185]

Baum, M. Extinction of avoidance responses through response prevention (flooding). *Psychological Bulletin*, 1970, *74*, 276–284. [256, 261]

Baum, W., & Rachlin, H. C. Choice as time allocation. *Journal of the Experimental Analysis of Behavior*, 1969, *12*, 861–874. [173]

Bechterev, V. M. *La psychologie objective*. Paris: Alcan, 1913. [25]

Bedford, J., & Anger, D. *Flight as an avoidance response in pigeons*. Paper presented at the Psychonomic Society, St. Louis, 1968. [327]

Beecroft, R. *Classical conditioning*. Goleta, Calif.: Psychonomic Press, 1966. [62]

Bem, D. *Beliefs, attitudes and human affairs*. Belmont, Calif.: Brooks, Cole, 1970. [35]

Bijou, S. W., Birnbrauer, J. S. Kidder, J. D., & Tague, C. Programmed instruction as an approach to teaching of reading, writing, and arithmetic to retarded children. In S. W. Bijou & D. M. Baer (Eds.), *Child development: Readings in experimental analysis*. New York: Appleton-Century-Crofts, 1967. [297]

Bilodeau, E. A. (Ed.). *The acquisition of skill*. New York: Academic Press, 1966. [341]

Blough, D. S., & Blough, P. M. Animal psychophysics. In W. K. Honig & J. E. R. Staddon (Eds.), *Handbook of operant behavior*. Englewood Cliffs, N.J.: Prentice-Hall, 1977. [187, 337]

Bolles, R. C. Species-specific defense reactions and avoidance learning. *Psychological Review*, 1970, *77*, 32–48. [250, 262–265, 327]

Bolles, R. C. *Theory of motivation*. New York: Harper and Row, 1967 (2nd ed., 1975). [113]

Bolles, R. C., Moot, S. A., & Nelson, K. Note on the invariance of response latency in shuttlebox avoidance learning. *Learning and Motivation*, 1976, *7*, 108–116. [242]

Borgealt, A. J., Donahoe, J. W., & Weinstein, A. Effects of delayed and trace components of a compound CS on conditioned suppression and heart rate. *Psychonomic Science,* 1972, *26,* 13–15. [285]

Bower, G. H., McLean, J., & Meachem, J. Value of knowing when reinforcement is due. *Journal of Comparative and Physiological Psychology,* 1966, *62,* 184–192. [286]

Brady, J., & Harris, A. The experimental production of altered states of consciousness: Concurrent and contingent behavioral models. In W. K. Honig & J. E. R. Staddon (Eds.), *Handbook of operant behavior.* Englewood Cliffs, N.J.: Prentice-Hall, 1977. [179]

Breland, K., & Breland, M. The misbehavior of organisms. *American Psychologist,* 1961, *16,* 681–684. [302, 309–312]

Broden, M., Hall, R. V. Dunlap, A., & Clark, R. Effects of teacher attention and a token reinforcement system on study behavior in a junior high school special education class. *Exceptional Children,* 1970, *36,* 341–349. [297]

Brogden, W. J. Sensory pre-conditioning. *Journal of Experimental Psychology,* 1939, *25,* 323–332. [66]

Brown, P., & Jenkins, H. M. Autoshaping of the pigeon's keypeck. *Journal of the Experimental Analysis of Behavior,* 1968, *11,* 1–8. [147, 320]

Brown, R. W. *A first language: The early stages.* Cambridge, Mass.: Harvard University Press, 1973. [368, 369]

Bucher, R., & Lovaas, O. I. Use of aversive stimulation in behavior modification. In M. R. Jones (Ed.), *Miami symposium on the prediction of behavior: Aversive stimulation.* Coral Gables, Fla.: University of Miami Press, 1968. [240]

Bugelski, B. R. Extinction with and without sub-goal reinforcement. *Journal of Comparative Psychology,* 1938, *26,* 121–134. [283]

Bullock, T. H., & Horridge, G. A. *Structure and function in the nervous system of invertebrates.* San Francisco: W. H. Freeman, 1965. [353]

Camp, D. S., Raymond, G. A., & Church, R. M. Temporal relationship between response and punishment. *Journal of Experimental Psychology,* 1967, *74,* 114–123. [228, 230]

Capaldi, E. J. A sequential hypothesis of instrumental learning. In K. W. Spence & J. T. Spence (Eds.), *The psychology of learning and motivation* (Vol. 1). New York: Academic Press, 1967. [178]

Capaldi, E. J. Memory and learning: A sequential viewpoint. In W. K. Honig & P H. R. James (Eds.), *Animal memory.* New York: Academic Press, 1971. [178]

Catania, A. C. Concurrent performances: A baseline for the study of reinforcement magnitude. *Journal of the Experimental Analysis of Behavior,* 1963, *6,* 299–301. [172, 241]

Catania, A. C. Concurrent operants. In W. K. Honig (Ed.), *Operant behavior: Areas of research and application.* New York: Appleton-Century-Crofts, 1966. [172, 173]

Catania, A. C. Reinforcement schedules and psychophysical judgment: A study of some temporal properties of behavior. In W. N. Schoenfeld (Ed.), *The theory of reinforcement schedules.* New York: Appleton-Century-Crofts, 1972. [162]

Catania, A. C., & Cutts, D. Experimental control of superstitious responding in humans. *Journal of the Experimental Analysis of Behavior*, 1963, *6*, 203–208. [122]

Catania, A. C., & Reynolds, G. S. A quantitative analysis of the responding maintained by interval schedules of reinforcement. *Journal of the Experimental Analysis of Behavior*, 1968, *11*, 327–383. [163]

Cautela, J. R. The problem of backward conditioning. *Journal of Psychology*, 1965, *60*, 135–144. [81]

Chomsky, N. *Syntactic structures*. The Hague: Mouton, 1957. [288]

Chomsky, N. Review of Skinner's *Verbal behavior*. *Language*, 1959, *35*, 26–58. [114, 140, 288, 370]

Chomsky, N. *Reflections on language*. New York: Pantheon, 1975. [114, 335, 366]

Chung, S. H., & Herrnstein, R. J. Choice and delay of reinforcement. *Journal of the Experimental Analysis of Behavior*, 1967, *10*, 67–74. [172]

Church, R. M. Response suppression. In B. A. Campbell & R. M. Church (Eds.), *Punishment and aversive behavior*. New York: Appleton-Century-Crofts, 1969. [230, 231]

Church, R. M., Wooten, C. L., & Matthews, T. J. Discriminative punishment and the conditioned emotional response. *Learning and Motivation*, 1970, *1*, 1–17. [234, 238]

Cowles, J. T. Food-tokens as incentive for learning by chimpanzees. *Comparative Psychology Monographs*, 1937, *14*, No. 5. [294]

Craig, W. Appetites and aversions as constituents of instincts. *Biological Bulletin of Woods Hole*, 1918, *34*, 91–107. [358]

Darwin, C. *The origin of species*. 1859. [20, 136]

Davenport, D. G., & Olson, R. D. A reinterpretation of extinction in discriminated avoidance. *Psychonomic Science*, 1968, *13*, 5–6. [256]

Denny, M. R. Relaxation theory and experiments. In F. R. Brush (Ed.), *Aversive conditioning and learning*. New York: Academic Press, 1971. [249]

Deutsch, R. Conditioned hypoglycemia: A mechanism for saccharin-induced sensitivity to insulin in the rat. *Journal of Comparative and Physiological Psychology*, 1974, *86*, 350–358. [98]

de Villiers, P. A. The law of effect and avoidance: A quantitative relation between response rate and shock frequency reduction. *Journal of the Experimental Analysis of Behavior*, 1974, *21*, 223–235. [172]

de Villiers, P. A. Choice in concurrent schedules and a quantitative formulation of the law of effect. In W. K. Honig & J. E. R. Staddon (Eds.), *Handbook of operant behavior*. Englewood Cliffs, N.J.: Prentice-Hall, 1977. [173]

Dews, P. B. Behavioral effects of drugs. In S. M. Farber & R. H. C. Wilson (Eds.), *Conflict and creativity*. New York: McGraw-Hill, 1963. [179, 180]

Dinsmoor, J. A., Flint, G. A., Smith, R. F., & Viemeister, N. F. Differential reinforcing effects of stimuli associated with the presence or absence of a schedule of punishment. In D. P. Hendry (Ed.), *Conditioned reinforcement*. Homeward, Ill.: The Dorsey Press, 1969. [286]

Ebbinghaus, H. *Memory: A contribution to experimental psychology*. Translated by H. A. Ruger and C. E. Bussenius. New York: Columbia University Press, 1913. [23]

Egger, M. D., & Miller, N. E. Secondary reinforcement in rats as a function of information value and reliability of the stimulus. *Journal of Experimental Psychology*, 1962, *64*, 97–104. [283–285]

Egger, M. D., & Miller, N. E. When is a reward reinforcing? An experimental study of the information hypothesis. *Journal of Comparative and Physiological Psychology*, 1963, *56*, 132–137. [285]

Eibl-Eibesfeldt, I. *Ethology: The biology of behavior*. New York: Holt, Rinehart and Winston, 1970. [346, 349, 350, 353, 354, 361, 365]

Eimas, P., Siqueland, E., Juscyk, P., & Vigorito, J. Speech perception in infants. *Science*, 1971, *171*, 303–306. [367]

Estes, W. K., & Skinner, B. F. Some quantitative properties of anxiety. *Journal of Experimental Psychology*, 1941, *29*, 390–400. [102, 224, 226]

Fantino, E. Choice and rate of reinforcement. *Journal of the Experimental Analysis of Behavior*, 1969, *12*, 723–730. [293]

Fantino, E. Aversive control. In J. A. Nevin (Ed.), *The study of behavior*. Glenview, Ill.: Scott, Foresman, 1973. [228, 231, 241]

Farthing, G. W. Effect of a signal previously paired with free food on operant response rate in pigeons. *Psychonomic Science*, 1971, *23*, 343–344. [273]

Felton, M., & Lyon, D. O. The post-reinforcement pause. *Journal of the Experimental Analysis of Behavior*, 1966, *9*, 131–134. [162]

Ferster, C. B., & Skinner, B. F. *Schedules of reinforcement*. New York: Appleton-Century-Crofts, 1957. [152, 165, 287]

Findley, J. D. Preference and switching under concurrent schedules. *Journal of the Experimental Analysis of Behavior*, 1958, *1*, 123–144. [173]

Flanagan, B., & Webb, W. B. Disinhibition and external inhibition in fixed interval operant conditioning. *Psychonomic Science*, 1964, *1*, 123–124. [162]

Flavell, J. H. *The developmental psychology of Jean Piaget*. Princeton, N.J.: Von Nostrand, 1963. [377]

Fodor, J. A., Bever, T. G., & Garrett, M. F. *The psychology of language*. New York: McGraw-Hill, 1974. [368]

Foree, D., & LoLordo, V. M. Attention in the pigeon: The differential effect of food getting vs. shock avoidance procedures. *Journal of Comparative and Physiological Psychology*, 1973, *85*, 551–558. [328, 329]

Foree, D., & LoLordo, V. M. Stimulus-reinforcer interactions in the pigeon: The role of electric shock and the avoidance contingency. *Journal of Experimental Psychology: Animal Behavior Processes*, 1975, *104*, 39–46. [328]

Gamzu, E. *Associative and instrumental factors underlying the performance of a complex skeletal response*. Unpublished doctoral dissertation, University of Pennsylvania, 1971. [324]

Gamzu, E., & Schwartz, B. The maintenance of key pecking by stimulus-contingent and response-independent food presentation. *Journal of the Experimental Analysis of Behavior*, 1973, *19*, 65–72. [277]

Gamzu, E., & Williams, D. R. Classical conditioning of a complex skeletal act. *Science*, 1971, *171*, 923–925. [148, 322]

Gamzu, E., & Williams, D. R. Associative factors underlying the pigeon's key pecking in autoshaping procedures. *Journal of the Experimental Analysis of Behavior*, 1973, *19*, 225–232. [322]

Garcia, J., Kimmeldorf, D. J., & Hunt, E. L. The use of ionizing radiation as a motivating stimulus. *Psychological Review,* 1961, *68,* 383–385. [312]

Garcia, J., & Koelling, R. A. The relation of cue to consequence in avoidance learning. *Psychonomic Science,* 1966, *4,* 123–124. [315–316]

Gardner, R. A., & Gardner, B. T. Teaching sign language to a chimpanzee. *Science,* 1969, *165,* 664–672. [374]

Gentry, W. D. Fixed-ratio schedule-induced aggression. *Journal of the Experimental Analysis of Behavior,* 1968, *11,* 813–817. [239]

Gibson, E. *Principles of perceptual learning and development.* New York: Appleton-Century-Crofts, 1970. [186]

Glass, A. V., Gazzaniga, M. S., & Premack, D. Artificial language training in global aphasics. *Neuropsychologia,* 1973, *11,* 95–104. [374]

Glazer, H. I., & Weiss, J. M. Long term interference effect: An alternative to learned helplessness. *Journal of Experimental Psychology: Animal Behavior Processes.* 1976, *2,* 202–213.(a) [144]

Glazer, H. I., & Weiss, J. M. Long term and transitory interference effects. *Journal of Experimental Psychology: Animal Behavior Processes.* 1976, *2,* 191–201.(b) [144]

Gleitman, L. R., & Rozin, P. Teaching reading by use of a syllabary. *Reading Research Quarterly,* 1973, *8,* 447–483. [379]

Goldstein, H., Krantz, D. L., & Rains, J. D. (Eds.). *Controversial issues in learning.* New York: Appleton-Century-Crofts, 1965. [29]

Gonzalez, R. C., Gentry, G. V., & Bitterman, M. E. Relational discrimination of intermediate size in the chimpanzee. *Journal of Comparative and Physiological Psychology,* 1954, *47,* 385–388. [215]

Goocher, B. E., & Ebner, M. *A behavior modification approach utilizing sequential response targets in multiple settings.* Paper presented at the Midwestern Psychological Association meetings, Chicago, 1968. [217]

Gray, P. H. Theory and evidence of imprinting in human infants. *Journal of Psychology,* 1958, *46,* 155–160. [363]

Guthrie, E. R. *The psychology of learning.* New York: Harper and Row, 1935. [29]

Guthrie, E. R. Association by contiguity. In S. Koch (Ed.), *Psychology: A study of a science* (Vol. 2): *General Systematic Formulations, Learning and Special Processes.* New York: McGraw-Hill, 1959. [29]

Guthrie, E. R., & Horton, G. P. *Cats in a puzzle box.* New York: Holt, Rinehart and Winston, 1946. [135, 343]

Gutman, A., Sutterer, J. R., & Brush, R. Positive and negative behavioral contrast in the rat. *Journal of the Experimental Analysis of Behavior,* 1975, *23,* 377–384. [280]

Hanson, H. M. Effects of discrimination training on stimulus generalization. *Journal of Experimental Psychology,* 1959, *58,* 321–334. [210]

Hearst, E. Stress induced breakdown of an appetitive discrimination. *Journal of the Experimental Analysis of Behavior,* 1965, *18,* 135–146. [238]

Hearst, E., & Jenkins, H. M. *Sign-tracking: The stimulus-reinforcer relation and directed action.* Austin, Texas: Psychonomic Society, 1974. [148, 321, 328]

Hemmes, N. S. Behavioral contrast in the pigeon depends upon the operant.

Journal of Comparative and Physiological Psychology, 1973, *85,* 171–178. [279, 280]

Henderson, J. D. The use of dual reinforcement in an intensive treatment system. In R. D. Rubin & C. M. Franks (Eds.), *Advances in behavior therapy 1968.* New York: Academic Press, 1969. [295]

Hendry, D. P. (Ed.). *Conditioned reinforcement.* Homeward, Ill.: The Dorsey Press, 1969.(a) [285]

Hendry, D. P. Reinforcing value of information: Fixed-ratio schedules. In D. P. Hendry (Ed.), *Conditioned reinforcement.* Homeward, Ill.: The Dorsey Press, 1969.(b) [286]

Herman, R. L., & Azrin, N. H. Punishment by noise in an alternative response situation. *Journal of the Experimental Analysis of Behavior,* 1964, *7,* 185–188. [231]

Herrick, R. M. The successive differentiation of a lever displacement response. *Journal of the Experimental Analysis of Behavior,* 1964, *7,* 211–215. [342]

Herrnstein, R. J. Secondary reinforcement and the rate of primary reinforcement. *Journal of the Experimental Analysis of Behavior,* 1964, *7,* 27–36. [292]

Herrnstein, R. J. Superstition. In W. K. Honig (Ed.), *Operant behavior: Areas of research and appplication.* New York: Appleton-Century-Crofts, 1966. [120]

Herrnstein, R. J. Method and theory in the study of avoidance. *Psychological Review,* 1969, *76,* 49–69. [257]

Herrnstein, R. J. On the law of effect. *Journal of the Experimental Analysis of Behavior,* 1970, *13,* 243–266. [163, 171]

Herrnstein, R. J. Nature as nurture: Behaviorism and the instinct doctrine. *Behaviorism,* 1974, *1,* 23–52. [304]

Herrnstein, R. J., & Boring, E. G. *A source book in the history of psychology.* Cambridge, Mass.: Harvard University Press, 1965. [19]

Herrnstein, R. J., & Hineline, P. N. Negative reinforcement as shock frequency reduction. *Journal of the Experimental Analysis of Behavior,* 1966, *9,* 421–430. [253, 257, 258]

Herrnstein, R. J., & Morse, W. H. A conjunctive schedule of reinforcement. *Journal of the Experimental Analysis of Behavior,* 1958, *1,* 15–24. [160]

Heth, C. D. Simultaneous and backward fear conditioning as a function of number of CS–UCS pairings. *Journal of Experimental Psychology: Animal Behavior Processes,* 1976, *2,* 117–129. [81]

Heth, C. D., & Rescorla, R. A. Simultaneous and backward fear conditioning in the rat. *Journal of Comparative and Physiological Psychology,* 1973, *82,* 434–443. [81]

Hilgard, E. R., & Marquis, D. G. *Conditioning and learning.* New York: Appleton-Century-Crofts, 1940. [259]

Hinde, R. A. *Animal behavior: A synthesis of ethology and comparative psychology.* New York: McGraw-Hill, 1970. [349]

Hinde, R. A., & Hinde, J. S. (Eds.). *Constraints on learning.* New York: Academic Press, 1973. [334]

Hineline, P. N., & Rachlin, H. Escape and avoidance of shock by pigeons pecking a key. *Journal of the Experimental Analysis of Behavior,* 1969, *12,* 533–538. [250, 327]

Hinrichs, J. V. Disinhibition of delay in fixed interval instrumental conditioning. *Psychonomic Science,* 1968, *12,* 313–314. [162]

Hobbes, T. *Leviathan,* 1651. [16]

Hoffman, H. S. Stimulus factors in conditioned suppression. In B. A. Campbell & R. M. Church (Eds.), *Punishment and aversive behavior.* New York: Appleton-Century-Crofts, 1969. [225]

Hoffman, H. S., & Ratner, A. M. A reinforcement model of imprinting. *Psychological Review,* 1973, *80,* 527–544. [362]

Huchinson, R. R., Azrin, N. H., & Hunt, G. M. Attack produced by intermittent reinforcement of a concurrent response. *Journal of the Experimental Analysis of Behavior,* 1968, *11,* 489–495. [239]

Hull, C. L. *Principles of behavior.* New York: Appleton-Century-Crofts, 1943. [16, 29, 207]

Hull, C. L. *A behavior system.* New Haven, Conn.: Yale University Press, 1952. [16, 199, 207, 288]

Hume, D. *Treatise of human nature.* 1739. [17]

Irwin, F. W. *Intentional behavior and motivation: A cognitive theory.* New York: Lippincott, 1971. [259, 261]

James, W. What is an emotion? *Mind,* 1884, *9,* 188–205. [35]

Jenkins, H. M. Generalization gradients and the concept of inhibition. In D. I. Mostofsky (Ed.), *Stimulus generalization.* Stanford, Calif.: Stanford University Press, 1965. [207]

Jenkins, H. M. Sequential organization in schedules of reinforcement. In W. N. Schoenfeld (Ed.), *The theory of reinforcement schedules.* New York: Appleton-Century-Crofts, 1970. [180]

Jenkins, H. M., & Harrison, R. H. Effects of discrimination training on auditory generalization. *Journal of Experimental Psychology,* 1960, *59,* 246–253. [199]

Jenkins, H. M., & Harrison, R. H. Generalization gradients of inhibition following auditory discrimination learning. *Journal of the Experimental Analysis of Behavior,* 1962, *5,* 435–441. [199]

Jenkins, H. M., & Moore, B. R. The form of the autoshaped response with food or water reinforcers. *Journal of the Experimental Analysis of Behavior,* 1973, *20,* 163–181. [148, 320]

Kamin, L. J. Effects of termination of the CS and avoidance of the US on avoidance learning. *Journal of Comparative and Physiological Psychology,* 1956, *49,* 420–424. [241]

Kamin, L. J. Predictability, surprise, attention and conditioning. In B. A. Campbell & R. M. Church (Eds.), *Punishment and aversive behavior.* New York: Appleton-Century-Crofts, 1969. [57, 90, 225, 334]

Kamin, L. J., Brimer, C. J., & Black, A. H. Conditioned suppression as a monitor of fear of the CS in the course of avoidance training. *Journal of Comparative and Physiological Psychology,* 1963, *56,* 497–501. [254]

Kazdin, A., & Polster, R. Intermittent token reinforcement and response maintenance in extinction. *Behavior Therapy,* 1973, *4,* 386–391. [179]

Kelleher, R. T. A multiple schedule of conditioned reinforcement with chimpanzees. *Psychological Reports,* 1957, *3,* 485–491. [294]

Kelleher, R. T. Fixed-ratio schedules of conditioned reinforcement with chimpanzees. *Journal of the Experimental Analysis of Behavior,* 1958, *1,* 281–289. [294]

Kelleher, R. T. Conditioned reinforcement in second order schedules. *Journal of the Experimental Analysis of Behavior,* 1966, *9,* 475–485. [289]

Kelley, H. Attribution theory. In M. R. Jones (Ed.), *Nebraska symposium on motivation.* Lincoln: University of Nebraska Press, 1967. [137]

Kello, J. E. The reinforcement-omission effect on fixed-interval schedules: Frustration or inhibition? *Learning and Motivation,* 1972, *3,* 138–147. [162]

Kemler, D. G., & Shepp, B. E. Learning and transfer of dimensional relevance and irrelevance in children. *Journal of Experimental Psychology,* 1971, *90,* 120–127. [205]

Kendler, H. H., & D'Amato, M. F. A comparison of reversal shifts and nonreversal shifts in human concept formation. *Journal of Experimental Psychology,* 1955, *49,* 165–174. [205]

Kendler, H. H., & Kendler, T. S. Vertical and horizontal processes in problem solving. *Psychological Review,* 1962, *69,* 1–16. [205]

Killeen, P. Reinforcement frequency and contingency as factors in fixed ratio behavior. *Journal of the Experimental Analysis of Behavior,* 1969, *12,* 391–395. [162]

Killeen, P. Preference for fixed-interval schedules of reinforcement. *Journal of the Experimental Analysis of Behavior,* 1970, *14,* 127–131. [292]

Kimble, G. A. *Hilgard and Marquis' conditioning and learning.* New York: Appleton-Century-Crofts, 1961. [145]

Köhler, W. *Gestalt psychology.* New York: Liveright, 1929. [29]

Köhler, W. Simple structural functions in the chimpanzee and the chicken. In W. D. Ellis (Ed.), *A source book of gestalt psychology.* New York: Harcourt Brace, 1939. [211–212]

Konorski, J. *Conditioned reflexes and neuron organization.* Cambridge: Cambridge University Press, 1948. [69]

Konorski, J. *Integrative activity of the brain.* Chicago: University of Chicago Press, 1967. [267, 271]

Kuhn, T. S. *The structure of scientific revolutions.* Chicago: University of Chicago Press, 1962. [301, 337]

Lashley, K. The problem of serial order in behavior. In L. A. Jeffries (Ed.), *Cerebral mechanisms in behavior.* New York: John Wiley and Sons, 1951. [288]

Lawrence, D. H. Acquired distinctiveness of cues, I: Transfer between discriminations on the basis of familiarity with the stimulus. *Journal of Experimental Psychology,* 1949, *39,* 770–784. [194]

Lawrence, D. H. Acquired distinctiveness of cues, II: Selective association in a constant stimulus situation. *Journal of Experimental Psychology,* 1950, *40,* 185–188. [194]

Lawrence, D. H., & DeRivera, J. Evidence for relational transposition. *Journal of Comparative and Physiological Psychology,* 1954, *47,* 465–471. [215–216]

Leaton, R. N., & Tighe, T. (Eds.). *Habituation: Perspectives from child development, animal behavior and neurophysiology.* Hillsdale, N.J.: Erlbaum, 1976. [56]

Lehrman, D. S. The physiological basis of parental feeding behavior in the ring dove (*Streptopelia risona*). *Behaviour,* 1955, *7,* 241–286. [357]

Lehrman, D. S. The presence of the mate and of nesting material as stimuli for the development of incubation behavior and for gonadotrophic secretion in the ring dove. *Endocrinology,* 1961, *68,* 507–516. [357]

Leitenberg, H. Is time-out from positive reinforcement an aversive event? A review of the experimental evidence. *Psychological Bulletin,* 1965, *64,* 428–441. [232]

Lenneberg, E. H. *Biological foundations of language.* New York: Wiley, 1967. [367, 368]

Lepper, M. R., Greene, D., & Nisbett, R. E. Undermining children's intrinsic interest with extrinsic rewards: A test of the "overjustification" hypothesis. *Journal of Personality and Social Psychology,* 1973, *28,* 129–137. [299]

Levine, F. M., & Fasnacht, G. Token rewards may lead to token learning. *American Psychologist,* 1974, *29,* 816–820. [298]

Liberman, A. M. The grammars of speech and language. *Cognitive Psychology,* 1970, *1,* 301–323. [399]

Liberman, A. M., Cooper, F. S., Shankweiler, D. P., & Studdert-Kennedy, M. Perception of the speech code. *Psychological Review,* 1967, *74,* 431–461. [379]

Locke, J. *An essay concerning human understanding,* 1690. [359]

LoLordo, V. M. Similarity of conditioned fear responses based upon different aversive events. *Journal of Comparative and Physiological Psychology,* 1967, *64,* 154–158. [271]

LoLordo, V. M. Facilitation of food reinforced responding by a signal for response-independent food. *Journal of the Experimental Analysis of Behavior,* 1971, *15,* 49–56. [272]

LoLordo, V. M., McMillan, J. C., & Riley, A. L. The effects upon food reinforced pecking and treadle pressing of auditory and visual signals for response-independent food. *Learning and Motivation,* 1974, *5,* 24–41. [273]

LoLordo, V. M., & Rescorla, R. A. Protection of the fear-eliciting capacity of a stimulus from extinction. *Acta Biologiae Experimentalis,* 1966, *26,* 251–258. [75]

Lorenz, K. The companion in the bird's world. *Auk,* 1937, *54,* 245–273. [362]

Lorenz, K. *Evolution and the modification of behavior.* Chicago: University of Chicago Press, 1965. [360]

Lorenz, K., & Tinbergen, N. Taxis and instinctive action in the egg-retrieving behavior of the greylag goose. In C. H. Schiller (Ed.), *Instinctive behavior.* New York: International Universities Press, 1957. [351]

Lovaas, O. I., & Simmons, J. Q. Manipulation of self-destruction in three retarded children. *Journal of Applied Behavior Analysis,* 1969, *2,* 49–53. [218, 240]

Lovejoy, E. *Attention in discrimination learning.* San Francisco: Holden-Day, 1968. [202]

Lyon, D. O. Some notes on conditioned suppression and reinforcement schedules. *Journal of the Experimental Analysis of Behavior,* 1964, *7,* 289–291. [227]

Lyon, D. O., & Felton, M. Conditioned suppression and variable ratio reinforcement. *Journal of the Experimental Analysis of Behavior,* 1966, *9,* 245–248. [226]

MacCorquodale, K., & Meehl, P. E. On a distinction between hypothetical constructs and intervening variables. *Psychological Review,* 1948, *55,* 95–107. [34]

Mackintosh, N. J. Stimulus selection: Learning to ignore stimuli that predict no change in reinforcement. In R. A. Hinde & J. S. Hinde (Eds.), *Constraints on learning.* London: Academic Press, 1973. [205]

Mackintosh, N. J. *The psychology of animal learning.* New York: Academic Press, 1974. [66, 178, 180, 199, 248, 279]

Mackintosh, N. J. A theory of attention. *Psychological Review,* 1975, *82,* 276–298. [202, 205]

Mackintosh, N. J. Stimulus control: Attentional factors. In W. K. Honig & J. E. R. Staddon (Eds.), *Handbook of operant behavior.* Englewood Cliffs, N. J.: Prentice-Hall, 1977. [192, 199]

Mackintosh, N. J., & Little, L. Intradimensional and extradimensional shift learning by pigeons. *Psychonomic Science,* 1969, *14,* 5–6. [205]

MacPhail, E. M. Avoidance responding in pigeons. *Journal of the Experimental Analysis of Behavior,* 1968, *11,* 625–632. [327]

Maier, S. F. Failure to escape traumatic shock: Incompatible skeletal motor responses or learned helplessness? *Learning and Motivation,* 1970, *1,* 157–170. [128]

Maier, S. F., & Seligman, M. E. P. Learned helplessness: Theory and evidence. *Journal of Experimental Psychology: General,* 1976, *105,* 3–46. [125–129]

Marler, P. A comparative approach to vocal learning: Song development in white-crowned sparrows. *Journal of Comparative and Physiological Psychology,* 1970, *71,* 1–25. [361]

McAllister, W. R., & McAllister, D. E. Post conditioning delay and intensity of shock as factors in the measurement of acquired fear. *Journal of Experimental Psychology,* 1962, *64,* 110–116. [252]

McAllister, W. R., & McAllister, D. E. Behavioral measurement of conditioned fear. In F. R. Brush (Ed.), *Aversive conditioning and learning.* New York: Academic Press, 1971. [249]

McGrew, W. C. *An ethological study of children's behavior.* New York: Academic Press, 1972. [365]

Meehl, P. E. On the circularity of the law of effect. *Psychological Bulletin,* 1950, *47,* 52–75. [112, 114]

Meichenbaum, D. H., Bowers, K. S., & Ross, R. R. Modification of classroom behavior of institutionalized female adolescent offenders. *Behavior Research and Therapy,* 1968, *6,* 343–353. [299]

Miller, N. E. Studies of fear as an acquirable drive. *Journal of Experimental Psychology,* 1948, *38,* 89–101. [250, 252]

Miller, N. E. Liberalizations of basic S–R concepts: Extensions to conflict behavior, motivation and social learning. In S. Koch (Ed.), *Psychology, a study of a science* (Vol. 2). New York: McGraw-Hill, 1959. [34]

Miller, N. E. Learning of visceral and glandular responses. *Science,* 1969, *163,* 434–445. [147]

Miller, N. E., & Carmona, A. Modification of a visceral response, salivation in thirsty dogs, by instrumental training with water reward. *Journal of Comparative and Physiological Psychology,* 1967, *63,* 1–6. [147]

Moore, J. W. Stimulus control: Studies of auditory generalization in rabbits. In A. H. Black & W. F. Prokasy (Eds.), *Classical conditioning II*. New York: Appleton-Century-Crofts, 1972. [78]

Morse, W. H. Intermittent reinforcement. In W. K. Honig (Ed.), *Operant behavior: Areas of research and application*. New York: Appleton-Century-Crofts, 1966. [168, 169]

Moscovitch, A., & LoLordo, V. M. Role of safety in the Pavlovian backward fear conditioning procedure. *Journal of Comparative and Physiological Psychology*, 1968, *66*, 673–678. [81]

Mowrer, O. H. On the dual nature of learning—A reinterpretation of "conditioning" and "problem solving." *Harvard Educational Review*, 1947, *17*, 102–148. [250]

Mowrer, O. H., & Lamoreaux, R. R. Fear as an intervening variable in avoidance conditioning. *Journal of Comparative Psychology*, 1946, *369*, 29–50. [249]

Neuringer, A. J. Effects of reinforcement magnitude on choice and rate of responding. *Journal of the Experimental Analysis of Behavior*, 1967, *10*, 417–424. [292]

Newman, F. L., & Baron, M. R. Stimulus generalization along the dimension of angularity. *Journal of Comparative and Physiological Psychology*, 1965, *60*, 59–63. [195–197]

Notterman, J. M. Force emission during bar pressing. *Journal of Experimental Psychology*, 1959, *58*, 341–347. [343]

Notterman, J. M., & Mintz, D. E. *Dynamics of response*. New York: Wiley, 1965. [343]

Obrist, P. A., Sutterer, J. R., & Howard, J. L. Preparatory cardiac changes: A psychobiological approach. In A. H. Black & W. F. Prokasy (Eds.), *Classical conditioning II*. New York: Appleton-Century-Crofts, 1972. [97]

O'Leary, K. D., Becker, W. C., Evans, M. B., & Saudargas, R. A. A token reinforcement system in a public school: A replication and systematic analysis. *Journal of Applied Behavior Analysis*, 1969, *2*, 3–13. [297]

O'Leary, K. D., & Drabman, R. Token reinforcement programs in the classroom: A review. *Psychological Bulletin*, 1971, *75*, 379–398. [10]

Pavlov, I. *Conditioned reflexes*. Oxford: Oxford University Press, 1927. [29–30, 40–42, 99]

Pavlov, I. *Lectures on conditioned reflexes: The higher nervous activity of animals* (Vol. 1) (translated by H. Gantt). London: Lawrence and Wishart, 1928. [101]

Peiper, A. *Cerebral function in infancy and childhood*. New York: Consultants Bureau, 1963. [71]

Peters, R. S., & Tajfel, H. Hobbes and Hull—Metaphysicians of behavior. *British Journal for the Philosophy of Science*, 1957, *8*, 47–65. [16]

Peterson, G. B., Ackil, J., Frommer, G. P., & Hearst, E. Conditioned approach and contact behavior toward signals for food or brain-stimulation reinforcement. *Science*, 1972, *177*, 1009–1011. [321]

Piaget, J. *The origins of intelligence in children*. New York: International Universities Press, 1951. [130]

Popper, K. R. *The logic of scientific discovery*. London: Huchinson, 1959. [32]

Premack, D. Toward empirical behavior laws: I. Positive reinforcement. *Psychological Review*, 1959, *66*, 219–233. [113]

Premack, D. Reversibility of the reinforcement relation. *Science,* 1962, *136,* 235–237. [113]

Premack, D. Reinforcement theory. In D. Levine (Ed.), *Nebraska symposium on motivation.* Lincoln: University of Nebraska Press, 1965. [113]

Premack, D. Language in chimpanzee? *Science,* 1971, *172,* 808–822. [374]

Prewitt, E. P. Number of preconditioning trials in sensory preconditioning using CER training. *Journal of Comparative and Physiological Psychology,* 1967, *64,* 360–362. [66]

Rachlin, H. Contrast and matching. *Psychological Review,* 1973, *80,* 217–234. [279]

Rachlin, H. *Introduction to modern behaviorism.* San Francisco: W. H. Freeman, 1976. [19]

Rachlin, H., & Green, L. Commitment, choice and self-control. *Journal of the Experimental Analysis of Behavior,* 1972, *17,* 15–22. [173–177]

Rachlin, H., & Herrnstein, R. J. Hedonism revisited: On the negative law of effect. In B. A. Campbell & R. M. Church (Eds.), *Punishment and aversive behavior.* New York: Appleton-Century-Crofts, 1969. [257]

Rackham, D. *Conditioning of the pigeon's courtship and aggressive behavior.* Unpublished master's thesis, Dalhousie University, 1971. (Cited in E. Hearst & H. M. Jenkins, *Sign-tracking: The stimulus-reinforcer relation and directed action.* Austin, Texas: The Psychonomic Society, 1974.) [320]

Rajecki, D. W. Imprinting in the precocial birds: Interpretation, evidence and evaluation. *Psychological Bulletin,* 1973, *79,* 48–58. [362]

Rescorla, R. A. Pavlovian conditioning and its proper control procedures. *Psychological Review,* 1967, *74,* 71–80. (a) [83–88]

Rescorla, R. A. Inhibition of delay in Pavlovian fear conditioning. *Journal of Comparative and Physiological Psychology,* 1967, *64,* 114–120. (b) [75, 252]

Rescorla, R. A. Pavlovian conditioned fear in Sidman avoidance learning. *Journal of Comparative and Physiological Psychology,* 1968, *65,* 55–60. [75]

Rescorla, R. A. Pavlovian conditioned inhibition. *Psychological Bulletin,* 1969, *72,* 77–94. [72, 77, 80]

Rescorla, R. A., & LoLordo, V. M. Inhibition of avoidance behavior. *Journal of Comparative and Physiological Psychology,* 1965, *59,* 406–412. [252, 270]

Rescorla, R. A., & Solomon, R. L. Two-process learning theory: Relations between Pavlovian conditioning and instrumental learning. *Psychological Review,* 1967, *74,* 151–182. [250, 257, 271]

Rescorla, R. A., & Wagner, A. R. A theory of Pavlovian conditioning: Variations in the effectiveness of reinforcement and non-reinforcement. In A. H. Black & W. F. Prokasy (Eds.), *Classical conditioning II.* New York: Appleton-Century-Crofts, 1972. [57, 60, 92–96, 103]

Revusky, S. H., & Bedarf, E. W. Association of illness with prior ingestion of novel foods. *Science,* 1967, *155,* 219–220. [317]

Revusky, S. H., & Garcia, J. Learned associations over long delays. In G. H. Bower & J. T. Spence (Eds.), *The psychology of learning and motivation: IV.* New York: Academic Press, 1970. [312, 313]

Reynolds, G. S. Behavioral contrast. *Journal of the Experimental Analysis of Behavior,* 1961, *4,* 57–71. (a) [131, 279]

Reynolds, G. S. Attention in the pigeon. *Journal of the Experimental Analysis of Behavior*, 1961, *4*, 203–208. (b) [201]

Reynolds, G. S. *A primer of operant conditioning.* Glenview, Ill.: Scott-Foresman, 1968. [180]

Reynolds, G. S., Catania, A. C., & Skinner, B. F. Conditioned and unconditioned aggression in pigeons. *Journal of the Experimental Analysis of Behavior*, 1963, *6*, 73–74. [364]

Richie, B. F. Can reinforcment theory account for avoidance? *Psychological Review*, 1951, *58*, 382–386. [259]

Richter, C. P. Experimentally produced behavior reactions to food poisoning in wild and domesticated rats. *Annals of the New York Academy of Sciences*, 1953, *56*, 225–239. [312]

Riley, D. A. *Discrimination learning.* Boston: Allyn and Bacon, 1968. [213]

Rilling, M. Stimulus control and inhibitory processes. In W. K. Honig & J. E. R. Staddon (Eds.), *Handbook of operant behavior.* Englewood Cliffs, N.J.: Prentice-Hall, 1977. [240]

Rizley, R. C., & Rescorla, R. A. Associations in higher order conditioning and sensory preconditioning. *Journal of Comparative and Physiological Psychology*, 1972, *81*, 1–11. [69, 289]

Roeder, K. D. *Nerve cells and insect behavior.* Cambridge, Mass.: Harvard University Press, 1963. [353]

Ross, R., Meichenbaum, D., & Bowers, K. *A brief summary of a case history of a correctional institution: Innovative treatment programs for delinquents.* Unpublished manuscript, University of Waterloo, 1974. [299]

Rozin, P. The evolution of intelligence and access to the cognitive unconscious. In E. Stellar & J. M. Sprague (Eds.), *Progress in psychobiology and physiological psychology* (Vol. 6). New York: Academic Press, 1976. [376–380]

Rozin, P., & Kalat, J. W. Specific hungers and poison avoidance as adaptive specializations of learning. *Psychological Review*, 1971, *78*, 459–486. [312]

Rudolph, R. L., & Van Houten, R. Auditory stimulus control in pigeons: Jenkins and Harrison (1960) revisited. *Journal of the Experimental Analysis of Behavior*, 1977, *27*, 327–330. [194]

Rzoska, J. Bait shyness, a study in rat behavior. *British Journal of Animal Behavior*, 1953, *1*, 128–135. [312]

Satinoff, E., & Henderson, R. Thermoregulatory behavior. In W. K. Honig & J. E. R. Staddon (Eds.), *Handbook of operant behavior.* Englewood Cliffs, N.J.: Prentice-Hall, 1977. [179]

Schachter, S., & Singer, J. Cognitive, social and physiological determinants of an emotional state. *Psychological Review*, 1962, *69*, 374–399. [35]

Schick, K. Operants. *Journal of the Experimental Analysis of Behavior*, 1971, *15*, 413–423. [110]

Schmidt, R. A. *Motor skills.* New York: Harper and Row, 1975. (a) [341]

Schmidt, R. A. A schema theory of discrete motor skill learning. *Psychological Review*, 1975, *82*, 225–260. (b) [341]

Schneiderman, N. *Classical (Pavlovian) conditioning.* Morristown, N.J.: General Learning Press, 1973. [59]

Schneiderman, N., Fuentes, I., & Gormezano, I. Acquisition and extinction of the classically conditioned eyelid response in the albino rabbit. *Science,* 1962, *136,* 650–652. [59]

Schwartz, B. Maintenance of keypecking in pigeons by a food avoidance but not a shock avoidance contingency. *Animal Learning and Behavior,* 1973, *1,* 164–166. [250, 327]

Schwartz, B. Behavioral contrast in the pigeon depends upon the location of the stimulus. *Bulletin of the Psychonomic Society,* 1974, *3,* 365–368. (a) [280]

Schwartz, B. On going back to nature: A review of Seligman and Hager's *Biological boundaries of learning. Journal of the Experimental Analysis of Behavior,* 1974, *21,* 183–198. (b) [315, 317, 330]

Schwartz, B. Positive and negative conditioned suppression in the pigeon: Effects of the locus and modality of the CS. *Learning and Motivation,* 1976, *7,* 86–100. [272–274]

Schwartz, B. Studies of operant and reflexive key pecks in the pigeon. *Journal of the Experimental Analysis of Behavior,* 1977, *27,* 301–313. (a) [324]

Schwartz, B. Two types of pigeon key pecking: Suppression of long but not short duration key pecks by duration-dependent shock. *Journal of the Experimental Analysis of Behavior,* 1977, *27,* 393–398. (b) [324]

Schwartz, B., & Gamzu, E. Pavlovian control of operant behavior. In W. K. Honig & J. E. R. Staddon (Eds.), *Handbook of operant behavior.* Englewood Cliffs, N.J.: Prentice-Hall, 1977. [148, 279, 321, 325]

Schwartz, B., Hamilton, B., & Silberberg. A. Behavioral contrast in the pigeon: A study of the duration of key pecking maintained on multiple schedules of reinforcement. *Journal of the Experimental Analysis of Behavior,* 1975, *24,* 199–206. [324]

Schwartz, B., & Williams, D. R. Two different kinds of key peck in the pigeon: Some properties of responses maintained by negative and positive response-reinforcer contingencies. *Journal of the Experimental Analysis of Behavior,* 1972, *18,* 201–216. [324, 343]

Scott, J. P., & Fuller, J. L. *Genetics and social behavior of the dog.* Chicago: University of Chicago Press, 1965. [363]

Seligman, M. E. P. CS redundancy and secondary punishment. *Journal of Experimental Psychology,* 1966, *72,* 546–550. [285]

Seligman, M. E. P. Chronic fear produced by unpredictable shock. *Journal of Comparative and Physiological Psychology,* 1968, *66,* 402–411. [103, 225, 226]

Seligman, M. E. P. Control group and conditioning: A comment on operationism. *Psychological Review,* 1969, *76,* 484–491. [103]

Seligman, M. E. P. On the generality of laws of learning. *Psychological Review,* 1970, *77,* 406–418. [330]

Seligman, M. E. P. *Helplessness.* San Francisco: W. H. Freeman, 1975. [103, 106, 125–129, 142–144]

Seligman, M. E. P., & Campbell, B. A. Effects of intensity and duration of punishment on extinction of an avoidance response. *Journal of Comparative and Physiological Psychology,* 1965, *59,* 295–297. [249]

Seligman, M. E. P., & Hager, J. L. (Eds.). *Biological boundaries of learning.* New York: Appleton-Century-Crofts, 1972. [330]

Seligman, M. E. P., & Johnston, J. C. A cognitive theory of avoidance learning. In F. J. McGuigan & D. B. Lumsden (Eds.), *Contemporary approaches to conditioning and learning.* Washington, D.C.: Winston-Wiley, 1973. [249, 258–262]

Seligman, M. E. P., Maier, S., & Geer, J. The alleviation of learned helplessness in the dog. *Journal of Abnormal and Social Psychology,* 1968, *73,* 256–262. [143]

Sevenster, P. Motivation and learning in sticklebacks. In D. Ingle (Ed.), *The central nervous system and fish behavior.* Chicago: University of Chicago Press, 1968. [365]

Shapiro, M. N., Miller, T. N., & Bresnahan, J. L. Dummy trials, novel stimuli, and Pavlovian trained stimuli: Their effect upon instrumental and consummatory response relationships. *Journal of Comparative and Physiological Psychology,* 1966, *61,* 480–483. [267]

Sheffield, F. D. Relation between classical conditioning and instrumental learning. In W. F. Prokasy (Ed.), *Classical conditioning.* New York: Appleton-Century-Crofts, 1965. [146, 322]

Shepp, B. E., & Eimas, P. D. Intradimensional and extradimensional shifts in the rat. *Journal of Comparative and Physiological Psychology,* 1964, *57,* 357–361. [205]

Shepp, B. E., & Schrier, A. M. Consecutive intradimensional and extradimensional shifts in monkeys. *Journal of Comparative and Physiological Psychology,* 1969, *67,* 199–203. [205]

Shettleworth, S. Constraints on learning. In D. S. Lehrman, R. A. Hinde, & E. Shaw (Eds.), *Advances in the study of behavior: Vol 4.* New York: Academic Press, 1972. (a) [334, 364]

Shettleworth, S. Stimulus relevance in the control of drinking and conditioned fear responses in domestic chicks (*Gallus gallus*). *Journal of Comparative and Physiological Psychology,* 1972, *80,* 175–198. (b) [328]

Sidman, M. Two temporal parameters of the maintenance of avoidance behavior in the white rat. *Journal of Comparative and Physiological Psychology,* 1953, *46,* 253–261. [243]

Sidman, M. *Tactics of scientific research.* New York: Basic Books, 1960. [337]

Sidman, M. Avoidance behavior. In W. K. Honig (Ed.), *Operant behavior: Areas of research and application.* New York: Appleton-Century-Crofts, 1966. [243]

Siegel, S. Conditioning of insulin-induced glycemia. *Journal of Comparative and Physiological Psychology,* 1972, *78,* 233–241. [98]

Siegel, S. Evidence from rats that morphine tolerance is a learned response. *Journal of Comparative and Physiological Psychology,* 1975, *89,* 498–506. [98]

Siegel, S. Morphine tolerance acquisition as an associative process. *Journal of Experimental Psychology: Animal Behavior Processes,* 1977, *3,* 1–13. [98]

Singh, D., & Wickens, D. D. Disinhibition in instrumental conditioning. *Journal of Comparative and Physiological Psychology,* 1968, *66,* 557–559. [162]

Skinner, B. F. Drive and reflex strength. *Journal of General Psychology,* 1932, *6,* 32–48. [304]

Skinner, B. F. The generic nature of the concepts of stimulus and response. *Journal of General Psychology,* 1935, *12,* 40–65. [109]

Skinner, B. F. *Behavior of organisms.* New York: Appleton-Century-Crofts, 1938. [29, 282, 288]

Skinner, B. F. 'Superstition' in the pigeon. *Journal of Experimental Psychology,* 1948, *38,* 168–172. [118–120, 319]

Skinner, B. F. Are theories of learning necessary? *Psychological Review,* 1950, *57,* 193–216. [48, 337]

Skinner, B. F. *Science and human behavior.* New York: MacMillan, 1954. [35]

Skinner, B. F. *Verbal behavior.* New York: Appleton-Century-Crofts, 1957. [138, 369]

Skinner, B. F. The phylogeny and ontogeny of behavior. *Science,* 1966, *153,* 1205–1213. [136, 331, 375]

Skinner, B. F. *Beyond freedom and dignity.* New York: Alfred A. Knopf, 1971. [6, 11, 16, 108, 136]

Skinner, B. F. *About behaviorism.* New York: Knopf, 1974. [34, 375]

Sluckin, W. *Imprinting and early learning.* Chicago: Aldine Press, 1965. [362]

Smith, M. C., DiLollo, V., & Gormezano, I. Conditioned jaw movement in the rabbit. *Journal of Comparative and Physiological Psychology,* 1966, *62,* 479–483. [58]

Smith, R. F., Gustavson, C. R., & Gregor, G. L. Incompatibility between the pigeon's unconditioned response to shock and the conditioned key peck response. *Journal of the Experimental Analysis of Behavior,* 1972, *18,* 147–153. [250]

Solomon, R. L. Punishment. *American Psychologist,* 1964, *19,* 239–253. [252]

Solomon, R. L., & Wynne, L. C. Traumatic avoidance learning: Acquisition in normal dogs. *Psychological Monographs,* 1953, *67,* Whole No. 354. [241]

Solomon, R. L., & Wynne, L. C. Traumatic avoidance learning: The principles of anxiety conservation and partial irreversibility. *Psychological Review,* 1954, *61,* 353–385. [254, 256]

Spence, K. W. The nature of discrimination learning to animals. *Psychological Review,* 1936, *43,* 427–449. [207–217]

Spence, K. W. The differential response in animals to stimuli varying within a single dimension. *Psychological Review,* 1937, *44,* 430–444. [207–217]

Spencer, H. *Principles of psychology* (3rd.), 1880. [20]

Staats, A. W. *Language, learning and cognition.* New York: Holt, Rinehart and Winston, 1968. [297]

Staats, A. W. *Social behaviorism.* Homewood, Ill.: The Dorsey Press, 1975. [294, 298]

Staats, A. W., Finley, J. R., Minke, K. A., & Wolf, M. M. Reinforcement variables in the control of unit reading responses. *Journal of the Experimental Analysis of Behavior,* 1964, *7,* 139–149. [296]

Staats, A. W., Staats, C. K., Schutz, R. E., & Wolf, M. M. The conditioning of reading responses using "extrinsic" reinforcers. *Journal of the Experimental Analysis of Behavior,* 1962, *5,* 33–40. [296]

Staddon, J. E. R., & Innis, N. K. Reinforcement omission on fixed-interval schedules. *Journal of the Experimental Analysis of Behavior,* 1969, *12,* 689–700. [162]

Staddon, J. E. R., & Simmelhag, V. L. The "superstition" experiment: A reexamination of its implications for the principles of adaptive behavior. *Psychological Review,* 1971, *78,* 3–43. [132–141, 238, 263, 319, 373, 375]

Stiers, M., & Silberberg, A. Autoshaping and automaintenance of lever contact responses in rats. *Journal of the Experimental Analysis of Behavior,* 1974, *22,* 497–506. [321, 324]

Stuart, R. B. Operant-interpersonal treatment for marital discord. *Journal of Consulting and Clinical Psychology,* 1969, *33,* 675–682. [296]

Stubbs, D. A., & Cohen, S. L. Second order schedules: Comparison of different procedures for scheduling paired and non-paired brief stimuli. *Journal of the Experimental Analysis of Behavior,* 1972, *18,* 403–413. [290]

Sutherland, N. S. The learning of discrimination by animals. *Endeavour,* 1964, *23,* 69–78. [202]

Sutherland, N. S., & Mackintosh, N. J. *Mechanisms of animal discrimination learning.* New York: Academic Press, 1971. [202, 205]

Switalski, R. W., Lyons, J., & Thomas, D. R. Effects of interdimensional training on stimulus generalization. *Journal of Experimental Psychology,* 1966, *72,* 661–666. [198]

Tait, R. W., Marquis, H. A., Williams, R., Weinstein, L., & Suboski, M. D. Extinction of sensory preconditioning using CER training. *Journal of Comparative and Physiological Psychology,* 1969, *69,* 170–172. [66]

Teitelbaum, P. The use of operant methods on the assessment and control of motivational states. In W. K. Honig (Ed.), *Operant behavior: Areas of research and application.* New York: Appleton-Century-Crofts, 1966. [179]

Teitelbaum, P. *Physiological psychology.* Englewood Cliffs, N.J.: Prentice-Hall, 1967. [71]

Terrace, H. S. By-products of discrimination learning. In G. H. Bower & J. Spence (Eds.), *The psychology of learning and motivation* (Vol. 5). New York: Academic Press, 1971. [279]

Thomas, D. R., Berman, D. L., Serednesky, G. E., & Lyons, J. Information value and stimulus configuring as factors in conditioned reinforcement. *Journal of Experimental Psychology,* 1968, *76,* 181–189. [285]

Thomas, D. R., Mariner, R. W., & Sherry, G. Role of pre-experimental experience in the development of stimulus control. *Journal of Experimental Psychology,* 1969, *79,* 375–376. [194]

Thomas, D. R., & Switalski, R. W. Comparison of stimulus generalization following variable-ratio and variable-interval training. *Journal of Experimental Psychology,* 1966, *71,* 236–240. [165]

Thompson, R. F., & Spencer, W. A. Habituation: A model phenomenon for the study of neuronal substrates of behavior. *Psychological Review,* 1966, *73,* 16–43. [56]

Thompson, T., & Boren, J. J. Operant behavioral pharmacology. In W. K. Honig & J. E. R. Staddon (Eds.), *Handbook of operant behavior.* Englewood Cliffs, N.J.: Prentice-Hall, 1977. [179]

Thorndike, E. L. Animal intelligence: An experimental study of the associative processes in animals. *Psychological Monographs,* 1898, *2,* Whole No. 8. [26–28, 43]

Thorndike, E. L. *Animal intelligence: Experimental studies.* New York: Macmillan, 1911. [26–28]

Thorndike, E. L. *Human learning.* New York: Appleton-Century-Crofts, 1931. [233]

Thorndike, E. L. *Fundamentals of learning.* New York: Teachers College, Columbia University, 1932. [233]

Timberlake, W., & Allison, J. Response deprivation: An empirical approach to instrumental performance. *Psychological Review,* 1974, *81,* 146–164. [114]

Tinbergen, N. *The Study of instinct.* Oxford: Clarendon Press, 1951. [185, 349, 354, 357]

Tinbergen, N., & Kuenan, D. J. Releasing and directing stimulus situations in *Turdus M. merula L* and *T. E. ericetorium Tarton.* In C. H. Schiller (Ed.), *Instinctive behavior.* New York: International Universities Press, 1957. [357]

Tolman, E. C. *Purposive behavior in animals and men.* New York: Appleton-Century-Crofts, 1930. [29]

Tolman, E. C. The determiners of behavior at a choice point. *Psychological Review,* 1938, *45,* 1–34. [29]

Trabasso, T. R., & Bower, G. H. *Attention in learning: Theory and research.* New York: Wiley, 1968. [202]

Trapold, M. A. Are expectancies based upon different positive reinforcing events discriminably different? *Learning and Motivation,* 1970, *1,* 129–140. [275]

Trapold, M. A., & Overmeier, J. B. The second learning process in instrumental learning. In A. H. Black & W. F. Prokasy (Eds.), *Classical conditioning II: Current research and theory.* New York: Appleton-Century-Crofts, 1972. [257]

Turner, L. H., & Solomon, R. L. Human traumatic avoidance learning: Theory and experiments on the operant-respondent distinction and failure to learn. *Psychological Monographs,* 1962, *76,* Whole No. 559. [261]

Ullman, L. P., & Krasner, L. (Eds.). *Case studies in behavior modification.* New York: Holt, Rinehart & Winston, 1965. [10]

Ulrich, R., & Azrin, N. H. Reflexive fighting in response to aversive stimulation. *Journal of the Experimental Analysis of Behavior,* 1962, *5,* 511–520. [239]

Ulrich, R., Stachnik, T., & Mabry, J. (Eds.). *Control of human behavior.* New York: Scott, Foresman & Company, Vol. 1, 1966; Vol. 2, 1970; Vol. 3, 1974. [10]

Vogel, R., & Annau, Z. An operant discrimination task allowing variability of response patterning. *Journal of the Experimental Analysis of Behavior.* 1973, *20,* 1–6. [345]

von-Frisch, K. *The dance language and orientation of bees.* Cambridge, Mass.: Belknap Press, 1967. [349, 357, 377]

von Uexküll, J. A stroll through the world of animals and men. In C. H. Schiller (Ed.), *Instinctive behavior.* New York: International Universities Press, 1957. [185, 354]

Wagner, A. R., Logan, F. A., Haberlandt, K., & Price, T. Stimulus selection in animal discrimination learning. *Journal of Experimental Psychology,* 1968, *76,* 171–180. [197]

Wagner, A. R., & Rescorla, R. A. Inhibition in Pavlovian conditioning: Application of a theory, In R. A. Boakes & M. S. Halliday (Eds.), *Inhibition and learning.* New York: Academic Press, 1972. [92–96]

Wagner, A. R., & Terry, W. S. Backward conditioning to a CS following an expected vs. a surprising UCS. *Animal Learning and Behavior*, 1975, *3*, 370–374. [81]

Warden, C. J., & Lubow, L. Effect of performance without reward on the retention of the maze habit in the white rat. *Journal of Genetic Psychology*, 1942, *60*, 321–328. [135, 343]

Watson, J. B. Psychology as the behaviorist views it. *Psychological Review*, 1913, *20*, 158–177. [25]

Watson, J. B. *Psychology from the standpoint of a behaviorist*. Philadelphia: Lippincott, 1919. [25]

Watson, J. B., & Raynor, R. Conditioned emotional reactions. *Journal of Experimental Psychology*, 1920, *3*, 1–14. [100]

Watson, J. S. Memory and "contingency analysis" in infant learning. *Merrill-Palmer Quarterly*, 1967, *13*, 55–76. [130]

Watson, J. S. Cognitive-perceptual development in infancy: Setting for the seventies. *Merrill-Palmer Quarterly*, 1971, *12*, 139–152. [130]

Westbrook, R. G. Failure to obtain positive contrast when pigeons press a bar. *Journal of the Experimental Analysis of Behavior*, 1973, *20*, 499–510. [279]

Wilcoxin, H. C., Dragoin, W. B., & Kral, P. A. Illness-induced aversions in rat and quail: Relative saliences of visual and gustatory cues. *Science*, 1971, *171*, 826–828. [318]

Williams, D. R. Classical conditioning and incentive motivation. In W. F. Prokasy (Ed.), *Classical conditioning*. New York: Appleton-Century-Crofts, 1965. [267–269]

Williams, D. R., & Williams, H. Automaintenance in the pigeon: Sustained pecking despite contingent non-reinforcement. *Journal of the Experimental Analysis of Behavior*, 1969, *12*, 511–520. [148, 323]

Wolfe, J. B. Effectiveness of token-rewards for chimpanzees. *Comparative Psychology Monographs*, 1936, *12*, No. 60. [294]

Wolff, J. L. Concept-shift and discrimination-reversal learning in humans. *Psychological Bulletin*, 1967, *68*, 369–408. [205]

Wolpe, J., & Lazarus, A. A. *The practice of behavior therapy*. New York: Pergamon, 1969. [105]

Wright, A. A., & Cumming, W. W. Color naming functions for the pigeon. *Journal of the Experimental Analysis of Behavior*, 1971, *15*, 7–17. [337]

Wyckoff, L. B. The role of observing responses in discrimination learning, Part 1. *Psychological Review*, 1952, *59*, 431–442. [285]

Zeaman, D., & House, B. J. The role of attention in retardate discrimination learning. In N. R. Ellis (Ed.), *Handbook of mental deficiency: Psychological theory and research*. New York: McGraw-Hill, 1963. [202]

Zeiler, M. D. The ratio theory of intermediate size discrimination. *Psychological Review*, 1963, *70*, 516–533. [217]

Zener, K. The significance of behavior accompanying conditioned salivary secretion for theories of the conditioned response. *American Journal of Psychology*, 1937, *50*, 384–403. [56]

Acknowledgements

Cover photograph. Boyarsky, Bill. "Pigeon Pecking," *Psychology Today*, 3rd edition. Photo by Bill Boyarsky. Permission granted by courtesy of Random House, Inc.

Figure 4.2 Smith, M. C., DiLollo, V., & Gormezano, I. *Journal of Comparative and Physiological Psychology*, 1966, *62*, 479–483. Figure 4, p. 481. Copyright 1966 by the American Psychological Association. Reprinted by permission.

Figure 4.3 Schneiderman, N., Fuentes, I., & Gormezano, I. *Science*, 1962, *136*, 650–652. Copyright 1962 by the American Association for the Advancement of Science.

Figure 4.9 Rescorla, R. A. *Journal of Comparative and Physiological Psychology*, 1967, *64*, 114–120. Figure 3, p. 119. Copyright 1966 by the American Psychological Association. Reprinted by permission.

Figure 6.2 Azzi, R., Fix, D. S. R., Keller, F. S., & Roche e Silva, M. I. *Journal of the Experimental Analysis of Behavior*, 1964, *7*, 159–162. Figure 2. Copyright 1964 by the Society for the Experimental Analysis of Behavior, Inc.

Figure 6.3 Herrnstein, R. J. *Operant Behavior: Areas of Research and Application*, edited by W. K. Honig, 1966. Figure 1, p. 36. © 1966, p. 36. Reprinted by permission of Prentice-Hall, Inc., Englewood Cliffs, New Jersey.

Figure 6.5 Staddon, J. E. R., & Simmelhag, V. L. *Psychological Review*, 1971, *78*, 3–43. Figure 3. Copyright 1971 by the American Psychological Association. Reprinted by permission.

Figure 7.7 Rachlin, H., & Green, L. *Journal of the Experimental Analysis of Behavior*, 1972, *17*, 15–22. Figure 2, p. 18. Copyright 1972 by the Society for the Experimental Analysis of Behavior, Inc.

Figure 8.3 Jenkins, H. M., & Harrison, R. H. *Journal of Experimental Psychology*, 1960, *59*, 246–253. Figure 2, p. 248. Copyright 1960 by the American Psychological Association. Reprinted by permission.

Figure 8.4 Terrace, H. S. *The Psychology of Learning and Motivation*, vol. 5, edited by G. H. Bower & J. Spence, 1972, 195–265. Figure 17, p. 240. © 1972. Reprinted by permission of Academic Press.

Figure 8.6 Newman, F. L., & Baron, M. R. *Journal of Comparative and Physiological Psychology*, 1965, *60*, 59–63. Figure 1, p. 61. Copyright 1965 by the American Psychological Association. Reprinted by permission.

Figure 8.7 Jenkins, H. M., & Harrison, R. H. *Journal of the Experimental Analysis of Behavior*, 1962 *5*, 435–441. Figure 2, p. 439. Copyright 1962 by the Society for the Experimental Analysis of Behavior, Inc.

Figure 8.8 Reynolds, G. S. *Journal of the Experimental Analysis of Behavior*, 1961, *4*, 203–208. Figure 1, p. 204. Copyright 1961 by the Society for the Experimental Analysis of Behavior, Inc.

Figure 8.11 Hanson, H. M. *Journal of Experimental Psychology*, 1959, *58*, 321–334. Figure 1, p. 324. Copyright 1959 by the American Psychological Association. Reprinted by permission.

Figure 9.1 Hoffman, H. S. "Stimulus Factors in Conditioned Suppression." In *Punishment and Aversive Behavior*, edited by B. A. Campbell & R. M. Church. © 1969, p. 187. Reprinted by permission of Prentice-Hall, Inc., Englewood Cliffs, New Jersey.

Figure 9.2 Camp, D. S., Raymond, G. A., & Church, R. M. *Journal of Experimental Psychology*, 1967, *74*, 114–123. Figures 1–3. Copyright 1967 by the American Psychological Association. Reprinted by permission.

Figure 9.3 Azrin, N. H. *Journal of the Experimental Analysis of Behavior*, 1959, *2*, 301–305. Figure 1, p. 302. Copyright 1959 by the Society for the Experimental Analysis of Behavior, Inc.

Figure 9.4 Camp, D. S., & Church, R. M. *Journal of Experimental Psychology*, 1967, *74*, 114–123. Figures 1–3. Copyright 1967 by the American Psychological Association. Reprinted by permission.

Figure 9.5 Church, R. M, Wooten, C. L., & Matthews, T. J. *Learning and Motivation*, 1970, *1*, 1–18. Figure 4, p. 15. © 1970. Reprinted by permission of Academic Press. New York.

Figure 10.1 Williams, D. R. *Classical Conditioning*, edited by W. F. Brodsky, 1965. Figure 17.1. Copyright 1965 by Irvington Publishers. Reprinted by permission.

Figure 10.2 Williams, D. R. *Classical Conditioning*, edited by W. F. Brodsky, 1965. Figure 17.2. Copyright 1965 by Irvington Publishers. Reprinted by permission.

Figure 10.3 LoLordo, V. L., McMillan, J. C., & Riley, A. L. *Learning and Motivation*, 1974, *5*, 24–41. Figure 3, p. 35. © 1974 by Academic Press, New York.

Figure 11.3 Garcia, J., & Koelling, R. A. *Psychonomic Science*, 1966, *4*, 123–124. Figure 1. Copyright 1966 by the Psychonomic Society. Reprinted by permission.

Figure 11.4 Gamzu, E., & Williams, D. R. *Science*, 1971, *171*, 923–925. Figure 1, p. 924. Copyright 1971 by the American Association for the Advancement of Science.

Figure 11.5 Williams, D. R., & Williams, H. *Journal of the Experimental Analysis of Behavior*, 1969, *12*, 511–520. Figure 1, p. 513. Copyright 1969 by the Society for the Experimental Analysis of Behavior, Inc.

Chapter 11, excerpts. Breland, K., & Breland, M. *American Psychologist*, 1961, *16*, 681–684. Pp. 682, 683. Copyright 1961 by the American Psychological Association. Reprinted by permission.

Figure 12.2 Herrick, R. M. *Journal of the Experimental Analysis of Behavior*, 1964, *7*, 211–216. Figure 2, p. 213.

Figure 12.3 Notterman, J. M. *Journal of Experimental Psychology*, 1959, *58*, 341–347. Figure 3, p. 343. Copyright 1959 by the American Psychological Association. Reprinted by permission.

Figure 12.5 Vogel, R., & Annau, Z. *Journal of the Experimental Analysis of Behavior*, 1973, *20*, 1–6. Figure 3, p. 4. Copyright 1973 by the Society for the Experimental Analysis of Behavior, Inc.

Chapter 12, excerpts. Chomsky, N. *Reflections on Language*, 1975, pp. 4 and 26. Copyright 1975 by Pantheon Books, a Division of Random House, Inc. Reprinted by permission.

Index